Learning Across Sites

The ever-evolving, technology-intensive nature of the twenty-first century work-place has caused an acceleration in the division of labour, whereby work practices are becoming highly specialised and learning and the communication of knowledge is in a constant state of flux. This poses a challenge for education and learning: as knowledge and expertise increasingly evolve, how can individuals be prepared through education to participate in specific industries and organisations, both as newcomers and throughout their careers?

Learning Across Sites brings together a diverse range of contributions from leading international researchers to examine the impacts and roles which evolving digital technologies have on our navigation of education and professional work environments. Viewing learning as a socially organised activity, the contributors explore the evolution of learning technologies and knowledge acquisition in net-worked societies through empirical research in a range of industries and workplaces. The areas of study include public administration, engineering, production, and healthcare, and the contributions address the following questions:

- How are learning activities organised?
- How are tools and infrastructures used?
- What competences are needed to participate in specialised activities?
- What counts as knowledge in multiple and diverse settings?
- Where can parallels be drawn between workplaces?

Addressing an emerging problem of adaptation in contemporary education, this book is essential reading for all those undertaking postgraduate study and research in the fields of educational psychology, informatics and applied informa-tion technology.

Sten Ludvigsen is Professor at InterMedia, University of Oslo. His research inter-ests focus on how digital learning resources are used and how relationships work in distributed settings, both in education and in the workplace.

Andreas Lund is Associate Professor at the Department of Teacher Education and School Development, University of Oslo. He has experience of teaching in high schools and his research interests include technology-mediated collective thinking and the pedagogical and technological co-design of learning environments.

Ingvill Rasmussen is currently undertaking a post-doctorate position at InterMedia, University of Oslo. Her research interests are learning and change connected to the use of computer technology in educational settings.

Roger Säljö is Professor of Education and Psychology of Education, University of Gothenburg. His research interests include learning, interaction and development in a sociocultural perspective.

New Perspectives on Learning and Instruction

New Perspectives on Learning and Instruction is published by Routledge in conjunction with EARLI (European Association for Research on Learning and Instruction). This series publishes cutting-edge international research focusing on all aspects of learning and instruction in both traditional and non-traditional educational settings. Titles published within the series take a broad and innovative approach to topical areas of research, are written by leading international researchers and are aimed at a research and post-graduate student audience.

Also available:

Transformation of Knowledge Through Classroom Interaction
Edited by Baruch Schwarz, Tommy Dreyfus and Rina Hershkowitz

Learning Across Sites

New tools, infrastructures and practices

Edited by Sten Ludvigsen,
Andreas Lund, Ingvill Rasmussen
and Roger Säljö

This first edition published 2011
by Routledge
2 Park Square, Milton Park, Abingdon, Oxon, OX14 4RN

Simultaneously published in the USA and Canada
by Routledge
270 Madison Avenue, New York, NY 10016

*Routledge is an imprint of the Taylor & Francis Group, an informa
business*

© 2011 selection and editorial material, Sten Ludvigsen, Andreas
Lund, Ingvill Rasmussen and Roger Säljö; individual chapters, the
contributors

Typeset in Galliard by
Pindar NZ, Auckland, New Zealand

Printed and bound in Great Britain by
CPI Antony Rowe, Chippenham, Wiltshire

British Library Cataloguing in Publication Data
A catalogue record for this book is available from the British
Library

Library of Congress Cataloging-in-Publication Data
Learning across sites: new tools, infrastructures and practices /
edited by Sten Ludvigsen . . . [et al.].—1st ed.
    p. cm.
  1. Educational change. 2. Teams in the workplace. 3.
Organizational learning. I. Ludvigsen, Sten.
  LB2806.L3836 2011
  658.3'124—dc22   2010002318

ISBN13: 978-0-415-58175-2 (hbk)
ISBN13: 978-0-415-58176-9 (pbk)
ISBN13: 978-0-203-84781-7 (ebk)

Contents

Foreword

This book has its origins in different strategic efforts in Norway and Sweden and from two major initiatives about learning, innovation and ICT in the European research area.

First, in 2002, InterMedia at the Faculty of Education, University of Oslo, was a partner in a major initiative for strengthening our understanding of societal transformation and the development of learning and ICT. Several research institutes and faculties have been involved in the strategic program, Competence and Media Convergence (CMC). The CMC program has been supported with a grant from the University of Oslo. This grant has given us the financial support necessary to arrange a series of international seminars and workshops as well as a special workshop where all the authors in this book met to further develop the ideas for their contributions to the project.

The second strand of support comes from the University of Gothenburg and two research initiatives. The first one is LearnIT, the research program on learning and ICT funded by the Knowledge Foundation in 2000. The second source of support at the University of Gothenburg is the national center of excellence, the Linnaeus Centre for Research on Learning, Interaction and Mediated Communication in Contemporary Society (LinCS). The founders of the Linnaeus Centre have collaborated with the Faculty of Education and InterMedia over a long period of time.

The third strand that must be mentioned is Kaleidoscope Network of Excellence in the 6th framework in EU (IST program). This program has given us, as European colleagues, excellent possibilities for international cooperation in the field of technology-enhanced learning.

The fourth strand is the EU project Knowledge Practices Laboratory (KP-LAB) (2005–2010, integrated project in the Sixth Framework, IST program), which adds new possibilities to such collaborations. Several of the chapters in this book address directly key issues in the KP-LAB project.

These different strategic efforts, centers, projects and networks collaborate at the personal as well as institutional levels, and this creates productive-structuring mechanisms for advancing our knowledge in order to promote a more complete understanding of learning in the 21st century. The projects and centers are also representations of how the networked society works. These different sources for intellectual collaboration provided the framework and the direction for this book.

We would like to thank all the scholars and funding agencies for their contributions to this book.

Chapter 1

Introduction

Learning across sites; new tools, infrastructures and practices

Sten Ludvigsen, Andreas Lund,
Ingvill Rasmussen and Roger Säljö

Existing and emerging practices

At the beginning of the 21st century we have seen how educational activities and work practices increasingly take place in networks and across multiple and diverse settings and contexts. One could say that society has become increasingly particularized into sectors and sub-sectors with an increasing division of labor. In each sector and sub-sector, the development of knowledge results in increasingly specialized work practices, which represent a particular configuration of professional languages, technologies and organizational arrangements. The consequence is that expertise and knowledge increasingly appear as in-depth specialization within local contexts. Such specialization creates obvious challenges for knowledge integration. Domain-specific knowledge is not always easy to translate into general insights, since the parallels to other settings and activities are not obvious. The implication is that knowledge does not travel easily between different settings, such as schools, workplaces, and leisure actives. This creates additional challenges when problems in society and its different institutions require solutions that go beyond the local context.

In this book the focus is how learning takes place in specific practices and under specific institutional conditions, but the ambition is also to probe into how what is specific and what is general relate to each other. Through the various contributions we aim to add to the understanding of what is unique about the many and diverse learning environments analyzed, and what may, potentially, emerge as more general features and dimensions in and across such contexts and settings. Specifically, we link this approach to emerging practices in the wake of the increased impact of digital and networked technologies. Such technologies represent both new contextual affordances and challenges, and they require an increased repertoire of collaborative capacity by professionals. Consequently, there is a need to unpack, concretize and, thus, increase our understanding of some of the many forms of collaboration as types of social practices. The title of this volume seeks to capture this intention. Through a number of (mostly) empirical and theoretical contributions, we seek to reveal how learning as a socially organized activity is enacted in and across sites, settings, and contexts.

The pace of the societal differentiation and advancement in knowledge production, both within and between our institutions, creates a set of dilemmas for the educational sector. There is a high degree of uncertainty about how to prepare people for new work practices, for what counts as knowledge, and what 21st century literacy and numeracy amount to. The problem can be stated as follows: In education the historical and social practices have been concerned with how learners accumulate knowledge. This knowledge has been seen as given in the sense that it has been developed in the humanities, the natural and social sciences and in other fields. We can talk about this pattern as a canon of representation (Wartofsky, 1979) that has emerged over millennia, and that sets the agenda for schooling. The students are expected to acquire this knowledge. This is understood as if knowledge is given. The problem with this historical canon is that students do not become socialized into asking questions and problematizing what has become accepted as the current knowledge, nor do they develop insights into the methods and procedures through which this knowledge is continually produced.

John Dewey formulated this dilemma almost a hundred years ago in his critical analysis of teaching and learning in traditional schooling. He argued that the problem is that the "statements, the propositions, in which knowledge, the issue of active concern with problems, is deposited, are taken to be themselves knowledge" (1966, p. 187). In other words, the products of inquiry and learning become the objects of learning, which implies that students seldom become familiar with the procedures through which knowledge emerges and is accounted for. One can argue that there are two competing historical scripts which are acted out as practices in educational settings. One is primarily concerned with existing knowledge and its acquisition and reproduction; the other is concerned with knowledge advancement and increasing learners' capacities to expand and go beyond what they already know, i.e. the focus is on making students able to understand and produce *new* and situationally relevant knowledge.

The consequence of this situation is an emerging gap between what counts as future-oriented practices and the practices historically developed in educational institutions (for recent discussions, see Hakkarainen *et al.*, 2004; Säljö, 2005; Sternberg & Preiss, 2005). Recent reports about the new challenges for the educational sector, such as the widely quoted volume *How People Learn* from the *National Science Foundation in the US* (Bransford *et al.*, 2000), and the OECD report *Innovation in the Knowledge Economy: Implications for education and learning* (2004), give some directions. However, the learning principles that have emerged from such reports appear as ideal descriptions. They hardly discuss what Olson (2003) has described as the deep tensions between, on the one hand, findings in educational psychology and the learning sciences, and, on the other, how one should understand the educational sector and schools as institutional phenomena.

With a high division of labor and specialization, learning and the development of competence is not something straightforward. On the one hand, we can make very general claims about robust principles for productive learning (see for example Sawyer, 2006). On the other hand, we know that these abstractions and general principles do not give much insight into how learning takes place *in situ* in the many kinds of very diverse settings where teaching and learning take place. Hence, we need studies and theoretical perspectives that make it possible to connect the abstractions to learning as forms of particularization. How individuals participate and interact in social settings need to be accounted for on the basis of a multilevel analysis perspective (Engeström, 1987; Säljö, 2000; Edwards, this volume; Ludvigsen, in press). One could argue that we need to study in depth how individuals meet, interpret, navigate around and engage with other participants, and how these activities are structured.

A society is transformed by and through new technologies, new types of artifacts, new forms of division of labor, and new arenas and institutions will create new conditions for learning. It is important to understand processes of development by studying specific institutions in education as well as in working life (Engeström, 1987; 2004), but also by studying new arenas such as CSCL (Computer Supported Collaborative Learning) settings and/or virtual/distributed environments and games (Crook, 1994; Gee, 2003; 2005; Stahl, 2006; Arnseth & Ludvigsen, 2006).

The trends referred to above call for a perspective on learning which takes learning as a socially organized activity as foundational (Säljö, 2000; 2005). This means that what people learn in specific settings is dependent on how activities are socially organized and how they have emerged as institutional practices. Such dependency does not imply that how and what we learn is given; such matters are, in principle, open to negotiation. But historical aspects of the current local practices create constraints as well as affordances. The implication of this argument is that we need to understand learning as genuine interdependence between human agency, socially organized activities and technologies. When we take learning as socially organized activities as a premise, this gives the analysts possibilities to describe and analyze learning on multiple levels.

Sociocultural perspectives

In discussions about learning in the 21st century, there is a need for a better understanding of learning processes at the individual as well as at the collective level. At the same time, the theoretical framework for learning has undergone several paradigm shifts. Behaviorist or associationist positions have been weakened through the impact of the "cognitive revolution" which came to dominate many scientific disciplines. However, during recent decades various sociocultural approaches to learning have made an increasingly greater impact in research and in the wider discussion. In particular this shift has been noticeable in research focusing on the interplay between ICT and learning in several settings. The unit of analysis has shifted from a focus on the individual, and/or on the isolated cognitive event, to a focus that includes attention to interactive, institutional and contextual features of human practices. As part of the more general social transformation that takes place through the digital technologies, the development within the specific field of ICT creates new conditions for learning and communication. Consequently, it seems reasonable to argue that a sociocultural theory of learning is a vital tool for understanding change and innovation in various sectors and practices in society.

The knowledge or information society can be analyzed and understood from many different perspectives. One major difference in research perspectives can be found between those in the social sciences who analyze society from above, and those who do it from below. Engeström and Middleton (1996, p. 2) formulate these positions as follows:

> Contrasting the studies of human agency in work with those primarily concerned with transformation of work over time can be characterized as comparisons between agency-driven microsociology-without-history and historically relevant macrosociology-without-agency.

This may be stating the argument in its extreme, but it does crystallize the differences between various positions that can be taken and the problems involved in this conflict between perspectives and their view on human agency and social structure. However, we think that the sociocultural perspective can represent a different approach to such problems. In sociocultural studies, human agency is obviously the basic premise (Wertsch *et al.*, 1993). Thus, by taking human agency as a starting point, we include cultural and historical aspects that become relevant for understanding the activities that participants perform *in situ* and over time. The implication of this scientific position is that social structures, patterns or milieus are not taken for granted, but studied as phenomena that are emerging within practices.

As agents in society we face ICT in several ways. It is through communication and interaction with fellow human beings and with technologies that we act and learn. New types of semiotic mediation are – and will become increasingly more – important. Convergence between different technologies and media brings about changes in conditions for meaning-making, which are important to understand when researchers intend to examine and explain what is meant by expressions such as digital competence or media literacy, and also when attempting to understand how such technological resources co-determine and even transform human interaction (Kress 2000; Erstad, this volume). Of particular importance in this context are studies of the interplay between communication, learning and ICT in different institutional settings. Changes in norms, division of labor and competences take place within all institutional settings in and across education as well as working life, but also in other sites and activities characterized by networking and gaming. One important aspect of this development is that institutional boundaries are challenged and appear as more blurred.

Learning as socially organized activity

We think that it is important in this introduction to elaborate what we mean by learning as socially organized activity. From new research in biology, we find that in terms of genetics humans are very similar to our biological relatives, the primates. About 98 or 99 per cent of the genetic material is said to be shared. This means that the significant difference between humans and primates is our capacity to create and share experiences, and to pass these experiences on to the next generation. We argue that if we do not understand how learning as specific activities are enacted, we simply cannot understand why and how people learn in different settings. We argue that the sociogenesis of human practices needs to be the core focus if we want to create further advancement in the learning sciences.

We build knowledge in different ways, through language and material artifacts and tools. It is in these socially organized activities knowledge is developed, organized, accumulated and passed on, or forgotten. Donald (1991) argues that the co-evolution of humans, technologies and societies resulted in the emergence of what he refers to as a theoretical culture in which the human brain functions in collaboration with an increasingly complex environment of symbolic representations and mechanisms for communicating. In this theoretical, or technology-supported, culture, we as a species continuously produce new types of representations, which are abstract and which may not be directly linked to any material objects. Such representational practices are essential features of how we work and learn in most areas of society.

However, the implication of this argument is that we need to study learning at multiple levels. We will now look at two key issues in this context: the unit of analysis and levels of descriptions. The notions of the unit of analysis and levels of descriptions imply that learning evolves along different timescales and across different settings (Lemke, 2000). It is common to differentiate between four levels in the sociocultural approach. These are: phylogeny, sociogenesis, microgenesis and ontogenesis (Engeström, 1987; Wells, 1999; Säljö 2000; Ludvigsen, in press). These levels are related and give us a specific focus for empirical studies. This means, first, that one can study individual learning without de-emphasizing the social and cultural aspects; second, that one can study how people learn and coordinate their activities in order to achieve a productive level of intersubjectivity and, third, that one can pay attention to how activity systems change learning at the collective as well as at the individual level. This last level is related to how the human species changes over longer periods of time (phylogeny).

The notion of a unit of analysis gives direction regarding which phenomenon one wants to study. If one wants to study how students develop a shared understanding, the focus is on how they are doing this through talk by using specific tools as resources. Here, the unit of analysis is the socially enacted talk, and how the tools mediate such practices. Or, we can study social activity systems, or even interaction between activity systems. We can follow individuals and groups or specific professions over time in order to deconstruct their learning trajectories. When deciding on a unit of analysis, we also decide what we can say something about. However, we have not described at what level of detail we want to study the phenomenon. For instance, do we mainly focus on the talk (i.e. the verbal activities), or do we include other features of interaction such as gestures, gaze, and so on? And do we differentiate between which parts of the talk we study; do we include interactional patterns, the emerging meaning-making, formal aspects such as grammar, and so on? The unit of analysis and levels of description constitute important premises for what kinds of more general statements one can make as a result of the analysis.

In the current volume we present a number of contributions where authors from different fields and with diverse disciplinary backgrounds connect general theoretical aspects of sociocultural perspectives to the particular, "lived" experiences that make up our social worlds. Across the diversity of chapters, we find quite a number of common themes and concerns. These will be addressed below. However, the themes that all the chapters touch upon can also be articulated as vital research questions, such as:

- How are learning activities organized?
- What kinds of tools and infrastructures are involved?
- What do participants learn?
- How are the social and cognitive aspects enacted?
- What are the competencies needed for participation in specialized activities?
- What counts as knowledge in multiple and diverse settings?

In sum, the answers to these questions give us important insights into the main theme of this volume; how learning, when embedded in social practices, takes place across sites and with new tools and infrastructures.

Chapters, sections, and themes

All chapters build on the analysis of situations and activities where "something new" is introduced into an environment, a setting or an institution. For example, one can introduce new types of ICT or other types of artifacts, or, alternatively, the phenomenon under study may be new as an object of learning. We want to examine situations where there is some kind of tension, breakdown or rupture. When there are ruptures, tensions or contradictions within and between different parts of an organization, a potential for new learning opportunities and activities emerges, as is emphasized in several of the chapters. Ruptures challenge the boundaries between social and cultural organizations and the technologies that are involved. The implication is that in the development of social order agents are expected to build new and relevant competencies. The increased complexity entails developing new types of communication and movement between diverse communicative practices. One assumption is that in order to do so, agents need to develop metacommunicative and metacognitive competencies to interpret and orient themselves towards the many and diverse demands and requirements that are situation and context specific.

This requires more than a 20th-century canon of competence which can be summed up in "the three Rs" – reading, writing, and arithmetic. However, what exactly a 21st-century canon entails is a question of much discussion, and the debate covers areas such as digital literacy, cultural competence, networked literacy, and – above all – capacity to take on complex and unexpected challenges. While we acknowledge that a new canon is currently only starting to emerge, we maintain that it is important to examine diverse sites where we can find indications of, or even established, practices that point in this direction. Consequently, the main sections in the current volume address sectors such as (i) school settings, (ii) higher education, and (iii) a range of workplaces.

However, from the many contributions in this volume, alternative and more thematically oriented categories materialize across the three main settings indicated above. We have endeavoured to present contributions as we find them typical of significant features of phenomena such as: *Developing professional expertise, Unpacking collaboration and trajectories of participation, Institutional development, Design environments and new tools and representations.* Several chapters cover more than one category, so this is a classification with some nuances – we leave further classification to the reader's discretion.

Given the title of the book, *Learning Across Sites: New tools, infrastructures and practices*, some readers may think there is a paradox when we argue that learning is situated while still taking place across sites. The manner in which we understand this is that as people, in their roles as students, workers or something else, move in and between institutional contexts, learning is never limited to single settings. A situated understanding of learning implies a focus on how previous knowledge and experiences become relevant and are used in accountable manners in new contexts. However, this must be studied *in situ*. Analytically, learning must be understood as a historical, social, and individual phenomenon. It is at the intersection between people's actions, the tools they use and the infrastructures they have access to that new conditions for learning arise and where new practices emerge.

Developing professional expertise

In this section, the focus is on challenges for established practices and the demands on agents and organizations to learn and accommodate to new circumstances in a range of work settings. As people engage in new types of work, orient themselves toward different objects of activity, or move between settings, the nature of expertise will have to change accordingly.

In Chapter 2, Edwards focuses on how we understand the development of professional learning and expertise. She argues that we need to take a new approach to this area of research. In many professions in modern society, people move between different settings and contexts as they perform their work. They are involved in what Edwards refers to as multi-agency collaboration, which means that representatives of different professions collaborate in the context of specific cases that are at the attention of several actors and agencies. Such boundary-crossing activities give the work a networked character. The empirical settings studied here are social care and teaching.

Engeström and Toiviainen, in Chapter 3, examine how we need to reconceptualize how we think about problems that arise when technologies are implemented in work settings. This reconceptualization implies understanding the development of professional expertise as horizontal movements. The central questions in this context are how to integrate theoretical principles of productive learning, the local user requirements, and technological solutions in the local institutions and their practices, in one and the same process. They investigate this problem area within three empirical settings: in research, in an engineering company, and in the context of software design.

Lahn's work gives an overview of how the notion of trajectory is conceptualized in different theoretical stances within a sociocultural tradition. This overview shows how different stances deal with learning over long periods of time. In addition, Lahn discusses how the concept of knowledge object can be understood in professional learning. He illustrates how the knowledge objects that are used for professional development vary between different professions.

Hakkarainen, Lallimo, Toikka, and White also address the role of knowledge networks in innovation and knowledge creation in Chapter 5. They argue that human expertise is collective in nature. The implication of this is that innovation in the knowledge society needs to be understood as development and formation within the context of networks of innovative knowledge-practices. The empirical settings studied are located in the fields of telecommunication and mechanical engineering.

In the study reported by Perret-Clermont and Perret in Chapter 6, the issue addressed is how a technical innovation changes the relationship between the industry and the technical-vocational educational system. In the watch and music-box industry in a village in Switzerland, the whole economic life was threatened by a new automatic system. The industry and the educational system urgently needed to change, but in which direction? What kind of knowledge and skills become relevant when implementing the new technologies? The interdependence between humans and artifacts are crucial to understanding such technological change. Managing such interdependence is typical of current and future professional expertise.

Unpacking collaboration and trajectories of participation

The concept of collaboration has been the subject of innumerable empirical studies and theoretical approaches. What emerges is that behind the term we see a plethora of configurations, where humans, tools, and spatio-temporal resources form object-oriented communities. In the contributions listed below, there are a number of such diverse collaborative configurations. Together they illuminate and problematize this crucial concept, and, thus, the chapters make a substantial contribution to our understanding of what collaboration entails and what learning implies in collaborative practices.

In Chapter 7, concepts such as timescales, intersecting trajectories of participation, learning and multiplicity are discussed by Ludvigsen, Rasmussen, Krange,

Moen, and Middleton. A review of key contributions to the concept of trajectory is the building block for this chapter. The empirical settings investigated are a school and a setting in which patients experience and deal with health problems.

In Chapter 8, Eklund, Mäkitalo, and Säljö develop insights into how a modern, technologically complex workplace operates when it comes to organizing learning for new members of staff. The firm in question provides IT support for a worldwide network that runs 24/7. The members of staff continuously need to assist customers with their local problems wherever they are in the world. The language used for such problem-solving is very complex when the problems of the clients are analyzed and related to the existing technology. To manage the work, the work practices are organized in teams where collective problem-solving strategies and continuous overlap in information are necessary ingredients for success.

In Chapter 9, Mørch and Skaanes describe how they have participated as researchers in the design and analysis of a web-based learning system that was introduced into a chain of petrol stations in Norway and eventually installed at 230 stations. Mørch and Skaanes analyze an emerging practice of technology-enhanced (web-enabled) workplace learning, and discuss their findings in terms of a conceptual framework that makes use of the concepts primary work and secondary work. In this framework, workplace learning is understood as an extension of secondary work, and more concretely associated with gap-closing primary and secondary work. They identify information-seeking as a key secondary work characteristic.

Crook discusses the concepts of collaborative experience in Chapter 10, and argues that we need to understand collaboration in terms of its cognitive, emotional and affective dimensions. To focus only on social interaction and tools will provide too limited a view of collaboration and learning. The empirical part of this chapter brings important insights into how students in a psychology course use digital resources, how they work together, and how tasks need to be constructed in order to make collaboration meaningful for the students.

In Chapter 11, Muukkonen, Lakkala, and Paavola seek to extend previous approaches to collaborative inquiry knowledge-building by adding a distinct focus on objects (in this respect their approach resembles that of Lund and Hauge below). They investigate two specially designed courses in higher education, where the ambition is to test a set of design principles. Networked expertise and collective orchestration of individual efforts are crucial in this type of collaboration.

Another way to unpack collaboration is shown in Stahl's study, Chapter 12, where small groups of students take part in virtual math teams. The students can sign up for math problem-solving online. The teams usually consist of three to four teenage students. The students only meet each other in the chat room in the math environment. The design of the environment has gone through a number of improvements in order to stimulate and scaffold the students' problem-solving activities, and it also provides good opportunities for studying group cognition. Stahl makes a detailed interactional analysis of what is going on in this environment.

In the chapter by Lund and Hauge, the focus is on object-orientation in collective knowledge construction in a cross-disciplinary project and with an ethical dilemma as the point of departure. The key concept in this chapter is the emerging object. The chapter gives a strong empirical account of how a group of learners collaborate and how they orient themselves towards the object and its representations in the classroom and with diverse technological resources at hand.

In Chapter 14, by Andriessen, Baker, and van der Puil, the concept of argumentation is in focus. The focus on explicit argumentation and dialogue is growing as an analytic perspective in research and as an instructional way of improving students' competence in different knowledge domains. The authors make a detailed analysis of how students perform a task in a computer-supported learning environment and where micro-conflicts is their key analytic concept.

In higher-education settings, Dysthe, Lillejord, Wasson, and Vines analyze "productive learning" with the ambition of showing how it ties into a cluster of concepts that concern activity and transformation. They investigate how the dialectic relationship between processes and products constitutes a relational space – or zone. Two case studies support their investigation, and they find that students in higher education benefit from being exposed to the divergent voices and conflicting perspectives of the research community.

Institutional development

Changing practices cannot be properly understood without taking the cultural-historical trajectories of institutions into consideration. A closer look at this often under-investigated aspect of human cognition and development is provided in several of the contributions in this volume, but in the following chapters such trajectories are in focus.

In the chapter by Schwartz and de Groot, a joint institutional developmental process between educational designers, teachers and researchers is documented. This developmental process leads to several breakdowns, which create new opportunities for learning to occur. New types of learning designs are accounted for in this chapter. The empirical context is in-service training for teachers.

In Chapter 17, Barnes and Sutherland investigate two important issues that concern how schools can develop more productive learning trajectories. Based on partnerships with schools and teachers, the authors have developed new tools for analyzing the teacher's practices. This is done in collaboration with the teachers, so the tools and ways of analyzing classroom interaction are more attuned to the teachers' work practices.

Erstad examines how multiliterate practices emerge and what the role of digital technologies is. The empirical data comes from different sources. The survey data is related to a large-scale ICT-based reform in Norway, and the corpus of qualitative data is based on a longitudinal study where the schools were followed over four years. The study is what we could call a multilevel study, where different research perspectives are deployed to understand how schools develop when different types of ICTs are introduced and used over time.

Design environments and new tools and representations

An important trend in the learning sciences during the last years has been the effort to design new environments and new ICT tools, which have the potential of enriching learning activities for the students. These design efforts involve new types of tools, but they also imply developing new social designs where students are given opportunities to work together in new ways.

In Chapter 19, Wegerif and De Laat reconceptualize the idea of higher-order skills, which is an important element of different learning theories. Using the notion of dialogue and dialogicality, the authors argue that successful learning includes the ability to recognize the perspective of others. Based on such a dialogical perspective on learning, they present two examples of designed environment, where dialogical ideas are concretized and implemented. Students' practices are analyzed in order to illustrate what the design affords in terms of assuming the perspectives of others.

In Chapter 20, by Järvela, Hurme, and Järvenoja, the focus is on how students develop strategies for self-regulation. The field of self-regulation and motivation is well developed in research, theoretically as well as and in terms of the number of empirical studies available in the literature. This study gives a distinct contribution to the issue of ontogenesis of such skills, and how students engage and express metacognitive knowledge related to the domain of mathematics. The environment that the students are using is designed for supporting individual and collective knowledge production.

Mercer, Gillen, Staarman, Littleton, and Twiner take the metaphor of the socio-cultural toolkit as their starting point. Based on this premise they critically examine the idea of technological innovations as agents for change in the educational sector. The empirical focus is on the use of interactive whiteboards in classrooms. They study different classrooms, teachers and knowledge domains in order to describe and understand how the interactive whiteboard is conceived and picked up as part of the practices of the teachers.

In the final chapter, Lindwall and Ivarsson investigate the uses of representational technologies in the context of learning the basics of kinematics in physics teaching. In a number of studies in mechanics environments, a particular tool referred to as Probeware has been shown to be one of the few learning environments which has proved to produce positive learning results. Probeware combines support for conceptual understanding with students' physical movements. In this chapter, Probeware is contrasted with another environment, Graphs & Tracks, in terms of the learning outcomes produced. Lindwall and Ivarsson use an interactional approach to explain the differences between the two environments, and, more generally, why Probeware seems to produce better results in terms of conceptual understanding.

The different sections provide rich descriptions and analyses of learning and knowledge construction. The sections together demonstrate and illustrate how important the social organization of learning is for the construction of knowledge, activity patterns and individual development in contemporary society.

References

Arnseth, H. C. and Ludvigsen, S. (2006). Approaching Institutional Contexts: Systemic versus dialogic research in CSCL. *International Journal of Computer-Supported Collaborative Learning*, 1(2), 167–185.

Bransford, J. D., Brown, A. L., and Cocking, R. R. (eds). (2000). *How People Learn: Brain, mind, experience, and school*. Washington DC: National Academy Press.

Crook, C. (1994). *Computers and the Collaborative Experience of Learning*. London: Routledge.

Dewey, J. (1966). *Democracy and Education*. New York, NY: The Free Press (original published in 1916).

Donald, M. W. (1991). *A Mind So Rare: The evolution of human consciousness*. New York, NY: Norton.

Engeström, Y. (1987). *Learning by Expanding: An activity – theoretical approach to developmental research*. Helsinki: Orienta-konsultit.

Engeström, Y. (2004). New Forms of Learning in Co-configuration Work. *Journal of Workplace Learning*, 16(1/2), 11–21.

Engeström, Y. and Middleton, D. (eds). (1996). *Cognition and Communication at Work*. Cambridge: Cambridge University Press.

Gee, J. P. (2003). *What Video Games Can Teach Us About Learning and Literacy*. New York, NY: Palgrave Macmillan.

Hakkarainen, K., Palonen, T., Paavola, S., and Lehtinen, E. (2004). *Communities of Networked Expertise*. Amsterdam: Elsevier.

Kress, G. (2000). Multimodality. In B. Cope and M. Kalantzis (eds), *Multiliteracies. Literacy Learning and the Design of Social Futures* (pp. 182–202). London and New York: Routledge.

Lemke, J. L. (2000). Across the Scales of Time: Artifacts, activities, and meanings in ecosocial systems. *Mind, Culture and Activity*, 7(4), 273–290.

Ludvigsen, S. (in press). What Counts as Knowledge: Learning to use categories in computer environments. In R. Säljö (ed.), *ICT and Transformation of Learning Practices*. Oxford: Pergamon Press.

OECD (2004). *Innovation in the Knowledge Economy: Implications for education and learning*. Paris: OECD.

Olson, D. R. (2003). *Psychological Theory and Educational Reform: How school remakes mind and society*. Cambridge: Cambridge University Press.

Säljö, R. (2000). *Lärande i Praktiken: Ett sociokulturellt perspektiv. [Learning in Practice: A sociocultural perspective]*. Stockholm: Prisma.

Säljö, R. (2005). *Lärand och Kulturella Redskap: Om lärandeprocesser och det kollektiva minnet. [Learning and Cultural Tools: Learning processes and the collective memory]*. Stockholm: Nordstedts Akademiska Förlag.

Sawyer, R. K. (ed.). (2006). *The Cambridge Handbook of the Learning Sciences*. Cambridge: Cambridge University Press.

Stahl, G. (2006). *Group Cognition: Computer support for building collaborative knowledge*. Cambridge, MA: MIT Press.

Sternberg, R. J. and Preiss, D. D. (eds), (2005). *Intelligence and Technology. The impact of tools on the nature and development of human abilities*. Mahwah, NJ: Lawrence Erlbaum Associates.

Wartofsky, M. W. (1979). *Models: Representation in scientific understanding*. Dordrecht: D. Reidel.

Wells, G. (1999). *Dialogic Inquiry. Towards a Sociocultural Practice and Theory of Education*. Cambridge: Cambridge University Press.

Wertsch, J. V., Tulviste, P., and Hagstrom, F. (1993). A Sociocultural Approach to Agency. In E. A. Forman and C. A. Stone (eds), *Contexts for Learning* (pp. 336–56). Oxford: Oxford University Press.

Section 1

Developing professional expertise

Chapter 2

Learning how to know who

Professional learning for expansive practice between organizations

Anne Edwards

> What we very quickly realised . . . is that we couldn't meet all the needs of every child and every family. So what we had to do was at least find access to people who could do that.
>
> (Practitioner involved in preventing the social exclusion of children and families in England in 2005)

Expansive practice

Research on the nature of expertise has been marked by a shift over the last decade or so. There has been a move from simply explaining it as an individual capacity to recognize the complications in a task, then foreground what is important and work on it (Schmidt, Norman & Boshuizen, 1990). It is now acknowledged that it may also be distributed across networks (Hakkarainen, Palonen, Paavola & Lehtinen, 2004, this volume; Nardi, Whittaker & Schwarz, 2002); is negotiated with others around tasks (Engeström & Middleton, 1996); and is a resource for joint action (Edwards, 2005; 2009). This shift recognizes, among other things, that some forms of work cannot be accomplished alone; that linear models of collaborative work no longer convince; and that some tasks are unpredictable and may involve flexible responses, which could not have been anticipated.

All of these approaches to expertise see it as a process of informed interpretations of the problems of practice and appropriate responses to those interpretations. The more distributed notions of expertise augment this explanation by recognizing that both interpretations and responses may be enriched if we bring into play the expertise of others. As we shall see, distributed forms of expertise are underpinning new forms of inter-professional collaboration. In many ways these practices are running ahead of ways of understanding and supporting them. This chapter is an attempt to better understand the competencies that are embedded in these emergent practices.

The analysis draws on cultural historical activity theory (CHAT) frameworks, which locate individual learning and development in environmental affordances for thinking and acting (Cole, 1996). A CHAT concept highly relevant to this chapter is the 'object of activity' as developed by both Leont'ev and Engeström. Leont'ev explained what he meant by object and its importance as follows.

> The main thing which distinguishes one activity from another, however, is the difference of their objects. It is exactly the object of an activity that gives it a determined direction. According to the terminology I have proposed, the object of the activity is its true motive.
>
> (Leont'ev, 1978, p. 62)

For example, it is easy to distinguish between a childcare setting where children's poor nutrition is the object of activity and is being worked on and transformed by careful feeding; and a setting where children's academic development is the primary object, with pedagogic practices being more important than careful feeding.

The idea of object-motive is a useful one because it asks us to recognize that the way we interpret a task or problem will shape the way we respond to it; and that our interpretations are shaped by the social practices of the situations in which objects of activity are located. In the first example of a childcare setting just given, we might interpret poor nutrition as primarily a problem of poverty and campaign for higher taxes, collecting money for families and so on; or we might see it as an outcome of family breakdown, teenage parenting and so on, and focus mainly on working with the carers of the children. When several people collaborate in working on an object, the usual outcome is an enriched or expanded understanding of the problem or task and a greater range of responses to it.

Engeström's later development of activity theory (Engeström, 1999) has more clearly located the object of activity within systems that are amenable to analysis, enabling us to examine how the patterns of work and the rules embedded in them constrain and reveal contradictions in how the object of activity is interpreted. Engeström's version of activity theory can take us some of the way towards explaining the processes and demands of inter-professional work. It helps us to see that an object of activity may be expanded by bringing to bear different perspectives when interpreting it, and that expansion of the object is likely to lead to changes in the configuration of the system in which it is located.

However, the focus on systems-level change in activity theory has meant that we still have some way to go to understand the actual practices that are the response to the expanded object of activity. This difficulty is compounded when these responses involve working across the boundaries of established systems. For example, a teacher and a social worker will have slightly different views of a child's non-attendance at school, which could allow a richer picture to be built and perhaps expand the shared object of activity, and which might in turn lead to an expansion of the activity systems inhabited by the two professionals. However, activity theory does not easily help us to tease out the negotiations that arise when the two practitioners work on supporting the child and her family. That is, it does not take us to the level of the professional competencies or attributes that come into play in these negotiations.

The chapters in this collection are shifting our focus to the level of practice by asking us to examine the competencies that arise when new tools are inserted into systems. In this chapter I follow that theme by using the conceptual tools of CHAT to look at (a) how an object of professional activity is expanded when new conceptual tools are brought to bear on it and (b) the development of expansive responses to these complex objects, which are made more challenging by the need to work across organizational boundaries.

The discussion will centre on the introduction of 'the prevention of social exclusion' as a new core concept in welfare and education services in England. Its introduction has led to major reconfigurations of local children's services and an expectation that professionals from different backgrounds will collaborate to disrupt children's trajectories of social exclusion to enable them to take up the opportunities for engaging with what society has to offer them. These collaborations call for new professional competencies and particularly a capacity to know how to contribute to and work with the expertise that is distributed across local systems. In particular I focus on the Children's Fund, which was a £980m national initiative (2000–2008) set up as a catalyst for developing systems and practices aimed at preventing social exclusion among 5- to 13-year-olds.

It was established with the expectation that new tools and new goals would lead to new ways of working; and as with many such initiatives a great deal of the learning that occurred was embedded within local sets of social practices and was short-lived. In this chapter I suggest that more attention needs to be paid to recognizing and sustaining ways of working with the new tools which reflect the demands of newly interpreted objects, if we are to take forward the knowledge that is embedded in emerging practices.

Working together to prevent the social exclusion of vulnerable children

The 1990s in Europe witnessed a refocusing of work with children and young people from disadvantaged backgrounds. These children came to be seen as vulnerable to social exclusion and likely to fail to engage with and contribute to society. Of course vulnerability is complex and may not be evident unless one looks across all aspects of a child's life: parenting, schooling, housing and so on. It was therefore immediately apparent that the welfare services which work with children needed to find ways of enabling collaboration between practitioners (Home Office, 2000; OECD, 1998).

As concerns with both youth disaffection and national economic competitiveness have grown, the prevention of social exclusion through early intervention and multi-professional working has become increasingly important and has been enshrined in a swathe of programmes which intervene in the early stages of vulnerability, which are not necessarily in the early years of life, by building protective factors such as sustained support around children. These factors are intended to disrupt emerging trajectories which look likely to lead to school failure and unemployment.

Professional learning and distributed expertise

In two recent studies[1] with colleagues, I have been examining how professionals learn to do the kind of responsive preventative work stimulated by these policies. As these studies have been located in the early days of policy-led changes in practices, much of the learning we have found has been on or beyond the boundaries of established organizational structures. They work outside their 'institutional shelters' (Sennett, 1999) in new forms of responsive collaborative practice while they focus on the transformation of children's trajectories. These trajectories are intrinsically mobile and unstable objects of activity: what Engeström calls 'runaway objects' (Engeström, 2005), which change as they are worked on and constantly move ahead of those who are working on them. Following the runaway objects that are children's trajectories, in order to move them towards social inclusion, is relatively new and quite risky work.

The learning involved is therefore not a matter of becoming an increasingly adroit participant in established professional practices; they often don't exist and if they do they may not offer the flexibility required for this new kind of responsive work (Edwards, Barnes, Plewis, Morris et al., 2006; Edwards, Daniels, Gallagher, Leadbetter and Warmington, 2009). This form of expansive practice requires the creation of new tools or new use of old tools and new competencies. Tools used by practitioners may be material and quite mundane, for example, a mobile phone solely for use at work seems to support flexible responses to children's trajectories. However, these tools may find themselves appropriated to sustain less expansive forms of practice unless attention is paid to how and why they are used on runaway objects.

The how and the why are necessarily intertwined with the use of material tools. New competencies need to accommodate an ongoing process of reinterpretation in response to the remaking of a child's trajectory as well as responsive negotiations of responses to those interpretations. Competencies need to be forward-looking: rather like Cole's 1996 development of Wartofsky's (1973) 'tertiary artifacts' i.e. tools for going beyond representations of what exists to enable imagined futures. Cole suggests that these function both internally by shaping our thinking; and externally by mediating our engagement with the world. By allowing us to look beyond the 'given' to what 'might be', tertiary artifacts resonate strongly with Engeström's notion of 'where to' tools. Giving the example of a care plan, Engeström suggests that they contain the 'core idea', and are used to sustain a long-term orientation on a complex object (Engeström, Pasanen, Toiviainen & Haavisto, 2005). The term 'tool' is more helpful than 'artifact'; as Cole suggests, tertiary artifacts can be seen as ways of thinking which can provide 'a tool for changing current praxis' (1996, p. 121).

Currently the core idea for policies aimed at the prevention of social exclusion is early intervention with a coordinated response which crosses occupational and organizational boundaries. Coordinating tools, such as Common Assessment Frameworks are being developed, but early comments from practitioners suggest that they are often used for record-keeping and accountability rather than being inspired by a sense of 'where to'. The challenge for professional learning, therefore, seems to be a matter of knowing how to interweave the core idea of the prevention of social exclusion with the use of material tools. There is considerable interest across studies of workplace learning in how people draw on the expertise of others; but this particular core idea, with its focus on runaway objects and working flexibly across often rigid boundaries, amplifies the challenges of doing so.

In one example of working with the expertise of others, Nardi and her colleagues (2002) examined the emergence of personal social or 'intensional' networks, describing them as the hidden underpinnings of organizational structures enabling work to be accomplished. Arguing that in new organizational modalities, 'It's not what you know, it's who you know', they traced the formation, maintenance and activation of networks in what they describe as netWORK which benefited both individual workers and their organizations. Here networks were presented as resource-laden and needing nurturing so that they could be accessed to accomplish the work identified by the netWORKER. There was, therefore, no attention paid to the joint use of 'where to' tools or expanded interpretations of runaway objects.

'Knotworking' (Engeström, Engeström, & Vähäaho, 1999) comes closer to meeting the kind of challenge offered by prevention by focusing on the bringing together of loosely connected people to work on complex tasks over relatively short periods. Knotworking certainly captures the ebb and flow of work as medical practitioners from different teams cooperate to save a life. However, while they may bring different expertise to bear, in this case they are all healthcare workers with a shared set of professional values and there is a system in place to enable the bringing together.

Gherardi and Nicolini (2002) look at collaboration across more distinct tribal boundaries in their study of how engineers, site managers and contractors in a building cooperative negotiated an understanding of safety that met their different criteria while working on a common building project. Using the metaphor of 'a constellation of interconnected practices' they suggested that learning can be seen as a form of 'brokering' which relates situated bodies of knowledge 'to the minimum extent necessary to "perform" the community'. There are certainly stronger resonances here with the longer-term negotiations associated with preventing social exclusion. However, the participants in this study were already connected and their expertise and priorities easily recognizable. Brokering or negotiating interpretations and responses across strongly boundaried traditions of practice is likely to be even more challenging.

The different approaches to understanding how people work with the expertise of others, which are exemplified by these studies, can be summarized as those which see the expertise as something that can be drawn on to assist action on objects of activity which have been interpreted by the primary actor; and those which recognize that other experts may also be involved in interpreting an object of activity with the result that responses to the now expanded object of activity are collaborative object-oriented actions. However, although both the Engeström *et al.*

and the Gherardi and Nicolini descriptions take more account of the interpretations brought to bear by the other experts than do Nardi *et al.*, neither of these studies examine collaboration across organizational boundaries on mobile runaway objects of the kind demanded by work on the prevention of social exclusion.

The National Evaluation of the Children's Fund (NECF)

The data discussed in this chapter are drawn from NECF. The Children's Fund comprised 149 partnerships, one in each local authority, across England. These partnerships set up boards, which consisted of senior representatives of local services such as education, social services and health as well as members of voluntary agencies. Their job was to commission the provision of local services such as breakfast clubs or play schemes, which aimed at preventing social exclusion through building protective factors around children and by encouraging inter-professional collaboration. As one section of the evaluation, we looked in some detail at sixteen of these boards as well as at four of the services commissioned in each of these partnerships in order to reveal the structures and processes that made for good outcomes for children.

The sixteen case studies were framed by CHAT and each ran over seven months with later shorter visits to enable us to capture change. Three researchers visited each partnership case study site for four days at four weekly intervals for seven months. In the visits we worked down each partnership from the strategic board in week one, to the service providers in the second visit, then to the children and families in the third visit. On the fourth visit we returned to look at service provision using insights from the children and families, on the fifth visit we returned to work with the boards. We made no visits in the sixth month but returned in the seventh month to give formal feedback and gather reactions to that feedback.

Evidence was collected primarily through interviews which were structured by CHAT, recorded, transcribed in full and then analysed using CHAT frameworks. We explored, for example, what people saw as the object of activity, what material and conceptual tools they were bringing to bear on the object they identified and how the work on the object was shared out. About 190 board members were interviewed and some of these were interviewed two or three times. We also interviewed about 150 practitioners using CHAT-based interviews; and worked with 185 children and young people and 184 carers to explore their experiences of what practitioners said they were doing.

In addition, we gathered evidence in structured workshops, which we described as DWR-lite, as they were based on the principles of developmental work research (Engeström, 2007) but were with different groups at each visit. For example, during our second visits we fed back our ongoing analyses to board members in workshops which were based on DWR. We offered their everyday understandings as mirror data in ways that revealed contradictions in the interpretations of the object of the activity of the board and used the analytic concepts of activity theory to drive forward their analyses of what the board was doing. That process was repeated in the third week with the service providers. We developed child-friendly versions of DWR for work with children; and ran a mixed board, practitioner and child and family DWR during the fifth visit.

We analysed the evidence from the interviews in two stages. In the three weeks between visits the team carried out initial analyses to prepare for DWR sessions. Then once the case studies had ended we started on more detailed CHAT analyses of the interviews and DWR sessions to produce case study reports. Once all the case studies had been completed we undertook cross-case analyses, which led to further analyses within cases. The data in this chapter are drawn from the 16 case studies and include evidence from board members, practitioners and children and their carers. They have been selected to illustrate analyses, which are also substantiated in final project reports (Edwards *et al.*, 2006; Evans, Pinnock, Beirens & Edwards, 2006).

Challenges for systems

The evaluation revealed some of the challenges of introducing a conceptual tool such as 'social exclusion' and examples of how they might be addressed. Let us look at these before moving on to examine the competencies needed for negotiating the alignment of practices.

Three important messages emerged about the impact of the new conceptual tool in these systems: the need to work on and understand the new tools which are inserted into systems; the need to provide spaces which could act as springboards for shifts in practice; and the need to think pedagogically when inserting new tools into existing practices.

Refining the tools

Two quite distinct categories of board became evident: 'stable boards', which politely assimilated the conceptual tools of prevention to existing schema; and 'developing boards' which started by treating prevention as an object in itself. In developing boards, interpretations of prevention were contested and worked on to fashion an understanding of it. These understandings then became the core ideas which were embedded in the tools which shaped they way they worked on their next object, which was usually how to commission services which worked at prevention in ways that took forward the boards' beliefs about prevention.

A comparison of the services commissioned by the two types of board revealed interesting differences. There was a strong tendency for stable boards to select services which already existed and to allow them to continue with existing practices with some 'rebranding' to meet funding criteria; while developing boards were more likely to expect services to reflect their careful thinking about the nature of prevention and to work in responsive and participatory ways with children and their families.

The messages from NECF to both local and national government arising from this evidence were: time needs to be allowed for working on new tools enshrined in policies; debate and contestation can be useful if focused on refining understandings; and compliance in using new tools may simply mask assimilation rather than rethinking.

Creating new spaces as springboards for new practices to emerge

The real challenge for inter-professional collaborations came at the level of service provision. Here we observed individual practitioners carving boundary-crossing paths as they helped vulnerable children to draw on the resources that other services in local networks, such as art therapy or sports clubs, could offer. These kinds of collaborations around children's trajectories were more likely to occur when new spaces, outside existing systems of service provision, were set up and sustained by workers employed by the Children's Fund.

These 'boundary zones' (Konkola, 2001) operated as neutral spaces where the values and professional priorities of each practitioner were respected, where information could be shared and where trust could be built. They were not activity systems working on a common and contested object, rather, they were places at the boundaries of established practices where local expertise could be made explicit so that it might be drawn on later.

> We try to have meetings in different places so that allows us to go to different projects; and in that way we have learnt about other people's projects and maybe been able to get an understanding and see where we can learn . . . you know, gain knowledge about that project.
> It's about understanding at a deeper level. It's about connections. Maybe you are not sure about the child we are thinking about; but as we talk it through there may be a connection and if not for that child, maybe for another.
> (Practitioners talking to NECF about learning to work
> across professional boundaries)

These neutral and benign spaces operated as springboards for horizontal linkages between practitioners as they etched new trails across local landscapes to gather resources round the trajectories of the children they worked with. The links they stimulated were, however, heavily situated in relationships with the practitioners they met there which increased their access to resources. The why and the how or core ideas of inter-professional work were rarely discussed in these meetings.

Services where the boards were unquestioning and 'stable' provided a useful lesson about an over-reliance on tried and trusted relationships for doing new work and lack of attention to the developing ideas that drive forward refreshed practices. In those partnerships we found no examples of practitioners working in boundary zones to build new networks of expertise and instead found several examples of pre-existing networks being used in ways which simply ensured that old pre-prevention practices continued unchanged. This lesson was important for partnerships with developing boards, as so many of the new inter-professional links were simply situated in specific relationships, that there was a danger that the only result of these local springboards would be new but easily fossilized networks.

Thinking pedagogically about inserting new tools

The problem was that there had been no analysis of how the Children's Fund would act as a catalyst and model. It focused on changing practices by setting up a funding system that was expected to fund services which would do new work. An opportunity for people to learn from the initiative was consequently lost. New preventative practices and their core ideas needed to be better understood so that they could be shared. Inter-professional work seemed to be driven by everyday concepts of doing the right thing for particular children by using local resources that could be trusted. But collaborations were not shaping or being shaped by stronger scientific conceptualizations, in the Vygotskian sense, of 'why' and 'how' which would enable them to work with people they did not know. One senior local authority worker lamented the lack of core ideas.

> If you search about and see where's the engine room, where all this learning is . . . (where it) is distilled and disseminated in a form that can really inform development, you can't find it.

Some people did recognize the need to conceptualize practice and to get to the point where the question 'where to?' might be raised. One practitioner responsible for sustaining a locality-based multi-professional group explained.

> I think the very first step is understanding about what the sort of issues are . . . Professions have very, very different ideas about need, about discipline, about responsibility, about the impact of systems on families . . . So I think the first step is actually to get some shared understanding about effective practices and about understanding the reasons behind some of them. Understanding some of the reasons why we are seeing these sorts of issues in families.

But even here the focus was on understanding each other's practices and rationales and not about thinking forward to new forms of practice. Indeed, we found little evidence of 'where to' tools for collaboration emerging naturally from the boundary zones we studied. The work that we observed was usually marked by an expectation that individual practitioners would do the boundary crossing on a case by case basis, drawing on their own interpretations of a child's vulnerability and drawing on local knowledge to access resources. There was very little sense of networked expertise being thought of strategically by the boards.

There were advantages to a lack of formality as it meant that practitioners could work quickly and flexibly in ways that were highly valued by the children and their families (Evans *et al.*, 2006). One challenge is therefore to enable that kind of flexibility across organizational structures which begin to see boundaries as important places to work and the networks that arise from them as important for preventative work. This challenge takes us to the competencies involved and how they might be sustained.

Challenges for practice

Although conceptualizations of practice did not arise naturally in boundary zones, they did surface in the light-touch version of DWR (Engeström, 2007) that we carried out with practitioners. There we worked with the contradictions inherent in everyday understandings to help people, among other things, to clarify the objects they were working on and to begin to develop the scientific concepts that might travel beyond their highly situated networks. In one session, for example, a practitioner explained that multi-professional work is only a matter of *adjusting what you do to other people's needs and strengths*. While that does not take us all the way to a description of the competencies needed for negotiating and adjusting, it is a good start.

Another helpful pointer to a core idea is Lundvall's idea of 'know-who' as an important competency.

> Know-who involves information about who knows to do what. But especially it involves the social capability to establish relationships to specialised groups in order to draw on their expertise.
>
> (Lundvall, 1996, p. 7)

Lundvall argues that know-who is embedded and learnt in social practice and cannot simply be codified into a register of names. He suggests that it is helpful to recognize the intertwining of tacit knowledge and codified knowledge; where codified knowledge such as a list of services and the resources they offer can be seen 'as material to be transformed' and aspects of tacit knowledge as 'tools to handle the material' (Lundvall, 1996, p. 11).

Lundvall's analysis of know-who as a capacity to 'draw on' expertise resonates more with the Nardi *et al.* (2002) notion of networks of expertise as resources to enhance one's own performance than it does with either knotworking or Gherardi and Nicolini's (2002) idea of 'constellations of interconnected practices'. However, the relationship that Lundvall suggests between externally provided tools such as lists of resources and the understandings involved in the ways they might be used is helpful for two reasons.

First, tools, such as lists, have the potential to be primary, secondary or tertiary artifacts (Wartofsky, 1973). That is, everything depends on how they are used. A list of local experts may be used in a compliant or primary artifact way, if a practitioner feels that 'I have to tell x what I'm doing, but I can't quite see why'. It may be used as a secondary artifact, when a child is referred on to another expert as part of an established system of onward referral. Or it may assume the function of a tertiary artifact, if used with a sense of 'where to', as a way of negotiating a web of responsive support around a child over time. These options take us to the second implication of an intertwining between what Lundvall describes as codified and tacit knowledge. There are qualitative differences in knowing-who which need to be recognized if we are to discuss competencies associated with using artifacts such as lists of experts. These qualitative differences point to the limitations of a focus solely on competencies.

From competency to responsible agency in expansive practice

While there is value in probing relationships between tools and competencies, an examination of individual competency gives only a partial picture of practice and may exclude attention to the social practices of the workplace and to the social identity of workers within particular settings. We therefore also need to look at practices and the identities they sustain. Holland and her colleagues, for example, have reminded us of the positional identities which reflect our readings of what we can do and who we might work with (Holland, Skinner, Lachicotte & Cain, 1998).

In the multi-professional collaborations we have been observing these are important issues, as so many of the workers who are doing the responsive work with children and families are relatively low status and largely working within accountability-led systems, with their collaborations with other professionals taking them outside those safe systems. For example, in the second study, 'Learning in and for Interagency Working' (Edwards *et al.*, 2009), more intensive DWR discussions revealed practitioners' need to 'rule-bend' in order to follow children's trajectories with other professionals. While it might be easy to establish a ladder of competency in which people learn how to know-who, it would be impossible to plan in that kind of instrumental way for learning the kind of flexible, rule-bending responsiveness that is needed for the forward-looking practices I have been describing.

We therefore need to go beyond analyses of competency to consider in more profound ways what we mean by expert practices which can ameliorate the social problems produced by the excessive individualism of late capitalism. This move involves bringing together three elements to form a more expanded notion of expertise. These are the individual agency evident when experts foreground what is important in a task when working with others; an ability to align one's actions with other people's strengths and needs; and a capacity to negotiate forward-looking responses for unpredictable objects of activity.

Elsewhere I have described a capacity to work with others to expand an object of activity and to align one's responses to those interpretations as 'relational agency' (Edwards, 2005; Edwards, Daniels, Gallagher, Leadbeater & Warmington, 2009;

Edwards and Kinti, 2009). I have described it as an enhanced form of agency which is necessary if practitioners are to be able to work responsively outside the safety of their institutional shelters. Knowing how to know-who is key to negotiating the fleeting collaborations that are a feature of the responsive work I have been describing. But what does knowing how to know-who look like and how is it accomplished?

Recognizing know-who

Know-who for responsive preventative work is not simply a matter of being well-networked. Networks can be unreflective, conservative and resistant to social change (Castells, 2000), as indeed were several of the long-established networks that we came across in the Children's Fund. The know-who which underpins relational agency is nearer to what Shotter describes as 'withitness thinking' (Shotter, 2005). Withitness thinking, Shotter explains, is a 'form of reflective interaction', where 'new possibilities of relation are engendered, new interconnections are made, new "shapes" of experience can emerge'. It is an expansive practice which presupposes an openness to the other as a source of learning and repositioning. He contrasts 'withitness thinking' with 'aboutness thinking' where the other is an object of consciousness and not another consciousness offering responses to which we in turn respond.

Know-who, which embraces withitness thinking, demands more than boundary crossing and brokering to access resources. It involves ongoing and unchoreographed movements of action and withdrawal based on constantly revised interpretations of a changing object and a recognition of and respect for the expertise of the other actors. It involves spontaneous responses, some rule-bending, a strong sense of one's own expertise and a focus on what 'might be' for socially excluded children. It is a high form of expertise and a marked shift from the cautious individual boundary crossing where children were helped to access other resources which we observed in much of the collaboration in the Children's Fund and which resonated with the Nardi *et al.* (2002) notion of NetWORK.

How is know-who accomplished?

A prerequisite for know-who is an ability to look outwards, to take the standpoint of another, an openness to what one sees and a capacity to critically reflect on what might impede object-oriented activity. There were some signs of it emerging in the Children's Fund.

The springboard boundary zones we saw in the Children's Fund were demanding the ability to look outwards with open minds as they built new relationships. They led practitioners to work against well-entrenched grains of inter-professional mistrust, as these quotations from practitioners illustrate.

Social Services could be seen in a very negative way, but because we have had the same person come along every week people have got to know her. They understand the reasons why they don't do this and why they do that, so they are less likely to be negative about it.

I've made new connections . . . for instance I've not worked much with schools before, so that was quite new for me . . . and I've made those links as strong as possible.

These new connections involved a growing ability to be professionally multilingual, able to speak across professional boundaries; and to be explicit about how expertise of different kinds leads to foregrounding different features rather than simply offering enriched ways of responding to one set of interpretations.

Experience of collaboration could also lead practitioners to question those practices which were invoked to strengthen boundaries.

One of the things that I think has dogged agencies is the cloak of secrecy. Now I think there is a difference between confidentiality and secrecy; a sort of jealously guarding their own territory.

An object-oriented, client-centred focus on children's trajectories seemed to be another important driver for flexible collaborations, as this practitioner explains.

My point is that you can put a group of people together, but it's about what they do when they get there. Because it just could be regrouping the same people doing the same tasks. But with [name of service] it's the way we work, having people grouped in a particular way to help the service user and delivering the service they want.

What also distinguished the more advanced forms of collaboration from what was simply boundary crossing to access support, was the length of commitment to a constantly renegotiated object of activity that collaboration required.

It comes down to a seamlessness of service . . . in terms of having the same people on a longer period of time to develop trust and gain knowledge and informed ideas about the family. Rather than passing them from pillar to post and back again.

However, this practitioner did not recognize that although she was describing 'withitness thinking' with other practitioners; 'aboutness thinking' drove relationships with the families. For many practitioners, negotiating practices with service users was a still some way down the line.

We can, therefore, begin to compile some of the organizational and personal features which are starting to contribute to the expansive practice necessary for the prevention of social exclusion. Organizational features include the opportunity to expand the object of activity; time to develop the tools for local use; providing boundary zones as springboards for inter-professional work; and a pedagogical approach to working with new ideas so that contradictions can be revealed and worked on to enable some 'where-to' thinking. Personal features can be summarized as a capacity to look outward and think relationally in inter-professional work for the prevention of social exclusion. It is therefore clear that more detailed work is still required at the inter-personal level.

Importantly, the expansive practice that arises in the settings that are enabling inter-professional work involves an ongoing interweaving of different professional interpretations of a mobile and transforming object with their responses to it. It is not simply a matter of coordination, brokering or accessing resources to work on the interpretations of a child's trajectory which has been made by one professional. Expansive practice consists of generative, forward-focused negotiations of interpretations and responses, which are propelled forward by the core idea, in this case a rich understanding of the prevention of social exclusion.

Concluding points

Attempting to make explicit the competencies embedded in the practices that are emerging in response to a new conceptual tool and set of policies has been a useful exercise. At the very least it has revealed more clearly than ever just how demanding work at the boundary sites of intersecting practices might be for both practitioners and the organizations they inhabit.

From a methodological perspective, the analytic resources of activity theory have provided ways of examining the interplay between objects, tools and the rules that constrain action. More recent work on boundary crossing, boundary zones, networks of expertise and runaway objects have helped to capture aspects of the mobility, uncertainty and risk inherent in professional collaboration in late capitalism. We now need to understand better, and make explicit, the micro-level negotiations which ensure that relational inter-professional practices are future-oriented and generative.

Know-who is a useful starting point for identifying those negotiations, but it also raises questions. These include understanding how interpretations and the aligning of responses are mediated. My current work is examining how the building of common knowledge in meetings is a prerequisite for the exercise of relational agency (Edwards, in preparation; Edwards and Kinti, 2009). Common knowledge contains the core ideas which are revealed when practitioners talk knowledgeably about what matters for them. However, as we show in the Edwards and Kinti paper, core ideas are not necessarily forward-looking and DWR methods can break through the contradictions that arise when new problems are tackled with old ideas.

Note

1 The two studies are: the DfES-funded National Evaluation of the Children's Fund with Marion Barnes, Ian Plewis, Kate Morris *et al.* (2003–2006) and an ESRC-TLRP

Phase III study, 'Learning in and for Interagency Working', with Harry Daniels, Jane Leadbetter, Deirdre Martin, David Middleton, Paul Warmington, Apostol Apostolov, Anna Popova and Steve Brown (2004–2007) (ESRC RES-139-25–0100).

References

Castells, M. (2000). Materials for an Exploratory Theory of the Network Society. *British Journal of Sociology, 51* (1): 5–24.

Cole, M. (1996). *Cultural Psychology*, Cambridge, MA: Harvard University Press.

Edwards, A. (in preparation). *Being an Expert Practitioner: A relational turn*. Dordecht: Springer.

Edwards, A. (2009). Agency and Activity Theory: From the systemic to the relational, in H. Daniels, K. Guttierez and A. Sannino (eds), *Learning and Expanding with Activity Theory* (pp. 197–211). Cambridge: Cambridge University Press.

Edwards, A. (2005). Relational Agency: Learning to be a resourceful practitioner, *International Journal of Educational Research, 43* (3): 168–182.

Edwards, A., Barnes, M., Plewis, I. and Morris, K. *et al.* (2006). *Working to Prevent the Social Exclusion of Children and Young People: Final lessons from the National Evaluation of the Children's Fund. Research Report 734*. London: DfES.

Edwards, A., Daniels, H., Gallagher, T., Leadbetter, J. and Warmington, P. (2009). *Improving Inter-professional Collaborations: Multi-agency working for children's wellbeing*. London: Routledge.

Edwards, A. and Kinti I. (2009). Working Relationally at Organisational Boundaries: Negotiating expertise and identity, in H. Daniels, A. Edwards, Y. Engeström and S. Ludvigsen (eds), *Activity Theory in Practice: Promoting learning across boundaries and agencies* (pp. 126–139). London: Routledge.

Engeström, Y. (2007). 'Putting Activity Theory to Work: The change laboratory as an application of double stimulation', in H. Daniels, M. Cole and J. V. Wertsch (eds), *The Cambridge Companion to Vygotsky* (pp. 363–382). Cambridge: Cambridge University Press.

Engeström, Y. (2005). Knotworking to Create Collaborative Intentionality Capital in Fluid Organizational Fields, in M. M. Beyerlein, S. T. Beyerlein and F. A. Kennedy (eds), *Collaborative Capital: Creating intangible value* (pp. 307–336). Amsterdam: Elsevier.

Engeström, Y. (1999). Activity Theory and Individual and Social Transformation. In Y. Engeström, R. Miettinen and R.-L. Punamäki (eds), *Perspectives on Activity Theory*. (pp. 19–38). Cambridge: Cambridge University Press.

Engeström, Y., Pasanen, A., Toiviainen, H. and Haavisto, V. (2005). Expansive Learning as Collaborative Concept Formation at Work, in K. Yamazumi, Y. Engeström and H. Daniels (eds), *New Learning Challenges: Going beyond the industrial age system of school and work*. (pp. 47–77). Osaka: Kansai University Press.

Engeström, Y., Engeström, R. and Vähäaho, T. (1999). When the Center Does Not Hold: The importance of knotworking, in S. Chaiklin M. Hedegaard and U. J. Jensen (eds), *Activity Theory and Social Practice*. (pp. 345–374). Aarhus: Aarhus University Press.

Engeström, Y. and Middleton (eds), (1996). *Cognition and Communication at Work*. Cambridge: Cambridge University Press.

Evans, R., Pinnock, K., Beirens, H. and Edwards, A. (2006). *Developing Preventative Practices: The experiences of children, young people and their families in the Children's Fund. Research Report 735*. London: DfES.

Gherardi, S. and Nicolini, D. (2002). Learning in a Constellation of Interconnected Practices: Canon or dissonance? *Journal of Management Studies, 39,* 419–436.

Hakkarainen, K., Palonen, T., Paavola, S. and Lehtinen, E. (2004). *Communities of Networked Expertise: Professional and educational perspectives.* Amsterdam: Elsevier.

Holland, D., Skinner, D., Lachicotte, W. and Cain, C. (1998). *Identity and Agency in Cultural Worlds.* Cambridge, MA: Harvard University Press.

Home Office (2000). *Report of Policy Action Team 12: Young people.* London: Home Office.

Konkola, R. (2001). Developmental Process of Internship at Polytechnic and Boundary-zone Activity as a New Model for Activity (in Finnish), cited in T. Tuomi-Gröhn, Y. Engeström and M. Young (eds), (2003). *Between School and Work: New perspectives on transfer and boundary crossing.* Oxford: Pergamon.

Leont'ev, A. N. (1978). *Activity, Consciousness and Personality.* Available at http://marxists. anu.edu.au/archive/leontev/works/1978 (accessed 11.08.2010).

Lundvall, B.-A. (1996). *The Social Dimension of the Learning Economy.* Druid working paper no 96–1 downloaded from Google Scholar (accessed 10.8.2005).

Nardi, B., Whittaker, S. and Schwarz, H. (2002). *NetWORKers and Their Activity in Intensional Networks, Computer Supported Cooperative Work, 11* (1–2), 205–242.

OECD (1998). *Co-ordinating Services for Children and Youth at Risk: A world view.* Paris: OECD.

Schmidt, H. G., Norman, G. R. and Boshuizen, H. P. A. (1990). A Cognitive Perspective on Expertise: Theory and implications, *Academic Medicine, 65* (10), 611–621.

Sennett, R. (1999). Growth and Failure: The new political economy and culture. In M. Featherstone and S. Lash (eds), *Spaces of Culture* (pp. 14–26). London: Sage.

Shotter. J. (2005). Wittgenstein, Bakhtin and Vygotsky: Introducing dialogically-structured reflective practices into our everyday practices. VIKOM Conference, Copenhagen. Available at http://pubpages.unh.edu/~jds/ (accessed 11.08.2010).

Wartofsky, M. (1973). *Models: Representation in scientific understanding.* Dordrecht: D. Reidel.

Chapter 3

Co-configurational design of learning instrumentalities

An activity-theoretical perspective

Yrjö Engeström and Hanna Toiviainen

Introduction

Despite available theory-based and participatory design approaches, there are persistent problems in the design and implementation of technology-mediated learning settings. How to integrate (a) demanding theoretical principles of productive learning, (b) user requirements of the local institutions, communities and practices, and (c) the technological solutions into one and the same process and a meaningful product? From the perspective of cultural-historical activity theory, combination and coordination of knowledge from multiple sources is not enough. What is needed is long-standing collaboration and co-configuration in which each partner will learn from others and move towards a collectively created new object. Activity theory also points to the importance of creating and using intermediate tools to make co-configuration design possible. Such intermediate tools, or boundary objects (Bowker & Star, 1999) need to be collaboratively created, contested and reconstructed in use.

Our analysis focuses on a long-term process of design that took place as collaboration between different stakeholder groups and aimed at creating a complex set of artifacts (Change Laboratory Tools, or CLT) for the purpose of facilitating learning in a work organization. Methodologically, the challenge differs from that of investigating short-term situational interaction commonly addressed in studies of design and learning thus far. We will analyze a design process in which three groups – namely (a) researchers, (b) in-house developers of a big engineering company (the users), and (c) software designers – searched for tools to support the implementation of the Change Laboratory (CL) method in a virtual and global corporate setting. How did they develop their multi-voiced dialogue and bring in their different elements of expertise? What does it take to achieve a shared object of design?

At the beginning of its work, the design team sketched an intermediate matrix tool to figure out the scope and structure of its potential object. The matrix combined the steps of the expansive learning (process) on the one hand and the elements of the prototypical setting of the Change Laboratory (structure) on the other hand. In the analysis, we will put particular emphasis on the emergence of hybrid language, hybrid concepts, and hybrid forms of knowledge. On the other hand, we will focus on disruptions, conflicts and tensions in the design process. Our analysis aims at constructing an initial conceptual framework for understanding and facilitating co-configurational processes of design and implementation of advanced instrumentalities of learning.

Theoretical framework

The significance of understanding and analyzing the object of the activity goes through all generations of the cultural-historical activity-theory research (Vygotsky, 1978; Leont'ev, 1978; Engeström, 2001, p. 135). There is no activity without an object. The object embodies the meaning, the motive and the purpose of a collective activity system. The object is not reducible to short-term goals; it is durable and gets reproduced in each cluster of actions vital to the activity. The object is given to the practitioners as "raw material." But it is also interpreted, constructed and changed by their actions. The object is key to the question "why?" in human conduct. It gives activity longevity and cohesive power (see Engeström & Blackler, 2005).

According to Stahl (2006, p. 19), activity theory "has no theoretical representation of the critical small groups in which the individuals carry on their concrete interactions and into which the community is hierarchically structured." His own theoretical perspective is represented by the diagram at the bottom on the right-hand side in Figure 3.1.

In the dominant tradition of small group research, groups are seen as ahistorical and acontextual entities which have their own universal organism-like dynamics (for critiques, see for example Fambrough & Comerford, 2006). To put an

[margin annotation, handwritten: Importance of vision (object)]

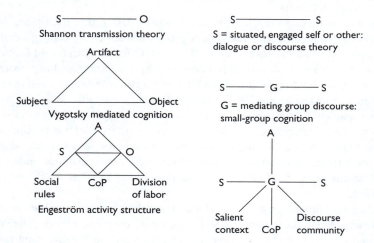

Figure 3.1 Gerry Stahl's comparison of representations of activity theory (left) and of the mediation of group cognition (right) (Stahl, 2006, p. 439)

abstract notion of "group" into a conceptual model of an activity system would violate the historicity of the cultural-historical approach. Instead, the nodes of "subject," "community," and "division of labor" in the triangular model of activity system (Engeström, 1987, p. 178) prompt the researcher and the practitioner to ask: What are the dominant patterns of organizing collaboration in this activity at present, what were they in its preceding historical forms, and what might they become in the future?

Activity theory is primarily interested in the historical evolution and transformations of different constellations of collaboration as vehicles for organizing object-oriented activity. In work organizations, teams have gone through important historical transformations during the decades after the Second World War (Engeström, 2008). At the moment, stable teams are typically being replaced by rapidly fluctuating forms of "knotworking" (Engeström, Engeström & Vähäaho, 1999; Engeström, 2005), as well as even more loose globally distributed "rhizomatic" or "mycorrhizae-like" patterns of collaboration (Engeström, 2006). *rhizomatic collaboration* Temporary interdisciplinary and inter-organizational projects and project groups, such as the design team studied in this chapter, may be regarded as meeting grounds between multiple activity systems, or possibly as emergent "boundary activity systems" (for critical analyses of projects, see Hodgson & Cicmil, 2006).

Stahl's own model (Figure 3.1) includes the notion of "salient context." What this might mean remains unclear. What is clear is the absence of the object in Stahl's model.

While common in various forms of interactionism and discourse studies (see Engeström, 1999), the absence of the object has consequences. First of all, it typically leads to the narrowing down of the analysis to the here-and-now, in other words, to very short slices of interaction with no history and no future. For instance the central data fragment analyzed by Stahl (2006, p. 250) in his book covers 28 seconds of classroom interaction. This "collaborative moment" is further analyzed as embedded in 10 minutes of "surrounding" classroom interaction. While such fine-grained analyses of discourse may be instructive, due to their isolation from more encompassing processes and historical changes, they have little to offer for researchers interested in problem-solving and learning embedded in complex transformations and design efforts typical to workplaces and professional networks.

The second consequence of the absence of the object is that the meaning and motive of the activity are taken for granted. In Stahl's crucial "collaborative moment," a group of 11-year-old boys discussed a classroom assignment which required them to compare and pair a number of different rockets represented on a computer screen. Stahl does not ask why this assignment was significant and for whom. What meaning and consequences – if any – did it have for the students? Because such an assignment obviously represents "hard science," it automatically carries a certain prestige. Prestigious triviality is indeed easy to take for granted.

In this chapter, we examine a co-configurational process of collaborative design (for the concept of co-configuration, see Victor & Boynton, 1998; Engeström, 2004; Virkkunen, 2006). What makes this process co-configurational is (a) that the object and intended product, a new kind of learning instrumentality, was regarded as a long-term project, with five years of time for design and experimentation and hopefully much more in actual use and constant reconfiguration, (b) the fact that multiple organizational entities and domains of expertise were involved without any one of them having a fixed authority position over the others, and (c) representatives of the eventual end users were actively involved in the design process.

The notion of an instrumentality refers to the entire toolkit used in an activity, understood as a multi-layered constellation, which includes both material and conceptual elements. As we pointed out recently, "the design and implementation of instrumentalities is obviously a stepwise process that includes fitting together new and old tools and procedures as well as putting into novel uses or 'domesticating' packaged technologies" (Engeström, 2007, p. 33).

The different organizational entities and domains of expertise involved in the process of collaborative design have their own social languages (Bakhtin, 1982). Thus, we approach the design process as a multi-voiced effort at constructing a shared object. We expect such a process to be riddled with and partially driven by contradictions that manifest themselves in collisions between the social languages, in the form of dilemmatic hesitations (Billig *et al.*, 1988) as well as open disagreements.

The context of the study

The project

The project aims to explore the potentials of technology-enhanced learning in different knowledge practices, namely those of school and university education, teacher education and work-related professional networks. The co-construction and dynamic interaction between the learning-theoretical, pedagogical, and technological developments is one of the main challenges set to the project.

Change Laboratory

Designing the technology to support the implementation of the Change Laboratory (CL) method in a "virtual" and global work setting is one of the components of the KP-Lab project. Change Laboratory is a method for developing work practices by the practitioners together with the interventionist-researchers. It was developed at the university of Helsinki, Center for Activity Theory and Developmental Work Research more than ten years ago and has ever since been implemented and elaborated in a variety of work organizations and networks (Engeström, Virkkunen, Helle, Pihlaja & Poikela, 1996; Ahonen, Engeström & Virkkunen, 2000; Ahonen & Virkkunen, 2003; Engeström, Engeström & Suntio, 2002; Engeström, Engeström & Kerosuo, 2003). The idea is to bring work redesign closer to the daily shopfloor practice while still keeping it analytical and oriented to radical concept shifts. The method supports expansive learning (Engeström, 1987) which involves major transformations of the work activity within and across work units and organizations. Figure 3.2 shows the prototypical layout of the Change Laboratory. It combines a set of conceptual tools with the image of a physical space, a room for analyzing and developing work.

While the Change Laboratory is a relatively well-established method in settings in which the participants are physically co-present, it has not been designed for geographically distributed and temporally asynchronous projects mediated primarily by ICT tools.

Design team

The participants of the CL design team were software designers from French and Finnish organizations, in-house developers from a consulting and engineering firm, and researchers from two Finnish research centers. The authors of this article are contributing to the research part of the project as a member of the expert panel (YE) and as a project researcher (HT). The former contributed to the formation of the matrix, the latter participated in the design team meeting analyzed in this chapter.

The long development session analyzed here was carried out among the Finnish partners orienting themselves towards the developmental interventions to be implemented in the company. Two in-house developers from the engineering company, two software designers (who in this particular meeting also came from the company), and one researcher (HT) participated in the focal meeting.

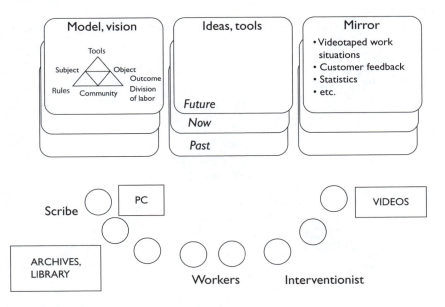

Figure 3.2 Prototypical layout of the Change Laboratory

The company

The piloting organization for the new Change Laboratory learning instrumentality is here called Forest Group. It is a globally operating consulting and engineering firm. There is a constant need for powerful learning instrumentalities that may enhance the employees' capabilities for co-configuration work in the globally distributed operations of Forest Group.

Analytical framework

Our analysis embraces several layers of the collaborative design work, which we depict in Figure 3.3. At the core there is the object of design that we call *new learning instrumentality* embedded in the context of the Change Laboratory (CL) method, to be reconceptualized for virtual and global corporate use.

In order to create a new kind of learning instrumentality we need, as the second layer, intermediate conceptual tools or boundary objects that facilitate co-configuration by bringing together the various perspectives and social languages. *The matrix tool* for designing the CL environment was such an intermediate device in the design team's work.

We expect the third potential layer in the collaborative design to be made up of *project talk*, which, at its best, may foster common ground and trust between the participants and link design work to the rest of the project. At its worst, project talk is formal discourse that functions as a "blanket" that obscures the object of design or as a "muffler" that silences discussion on contradictions and contested perspectives.

Finally, the different social languages brought in by the professionals are expected

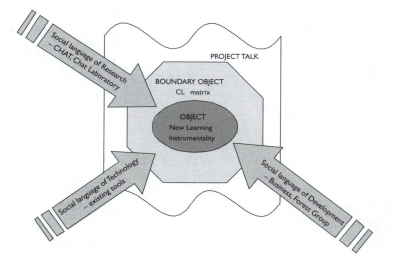

Figure 3.3 Analytical framework

to permeate all these layers, become audible and get mixed in with the meeting talk. We will briefly describe each of the elements of the framework.

The object of design

The initial definition of the object of design – a set of the Change Laboratory tools for enhancing learning in professional networks – can be found in the project documents produced in the application and planning phase. The overall pedagogy-oriented assignment was formulated as follows.

> Educational or workplace communities will be supported in reflecting on and transforming their knowledge practices and other activities by developing Change Laboratory Tools (CLT). Toward that end, the CLT help the participants in making their practices and activity structures visible. The idea of CLT is to structure the users' activities in a way that help them address issues critical for deliberate transformation of prevailing practices. Accordingly, Video-taped story-telling and Map-It Tools (–) can be used with CLT, but also separately.
>
> (Knowledge Practice Laboratory, 2006, p. 25)

The technology-oriented task assignment was titled "Change Laboratory Services."

> This task will handle the integration of the Change Laboratory tools within the KP-Lab shared space. Technology assessment, requirement analysis, and design will be the activities performed during this first period.
>
> (Knowledge Practice Laboratory, 2006, p. 97)

But the technological design of the CL tools was only one side of the task. The other side dealt with the knowledge practices of the company in which the CL tools were to be implemented in the piloting phase.

The planning of the CL will start by specifying the organizational unit with which the piloting process may be implemented, focused at the analysis and development of the business concept and the learning activity. The representatives of customers and other stakeholders will be invited to participate, at least acting as a mirror for Forest Group's activity. The case will present an opportunity to pilot first versions of KP-Lab tools, such as Change Laboratory-tools and video annotation tools.

> (Knowledge Practice Laboratory/WP10, 2006)

The matrix as a boundary object

The matrix for designing Change Laboratory tools, shown in Table 3.1, was sketched in the meeting preceding the one we analyze in this article. It became an intermediate tool, a boundary object, which organized the collaborative design effort. Before, the design team had found it somewhat difficult to establish a link between the features of the Change Laboratory and the ICT tools and technologies achievable through the project. The matrix was composed of the basic concepts and elements built in the CL method, with the idea of keeping together both the steps of the CL procedure ("process") and the elements of the CL setting ("structure") through the design process.

The grid was meant to be filled in with the learning tools needed in different phases of the CL. In the first meeting where the matrix was used, participants ended up listing the tools in the column left, under the "Steps of expansive learning," while other cells remained untouched. To save space, only a part of this filled-in column is shown in Table 3.2.

Project talk

Project talk typically contains names and abbreviations as well as organizational-bureaucratic procedures, timelines and deadlines that connect the participants to the project and to each other but often do not effectively communicate to outsiders. We are interested in project talk to the extent it facilitates or prevents the participants' work on the object of design.

Social languages

The three identifiable social languages of the design team were those of the company's in-house development, the software design, and the intervention research. For short, these three may be called the language of development, the language of technology, and the language of research. Each of these carried a special domain of knowledge to the team, namely that of business, information and communication technology, and cultural-historical activity theory respectively. In our data, the participants' utterances seldom represent a specific social language in a pure and well-bounded form. To some extent, this may be due to the fact that in this meeting the software designers were also employees of the same company as the in-house developers. The following three excerpts exemplify some characteristics of the three social languages.

In-house developer: If we think about the Forest Group case which may be the easiest, concretely think about the case of our IT organization that NN was talking about, in other words, it is distributed . . .

Software designer: In addition, are they all built on the same platform, these annotations? In that case one could dig and mine, kind of, if they were in the same place . . .

Researcher: In the beginning, I guess, the models of the past are emphasized and strongly the ethnography of the present, which is . . . Kind of this mirror, mirror material. And then, gradually, as they start to plan, then the ideas and the tools are emphasized and then the present and future . . .

Table 3.1 The matrix in the beginning of the design meeting

Layout of change laboratory

Steps of expansive learning	Workers	Scribe	Interventionist	3 x 3 Wall table: past, present, future	Model vision	Ideas/ tools	Mirror	Video	PC	Archive library
1 Charting the situation										
2 Analyzing the situation										
3 Creating a new model										
4 Concretizing and testing the new model										
5 Implementing the new model										
6 Spreading and consolidating										

Table 3.2 Filled-in matrix column at the end of the design meeting

Steps of expansive learning

Kick off meeting
Processes, tools, virtual environment, virtual coffee breaks

Creating Virtual Change Laboratory Infrastructure and procedures
Asynchronous and synchronous virtual sessions
Organizing archive and library
Virtual shared space 3 × 3 + other tools

I Charting the situation

I.I Interview and virtual interview (map it?)
    Requirements for virtual interview?

I.2 Video and annotation

I.3 Wikipedia and blog
    Who knows and what?

I.4 Data mining

I.5 Virtual sessions

I.6 Virtual shared space 3 x 3 + other tools

2 Analyzing the situation

Mirror material in share space

Archive library

Modeling tools (triangle model of activity)

Virtual whiteboard

3 Creating a new model

Modeling tools (triangle model of activity)

(continues . . .)

Data

Our data covers a sequence of six design meetings in which the matrix tool was generated, used and modified by the participants. This chapter is focused on the second one of these meetings, held on June 1, 2006. The meeting lasted two hours and twenty minutes. It was video- and audio-recorded and transcribed. After the sixth meeting, the participants went on to design the first digital presentation of the 3 × 3 wall tables central in the Change Laboratory setup. The ensuing new series of meetings was called "mock-up meetings."

We first divided the transcript into main episodes by identifying shifts in the general topic of the discussion. This is made visible in Table 3.4 that covers the first 60 minutes of the meeting. The main episodes of talk were further divided into more detailed sub-episodes on the basis of the new elements introduced to the topic at hand. For example, a speaker articulated a contradiction or dilemma related to the design (episode 3.1) or suggested the use of a digital tool, which raised additional questions (episode 8.1).

Table 3.3 Episodes of talk during the first 60 minutes of meeting 2 (episodes analyzed in detail are marked in bold)

Disc 1/time	Episode		Initiative	
0:00:25	1	Preparing the matrix	Dev1:	How do we present and use the matrix?
0:02:40	2	Workplace chat	Dev2:	This tastes good!
0:04:25	3	Negotiating the use of the matrix	Res:	This is a primitive Word table, as you can see . . .
0:05:04– **0:06:34**	**3.1**	**Design contradiction between innovative ideas and existing tools**	**Dev2:**	**What we talked about afterwards last time . . .**
0:06:13	3	Continues	Res:	Who is going to be the scribe?
0:13:35	4	Understanding multimedia annotation	Dev2:	By the way . . .
0:16:45	5	Presentation of the CL sessions in the matrix	Dev2's notion on the presentation of the sessions in the matrix	
0:17:34	**6**	**Breakthrough in defining the core of design**	**Tec1:**	**I think this is the phase where . . .**
0:22:05	7	Filling in the matrix	Res:	But we could go back to . . .
0:31:09	8	Need for structuring data-gathering in the "virtual" CL	Dev2:	Can we? How should I put it?
0:35:40– **0:38:16**	**8.1**	**Design dilemma of an existing tool**	**Dev2:**	**Let's put Map-it tool in there!**
	8	Continues	Dev2:	What kind of tool do you would imagine there should be?
0:44:43	9	Use of Wiki	Tec2:	From Wikipedia it occurred to my mind that . . .

(continued on next page)

Table 3.3 (continued)

0:51:13	10	Using "who-knows-what" tools	Tec2:	I got just a cheap idea from that wiki …
0:55:28	11	Interventionist's blog and information sharing in the CL	Tec1:	And then, certainly, be it wiki or blog …
0:56:54– 1:02:02	12	Meaning of the 3 x 3 table as the core of design	Dev1:	Is the idea (–) wallpaper?

In the rest of this chapter, we will restrict our analysis to sub-episode 3.1, epi-sode 6, and sub-episode 8.1 (marked in bold in Table 3.4). The choice of these three episodes is based on the theoretical and practical emphasis we put on the *tension-laden formation of the object*. The three episodes represent intense phases in which the object of the design was first problematized in contradictory terms, then jointly formulated in an enthusiastic manner, and finally re-problematized in dilemmatic terms. In the three sections that follow, we will analyze each of the three episodes in a temporal order. The speakers are marked with symbols Dev1 and Dev2 (in-house developers), Sof1 and Sof2 (software designers), and Res (researcher).

Design contradiction between innovative and existing tools

A tension between the innovative design of new Change Laboratory tools and the exploitation of the existing technological solutions and tools went through the meeting and shaped the use of the matrix. This tension is not unique to this case but is commonly encountered in projects designing tools and environments for different contexts of learning. Existing tools may be technologically ready to be used and make the design task look easier. The existing tools have exchange value in that they can bring quickly concrete outcomes to the project or credit for the partner who has introduced a given tool. Also, by using ready-made tools partners can save in design expenditures. Compared to this, the innovative solutions are technologically and pedagogically, as well as economically, much more risky and uncertain – but also much more interesting. They have great potential use value for the project (for a theoretical discussion of exchange value and use value, see Engeström, 1987, pp. 82–91).

The focal contradiction was addressed at the beginning of the design team meet-ing (time 0:05:04–0:06:034) in an episode produced by an in-house developer, the researcher and a software designer. However, none of the social languages dominated the articulation of the contradiction. The discursive turns were saturated by project talk encouraging the free-floating of ideas.

From episode 3.1

01 *Dev2:* What we talked last time afterwards, you [Tec1 and Tec2] were there, that we could consider having kind of two-level ideas, those that are feet-off-the-ground which are not necessarily implemented as such, and then stuff like video annotation, it's, kind of, *unimaginative*. We don't need to- then consider where to (.) where to go. (.) Particularly to this [Res: # Right.] "creating a new model" we can, it's I think one of those– (.)

02 *Res:* Yes I think that we in this phase can put forth ideas [Dev2: Yeah!] very freely.

03 *Dev2:* And then come [Dev1: That's what we should do I think. Res: Yes.] And we do have five years so . . .

04 *Res:* Yes [he-he].

05 *Dev2:* But kind of come from there . . .

06 *Res:* Yes right just this way. [Dev2: downwards so] Especially in this start-up phase so . . .

07 *Sof1:* Just so that not straightforwardly translate existing tools into virtual ones (sort of), [Dev2: Right!] but could we think of finding some new, kind of more innovative tools.

The question was thus not whether to choose ready-made tools or create new ones, but how to combine these two in collaborative design. Both were needed, which is what Dev2 (turn 1) described as "two-level ideas." In a situation such as this, the options seem to be to move either top-down or bottom-up, in other words, from innovative ideas to existing technologies or from existing technologies to innovative ideas. The participants supported the former direction. How this might be accomplished, what "coming downwards" would mean in practice, was not articulated.

Perhaps more importantly, the contradiction between existing technologies and new ideas was not explicated in substantive terms. It remained unclear in just what ways the two might collide. Thus, the contradiction remained latent and underdeveloped in this phase.

Breakthrough in defining the core of design

Episode 6, also from the first half an hour of the meeting (time 0:17:34–0:22:04), generated a potential solution to the design dilemma. It was initiated by a software designer whose opening question may be interpreted, in the context of the meeting, as a boundary-crossing attempt between the social languages of technology and research (turn 1). After receiving an approving answer from the researcher (turn 2), he elaborated the idea more in terms of technology (turn 3).

From episode 6

1   *Sof1:*   I think this is now (.) a phase where – So is there a kind of core
                    on which it is every time done, is it this "wall table" or this one
                    including the "past present future," around which every time,
                    kind of, that could be if we think about the tool, [Res: Yes?] so
                    a kind of the core of the tool?

2   *Res:*   Yes, ri-right actually you could say it is [Tec1: Okay.] it is right
                    in the focus of use and it is elaborated [Tec1: Mm.] all the time
                    so yes it is . . .

3   *Sof1:*   . . . So it would be somehow on the screen if it's now on the
                    wall it would then be on the screen, and around it, it is filled in
                    with these other tools or somehow . . .

This suggestion by the software designer (turns 1 and 3) gained support from an in-house developer, from the researcher, and from others as well. It was followed by approving words "yes," "right," "that's what I mean." The software designer was elaborating the idea of putting the 3 × 3 wall table (see Figure 3.1) into the center of the design by arguing that it would integrate both the structure and the process of the Change Laboratory into the design (which was the idea of the matrix tool as well). The object of collaborative design began to take shape and, simultaneously, seemed to provide a model for the design procedure. A sense of shared understanding and innovation was expressed in overlapping talk in an enthusiastic tone.

From episode 6

25   *Dev1:*   (--) one could say that once it is clear [what is done in each
                    CL-phase], then ask what are the tools [Tec1: Yeah!], yes, [Res:
                    Mm.] and then we could think a little bit what are the future
                    tools. [Tec1: Yes. Yes (–)] Something. [Res: Yeah.] And then
                    return to this #
                    [A lot of overlapping talk]

This is not "coming downwards" as was phrased in episode 3.1 when the team was dealing with the design dilemma, but "returning" to the 3 × 3 table after discussing the learning tools connected to each phase of the CL process. This episode was a breakthrough in defining at least tentatively the core of the design, the object of collaboration beyond the design deadlock resulting from the dichotomy between innovative and existing tools. At least in this case, an expansion of the object of design involved crossing the boundary between the languages of technology and research.

   The participants agreed on a two-step procedure: (1) studying the Change Laboratory process step by step and deciding which tools are needed in each phase;

(2) going back to the 3 × 3 table and placing the tools in the table. A timeline was added to the CL-layout picture right under the 3 × 3 table to point out that the table's tool constellation will look different in different phases of the CL process. However, the strong agreement and sense of breakthrough did not eliminate the design tension that also in this episode was audible in comments like "if we could find some steps that are 'easy' to fill in" and "at least we get crazy ideas."

Design dilemma of an existing tool

The third excerpt of this analysis is situated in the middle of the long episode 8.1 (time 0:35:40–0:38:16) addressing the design (by filling in the matrix) of the first two steps in the CL process, "Charting the situation" and "Analyzing the situation." The question was: What kind of more structured and visualized tools are possibly needed to carry out the start-up interviews in a virtual space compared to the traditional face-to-face interviews? An in-house developer suggested the use of the Map-It tool, one of the promising tools introduced to the KP-Lab project already in the planning phase. On the other hand, the design team members, the initiator included, knew that the tool in question was not associated to carrying out interviews. In general, the use of it had been explicated in the "Description of Work" of the project, but the implementation had not been discussed thus far in relation to the CL design.

Would the adoption of an existing tool represent one of the "easy" solutions mentioned before in the design meeting? Or would it require a lot of tailoring and modification to fit this specific context? It is interesting to look into a piece of discourse on the potential of the given tool and observe a moment when existing technology enters the design of a learning instrumentality.

From episode 8.1

01	*Dev2:*	# . . . the reason why I suggested Map-It to interviews was that it is in a sense mind-map-based [Res: Mm?], I don't know it too well, it came to my mind that it might simultaneously save the data "elegantly."
02	*Tec1:*	. . . that process, [would it save] the process, what is being done? Perhaps? [he-he]
03	*Res:*	Yes? [he-he; expressions of insecurity.] So how did you think that for interviewing – this kind of mind-map type?
04	*Dev2:*	For interviewing in a sense that it allows you to create a kind of process based on which . . .
05	*Res:*	Mm. [Doubting.]
06	*Tec2:*	# Does it save a kind of text [# Tec1: yes-;
	Dev2:	I don't exactly–] and the image, and, the session (–)
07	*Tec1:*	But I don't understand, does it save how it *evolves* or does it only save the outcome?

08	*Tec2:*	# right the information (–)
09	*Dev1:*	# Are you talking about Map-It? The idea is in the first place that during the meetings a need to make notes would be in minimum, it would be prepared as much as possible [Dev2: Yes.] and then they would simply be collected – that's one of their points that we could get [Tec2: (summarizing type of)] Yeah. I also lack knowledge about it.
10	*Res:*	mm
11	*Tec2:*	# (–)
12	*Dev1:*	# But it has (it is more like) data-gathering organizing for decision-mak- it won't maybe . . .
13	*Dev2:*	# That's what came to my mind- Well I don't know why it wouldn't be suited for interview?
14	*Dev1:*	# well no-no. (.) But the point is anyway that it allows collecting the ideas at the same time so-. I got two points (in the video demonstration), one thing is that it [a meeting] is well prepared, so that it is possible to run with a minimum effort, and the report is created simultaneously. [Tec2: (–)] Right. So in that sense, why couldn't we use it here.
15	*Res:*	Well yes I don't [Dev2 continues] # I may not get the point . . .

The design through an existing technological solution appears to be neither easy nor linkable to the pedagogical context that was the object of design. Unlike in the breakthrough, the social languages were not interwoven. The predominantly audible language of technology remained isolated from the other potentially available social languages. The technology talk conveyed in this case a lack of knowledge, uncertainty, and a lot of open questions about the usability of the tool. The design dilemma was elaborated by means of "but" and "maybe" talk. Even positive expectations were expressed in a negative form: "I don't know why it wouldn't be suited for interview" and "why couldn't we use it here" (turns 13 and 14). The episode was concluded by emphasizing the user needs that set requirements even to the ready-made tools (turns 19–21).

From episode 8.1

| 19 | *Res:* | M–m? (.) Right, I just don't know it well enough to get any special images of it [he-he] but well maybe, we can add Map-It there but we can of course try to describe our needs, in that way somebody [who knows Map-It] # may even comment on it – Yes? |
| 20 | *Dev2:* | # But my question is also whether it is possible for Map-It that is ready-[made] to bring our needs. Easily- I don't know it well enough either. |

21   *Tec2:*   # We should (find out) what is required from the program in
                      question [Dev2: Yeah.] and then make a survey of the cor-
                      responding programs by which the data can be stored (–).

The whole episode actually demonstrates a bottom-up design effort that remained
somewhat detached from the core of the design. At the same time, it had creative
potential. An existing tool was introduced by a participant in a way that might
expand its present use and build bridges between the preconditions of the project
and the design needs of the Change Laboratory, between the existing and the
innovative.

Challenges for research on designing learning instrumentalities

It is now time to return to our analytical framework and discuss what these partial
findings suggest as challenges for enlarging the scope of analysis to a more encompassing series of collaborative design actions.

The three episodes seem to represent the beginning of a spiral-like movement
between the formulation of a contradiction, a breakthrough-like resolution of the
contradiction, and a reappearance of the contradiction in a more subtle, dilemmatic
form. It seems indeed plausible that the tension between new theoretical ideas
and existing technologies can only be resolved through multiple iterative cycles of
problem-solving and learning of the kind exemplified by the three episodes.

These cycles have a history and future in the trajectory of design. It seems
reasonable to include them in the analytical framework and subsume to a closer
study in the analysis of longitudinal processes of collaborative design. Are these
minor cycles just accidental and sporadic in the process of design? Or do they reveal
dynamics gradually molding the object of design, suggesting a connection to the
cycles of expansive learning? In the latter case, how can we methodologically trace
and document transitions from cycles of local design actions to expansive object
creation and learning at other (e.g. project-wide, company-wide, network-wide;
see Toiviainen, 2003) levels of design activity?

The first episode we analyzed seemed to be flavored with project talk including
an optimistic orientation towards innovative development work. There was strong
agreement but the object of agreement was defined in loose terms and remained
detached from the contents and implementation of the Change Laboratory. In
the second episode, the social language of research seemed to become universally
accepted, as the participants expressed their enthusiasm for the notion of the
"core." The breakthrough potential of this episode was reflected in efforts of
bridging the language of research and the language of technology.

Nevertheless, the latter was still "waiting for its turn," as exemplified by the
expression "and then we could think a little bit of what are the future tools." In
the third episode, the social language of technology took a dominant role, almost
as a troublesome interruption of the future-oriented hubris. For the time being,

the technological language was not rich enough to bring a solution to the design contradiction.

An investigation of the first months of the design process shows that the participants' voices seldom represented one of the three social languages in a pure form. While one of the languages may have dominated in any given episode, the participants were rather fluidly and subtly moving across the three languages. On the other hand, this movement and mixing of social languages involved tensions and conflicts that often found their expression in doubts and hesitations. Is the blending of the social languages typical throughout the process or will they have to polarize in order to contribute to expansive object construction? The problems of the language of technology in the third episode analyzed above suggest a need for the consolidation of the technology. The social languages may have to diverge again and participate in conscious negotiation on a shared hybrid language, to make the creation of a shared object possible.

Conclusion

We argue that collaborative design is a process of cognition and learning that orients itself toward the construction of an object. The creation of a new object involves multiple social languages and is riddled with contradictions, something that is typically not captured by micro-analyses of collaborative moments. To deal with such a movement, participants need meta-tools that mediate and facilitate the identification and acknowledgment of contradictions and potential solutions. We anticipate that the design contradiction discussed above will become even more compelling and complex later on in the project as the end users step more directly into the collaborative design. In the data analyzed for this chapter, the social language of development remained conspicuously weak.

Our first conclusion is that collaborative design is a learning process that is actualized in the construction of the object of collaboration. It is a long process without shortcuts or straightforward adoption of easy, ready-made technical solutions. In this case, the emerging object of design was a new learning instrumentality. Without constant questioning, reopening, and redefining of the object, collaborative design and learning easily become processes for their own sake – perhaps interesting but hardly productive.

Second, the object of design is in itself contradictory. In the case analyzed in this chapter, the inner contradiction of the object manifested itself above all as a tension between the existing tools and new innovative ideas that defined the core of the design. One could argue, as is often heard, that creativity is in the combination of existing tools in a new context. However, such a combination is a contradictory issue that cannot be accomplished without the creation of new intermediate tools and hybrid social languages.

Third, the contradictory object is worked out through multi-voiced dialogue. To master this, participants need to learn to identify and recognize the characteristics of their social languages and to take advantage of their complementarity. In practice, social languages do not appear in pure form but are mixed. The languages take shape in interaction with the object under creation. In our data, the centrality of the CL and the matrix molded the meeting talk, while even the in-house developers' talk seldom articulated issues devoted purely to the company's developmental and business needs. Our data also allows further examination on how project talk may intervene in the social languages, how it may contribute to dealing with tensions and eventually to the construction of the object.

Our fourth concluding point addresses the importance of intermediate boundary objects in mastering the design as a complex learning process. In this case, the matrix tool for designing the new Change Laboratory learning instrumentality was used to mediate the design. Boundary objects are temporary objects of collaboration but also hybrid tools typically not taken as ready-made and unmodifiable. While it stems from activity theory, the design matrix does not represent the customary conceptual presentation of the Change Laboratory. Being a matrix, it is rather a translation of a theoretical model into a form more accessible to design.

A design setting almost inevitably brings with it the risk of technological domination, forcing theory and methodology to adopt the language of technology. On the other hand, if co-configuration as a new mode of collaboration is applied to design, the technology challenge must be faced and dealt with.

References

Ahonen, H., Engeström, Y., and Virkkunen, J. (2000). Knowledge Management – The Second Generation: Creating competencies within and between work communities in the Competence Laboratory. In Y. Malhotra (ed.), *Knowledge Management and Virtual Organizations* (pp. 282–305). London: Idea Group Publishing.

Ahonen, H. and Virkkunen, J. (2003). Shared Challenge for Learning: Dialogue between management and front-line workers in knowledge management. *International Journal of Information Technology and Management*, 2, 59–84.

Bakhtin, M. M. (1982). *The Dialogic Imagination: Four essays.* Austin: University of Texas Press.

Billig, M., Condor, S., Edwards, D., Gane, M., Middleton, D., and Radley, A. R. (1988). *Ideological Dilemmas: A social psychology of everyday thinking.* London: Sage Publications.

Bowker, G. C. and Star, S. L. (1999). *Sorting Things Out: Classification and its consequences.* Cambridge: The MIT Press.

Engeström, Y. (2008). *From Teams to Knots: Activity-theoretical studies of collaboration and learning at work.* Cambridge: Cambridge University Press.

Engeström, Y. (2007). Enriching the Theory of Expansive Learning: Lessons from journeys toward coconfiguration. *Mind, Culture, and Activity*, 14, 23–39.

Engeström, Y. (2006). Development, Movement and Agency: Breaking away into mycorrhizae activities. In K. Yamazumi (ed.), *Building Activity Theory in Practice: Toward the next generation* (pp. 1–43). Osaka: Center for Human Activity Theory, Kansai University.

Engeström, Y. (2005). Knotworking to Create Collaborative Intentionality Capital in Fluid Organizational Fields. In M. M. Beyerlein, S. T. Beyerlein, and F. A. Kennedy (eds), *Collaborative Capital: Creating intangible value* (pp. 307–336). Amsterdam: Elsevier.

Engeström, Y. (2004). New Forms of Learning in Co-configuration Work. *Journal of Workplace Learning*, 16, 11–21.

Engeström, Y. (2001). Expansive Learning at Work: Toward an activity theoretical reconceptualization. *Journal of Education and Work*, 14, 133–156.

Engeström, Y. (1999). Communication, Discourse and Activity. *The Communication Review*, 3, 165–185.

Engeström, Y. (1987). *Learning by Expanding: An activity-theoretical approach to developmental research*. Helsinki: Orienta-Konsultit.

Engeström, Y. and Blackler, F. (2005). On the Life of the Object. *Organization*, 12, 307–330.

Engeström, Y., Engeström, R., and Kerosuo, H. (2003). The Discursive Construction of Collaborative Care. *Applied Linguistics*, 24, 286–315.

Engeström, Y., Engeström, R., and Suntio, A. (2002). Can a School Community Learn to Master its own Future? An activity-theoretical study of expansive learning among middle school teachers. In G. Wells and G. Claxton (eds) *Learning for Life in the 21st Century: Sociocultural perspectives on the future of education*. London: Blackwell, (pp. 211–224).

Engeström, Y., Engeström, R., and Vähäaho, T. (1999). When the Center Does Not Hold: The importance of knotworking. In Chaiklin, S., Hedegaards, M., and Juul Jensen, U. (eds) *Activity Theory and Social Practice*. Aarhus: Aarhus University Press, (pp. 345–374).

Engeström, Y., Virkkunen, J., Helle, M., Pihlaja, J., and Poikela, R. (1996). Change Laboratory as a Tool for Transforming Work. *Lifelong Learning in Europe*, 1, 10–17.

Fambrough, M. J. and Comerford, S. A. (2006). The Changing Epistemological Assumptions of Group Theory. *The Journal of Applied Behavioral Science*, 42, 330–349.

Hodgson, D. and Cicmil, S. (eds) (2006). *Making Projects Critical*. Basingstoke: Palgrave.

Knowledge Practice Laboratory (2006). Integrated project. Annex 1 – Description of Work. (Corporate document, no. KP-Lab;27490.) Retrieved on April 25, 2006, from KP-Lab project website: http://www.kp-lab.org/intranet/consortium-issues/official-documents/6_027490_0_0_cont_core_3

Leont'ev, A. N. (1978). *Activity, Consciousness, Personality*. Englewood Cliffs: Prentice-Hall.

Stahl, G. (2006). *Group Cognition: Computer support for building collaborative knowledge*. Cambridge: MIT Press.

Toiviainen, H. (2003). *Learning Across Levels: Challenges of collaboration in a small-firm network*. Helsinki: Department of Education, University of Helsinki.

Victor, B. and Boynton, A. (1998). *Invented Here: Maximizing your organization's internal growth and profitability*. Boston: Harvard Business School Press.

Virkkunen, J. (2006). Hybrid Agency in Co-configuration Work. *Outlines: Critical Social Studies*, 8, 61–75.

Vygotsky, L. S. (1978). *Mind in Society: The development of higher psychological processes*. Cambridge, MA: Harvard University Press.

Chapter 4

Professional learning as epistemic trajectories

Leif Christian Lahn

Introduction

In this chapter we want to make a theoretical exploration into the concept "learning trajectory." It has become widely circulated in many fields, and, not surprisingly, different authors in different academic traditions use the term quite differently. Our intention here is not to do a conceptual cleansing. We will restrict ourselves to the literature on professional learning and development where it has become more and more common to talk about "learning trajectories." This state of the art concept is understandable for several reasons. First, it reflects a more common discontent in many fields of research with static notions like "competence," "expertise." Second, to speak of trajectories rather than a developmental process makes the diversity and multidimensionality of learning processes more salient. And third this term points to the embeddedness of trajectories in systems that varies along temporal and spatial dimensions. Professionals are members of a range of different institutions at the same time, and these may work together to provide very distinct learning opportunities. For example, career patterns (Brown, 2002) may tune the interests of individuals to a lifelong learning commitment, whereas a new tool may interact with such a trajectory and either force the practitioner into updating her skills or in resisting a change of working conditions. For members of professional communities, issues related to their knowledge domain are of strategic importance since it defines what they are and what they are entitled to do. Besides, modern working life is said to be characterized by "epistemification" (Stutt & Motta, 1998) as production processes become increasingly knowledge-dependent, and our use of codified knowledge is usually mediated by new technologies. By implication, trajectories that somehow link to these knowledge concerns may be crucially important when our theme is professional learning. We refer to them as "epistemic trajectories."

Another reason for using the term "epistemic trajectories" is that it may bring to the fore issues of knowledge that have been taken off the scene for some years (Muller, 2000). Professional learning and development is understood in general terms, disregarding the distinctive regulating qualities of knowledge. It may shape the way experts formalize their "communities of practice" and reproduce their disciplines and modes of transmission (Bernstein, 1996). For example, nurses will update their skills according to an educational regime that is quite different from accountants or lawyers. Researchers may easily attribute these variations to distinct personal preferences among practitioners or to workplace provisions, and be blind to the societal division of knowledge that regulates the local level.

So in this chapter we will discuss why it may be fruitful to use the concept of trajectory when studying professional learning. We need to make some comments on what is meant by "learning trajectories," and how it differs from "epistemic trajectories." Often these conceptual issues are part of a larger methodological discussion on units of analysis and the scaling of observations. Our explorations in this field are inspired by an ongoing Norwegian research project "Professional learning in a changing society" (ProLEARN, see www.pfi.uio.no/prolearn/) that studies the transition from school to professional work in nursing, teaching, engineering and accounting. It seeks to combine longitudinal approaches and multilevel studies. Some promises and pitfalls associated with such a design will be addressed.

Perspectives on learning trajectories

For our purpose it may be useful to make a rough classification of learning trajectories into three categories: Educational learning trajectories, informal learning trajectories and organizational learning trajectories. They are shown in Table 4.1 together with the fourth. The first category could also be referred to as didactic. It describes the formal stages in a school subject when these are constructed on the basis of an understanding of the students' learning processes. The second is better known through labels like "lifetime learning trajectories" (Gorard, Rees, Fevre & Welland, 2001), "learning careers" and is used within adult education and life course research as terms that underline informal and multi-linear processes of personal development. The third, that we have called "organizational learning trajectories," is a generic term that includes both ladders in occupational careers and more horizontal moves that turn newcomers into proficient professionals.

Different metaphors of learning may overlap with the categories above. It may be useful in our elaboration of the concepts "learning trajectories" and "epistemic trajectories" to adopt Sfard's (1998) well-known dichotomy between the acquisition metaphor and the participation metaphor of learning that has recently been extended by Paavola and Hakkarainen (2005) to include a third metaphor, the knowledge creation metaphor.

The acquisition metaphor sees the human brain as a storehouse where learning takes place when information chunks are accessed in one situation, piled up in memory and retrieved for implementation in new situations. In contrast the second, the participation metaphor, understands social practice as the locus of human development; and the third will emphasize the mediated character of collective learning processes. Of course these distinctions are like caricatures that highlight only a few salient features and leave a lot of space for overlapping positions. In order to sharpen the categorization we have added a reference to theoretical basis.

Table 4.1 A typology of learning trajectories

	Educational learning trajectories	Lifelong learning trajectories	Community learning trajectories	Epistemic trajectories
Metaphors of learning	Skills acquisition	Participation	Knowledge creation	
Theoretical basis	Cognitive psychology	Narrative theory/personality psychology	Social theory, cultural studies	Sociology (of knowledge/professions), system theory
Process characteristics	Individual learning of a new task or differences in strategies between novices/experts	Personal reconstructions of life episodes	Collective sense-making of past, present and future events	Knowledge development as mediated network relations
Didactical implications	Instructional design in subject area or specific learning of cognitive strategies	Reflection on personal lifelines and/or professional contexts	Sharing of embedded knowledge	Reorganisation of "epistemic infrastructure"
Analytical levels and time scales	Individual learner on learning tasks ("lesson") or problem-solving tasks	Individual learner in professional contexts and life-cycles	Interactive level and socialization into professional communities	Network level and different time scales
Methodological preferences (type of data and data-collection)	Task analysis through verbal protocols. Learning logs	Biographical methods. Historical analysis	Ethnographic approaches	Shadowing action research

The literature on educational learning trajectories draws mainly from "hard core" information processing models of human cognition or constructivist accounts with a sensitivity for contextual contingencies. The lifetime perspective leans on narratology and research on life histories. In line with different "turns" within the social sciences this tradition has moved in the direction of contextualism during the last decades. The same could apply to the concept "community learning trajectories" that includes both theories of social participation that take individual minds interacting with others as a point of departure – and those that focus on social context as an infrastructure for human learning. The latter may coincide with approaches that address knowledge issues, and that are indicated in the right column.

When discussing the different approaches delineated below, we will go through the themes that are listed in the left column. After providing a theoretical positioning, we take a closer look at their understanding of learning trajectories. What is learned and how? Does the analogy with trajectories make us more attentive to aspects of professional learning than a more prosaic term like "learning process"? In answering these questions, we will explore the didactical implications of the different frameworks which are closely related to the process characteristics. They are all addressing the HOW-dimension of professional learning, but didactics refers here to the formalization of learning strategies that more or less reflects the different interpretations of processes. The two last categories on analytical levels/time scales and methodological preferences point to contrasts in research focus and approaches. In the following sections we will first discuss the three perspectives on "learning trajectory" and then argue that they tend to neglect knowledge issues that, as pointed out above, are important when we deal with professional learning. So we bring back knowledge through a discussion of Karen Knorr Cetina's (1997) concept "epistemic object." In our final discussion some limitations in her framework are identified, but still we want to welcome further explorations into epistemic trajectories.

Mapping thinking strategies in flexible professional work

The term "educational learning trajectories" includes two research traditions that have a legacy in cognitive psychology. The first has coined "hypothetical learning trajectories" (HLT) and is a conceptual framework and methodology for studying the steps taken by students to become proficient in a knowledge domain, for example mathematics (Clements & Sarama, 2004). From detailed observations of individual strategies it derives a prescribed teaching sequence. The second tradition is closely associated with the research on expertise and is more relevant when we are dealing with professional learning.

In a nutshell cognitivistic studies of expertise depart from the idea that differences in thinking processes could be derived from concurrent verbalization on the part of problem-solvers as they work on academic tasks. The usual set-up is to compare the strategies of inexperienced and experienced subjects in specific academic or professional domains like legal (Ashley, 1988) or clinical reasoning (Kassirer & Kopelman, 1991). These could include a set of algorithms "operationalizing" diagnostic hypothesis generation and refinement, use and interpretation of diagnostic tests, causal reasoning, diagnostic verification, therapeutic decision-making, and so on. The "long way" from novice to expert performance is understood as a gradual proceduralization of rule-based behavior that improves the efficiency of professional performance. After years of practice, less attention is paid to detailed operations and more to contextual cues and alternative lines of action. This combination of cognitive routinization and reorientation is at the core of the Dreyfuses' model of competence development (Dreyfus & Dreyfus, 1986). The later is often referred to as a prototype defining the stages that an apprentice must pass on her way to proficiency in an expert domain.

The classical information-processing approach to skill acquisition may provide a valid account of mastery in restricted and stable domains like chess and formal logics, but it is now widely recognized that a less linear process must be assumed when we observe the progression of candidates in "open" problem areas like management (Sternberg & Horvath, 1999) or teaching (Ropo, 2004). Recent reviews of expertise research include a large variety of new concepts and approaches that has been introduced to account for skill acquisition in a complex and flexible working life (Charness, Feltovich, Hoffman & Ericsson, 2006; Feltovich, Spiro & Coulson, 1996). They confirm the conclusion that the amount of practice is a poor predictor of expert performance, and that the transition into mastery of task is often a complex and dynamic process. More attention is now paid to contextual variables that provide the practitioners with a wide selection of problems and scaffolds that support an effective reorganization of knowledge. Besides, the learner is being conceived as an active designer of his or her own learning environment. Progress in expert performance is, according to Ericsson (1997), dependent on deliberative practice, on switching to "deep" strategies in a knowledge domain and on involvement in self-regulatory moves like rehearsing a successful solution or mentally simulating a set of alternatives.

Based on these short glimpses from research on expertise one could question the validity of a linear and unidimensional representation of conceptual learning and instructional design – and it seems justified to be doubtful about "trajectory" as a generative metaphor for professional learning (Schön, 1983). At the conceptual level it is problematic to maintain the notion of a default pattern in expert development. Instead a wide variety of flexible paths must be assumed. Their starting- and endpoints will not be easily defined, making any reference to a "trajectory" misleading. Another criticism is methodological and refers to the circularity involved in the following steps: First to collect observational and self-reported accounts of problem-solvers doing "thinking aloud," then to translate these data into information-processing concepts and finally to use these to explain differences in human proficiency as brain mechanisms.

The mentalistic flavour of the cognitivist approach may be counterbalanced by its emphasis on systematic and detailed observation of task performance. Of course a successful use of these guidelines depends on a deep understanding of the professional domain on the part of the designers. Another strength that can be attributed to this tradition is its insistence on process descriptions – although the trajectories to be accounted for are rather short-lived. In recent studies of professional and vocational learning "learning logs" have become increasingly popular (Achtenhagen, 2001; Fuller & Unwin, 2002). Compared with "think aloud" techniques, they do not carry the theoretical burden of mentalism. Besides, these logs are often extended in time and space. However, this scaling varies to a considerable degree between different approaches. On one hand qualitative-oriented researchers have derived guidelines from diary methods, whereas others use precoded questionnaires with low demand on response elaboration. The latter alternative has attracted a growing popularity in research on screen-based work thanks to computer programs that allow a continuous logging of users' "navigational patterns" or e-portfolios (Deakin, Côté & Harvey, 2006). These reports could be linked to video-data in case of cooperative performances.

In sum, when using methods for mapping educational learning trajectories, one should be attentive to the framing of the target behavior and the sampling of time and spaces. This last point reminds us that professional performance and learning events may take the shape of shorter or longer cycles. For example, when we contrast the surgical work and training episodes of medical doctors and nurses with the defence of a lawyer and the familiarization of students in legal argumentation. Clearly, these situations differ in formats – in terms of "body language" on the first and formalized language in the second. In addition, the expert surgeon may gain practical experiences of cases, whereas the law students are offered written material to work on.

Biographies and lifetime learning trajectories

The term "learning trajectories" is widely circulated within the research literature on adult and lifelong learning and has been defined in a number of ways. For our purpose one could distinguish between an autobiographical and life-course-oriented approach and a historical and work-oriented approach. The former is for example represented by different texts on "lifetime learning trajectories" (Gorard et al., 2001) – sometimes implying that earlier stages in life have a determining influence later. The other tradition puts a heavier emphasis on the social and institutional context of the learner and provides a more dynamic model of professional development. Another difference is methodological – respectively a preference for diary methods and narrative analysis or qualitative interviews and discourse analysis. Both research strands differ radically from the theoretical framework of cognitivism, even if they tend to preserve the individual learner as unit of observation. This is less clear in the historical approach. Of course both frameworks use an extended temporal and spatial span for learning – compared with the educational learning trajectories we reviewed above.

The standard procedure in autobiographical and narrative positions is to ask the learners to report on distinctive episodes and transitions across life phases and sectors (school, work, family life, friends). These events are subsequently drawn together into "learning trajectories" or "learning histories." According to the traditional script this assembly was to represent a basically linear representation of personal life courses. However, recent models have reinstated context and acknowledged that "prior scripts" are co-constructed as the storyteller is telling her story in a particular way for a particular purpose, implanting metanarratives that are useful for what she wants to present and for what she thinks the researcher wishes to hear (Cary, 1999). Such a turn does not only represent a reflective stance on the interactive production of data, but also a greater acceptance of the contextual framing of the lifetime learning trajectories as experienced by the storyteller, and of her ability to continuously redesign these contours as she lives her life (Helms Jørgensen & Warring, 2002). Thus the two approaches delineated above seem to converge in recent literature.

The biographical and contextualistic perspectives on learning trajectories have been strongly represented by Danish researchers (Olesen, 2003; Helms Jørgensen & Warring, 2002; Dreier, 1999). Some of the nuances between the various groups may be relevant for our present discussion. Olesen (2003), basing his argument on critical theory and personality psychology, develops a conceptual platform that captures the historicity of biographies and the striving of the storyteller (the self) to make conflicting experiences into meaningful accounts of herself – to another. In line with other scholars he advocates a research strategy that invites the storyteller into "theorizing" as a collaborative process (Goodson & Sikes, 2001). In Olesen's account the learning trajectory seems to be a subjective reconstruction of complex life experiences, whereas Helms Jørgensen and Warring (2002) and Dreier (1999) introduce an external perspective on these biographical productions through concepts like "learning environments" and "space of action." Thus one could speak of "subjective" and "objective learning trajectories" – although such a distinction would not do justice to the different Danish authors referred here, since there is a strong family resemblance in their positions.

For our present discussion of "learning trajectories" these short glimpses from life history research highlight the following points. First we demonstrate how the concept "trajectory" is turned into a multidimensional category, and that more attention is paid to dynamic processes. In light of the distinctions between subjective/objective and personal/interactive introduced earlier, continuity in professional development may be a function of a personal project, a standard career pattern in a specific expert culture or an accepted way of describing events leading up to the present state of affairs. In general one could observe in the literature a stronger emphasis on the institutional framing of biographies – turning the attention away from the life of professionals to their professional life. Also the joint construction of personal narratives by storyteller and researcher has become more and more recognized as a valid interpretative framework.

In the objectivist or contextual tradition career opportunities and social position are typically used as indicators of a productive occupational life (Lahn, 2003) mediated by workplace characteristics. Rarely do we find any reference to knowledge ecologies in the trajectory of experts. This contrasts with the fact that professionals often make occupational choices that lead them into the forefront of their expertise. In more general terms one could say that the life history approaches tend to neglect the "what" issues related to professional knowledge. When the domain of jurisdiction and identity formation is left out of the interpretational scheme, the importance of institutional contexts designed for learning may be underestimated. This is problematic from a methodological point of view. If diaries and portfolios are collected on a lifeline basis, the learning qualities attributed to episodes may be quite doubtful. It would be more justifiable to identify those patterns in relation to contexts where learning is attended to – for example, in the supervision of new nurses.

It is not easy to make any identification of clear-cut didactical programmes associated with the various frameworks presented above. As already mentioned, the research strategy of Olesen includes the prospects of theoretical reflection and knowledge creation in the interaction between storyteller and researcher. Similar aims have been proposed within the Anglo-American tradition where a range of methods are devised to support self-reflection and lifelong learning strategies (Mezirow, 1997). Within the more contextualistic camp, similar programmes are complemented by models for the redesign of learning environments, and so on. But it is safe to conclude that the conceptual framework indicated by lifetime learning trajectories is mainly introduced to enrich our understanding of human development in complex environments – where professional life is one such sector.

Community participation as trajectories

From the booming literature on social constructivist approaches to learning, the theoretical frameworks of Jean Lave, Etienne Wenger, John Seely Brown and others seem the most relevant ones when we study professional learning – since they take their empirical evidence from expert communities in working life. One of the main conceptual pillars in the edifice of Lave and Wenger (1991) is "legitimate peripheral participation." It draws our attention to the following qualities of occupational learning environments: The novice enters a field partly structured for training purposes where the curriculum may be defined through the allocation of tasks – a so-called embedded pedagogy. She attains a mixed professional identity as both a member of a global expert community and as apprentice. These definitions are institutionalized at the workplace in the format of more or less informal contracts that also partly regulate the tacit expectations attributed to the output of novices as they progress towards an identity as experts in their community. The access to these contexts is often mediated by tools or technologies that are both transparent to expert members of a community and problematic, since they are constantly replaced by new versions or configurations. Thus, experienced practitioners are asked to take on the role of learners.

Wenger (1998) tends to blur the distinctions between learning, identity and trajectory – by claiming that "As trajectories, our identities incorporate the past and the future in the very process of negotiating the present" (p. 155), and that learning is an event on these trajectories. One plausible interpretation of learning trajectory in these and other passages would be: It represents a mental construction that synthesizes experiences and projections from the past, the present and the future – as a "metascript" (Wenger, 1998) that impacts on our perception and actions in situations, and that are at the same time shaped by these instantiations. In more general terms Wenger uses the concept "trajectories" to amplify the temporal character and recursiveness of identity formation and learning which subsequently is viewed as aspects of all human activity. They are conceived as a "shared repertoire of communal resources" that can be used appropriately.

However, Wenger vacillates between different understandings of the term "trajectory." In the following extract it is not clear whether he refers to subjective (individual/collective) patterns of identity formation or structural attributes of communities and work organizations: "Identities are defined with respect to the interaction of multiple convergent and divergent trajectories" (1998, p. 154). The latter interpretation is strengthened by the many references that are made in his texts to different types of transitions within and across professional communities. Wenger introduced a series of so-called boundary-crossing devices that facilitate these movements, like structures for negotiation and brokering of knowledge and skills, for overlapping membership and multiple commitments, like in project organizations. At the core of these distinctions is a concern with "psychosocial contracts" of authorization, advancement, performance and so on. They seem to be institutional categories ("paradigmatic trajectories") and do not classify patterns in human action (or learning content, Eraut *et al.*, 2005). To conclude, a reference to "cultural learning trajectory" would take care of the subjective aspects as well as the objective – understood as cross-cultural infrastructures.

Although the concept of "trajectory" summarizes some structural characteristics of expert communities and formal institutions, its main function in the social learning theory of Wenger is to draw our attention towards a temporal order that shapes collective interactions, which are recursively transformed through this practice. And, of course, "shared learning histories" may be at the base of identity formation. The societal level is accounted for by tying the different contexts together (see also Dreier, 1999; Edwards, 2005). It is, so to speak, constructed from below. As a critical comment one could claim that learning trajectories in professional work may be shaped by the larger socio-economic environment and by institutional contingencies that are not necessarily present at the community level. For example, one important distinction in studies of occupational careers is whether these are embedded in a welfare state or a market liberal system (Lahn, 2003). From the sociology of professions we also learn that strategies for competence development in professional groups are often motivated by a protection or expansion of a field of jurisdiction (MacDonald, 1995; Freidson, 2001) rather than an updating of operative skills. Without going into the debate on professionalization strategies it suffices for our discussion to point out that professional development and learning could be seen as boundary crossing from an interactional point of view and boundary demarcation from a sociological position. Another transformation that is not easily observed at the interactional level within the workplaces is the progression (or regression) of knowledge domains and disciplines. These processes may be slow and only discernible if the researchers apply a longer timescale in their studies than what is prescribed by Wenger and others.

In sum the cultural perspective not only decenters learning from the inside of human minds to the socio-material context, but also extends it to a wider spatio-temporal field called the "community of practice." At the same time the symbolic processes that go into the formation of professionals, are given greater attention and extended into issues of motivation and social identification. The pitfalls of cognitivism are avoided by reducing the subject to a mediator or broker between trajectories and specific events. Like artifacts and mental representations in general, professional knowledge is seen as a "structuring resource" (Lave, 1988) that interacts with its use and recursively transforms itself, whereas the learning process partly takes on the characteristics of occupational socialization. Thus, it loses some of the domain specificity that remains a hallmark of the psychological research on expertise.

This approach to professional learning derives its methodological ballast from ethnographic studies of craftwork and apprenticeship (Chaiklin & Lave, 1996). As pointed out above, the merit of such a strategy is to enrich our understanding of the complex social processes that shape the individual learner. Its limitations are evident when we study modern working life. The learning environments are drawn with quite small circles, and systemic dislocations between professional domains tend to be left out of the analytical apparatus. Likewise the more global character of academic knowledge is rewritten as "resources" that transform the context of use and is shaped by it. Within such a framework one would anticipate that practitioners seek new competence not because it is needed for operational reasons – but for symbolic purposes. The latter could be illustrated by nurses adopting more evidence-based methods to compete with other professional groups with a stronger academic standing. Finally, it is justifiable to interpret the "metascripts" that Wenger equates with trajectories in communities of practice, as collective representations that are constructed from shared practices. Through a process of individual sense-making, multiple passages are transformed into a more-or-less coherent identity as professional. However, one could alternatively envisage a more dispersed process where the practitioner adopts typifications of their trade or professions from "above" and enact these in different local contexts – constructing a personal system of multiple identities. Anyway the literature on communities of practice is quite vague on how trajectories of participation are translated into identities or learning.

Bringing back knowledge

The three types elaborated above, the educational, the lifelong and the cultural, lean on different academic traditions. They could be compared and contrasted along some key dimensions. The first revolves around the dichotomy of "subjective" and "objective" where trajectories are constructions of the individual mind, human interactions or the cultural mind on one side and structural or systemic characteristics on the other. The second source of variation is the different timescales that are used within the research traditions that we have reviewed. A trajectory ranges from students' performance on school tasks to life-course transitions or cultural typifications of collective experiences. A third dimension that is related to both analytical levels and spatio-temporal scaling is content. Do trajectories refer to cycles of individual problem-solving, learning processes, paths of participation, cultural/institutional patterns? As pointed out several times, it is far from clear what is learned – and thus what is put on a trajectory. In both the life history and the community approach, the concept of learning is quite open – or diluted. Within the cognitivist tradition, it has a more circumscribed meaning and reflects the specifics of the knowledge domain. However, the first part of the term "learning trajectories" primarily indicates the role of the trajectories and not necessarily their content. If this aspect should be highlighted, notably their knowledge content, it may be more useful to talk about "epistemic trajectories."

If we reintroduce knowledge (Muller, 2000) into research on professional learning, our understanding of the interface between schooling and work practice may have to be revised. Professionalism is often associated with expert groups being awarded the jurisdiction of an occupational field. The intellectual basis for such an institutional contract could be traced back to a system of educational requirements and certification schemes. However, the transfer of knowledge from higher education to the appropriate sector of work is rarely a simple one-to-one process. Chemical engineers have a stronger foothold in their discipline than mechanical engineers, whereas the teaching and health-caring professions seem to base their occupational practice on "tacit skills" (Lahn, 1995) possibly acquired outside formal educational regimes. This variation in the interplay between formal education and professional expertise does not only determine how transitions from school into work are structured, but also the extent to which a continuous training is provided. In other words, professional knowledge structures contain the "knowledge of how to acquire new knowledge" (MacDonald, 1995) – at an individual and communitarian level but also at an institutional level.

In our introductory sections we approached the term "epistemification." It needs some further clarification and should include both the transformation of work tasks into textual processing and a larger societal complexity. In many sectors more space is provided for the redefinition of expertise as practitioners from different fields are brought together to discuss boundary-crossing solutions to emergent issues. In addition, higher education has become the admission ticket to working life. A new societal division of knowledge is put on the agenda and should be a mandatory horizon for studies of professional learning. As a theoretical reflection on these historical lines Knorr Cetina (1999) talks about "epistemic cultures." Her main argument is that scientific production and social organization diffuse into other sectors of modern societies, and that this trend is supported by the ubiquitous construction of "object-centered relationships." Since practice is dispersed and opened up for multiple participation and interdisciplinary efforts, traditional ties loose their binding force (Jensen & Lahn, 2005) and have to be reinvented. So-called epistemic objects are providing the energy and structuring resources for the construction of new practices. These objects can be interpreted as both material instantiations of professional knowledge and "agents" that reshape their epistemic infrastructure (Hakkarainen, Pelonen, Paavola & Lehtinen, 2004). For example, electronic patient journals combine the format of medical records, hospital routines and new media into a hybrid system that supports knowledge creation (Bruni, 2005). Thus epistemic objects redefine workers into learners and learning into a distributed process. The latter must be given a very different representation as a trajectory than the ones proposed by Wenger – since it does not follow the centripedal socialization pattern suggested by the term "communities of practice." This logic is brought one step further in the studies of Jan Nespor (1994) who observed students in physics and business as they prepare for transitions into profession work. These movements into the disciplinary apparatus are described as an activity that not only is regulated by local interactions, but that recruits processes and space elsewhere (op. cit., p. 10). His unit of analysis is the system of elements where various trajectories intersect, for example the hybrid construction of lectures, knowledge domain, presentations sheets, notebooks, auditoriums, and through which students have to move to accomplish the defined identities and interests – as an "obligatory passage point" to use the expression of Callon (1986). Nespor refrains from putting trajectories on different levels, for example in "personal learning trajectories" and "institutional learning trajectories," and replaces it with a "network that constructs space-time relations" (1994, p. 131). "Learning" is segments of motion "which follow the shapes of more stable institutional or disciplinary networks" (ibid.), and which is stabilized by artifacts like the ones we have listed above.

When learning and knowledge development are seen as changes in mediated network relations, attention is directed towards three processes. First, the ubiquitous character of "epistemic objects." Modern artifacts like new media and ICT are "colonializing" all life spheres. They are far from transparent for the users and have to be learned. Second, these objects are representing knowledge – and in the context of professional work, changes of tools tend to imply that expert knowledge is redefined and transformed. Third, complexity is amplified by their infiltration of networks that often include both new technologies and institutional reconfigurations. For example, the shift from doing design on drawing boards to computer-assisted design can be summarized as a radical transformation and restructuring of engineering skills, professional rankings, career trajectories, division of work tasks, and interorganizational collaboration (Lahn, 1995). In this way we may justify the reference to "mediated network relations" that embed and afford professional resources. In a didactical perspective the task is literally expanded since the learning environment is distributed, and different knowledge domains are fused in order to cope with problems that require an interprofessional response.

Paavola and Hakkarainen (2005) have devised strategies for the redesign of such "epistemic infrastructures."

Concluding note

In this chapter we have reviewed different understandings of "learning trajectory." As pointed out, one of the merits of the cognitive approach is that it goes deeply into issues of knowledge content, which is important when dealing with learning in expert cultures. Researchers taking a life history and community perspective tend to leave out the specificity of professional domains of their analytical framework. Thus, for programmatic reasons, we want to bring back knowledge into our discussion. In doing this turn we have been inspired by the research of Knorr Cetina and one of her key concepts, "epistemic object." However, there are some problems associated with such a move that need to be commented on.

It is evident that the concept of "knowledge" in the literature on expertise on one side and Knorr Cetina's texts on the other are miles apart. Her theoretical position has family resemblance with community approaches in underlining the social-constructed character of professional knowledge. She then adds the objectual element in collective epistemic processing. The issue of knowledge content is taken care of by her field studies of scientists working at CERN and currency dealers in Swiss banks. In reflecting on the general validity of her conceptual framework, Knorr Cetina (1999) suggests that it can be seen as providing "templates" that sensitize observations in other contexts. Thus "epistemic object" cannot be given a fixed definition. It has to be interpreted in relationship to a field of practice. There is a conflict between conceptual clarity and richness in her texts, and here we follow Engeström (2005) in pointing out the need for a historical analysis that may bridge a complex and an abstract understanding of professional learning.

This brings us to a related area of concern when adopting the vocabulary of Knorr Cetina and others. How do we study "trajectories" within this paradigm? The most critical question is related to the issue of analytical levels. Both Knorr Cetina and Nespor are using interactional data and refrain from doing any "exogenic" study of historical or other metalevel trajectories. Of course there is no clear-cut answer to how these processes are developmentally coupled (Beach, 1999), but Knorr Cetina and Nespor seem to circumvent such problems by adopting a flat model of "mediated network relations." This step also represents a conceptual drift that makes their concept of knowledge just as blurred as the ones to be found in the literature on "communities of practice." Thus the texts of Knorr Cetina and others may deliver some "templates" in our attempt to bring back knowledge in studies of professional learning. But as suggested above, other theoretical positions have to be recruited in this campaign. Still there is a need to preserve the concept "epistemic trajectory" in order to remind ourselves that issues of knowledge content and its dynamics are important when studying expert communities.

References

Achtenhagen, F. (2001). Some Hints on the Success and Failure of Self-directed Learning at the Workplace. In L. F. M. Niewenhuis and W. J. Nijhof (eds) *The Dynamics of VET and HRD Systems*. Enschede: Twente University Press.

Ashley, K. (1988). Arguing by Analogy in Law: A case-based model. In D. Helman (ed.) *Analogical Reasoning: Perspectives of artificial intelligence, cognitive science and philosophy*. Dordrecht: Kluwer.

Beach, King D. (1999). Consequential Transitions: A sociocultural expedition beyond transfer in education. *Review of Research in Education*, 24, 124–149.

Bernstein, B. (1996). *Pedagogy, Symbolic Control and Identity: Theory, research, critique*. Lanham: Rowman & Littlefield.

Brown, D. (ed.) (2002). *Career Choice and Development*. New York: Jossey-Bass.

Bruni, A. (2005). Shadowing Software and Clinical Records: On the ethnography of non-humans and hetergeneous contexts. *Organization*, 12, 357–378.

Callon, M. (1986). Some Elements of a Sociology of Translation: Domestication of the scallops and the fishermen of St Brieuc Bay. In J. Law (ed.) *Power, Action and Belief*. London: Routledge & Kegan Paul.

Cary, Lisa J. (1999). Unexpected Stories: Life history and the limits of representation. *Qualitative Inquiry*, 5, 411–427.

Chaiklin, S. and Lave, J. (1996). *Understanding Practice*. Cambridge: Cambridge University Press.

Charness, N., Feltovich, P. J., Hoffman, R. J. and Ericsson, K. A. (eds) (2006). *The Cambridge Handbook of Expertise and Expert Performance*. New York: Cambridge University Press.

Clements, D. H. and Sarama, J. (2004). Learning Trajectories in Mathematics Education. *Mathematical Thinking and Learning*, 6, 81–89.

Deakin, J. M., Côté, J. and Harvey, A. S. (2006). Time Budgets, Diairies, and Analyses of Concurrent Practice Activities. In N. Charness, P. J. Feltovich, R. J. Hoffman and K. A. Ericsson (eds). *The Cambridge Handbook of Expertise and Expert Performance*. New York: Cambridge University Press.

Dreier, O. (1999). Personal Trajectories of Participation Across Contexts of Social Practice. *Outlines*, 1, 5–32.

Dreyfus, H. and Dreyfus, S. (1986). *Mind Over Machine*. New York: Basic Books.

Edwards, A. (2005). Understanding Mind in World: The Vygotskian legacy. *Contexts, Communities, Networks: Mobilising learners' resources and relationships in different domains*. Seminar one, 15–16 February 2005, Glasgow Caledonian University.

Engeström, Y. (2005). *Developmental Work Research: Expanding activity theory in practice*. Berlin: Lehmanns Media.

Eraut, M., Maillardet, F., Miller, C., Steadman, S., Ali, A., Blackman, C. and Furner, J. (2005). What is Learned in the Workplace and How? Typologies and results from a cross-professional longitudinal study. *EARLI 11. Biannual Conference, Nicosia*, August 23–29, 2005.

Ericsson, K. A. (ed.) (1997). *The Road to Excellence: The acquisition of expert performance in the arts and sciences, sports, and games*. Mahwah, NJ: Erlbaum.

Feltovich, P. J., Spiro, R. J. and Coulson, R. I. (1996). Flexibility in Contexts Characterized by Complexity and Change. In P. J. Feltovich, K. M. Ford, K. M. and R. R. Hoffman (eds) *Expertise in Context. Human and Machine*. Menlo Park, CA: The MIT Press.

Freidson, E. (2001). *Professionalism. The Third Logic*. Chicago: The University of Chicago Press.

Fuller, A. and Unwin, L. (2002). Developing Pedagogics for the Contemporary Workplace. In K. Evans. (eds) *Working to Learn: Transforming workplace learning*. London: Kogan Page.

Goodson, I. and Sikes, P. (2001). *Life History Research in Educational Settings. Learning from Lives*. Buckingham: Open University Press.

Gorard, S., Rees, G., Fevre, R. and Welland, T. (2001). Lifelong Learning Trajectories: Some voices of those in transit. *International Journal of Lifelong Education, 20*, 169–187.

Hakkarainen, K., Pelonen, T., Paavola, S. and Lehtinen, E. (2004). *Communities of Networked Expertise. Professional and Educational Perspectives*. Amsterdam: Elsevier.

Helms Jørgensen, C. and Warring, N. (2002). Learning in the Workplace: The interplay between learning environments and biography. *ESREA Conference on Adult Education and the Labour Market VII*, May 30–June 1, 2002.

Jensen, K. and Lahn, L. C. (2005). The Binding Role of Knowledge: An analysis of nursing students knowledge ties. *Journal of Education and Work, 18*, 307–322.

Kassirer, J. P. and Kopelman, R. I. (1991). *Learning Clinical Reasoning*. Baltimore: Williams and Wilkins.

Knorr Cetina, K. (1999). *Epistemic Cultures: How the sciences make knowledge*. Cambridge, MA: Harvard University Press.

Knorr Cetina, K. (1997). Sociality with Objects: Social relations in postsocial knowledge. *Theory, Culture and Society, 14*, 1–30.

Lahn, L. C. (1995). *Yrkeskompetanse i Støpeskjeen (Professional Competence in a Melting Spoon)*. Thesis for dr.polit. University of Oslo.

Lahn, L. C. (2003). Competence and Learning in Late Career. *European Educational Research Journal, 2*, 126–140.

Lave, J. (1988). *Cognition in Practice*. Cambridge: Cambridge University Press.

Lave, J. and E. Wenger (1991). *Situated Learning: Legitimate peripheral participation*. New York: Cambridge University Press.

MacDonald, K. M. (1995). *The Sociology of Professions*. London: Sage Publications.

Mezirow, J. (1997). Transformative Learning: Theory to practice. *New Directions for Adult and Continuous Education, 74*, 5–12.

Muller, J. (2000). *Reclaiming Knowledge: Social theory, curriculum, and education policy*. London: RoutledgeFalmer.

Nespor, J. (1994). *Knowledge in Motion: Space, time and curriculum in undergraduate physics and Management*. London: The Falmer Press.

Olesen, H. S. (2003). The Learning Subject in Life History: A qualitative research approach to learning. In M. H. M. B. Abrahão (red.), *The Autobiograph Research: A methodological and practical discussion*. Porto Alegra, Brasil: EDIPUCRS.

Paavola, S. and Hakkarainen, K. (2005). The Knowledge Creation Metaphor: An emergent epistemological approach to learning. *Science and Education, 14*, 535–557.

ProLEARN (2004). Professional Learning in a Changing Society. Online. http://www.pfi.ui.no/prolearn

Ropo, E. (2004). Teaching Expertise: Empirical findings on expert teachers and teacher development. In Boshuizen, P. A., Bromme, R. and Gruber, H. (eds). *Professional Learning: Gaps and transitions on the way from novice to expert*. Dordrecht: Kluwer Academic Publishers.

Schön, D. A. (1983). *The Reflective Practitioner: How professionals think in practice*. New York: Basic Books.

✓ Sfard, A. (1998). On Two Metaphors for Learning and the Dangers of Choosing Just One. *Educational Researcher, 27*, 4–13.

Sternberg, R. J. and. Horvath, J. A. (eds) (1999). *Tacit Knowledge in Professional Practice: Researcher and practitioner perspectives.* Mahwah, NJ: Lawrence Erlaum.

Stutt, A. and Motta, E. (1998). Knowledge Modelling: An organic technology for the knowledge age. In M. Eisenstadt and T. Vincent (eds). *The Knowledge Web: Learning and collaboration on the net.* London: Kogan Page.

✓ Wenger, E. (1998). *Communities of Practice: Learning, meaning, and identity.* Cambridge: Cambridge University Press.

Chapter 5

Cultivating collective expertise within innovative knowledge-practice networks

Kai Hakkarainen, Jiri Lallimo, Seppo Toikka and Hal White

Introduction

The present paper examined human expertise from three perspectives, i.e. knowledge acquisition, participation, and knowledge creation (Paavola *et al.*, 2004; Hakkarainen *et al.*, 2004). Implications of these theoretical perspectives will be illustrated by reporting results of two ongoing investigations of professional expertise. Based on consideration of the latter two perspectives, it is argued that human expertise is collective in nature and cannot be understood as mere individual and mental process (knowledge-acquisition perspective). We consider the metaphors as heuristic tools that assist in examining various aspects of learning. While the first two have been extensively examined and investigated, the third aspect is mostly unknown territory. Yet, in order to have a *holographic* view of learning one needs to take all of the perspectives, simultaneously, into consideration.

Knowledge-acquisition perspective on expertise

Investigators have examined cognitive processes related to higher-level competencies since the 1970s. Expert studies revealed, contrary to researchers' expectations, that domain-general reasoning processes or memory-skills did not substantially diverge between experts and novices. The *knowledge-acquisition perspective* on expertise assumes that experts' exceptional performance is based on a large body of well-organized and usable *crystallized knowing* that assist them in separating essential from unessential aspects of problem-solving (see Baltes, Staudinger, & Lindenberg, 1999; Krampe & Baltes, 2003; and Bereiter & Scardamalia, 1993). Experts on this view pursue challenging objectives by relying on limited resources of *fluid knowing*, develop new practices and procedures that transform novel activity into routines (*crystallized knowing*), thereby, releasing new resources for carrying out even more challenging projects. Activity becomes gradually easier as agents accumulate crystallized knowing embodying solutions to frequently encountered problems and develop routines for dealing with initially messy and problematic situations. According to this view, experts outperform novices because they have acquired a rich body of crystallized patterns of solving problems that enable meaningful and effective functioning in familiar (both frequently and infrequently encountered) situations.

Participation perspective on expertise

The above description of psychological research on expertise provides an individualist and mentalist picture of human expertise. From the *participation* (*dialogical*) *perspective*, in contrast, the development of expertise involves transforming participation from peripheral to central as a function of appropriating collective practices (Lave & Wenger, 1991). Experts' bodies of crystallized knowing do not emerge from depths of their mind but are internalized and appropriated from historically developed expert cultures. Expertise is a matter of growing up and participating in social communities and learning to function according to their shared practices, norms, and values, as Lave and Wenger (1991) have proposed. Consequently, expertise is not only a mental, but a socially and materially distributed, process (Hutchins, 1995). Such a position involves questioning the Cartesian separation between internal (mental) and external (material) processes and encourages one to examine the human mind as a flexible, permeable, and extended system that can be integrated with external instruments and other agents, toward a higher-level intellectual system (Clark, 2003; Donald, 1991; Vygotsky, 1978).

Moreover, expertise relies on merging or fusing cognitive processes within various communities and networks (Hakkarainen *et al.*, 2004). Collective fusion of cognitive efforts allows human beings to pursue projects and enterprises that go beyond an individual's intellectual resources. Human minds are not isolated entities, but merge and fuse so as to constitute collective cognitive systems. A beautiful example of such systems is so called *transactive memory* (Wegner, 1986; Moreland, 1999) that emerges spontaneously through even short joint practices and shared object-oriented working but breaks down if people switch groups. It assists in managing daily activities, such as finding things, participating in meetings, remembering memorable days, and provides accurate metaknowledge concerning distribution of knowledge and competencies that helps to coordinate collective activities and achieve better results than would otherwise be possible. Workmates and colleagues function as an external memory that allows us to manage various daily activities, such as other non-routine events. Socially distributed cognitive systems may represent expertise that is homogeneously (e.g. rowing team) or heterogeneously (baseball team) distributed (Johnson *et al.*, 2000). People are more and more often working in multi-professional teams in which mere *vertical* development of expertise within one's domain is not sufficient; rather, people need to engage in *horizontal* learning as well, relating and fusing their expertise to that of their fellow team members (Engeström, Engeström, & Kärkkäinen, 1995).

Toward a knowledge-creating perspective on collective expertise

The acquisition and participation perspectives may be seen as two diverging, fundamental approaches to expertise (Sfard, 1998). The present investigators have argued, together with Sami Paavola (Paavola, *et al.*, 2004), that understanding learning and expertise in knowledge society may require a third perspective that addresses innovative processes of creating knowledge or transforming social practices. From the *knowledge-creation perspective*, expertise does not primarily involve acquiring already existing knowledge or growing up to a stable community, but making deliberate efforts to transform prevailing knowledge and practices. We call such processes "knowledge creation" to highlight their novelty and a shift from routine ways of understanding. As stated, our theory considers knowledge creation as a socially distributed process; further, not mere dialogic interaction between minds. Collective expertise appears, rather, to be a *trialogical* process, that is, members focused on developing shared objects of activity. These mediating objects may, for instance, be ideas, theories, designs, concrete products or practices being reflected on. Collective expertise appears to coevolve in sustained and deliberate processes of working with trialogical objects of activity (Paavola *et al.*, 2004).

Knowledge-intensive work takes place in a turbulent second-order environment (Bereiter & Scardamalia, 1993) in which the criteria of success are dynamically tightening as a function of other players' success. Such environments require expert communities to engage in constant innovation and social transformation in order to successfully meet challenges that are novel to all participants involved. Knorr Cetina (2001, p. 178) argued that the traditional conception of practices as being based on repeated routines does not accurately characterize epistemic communities that are engaged in deliberate and systematic "reinvention" of their knowledge practices so as to elicit novelty and innovation. Consequently, we propose that collective expertise typical for our times may be considered to be cultivated in *innovative knowledge communities* rather than traditional communities of practice (Hakkarainen *et al.*, 2004; Paavola *et al.*, 2004). Yet, the communities in question rely on social practices, knowledge practices tailored to promoting continuous innovation and change. Analogously, with crystallized and fluid knowing, these practices allow communities to pursue novelty, and transform it to routines, in order to release resources for reaching again to work at the edge of the competence.

Two theme issues of respected journals have recently focused on examining the transforming nature of the objects of modern professional activity (Engeström & Blackler, 2005; Kaptelinin & Miettinen, 2005). In knowledge-intensive work, experts are not just working with more and more complex objects. These objects, further, are not usually pre-determined, but tend to be fluid and slippery, being constantly transformed and repeatedly re-defined in the course of activity. As a consequence of the breaking down of intra- and inter-organizational boundaries, the objects appear, in many cases, to be hard to specify, fragmented or only

partially mastered by an individual or team working with them. These resemble
what Rheinberger (1997) and Miettinen and Virkkunen (2005) call *epistemic
objects*, as distinguished from technical ones. While the technical objects represent
instruments connected with well-known, routine procedures, the epistemic ones
prevail at the edge of their epistemic horizon and encompass what the investigators
do not yet know. These dynamic objects function as originating sources of novel
conceptualization and innovative solutions. The creative nature of knowledge work
appears to be characterized by sustained work at the edge of the unknown.

The concept of "object" has *philosophic* roots in Marx's and Hegel's studies,
and *psychological* roots in activity theory as developed by Vygotsky (1978) and
elaborated by Engeström (1987). Activity theorists have recently started analyzing
knowledge-intensive work taking place in inter-organization zones of interlinked
activity systems and focusing on objects transcending organizational boundaries.
Doing new things is difficult both for individuals and their communities, but necessary when practices embedded in the interacting activity systems are not sufficient
to solve and conceptualize contradictions arising within the network or in relation
to its broader environment. In a similar vein, actor-network theory (ANT, Latour,
1999; Miettinen, 1999), grounded in a rich body of ethnographic science and
technology studies, emphasizes how human activity takes place in heterogeneous
networks of humans and artifacts. Actor networks represent temporary constellations of people, institutional agents, and artifacts that are mustered together to
work on a shared object across organizations' boundaries. Knowledge practices
are deeply embedded in heterogeneous networks and various affordances provided
by artifacts.

In what follows, we present two cases based on our work-in-progress in which
collective expertise has been studied in complex workplace settings. The studies
address both dialogical (participation perspective) and trialogical (knowledge creation) aspects of expertise. The first study looks into the role of mediating artifacts
and technology-enhanced practices in design work, the second study concerns
hybrid expertise as socially distributed and relative expertise in an ICT company.
While we acknowledge importance of engaging in broader ethnographic workplace
studies, the present investigations mainly relied on interviews and social network
analysis.

Case I. The role of knowledge artifacts in engineering design

Problem and focus of the study

Case study 1 addresses knowledge networks of five mechanical engineering companies' design processes (Björkstrand & Lallimo, 2006). The project addressed the
transforming nature of objects and instruments of engineering design work. Due
to the introduction of new ICT tools in the engineering design process, knowledge
artifacts, such as product plans, digital models, development documents, and so on,

are easy to modify and reuse in future projects. Modifying already existing plans, instead of designing from scratch, saves considerable amounts of time and money and is preferred whenever possible. Although the distribution and modification of the artifacts is considered as a relatively easy task, the workers constantly face problems in effective reuse of the artifacts in new projects. They may have to work through multiple representations (text, drawings and formulas, both digital and on paper), finding relevant pictures, identifying most recent versions. Modern engineering products may involve tens of thousands of components that are difficult to manage without advanced computer aided design (CAD) programs.

The study was conducted to chart the present practices and challenges of using ICT tools in creation, distribution, use and reuse of knowledge artifacts in product engineering companies. The companies manufactured quite different products, such as specific electronic lightning systems, industrial lifts, military ATV's, and soapstone fireplaces. The companies represented medium-size enterprises (250–700 employees) divided into many operational sections, operating mainly in international markets. Also, the companies were undergoing a transition from using 2D CAD to more flexible 3D software promoting reuse and modification of design documents. The 3D instruments are integrated with product data management systems (PDM) and merge design and manufacturing in a novel way. To investigate the role of design and production systems in knowledge creation the following questions were explored:

- What kind of knowledge artifacts do engineers create and what kind of tools and knowledge is used to produce them?
- How does individual and collective expertise relate to production, use, and reuse of design artifacts in design processes?

Methods

Data collection was conducted by a series of semi-structured interviews in each company. First, the key persons to be interviewed were identified, together with company representatives with respect to role and experience in the company. They covered different functions linked to product development from sales to design and manufacturing. There were 30 people interviewed. Half of the interviewees were designers, the rest representing management, sales, production, or research and development. The interviews were structured to address three main categories as follows.

1   Charting the professional background on the interviewee and his perspective on the historical development of design work.
2   Charting the social network required for managing knowledge of the design process.
3   Finding out how technological and social aspects of knowledge management were combined in the interviewee's work.

On average, the interviews took 74 minutes; altogether there were about 500 pages of transcribed data to be analyzed. Further, the interviewees were also asked to construct a sociogram map (ego-centric network) of the people and tools they interacted with during the design process. Audio-recorded interviews were transcribed and analyzed using qualitative content analysis with a special focus on the accounts of producing, using, and sharing of knowledge artifacts, and in respect to instrument usage while producing artifacts. Although the study focuses on discursive entities (participants' beliefs) rather than their practices, their central position in the investigated companies' knowledge networks allowed them to provide relevant and useful information for the present study.

Results

The main finding of the study was that, contrary to the often used, linear-waterfall model of design process where knowledge is processed and then passed on from one phase to the next, the people described the design system as a dynamic network of intertwined design practices and processes. The dynamic network contained several different expert practices connected through knowledge-sharing tools and design-related artifacts. These networks were in a constant state of fluctuation where some knowledge artifacts could be central in the network at a given time; be "left out" after some time, then "re-invited" again.

The second finding was that the accounts of use of knowledge artifacts were, to a great extent, inseparable from the specific network in which they were produced. For example, the correct interpretation of a design document could require knowledge of any or all of the following knowledge practices:

1   General expert practice (e.g. knowledge of engineering notation and design tools).
2   Company practice (e.g. historically formed practices in the company, such as internal quality management, the documentation practices in the company).
3   Knowledge-network practice (e.g. a deviation from the general company practice because of a specific need for individual practices arising from the network going beyond boundaries of the enterprise in question).

The excerpt below illustrates an interviewee's description of different ways in which designers join a project network. Before an official (company practice) assignment to the designer is made, the sales representative may negotiate details of documents with a designer, but this requires that the sales representative be familiar with the designer and aware of the specific knowledge-network.

Researcher: In what phase do you come in to a project? If a deal is under negotiation, when do they turn to you?
Designer: There are very diverse situations; like sometimes there might be a call from the sales manager calling from a customer meeting that

if it's possible to do this and this, and I tell my own opinion if it is or not; and sometimes it's decisive if it can be done in our automation line and they know it best at the production and then what are resources for design and schedules that Tom (head of design team) knows best. And depending on personal kind of relationships you have, do people know each others' expertise – that for example we have a new sales guy that he has never asked me for any comments; and then Mike (sales manager) calls very openly where we know each other . . .

Further into the interview the designer describes how discussion around certain design documents often addresses different expertise, such as designers' ability to identify past designs that can be exploited, or to evaluate how modifications to these designs relate to the production processes.

Designer: [I]f a customer needs fast some model that you know is similar to an existing product, then there's no sense to use design resources when you first offer an existing product slightly modified and offer it as a express shipment that they get to concretely hold it in their hands, because we have noticed that 3D image is not always true even if there are all figures and programs and other . . . when you aluminum sheet this way or this way, it bends differently and minimizing material loss has taught us that there are different tensions where a novice would think that it's a bundle of 1 mm aluminum it's all the same stuff; but you need to know in what alignment it is there.

In all the investigated sites the main focus of deliberate transformation of design practices was on production and reuse of design documents. Most of the sales actions in the companies could be described as mass-tailoring; selling existing designs that were "tailored" to fit the customer's needs. Implementation of a new 3D design system forced the companies to reflect on their way of working. None of the five companies had detailed company-level instructions for how to conduct design work and the database of existing designs was the only common reference point among designers. However, the databases were arranged according to the end product and project description (date, customer, etc.), while designers were usually looking for existing documents that addressed a certain design problem. To find the relevant document, they had to rely on their own knowledge of past projects or find someone who had this knowledge as the artifacts did not explicitly contain this information.

A designer with over 20 years of experience in the company described the challenges for a new worker as follows:

Researcher: When a new employer comes to the company, what would be for her the most difficult things to learn?

Designer: Hardest for her would be to learn those labeled products . . . the product repertoire is so wide that when an employer says that now I have this [product label] that she would identify what kind of [design] it is . . . you get this knowledge when products evolve . . . something that has been made '83, and there are no proper documents, but everyone who was working here back then remembers what it is. But for someone new, she sees a [product] code and drawing but if she is asked 'what was the old corner-light for NR railway carriage', she doesn't know.

In many cases, knowledge of heterogeneous and diverse practices was required. For example, many designers stated that when examining a production drawing, they could identify which one of their co-workers had made it, just by the knowledge of different individual design practices. Also the range of different knowledge artifacts used was diverse, ranging from hand-written notes, paper copies and photos to computer-based 3D graphs and concrete prototypes with exact physical properties. Design practices were heterogeneous; traditional drawing board design co-existed with 2D and 3D design practices.

Knowledge artifacts within a development process could serve multiple functions as objects of activity, as mediators or as boundary objects between different expert practices within the network. For example, all companies were implementing a product data management system (PDM) that linked the component data, prices and design drawings. This mediated the design activity by presenting the designers with clear constraints considering the production timetable and production costs. What the designers would consider as the best solution would often be impossible to produce within time or would cost significantly more than another solution; one that, for instance, the project manager would think was the best solution. The PDM was also the boundary object that personnel from both practices referred to in their accounts of design processes.

In one of the companies PDM was officially introduced as an answer to linking archived project documents to design processes. A young engineer was hired to the company as an expert of 3D CAD and PDM systems. In the following excerpt, he describes the rationale of introducing a design standards protocol:

Researcher: Does the design standard mean that there would be general guidelines of what knowledge is stored in the system when a product is designed?

Engineer: Yes and that all knowledge could be found in principle or at least information about where you can find it . . . in the old system a quite big problem is that in the server there is a designated folder with subfolders and they don't guide you at all; you need to basically know that this was done this year if we want to find specific product models. But of course PDM would now fix it if we will get it in people's minds that they should put data in PDM.

Next, the researcher asked how the implementation of the new system was advancing and the engineer identified problems related to individual documentation practices, the varying company practices in different departments and general issues of "translating" old 2D design documents into 3D modeling documents.

Researcher: How much does there seem to be resistance for change? It would be understandable that there would be.

Engineer: There is that quite a lot, and then you don't really start to use it. Usually that is the only thing that, well you don't have time, and then people forget what they have learned, and suddenly you are back where you started from . . . . [I]n the custom product department, the big problem seemed to be that the design cycle is so fast that you just design a model that looks right and don't design the interior parts and send it to the customer, because the problem is that the catch percentage [percentage of offers that lead to a contract] is so small; then how much work do you put into the initial design . . . the new system is terribly good as it gives you straight away so much that you can create the drawings much easier than with the old one. But the other side is that the old system has so much existing material, and you should create new material for the new system.

Several distinctive differences in work practices between individual designers within a company could be identified. Young designers, fresh out of school, had in general better skills in new design tools, such as 3D CAD, and often identified contradictions in the company practices. On the other hand, older workers stated that it took them years before they attained knowledge about the specific knowledge-networks. Such processes were, e.g. developing transactional memory and learning the design marks of other designers; something that could help them identify the creator of an old useful design document in case the original creator was not recorded.

In the investigated companies, the development of work included the introduction and integration of new design and production tools, such as 3D CAD and PDM systems, to support knowledge-management in design projects. The companies had, further, development teams, for testing and quickly validating ideas, which were working closely together with design teams. Projects were initiated both by management to develop a new product type for the market and by shop-floor-level ideas. The development team manager for the company producing soapstone fireplaces described one instance of shop-floor idea development as follows:

. . . I was thinking about another method for attaching together 1 inch thick stones . . . we brainstormed how we could come up with a new method and in practice I drew a while with AutoCAD and then another [person] came from the production who has been [working] there for ten, fifteen years . . . we looked at it together and then we went to the Model Master [person who makes prototypes], and he thought about it . . . then another designer came along to see that this would go here and that there and then we ordered the stones. And in the next day we put it together, and there was the whole group watching how it is possible to make. So the shop floor was really crowded and everybody was commenting . . .

The above excerpt describes how an idea of a new production method transformed into a design drawing, produced with 3D CAD tool, and further into a concrete prototype. It also describes the different expertise required to produce the artifacts. The study of expertise in the context of design projects could not be separated from the cultural-historical development of the company practices or from the development of practices within the knowledge networks. Furthermore, the construction of a common object between the different practices was often mediated by software that allowed users to offer different representations of the "object-in-progress." The design documents, plans and drawings are trialogical in nature; in the subjects' accounts the design activity was organized around deliberate collective transformation of the object in which the knowledge artifacts played a significant role.

Case 2. Combining individual and collective expertise in design-intensive work: knowledge brokering and hybrid expertise within ICT company

Problem and focus of the study

The second study addressed collective knowledge networks in a company developing collaborative technology for national and international markets. The purpose of the present study was to gain understanding of knowledge flow and knowledge creation in multi-professional, knowledge-intensive work, which takes place in increasingly flatter organizations. The ICT company under study had faced problems of combining the product-related technical knowledge, which was possessed in the technical-development function, and the customer-related knowledge possessed by the sales function. The researchers were invited to the company in a situation where the company had launched initiatives to develop ways of knowledge-sharing and creating new knowledge and products. This is a typical case in the field of knowledge-intensive work, where the existing information gets out-of-date quickly, and the creation of new products and knowledge is dependent on how the knowledge is shared and developed in heterogeneous expertise settings. Thus, the question of the organization of knowledge creation bounced back to exploring how the vertical, oftentimes dispersed, expertise and multi-professional work settings were interrelated and how their co-development takes place. Putting it in other words, in the company, the *horizontal learning and expertise* (Engeström, Engeström, & Kärkkäinen, 1995) was needed to cross boundaries of expertise domains. The framework of the study relies on notions of how individual expertise and collective knowledge networks are tightly intertwined. In multi-professional work, particularly, the expertise of various individuals constitutes distributed, however interlocked, participation frameworks, by which differing domain knowledge and working practices are linked together.

Together with their colleagues, the present investigators conducted a study focusing on organizational communication structures and practices of sharing the existing crystallized knowledge and enabling fluid knowing around new products. In the reported study particularly, we explored the central actors' interaction network, and their knowledge-brokering practices. Knowledge brokering supports the knowledge flow between otherwise separated organizational functions and people. Knowledge brokers are entrepreneurs, who are capable of combining existing resources in new ways. As we illustrate in this study, their special kind of expertise may be represented as a form of *hybrid expertise* through which an expert culture's knowledge is "translated" and transformed into something new that participants of other expert domains can understand (Howells, 1998; Sverrisson, 2001). For example, in the field of ICT development, an individual possessing profound technical, sales and marketing expertise, and knowledge about customers, represents hybrid expertise. In order to understand collective knowledge networks from the point of knowledge sharing and creating new products and knowledge, we particularly explored the following questions:

- What are the knowledge brokers' positions in the communication network?
- What elements of expertise and working practices are linked to brokerage activity?

Methods

The company understudy produces business-to-business groupware, internet and intranet solutions to the organizational and public sector. It has sales offices, development centers, and partner companies employing about 1000 workers worldwide. Particularly, the research was carried out with a unit consisting of 119 people. The study presented in this chapter belongs to a series of studies conducted during a three-year research period, focusing on management and facilitation of knowledge in multi-professional settings.

The data were collected and analyzed by two methods. First, by using social network analysis (SNA) (Wasserman & Faust, 1994) and a suitable questionnaire format, each worker of the company evaluated his/her communication links related to all other workers in the company. They were asked from whom they receive information concerning different products or customers and to whom they turn for advice in different questions. By this means, the structures of interaction network and epistemic network positions of individual people of the company could be explored. For the particular purposes of this study, nine central actors who had an above-average *betweenness centrality value* in all aspects of the questionnaire, were identified as knowledge brokers. The *betweenness centrality value* indicates the extent to which an actor is situated between others in the network, in terms of mediating information between them.

After conducting SNA, nine knowledge brokers were interviewed about their practices of sharing and developing knowledge. The semi-structured interviews concentrated on their working background and competencies, and on the working practices concerning knowledge-brokering. Interviews that took on average 100 minutes were transcribed word for word and content analyzed. Constructing the analytic scheme was assisted by several documented workshops (results reported elsewhere). The categories for analyzing the brokerage were constructed in several rounds of iterative analysis, and convey the various elements of knowledge-brokering.

Results

The results indicate how human actors may function as intermediaries between various parts of heterogeneous networks. According to social network analysis, the knowledge brokers' position in communication networks was characterized by an exceptionally thick communication network (involving above average communication links) across organizational functions and diverse people, and thus a central position in the communication flow. This is exemplified in Figure 5.1.

By assessing the knowledge brokers' betweenness centrality value, they could be considered to be in a favored position to the extent that, more than the other workers, they were positioned on the geodesic paths (shortest paths in a network between actors) between other pairs of actors in the network. Thus, their position in the network highlighted the possibility that they were exposed to extensive information circulation in the network.

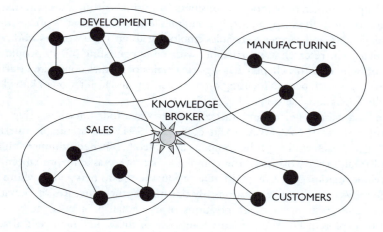

Figure 5.1 Knowledge broker, marked as a star, mediating knowledge across people and organizational functions

The interview data emphasized that knowledge-brokering takes place in a specific context; elements such as hybridization of otherwise separated domains and organizational units, relational knowledge of organizational potentials and pitfalls, and transactive knowledge of an organization's resources were brought up. Knowledge brokers' objects of work were on two main levels. First, in their daily work they worked on their primary appointments as sales managers, product managers, or support managers. The second level of work could be described as managing and coordinating the multi-professional objects of work, which were highly emergent in nature. These objects, or ill-defined problem-solving situations, could not be seen beforehand – one reason being because they were generating and enabling fluid knowing around new demands from the customers, which had no existing, crystallized solutions inside the company.

Hybrid expertise of the knowledge brokers did not emerge from scratch, but had required lengthy efforts of working in and with various domain fields and people. Such efforts are indicated in the following excerpt describing the work of the product manager, who had a background originally in psychology and usability, and who had later educated himself in technical product development. The excerpt illustrates the hybrid nature of combining and translating the requirements from the customers for the understanding of technical development, and also the other way around:

> My present job description is versatile. It consists of managing the requirements raised mainly by customers for existing and new products, and also coordinating this development process between customers and the company. One important aspect of this was developing the roadmap for the product together with my superiors. Also describing product's fact sheets and product overviews for salespeople and customers including the technical elements.

Nishiguchi's (2001) distinction between functional and relational skills is useful in analyzing knowledge-brokering. "Functional skills" refers to skills of exploiting already existing knowledge and competence for accomplishing specific tasks and pre-given goals. "Relational skills," by contrast, refers to "capabilities of a requisite variety to connect and reorder one's own and other's functional skills as necessary in relatively localized field or context of activities" (p. 216). Relational knowledge of the organization was brought up by the development services manager, who had vast experience of working in the company:

> I'm involved in product development to pretty much everything which is not the actual technical development, that is, productization and the related services, and customer support. I consider my work more like managing people's work; I do not concentrate on any specific element of the product. Because of that, in order to make some decisions I have to crosscheck the aspects from several people. That I do also for showing the possible pitfalls of single peoples' perspectives.

In an organization trying to combine different fields of expertise, it becomes remarkably important to know who has the expertise, and how accessible it is. This was illustrated in the interviews as the form of transactive knowledge. As stated by the services manager, who had a long history working in the company and several people:

> People come to ask me about old solutions and who has done something in previous projects. For me it is important to assure that people have the knowledge they should have. Its also important to make sure that many people know where the knowledge exists, because that information does not keep inside of my head or memory only.

In organizational transactive memory, its two-sided nature appears to be important; on the one hand, the services manager had the transactive knowledge about who knew what, and on the other hand, the other people knew that the services manager had the transactive organizational knowledge.

The most central knowledge brokers formed a kind of meta-brokering network. This interaction network worked as a means of gaining insight from different ground-level working activities and sharing it with other knowledge brokers. Such interaction indicates that knowledge brokers not only transfer information from one part of an organization to another, but that they are heavily bound to combine and develop new knowledge using their brokering position. The knowledge-brokering activity was connected to both formal hierarchical structure (e.g. certain knowledge brokers being in a management position with several horizontal links) and informal horizontal relations, representing links which were based more on trust and personal relationship than exact contracts. For example, certain knowledge brokers connected people through informal relations and intentional relations across organizational boundaries.

An essential foundation of the brokers' networking activities were different organizational artifacts, such as technologies, documents and manuals, and practices using an organization's ICT systems. In problem situations, the brokers not only consulted other fellow experts, but heavily relied on a variety of bug reports, manuals, quality books, and other material. Knowledge brokers referred to these artifacts when helping others to pilot their work. Knowledge brokers used various artifacts to transform their knowledge and skills to other domains by writing, for instance, "white papers" to explicate promising technological possibilities for the sales department and other non-technical departments. These documents were a reference point for developing product features or new working practices. These mediating artifacts represented transformative brokering from one field to another, involving the elaboration of a shared object of work. Through the brokering activities, different domain fields' overlapping interests or potential complications were explained and made visible. They functioned as boundary objects (Star, 1989) that assisted stakeholders' interaction, knowledge sharing, and negotiation of knowledge advancement.

Summarizing the findings, the study indicated how the network of human actors and artifacts complement an interwoven system. Different vertical fields of expertise are bridged by elements of hybrid expertise, which are constituted by people and mediating artifacts. The findings highlight the relevance of knowledge-brokering in heterogeneous settings, but also the vulnerability of the network when the knowledge-brokering is exhibited in only a few people. In addition, the design and use of mediating artifacts, e.g. boundary objects, remains most relevant for organizations that rely on work between various overlapping working domains. Knowledge brokers do not simply link crystallized knowledge in an information network; they cannot merely be characterized as the ones who possess metaknowledge about organizational resources. In addition, they receive the freshest ideas from multiple and diverse sources, enabling them to create fluid syntheses of knowledge. The knowledge-brokering is double-edged; on the one hand it serves the new hybrid solutions for the company, on the other hand it constitutes bottle-necks of information flow. The interviews brought up contradictory knowledge-brokering situations and work practices which had led to biased treatment of information. This study implies that knowledge-brokering is heavily bound to the system to which it is linked, and whose knowledge and communication structures it serves.

Discussion

Research on expertise is only now moving toward addressing real-world expertise taking place in collective knowledge networks. The two presented case studies indicate that there are essential collective aspects of expertise that are easily lost if expertise is considered apart from heterogeneous networks of activity. The investigations revealed that it was quite inadequate to describe the participants' expertise individually; the professional competencies analyzed were usually defined relationally and frequently involved hybridization across internal (research and developments, design, marketing, manufacturing) and external (customers, subcontractors) practice fields. The studies revealed various ways in which expertise is shared among the participants, mediated by artifacts, and cultivated by workplace communities' shared practices.

The studies revealed that the social and technical organization of work was under constant transformation within the organizations, which forced the participants to struggle with frequent discordination or breakdown of activity. These expert communities had cultivated specific knowledge practices to systematically deal with novel, unanticipated problems emerging, for instance, while moving toward mass-customization. Many of the organizations investigated had created special product-development laboratories involving certain experts, many of them self-educated old-timers, who were allowed to pursue, fulltime, new innovations and explorations. These experts functioned as knowledge-practice brokers who helped the expert community to carry out routine and innovative practices in parallel. Rather than working with traditional well-defined and stable objects, all of the expert communities were working with fluid objects (Law & Singleton, 2005; Engeström & Blackler, 2005) that were under constant redefinition. Simultaneously with relying on standard solutions, the communities were developing highly customized products and services. The heterogeneity of knowledge practices both within and across the organizations was striking. Tradition and innovation, exploitation and exploration (cf. March, 1999) appeared to co-exist across extended periods of time in terms of 3D design environments merging with drawing boards and 2D CAD applications.

The trialogical approach to learning appears to be highly beneficial in order to properly acknowledge the constitutive role of objects in experts' personal and collective activity. The trialogical objects that the participants of the two cases worked on showed variety; from marketing plans, white papers, and engineering designs to software applications, engineering products, and journal articles. While experts often discuss their work in face-to-face meetings, a great deal of their activity takes place in creating, elaborating, and commenting on various types of epistemic artifacts, such as plans, designs, and white papers. Trialogical objects have a central role in human discursive practices in terms of incorporating the "materiality" of knowledge. Technologies, texts, and the physical environment perform the role of anchoring knowledge and interactional infrastructures between humans and non-humans (cf., Latour, 1999). A field of practices can be regarded as "a network of fragmented and distributed knowledge held together by the power to associate heterogeneous elements" (Gherardi, 2006, p. xxiii). Expert work, as we know it, is always embedded in an extremely complex body of historically evolved knowledge, instruments, and practices.

References

Baltes, P. B., Staudinger, U. M. and Lindenberg, U. (1999). Lifespan Psychology: Theory and application to intellectual functioning. *Annual Review of Psychology*, 50, 471–507.

√ Bereiter, C. and Scardamalia, M. (1993). *Surpassing Ourselves. An inquiry into the nature and implications of expertise.* Chicago: Open Court.

Björkstrand, R. and Lallimo, J. (2006). Knowledge Intensive Design System: An attempt for better engineering environment. In J. Malmqvist and F. Berglung (eds), *Proceedings of 1st Nordic Conference on Product Lifecycle Management – NordPLM'06*, (pp. 243–253). Göteborg, Sweden, January 25–26, 2006. ISBN 91-975079-3-8.

Clark, A. (2003). *Natural-born Cyborgs: Minds, technologies, and the future of human intelligence.* Oxford: Oxford University Press.

Donald, M. (1991). *Origins of the Modern Mind: Three stages in the evolution of culture and cognition.* Cambridge, MA: Harvard University Press.

Engeström, Y. (1987). *Learning by Expanding.* Helsinki: Orienta-Konsultit.

Engeström, Y. and Blackler, F. (2005). On the Life of the Object. *Organization*, 12, 307–330.

Engeström, Y., Engeström, R. and Kärkkäinen, H. (1995). Polycontextuality and boundary crossing in expert cognition: learning and problem solving in complex work activities. *Learning and Instruction*, 5, 319–336.

Gherardi, S. (2006). *Organizational Knowledge: The texture of workplace learning*. Malden, MA: Blackwell.

Hakkarainen, K., Palonen, T., Paavola, S. and Lehtinen, E. (2004). *Communities of Networked Expertise: Professional and educational perspectives*. Amsterdam: Elsevier.

Howells, J. (1998). Management and Hybridization of Expertise in Network Design. In R. Williams, W. Faulkner and J. Fleck (eds), *Exploring Expertise: Issues and perspectives* (p. 265–285). London: Macmillan.

Hutchins, E. (1995). *Cognition in the Wild*. Cambridge, MA: MIT Press.

Johnson, P., Heimann, V. L. and O'Neill, K. (2000). The Wolf Pack: Team dynamics for the 21st century. *Journal of Workplace Learning*, 12, 159–164.

Kaptelinin, V. and Miettinen, R. (2005). Perspectives on the Object of Activity. *Mind, Culture, and Activity*, 12, 1–3.

Knorr Cetina, K. (2001). Objectual Practices. In T. Schatzki, K. Knorr Cetina and E. Von Savigny (eds), *The Practice Turn in Contemporary Theory* (pp. 175–188). London: Routledge.

Krampe, R. and Baltes, P. (2003). Intelligence as Adaptive Resource Development and Resource Allocation: A new look through the lenses of SOC and expertise. In R. Sternberg and E. Grigorenko (eds), *The Psychology of Abilities, Competencies and Expertise*. Cambridge: Cambridge University Press.

Latour, B. (1999). *Pandora's Hope*. Cambridge, MA: Harvard University Press.

Lave, J. and Wenger, E. (1991). *Situated Learning: Legitimate periperal participation*. Cambridge: Cambridge University Press.

Law, J. and Singleton, V. (2005). *Object Lessons. Organization*, 12, 331–355.

March, J. G. (1999). *The Pursuit of Organizational Intelligence*. Oxford: Blackwell.

Miettinen, R. (1999). *The Riddle of Things*: Activity Theory and Actor-Network Theory as Approaches to Studying Innovation. *Mind, Culture and Activity*, 6(3), 170–195.

Miettinen, R. and Virkkunen, J. (2005). Epistemic Objects, Artefacts and Organizational Change. *Organization*, 12, 437–456.

Moreland, R. L. (1999). Transactive Memory: Learning who knows what in work groups and organizations. In L. L. Thompson, J. M. Levin and D. M. Messick, (eds), *Shared Cognition in Organizations: The management of knowledge* (pp. 3–31) Mahwah, NJ: Lawrence Erlbaum.

Nishiguchi, T. (2001). Coevolution of interorganizational relations. In I. Nonaka and T. Nishiguchi (eds), *Knowledge Emergence: Social, technical, and evolutionary dimensions of knowledge creation* (pp. 202–222). Oxford: Oxford University Press.

Paavola, S., Lipponen, L. and Hakkarainen, K. (2004). Modeling Innovative Knowledge Communities: A knowledge-creation approach to learning. *Review of Educational Research*, 74, 557–576.

Rheinberger, H. J. (1997). *Toward a History of Epistemic Things: Synthesizing proteins in the test tube*. Stanford, CA: Stanford University Press.

Sfard, A. (1998). On Two Metaphors for Learning and the Dangers of Choosing Just One. *Educational Researcher*, 27, 4–13.

Star, S. L. (1989). The Structure of Ill-structured Solutions: Boundary objects and heterogeneous distributed problem solving. In L. Glasser and M. N. Huhns (eds), *Distributed Artificial Intelligence*, Vol. 2. London: Pitman.

Sverrisson, Á. (2001). Translation Networks, Knowledge Brokers, and Novelty Construction: Pragmatic environmentalism in Sweden. *Acta Sociologica*, 44, 313–329.

Vygotsky, L. S. (1978). *Mind in Society: The development of higher psychological processes*. Cambridge, MA: Harvard University Press.

Wasserman, S. and Faust, K. (1994). *Social Network Analysis. Methods and applications.* Cambridge: Cambridge University Press.

Wegner, D. M. (1986). Transactive Memory: A contemporary analysis of the group mind. In B. Mullen and G. R. Goethals (eds), *Theories of Group Behavior* (pp. 185–208). New York: Springer-Verlag.

Chapter 6

A new artifact in the trade

Notes on the arrival of a computer-supported manufacturing system in a technical school

Anne-Nelly Perret-Clermont
and Jean-Francois Perret

Introduction

In the following chapter we will report experiences and insights from an intensive, three-year-long study in a vocational school (École Technique de Sainte-Croix), situated in the northwest of Switzerland, in a moment of change. The arrival of a new artifact – a computer-supported manufacturing system – was at the origin of the study. For us, readers of activity theory (Scribner, 1984; Lave, 1988; Säljö, 1999; Engeström and Miettinen, 1999), this has proven a wonderful event to observe: humans and non-humans, resistances, discourses, actions, conflicts, institutional changes, and perhaps learning. Transformations occur not only at the level of the individual and inter-individual action and thinking. Concomitant and consequential changes of the "event" (this entrance of a complex new artifact in a learning environment) will also be observed at the social, institutional, political and economical levels. Yet, in the school, these changes were not always reflected upon or even noticed by learners and teachers. This resulted in diffuse and sometimes strong anxiety in these persons. It has offered researchers a unique opportunity to perceive the interdependence between artifacts and people; to observe the resistance to or search for the transformation of the activities, and the explicit and implicit learning that was occurring. The potentially complex transformative effects of the introduction of this new technology into the teaching of small-scale precision engineering had not been expected by the partners.

We will try to give the reader a chance to have a taste of what this has meant. The situation is complex because the school is quite dependent on the local watch-making area, which is supported by its traditions of professionalism and quality, but is at the same time undergoing the strong impact of globalization. An observational study of three years is a multidimensional enterprise, and the lessons that can be learned are quite numerous. Here, to make it short, we will adopt a narrative tone in order not to hide the complexity of the reality observed, and to account for its deployment in time. Other publications permit a more in-depth approach, either to the whole study or to some specific aspects (essentially Perret and Perret-Clermont, 2004; but also Golay Schilter *et al.*, 1997, 1999; Perret

1997, 2001; Perret-Clermont *et al.*, 2000, 2001; Kaiser *et al.*, 1999, 2000; Marro 1997, 2004).

Special attention was paid first to what the arrival of a major new artifact (a computer-supported manufacturing system) has meant for teaching arrangements and students' learning. In trying to account for the changes observed, we have come to realize the interdependency of different activity systems: the local school, other competing schools, the cantonal state, the federal state, the trade, the lobbies that voice the technological needs of local firms, the employment market, and so on. All participate in defining what happens in the school at a given moment. In parallel, students and teachers develop their own understanding of what is happening. Obviously, there are clashes, paradoxes, unawareness, born from competing demands, misunderstandings, prejudices, personal goals, and so on. Our own growing awareness of this complexity, as well as our efforts to spell it out, will lead us into reconsidering what is "learning" and "teaching" in such a socio-technical setting.

Questions from the field and questions from theory: setting up an investigation

The recent development of computer-supported technologies has profoundly affected workplaces and is transforming, sometimes inconspicuously, the social organization of the professional and educational fields. Schools and political authorities are aware of the need for changes. The Jura Mountains, which depends on the small mechanics and watch industry, needs to meet the new challenges of the trade in order to survive economically. But nobody really knows how vocational education should be reorganized in order to meet the multilevel changes of technology. Providing students with the opportunity to develop adequate skills, attitudes and competencies that will allow them to "join society," as apt citizens but also as employees or entrepreneurs in professional activities requiring a high level of performance is a pressing goal (Gilomen, 2002; Trier, 2000, 2003; Perret-Clermont *et al.*, 2004). Local firms strive to maintain their tradition of creativity and quality, in order to keep up with the changes in the market. This means that they also have to remain sufficiently attractive to young people.

We were looking for an opportunity to contribute to a better understanding of these transformations when Roland Bachmann, a friend and director of a technical school, asked for help. He was looking for independent interlocutors to reflect upon the contradictory pressures that he was trying to deal with in a growing climate of uncertainty.

We agreed that we would enter his school as observers, as would ethnographers in a new field (Delbos and Jorion, 1984), i.e. trying to learn the language and the worldviews of the partners, observing and taking notes, asking questions and making interviews, sometimes interfering as a way to test intuitions. But our theoretical background was not going to be anthropology. We would look at the school's activity through the "lenses" of a cultural-historical psychology and activity theory, calling attention to the individual learners and teachers as well as their contexts, but also to the interdependency between thinking, technologies, norms, roles, identities and goals (Resnick *et al.*, 1997; Martin, 1995; Verillon and Rabardel, 1995; Latour and Weibel, 2002; Engeström and Middleton, 1996; Ludvigsen *et al.*, 2003). We would draw upon our ongoing work regarding the psycho-social processes involved in teaching-learning situations (Perret-Clermont and Carugati, 2001; Perret-Clermont and Iannaccone, 2005); and, in particular, we would again pay attention to the discrepancies between the wishes of the designers of an educational setting and what really happens as seen from the side of the recipients of the pedagogical offer (Perret, 1985; Muller Mirza, 2005; Marro and Perret-Clermont, 2000; Willemin, Perret-Clermont and Schürch, 2006; Zittoun, 2006).

Our interlocutor, director of a technical school, was concerned about the anxiety and as a consequence the discouragement he sensed in staff and students. The area around the school was depressed because of difficulties in the local industry. He was hoping to find ways to boost the school's development and imagined receiving support for that from the area. One of his major steps in this direction was the (expensive) acquisition of a computer-supported manufacturing system (CSMS) to be used as a didactic tool in the workshops of the school. He had managed to get subsidies, reorganize the building to house it, advertise the acquisition in order to attract new students, yet he was left with unsolved problems regarding the curriculum and the teaching: how could the skills required by such a technological device be taught? Would the staff engage in the necessary efforts to adapt? Would the representatives of the profession, who participate as experts in the students' final examinations, acknowledge the learning of these new skills which were not (yet) part of the official curriculum? Would the students perceive and appreciate this modernity?

This school had a long tradition in the acquisition of financial resources by selling the work done in the school: the professors of the school have a record of new technical advances developed by themselves (in numerical control, for instance) and they had been successfully selling this technology and training courses to enterprises in Switzerland and abroad. Student's work performed with it was also sold to local firms. But how would this be done now?

The CSMS has not been developed by the school and comes in as an outsider. It doesn't seem likely that the school will get orders from industry, for products made with this technology. The school could still hope to sell training courses to future users of CSMS, but that was really the point: how should such training be organized? The new machine seems to disorganize the school, the curriculum, and the professors' agendas. And, furthermore, this technology always has bugs and breakdowns and seems unreliable when planning lessons!

We knew that other changes were simultaneously taking place on the wider scene: technical schools were being reorganized at the cantonal level; the local market was suffering from unemployment and less likely to ask for the school's offers; the student population was changing due to demographic shifts in society, etc. As we expected that the anxiety that was rapidly increasing in the school did not have its causes (or solutions) only within the teaching-learning process, we readied ourselves to inquire about the interdependency between different factors, by paying close attention to the crisis and to the contradictions encountered by the school in its attempts to adapt. The director agreed with this plan: the study of the entry of this artifact (CSMS) into the school was going to be considered as the principal object of study for itself, but also as a "critical event" to serve as an analyzer of the processes at different levels: individuals (teachers, learners, administrative staff); interpersonal relations; role distributions; social representations of learning and teaching; understanding of the technological change; time perspective; social positioning of the school among other schools; relations to the local enterprises and to the state.

A grant of the Swiss National Science Foundation, in a program dedicated to the analysis of changes and efficiency in the educational system, allowed us to set up a three-year-long observation plan starting for two years with: visits to the school and to its partners; reading of archives and other written sources; participant observations, for long periods of time, in classes, workshops, staff meetings, meals, open days; feedback meetings; interviews; and a questionnaire given to the students. This enabled us to better understand certain important elements of the scholastic, professional and existential problems encountered. On this basis, a specific activity was then chosen to become the center of the observations of our third year of study: namely the practical training sessions devoted to computer-supported manufacturing. It became a privileged observation point from which to identify, along with the professors, what they considered to be "traditional know-how" and "theoretical knowledge" required by the CSMS activity. (The teachers were unaware of activity theory and it was not our aim to teach them such a perspective. We only wanted to access their understanding of the situation in their own terms. But of course we were quite aware of the misleading aspects of these very common distinctions between theory and practice, know-how and formal knowledge.)

Special attention was paid to observing how the students interact with the CSMS, and among themselves or with their teacher, when working in small groups on the machine, and to how they interpret what is happening. We were expecting to see reflected here, at this level of micro-analysis, a certain number of psychological and social elements of the wider reality of the lives of the students and of the school.

A narrative account of some observations

The Jura Mountains, in the northwest of Switzerland, has a long history of clock-making and small mechanics, along with cultural and organizational traditions to cultivate the numerous skills required (technical, artistic, mathematical, commercial, etc.). This area has also developed institutional settings for their transmission, which have varied in time: each technological innovation has brought changes in the components of the trade, has put new demands on professional education, and required specific social organizations.

Traditionally, in Switzerland, a large proportion of apprentices are mostly trained by working directly with a master in a (often small) firm, a well-defined community of practice in which the learner gradually moves, according to a defined itinerary, from the status of peripheral participant (paying to have the chance to observe the trade) to the status of certified professional, earning his or her income by being fully involved in the professional activity. This practical training is complemented by some formal teaching. It is a "dual system": on one hand, the apprentices spend most of their time in the firm's workshops but also go, for a series of hours per week, to a professional school to benefit from lessons designed to serve as background to understand the trade in which they are being trained. The learners belong to two different, relatively independent, activity systems: the firm and its workshops, and the school and its classes (but there is an overlap as the firms often participate in deciding what should be taught and in assessing the student's final examinations).

In watch-making, earlier perhaps than for some other professions, it became clear that the basic knowledge required from professionals was very demanding and could not be dealt with in a day or two of lessons given just as a complement to the know-how acquired in the workshops. At the end of the 19th century, this gave birth to full-time technical schools. The Sainte-Croix is one of them. These professional schools (écoles de métiers) are seen as bridges between school and work. This implies a tension in the school workshops, as they oscillate between school activity and industrial activity. Teachers manage this tension by setting up "authentic" activities that reflect the "reality" of the trade.

These schools receive financial support from the state. But this economic input has always proven insufficient: the schools themselves have had to be largely self-supported, via the acquisition of funding, by carrying out mandates, or by selling innovations or training. As a consequence, their staff cannot at all be identified with the figure of a "teacher" (in the role of a teacher in compulsory education), but rather with that of a professional engineer who develops products, and takes part in production via mandates that the students execute both as an opportunity to practice their newly acquired skills and as a means to finance the school. In these schools, students are not just learners: they are also invited as (peripheral) participants in part of the development and production activity.

Two different activity systems are present in only one organizational entity: namely the activity of the school as a school, and the activity of the school as a firm. These two systems overlap: when needed, the teaching is modified in order to cope with the production demands; the teachers (or "professors") are aware that they have to keep their professional knowledge updated. Of course, the school is not an isolated activity system: it interacts with the public authorities, that contribute to its financing and edict regulations for the recognition of the diplomas; the school equally interacts with the economic sector of the region – and gradually with the whole country and abroad as the globalization process increases – in order to acquire mandates and offer or sell advice and training (as the school presently does in Brazil).

New technologies and fear of an economic threat in the Jura Mountains

In the 1970s, the school had already introduced computer numerical control (CNC) and carried out pioneering work in designing and selling new systems. This had changed part of the content of the teaching but not the format, because CNC kept requiring *individual work* from the technician. In the early 1990s, as in earlier circumstances on the arrival of a new technology, when computer-integrated manufacturing (CIM) emerged, schools and trades were shaken by what they perceived as a new threat and challenge. But they had the feeling that this change would be more important than previous ones because relying on *team work*: the technological advancement was not coming in support to the individual worker's action but automating a whole production chain and hence completely redefining the workers' tasks and status.

In the little mountain town of Sainte-Croix, the seat of a renowned (typically Swiss) watch and music-box industry, it is the arrival of a small low-cost music-box, produced by fully automated systems on the other side of the earth, that created a turmoil: it made evident the fact that traditional technology could not compete anymore. The whole local economic life was suddenly seen to be at risk. The firm immediately reacted by acquiring a computer-integrated manufacturing system. But such an expensive device was to create a new problem because, in order to be profitable, it had to run all day and night. This meant that, contrarily to former machines, it was not possible to stop it in order to train the staff to use it. A specific teaching space had to be organized. The firm therefore turned to the technical school, across the street: the school would buy a "didactic" machine (with some financial support from the federal state's action in favor of new technologies) and organize courses both for its students during the day and for adult workers in the evening.

A technological source of worries and conflicts

The arrival of this new technological device in the school was not inconspicuous. Not only was it very expensive and the source of a lot of pride ("our school is acquiring top technology") but also of gossip; it was very cumbersome and required the reorganization of the building to free a whole floor for it.

Members of the school staff were worried: would the new technology render classical machining skills obsolete and deprive them of their jobs? The students were preoccupied: "What are we training for? Will we end up in silly jobs, just looking after a machine that does everything by itself? Mere button-pushers?" The staff were aware of major changes on the horizon, but didn't really know which changes they ought to introduce into the curriculum, ending up with minor adaptations – but these were not understood by the representatives of the trade on the board of examiners of final diplomas: they were sceptical and kept requiring the traditional skills without giving much credit to the new know-how. Indeed, the identity and ethos of the trade were questioned: "This type of manufacturing cannot compare with traditional quality. A good worker should master his piece all along the machining process." Conversations were intertwined with the ideas of "Swiss identity" and "traditional quality."

It then appeared, as a matter of fact, that the local firm did not need to train anybody anymore: new qualified computer engineers had been recruited and the established technicians set in the role of helpers to those experts; the under-qualified part of the staff had none of the necessary prerequisites that could allow them to benefit from a training program on the didactic machine. Therefore, the collaboration between the school and the firm on this issue was stopped, with discouragement as a consequence. In the meantime, the member of staff in charge of the didactic machine was spending many more hours than foreseen trying to master it, in order to make proper demonstrations to the students who were very critical towards any bug!

The CSMS machine had in some manner been "pushed" into the school as a "must" in order to remain up to date. The firm and the school had been col-laborating for decades. But, eventually, the change was too large to be dealt with by means of this traditional cooperation. It was creating much deeper disruptions than foreseen within role distributions, material arrangements of the building, school program, learning modalities and hiring policy. Directors, professors, work-ers, students, political and school authorities had different goals. They co-existed without clear awareness of the contradictions.

Another problem arose a year later, when the school understood that the assem-bling chain of the computer-supported system had been delivered to them without all the necessary software "because of insufficient pre-definition of the require-ments." But nobody in the school could even imagine what these requirements should have been.

What should be learned?

We had been called into the school in order to evaluate the relevance of past and present learning processes and discuss readjustments. Tradition had established a step-by-step introduction for the learners of the various professions (mechanics, electronics, etc.), starting from basic skills (e.g. filing) up to the final masterpiece that the apprentice would do on his own to demonstrate his expertise. Now, fol-lowing the "step by step" tradition of teaching, the director and teachers were trying to rearrange the curriculum to include a theoretical introduction to CSMS. Of course, this meant also a reconsideration of the time allocated to the traditional contents of the teaching, threatening the occupational time (and hence the salaries) of some of the teachers. This meant more things to learn.

Some professors started criticizing the long weeks spent by the novices in learn-ing how to file with precision, when later the computer-supported machine would do it automatically; but others would argue (justly, according to Martin, 1995) that a first hands-on experience with the matter to be filed would subsequently prove very useful towards understanding the automated processes and to know how to adjust it according to the type of metal. Some teachers were used to give more space gradually to the students' own activity (production of machined objects) and would not give this up in favor of theoretical courses on the programming of computer-supported manufacturing. The staff valued neat and precise work from the students. In their opinion, this was not possible anymore in (bugging, complex) digital manufacturing – and the ethos of quality of the whole profession was considered to be at risk. The capacity to plan work within precise periods of time (in the final examination the students have to demonstrate their capacity to accomplish all interdependent parts of a difficult task in a limited amount of time) was equally important to them: but the computer-supported manufacturing is so frequently stopped by bugs or unforeseen programming problems that this quality seemed difficult to cultivate! Hence, some of the professors were very sceptical about the educational value of the new technology. And students, at times, reflected the same point of view.

There was a growing awareness that students were mostly trained to work on their own and demonstrate individual competencies, but that they would need now to learn social skills in order to be prepared for teamwork. The school did not have the proper culture for that: some teachers would tell us they had "no idea how social skills should be taught." In the questionnaires on how they learn, students responded in a very ideological way, feeding us back statements such as: "by practicing, practicing, practicing . . ."; "to repeat something many times is the best way to learn"; "you have to listen very attentively"; "it is important to work on your own"; "no, I don't ask help from the teacher or from my colleagues." But when visiting classes and workshops, we could observe students helping each other all day long, asking questions, imitating gestures, and teachers moving from one student to another giving them hands-on support, and so on. But the staff were unaware of these social skills and, as a consequence, were not explicitly fostering them.

Diagnosing the "bugs": a major challenge not recognized as such

It was found that the students' lack of trust in the "didactic machine" ("it is not a real machine," "firms work on different machines"), which they had not made explicit, notably interfered with their motivation. The professor thought he had to demonstrate elegant examples of perfect production with the CSMS. Yet, from our observations, it is now clear that the expertise in CSMS resides, to a greater extent, in the capacity to diagnose inevitable "bugs" properly rather than in the preparation of a "perfect" demonstration in front of the classroom. In fact, what might have initially appeared as "bugs" were not bugs but necessary adjustments for a complex machine. Yet, this community (professor and students) had a spontaneous sense of it: whenever the machine broke down and the professor would ask for help, the atmosphere would change from that of a classroom (with its childish ritual fights for less possible efforts and best possible grades) to a positive novice-expert relationship collaborating to solve the problem. In those moments, the students were actively learning about the functioning of this technology and taking responsibility for making it work, but this was not considered a learning experience, just as a moment devoted to helping so that the computer-supported manufacturing could start again! In these moments of breakdown and de-bugging, the traditional border between students and teacher was challenged and the whole process was weary by lack of understanding the diagnosis referring to the causes of "bugs" as a major task to be managed and learned online. Students would concentrate on how to finish the machining on time to catch their train as soon as the school bell would ring. And the teacher would make many efforts for little reward.

A parallel change in the larger landscape impacts the school

While "The Machine" was becoming a nightmare for the whole school, the local economic crisis, induced by these major competitive and technical challenges, encouraged the firms of the area to refuse the traditional economic role of the school. The local enterprises did not want to finance any more mandates to the school and they even asked the state to forbid the school to undertake any financially profitable activity. They were now considering it as an economically unfair competition. The state was to make it a full state school and support all its costs. At first, the staff didn't mind this pressure: a state status would offer them more security, longer holidays, and so on. But discontent was slowly growing, and professors were becoming bitter: their technological initiatives were not being rewarded anymore and were considered as having nothing to do with the state school plans – they were even perceived as disturbing them!

Lessons learned from these observations

Paradoxes and conflicts are likely to engender new learning (Yamazumi, Engeström and Daniels, 2005). But potential gains in terms of knowledge acquisition are likely to be submerged by a tide of other preoccupations, if special care is put into retrieving this new knowledge and disseminating it.

Retrieving knowledge first requires acknowledging that such a new learning is taking place. "Acknowledging" means that knowledge and know-how exist only if they become a conscious reality via social recognition. Second, it requires paying specific attention not only to the gain in knowledge that is produced via this learning, but also to the actors' own understandings of what is happening: are they aware of any knowledge production? Are they dealing with these activities and their changes in terms of learning and knowledge gains? It may well be that the actors, far from perceiving the events as opportunities for learning, attribute breakdowns to their (in)competencies, or to factors standing out of their reach and that, in consequence, they neglect trying to understand. The retrieval and transfer of learning, gained during the changes in the activity system, require an understanding of oneself (or of one's community of practice) as an active source of new learning and as a stakeholder of knowledge and know-how. Knowledge exists if individuals and groups maintain some kind of responsibility to retrieve it, which equally implies the responsibility to transmit it and some kind of recognition of one's role and competencies in this circulation of knowledge.

How does one acquire knowledge within change processes? Individuals and groups need special and secure "thinking spaces" (Perret-Clermont, 2004) to reflect upon the cognitive, technical, social and economic events, their meanings and their alternatives. They also need secure spaces to securely test their understandings of the processes involved. But such spaces are rare in schools: the dominant ideology of teaching and learning relies upon a dependence of novices on experts, considered as possessing context-independent knowledge, from which universal solutions can be deduced top-down (Perret-Clermont and Iannaccone, 2005). This epistemological perspective comforts hierarchies, but is very emotionally demanding, especially when supposedly "universal" knowledge fails to apply to the complexity of singular new situations, as is often the case with technological change.

On the contrary, if learning is understood as the result of a mix between, on one hand, experience retrieved from the past offering mediations to decipher present experience and, on the other hand, lessons learned from present inquiry turned towards a creative future, then it becomes clear that learners should be offered learning opportunities that are not the mere "spelled out" transmission of dominant knowledge. Open "thinking spaces" are required for such a learning to occur and to be acknowledged: open but bounded like game-fields (the "ball" has to remain on the field, i.e. thoughts have to concentrate on the matter), in which individuals, groups and communities can test actions and thoughts via trials and errors, debates and argumentation, experiments and investigations. They can, of course, opt to change the field boundaries and the rules of the game (change matter, of zone of enquiry, conceptual tools, etc.) but this, also, has to become an object of thought. These thinking spaces need some kind of "protection": by this we mean, as mentioned above, that the social architecture of these spaces has to allow that actions and thoughts be tested and discussed without taking undue risks (for health, finances, reputation, etc.). Creating such thinking spaces means creating opportunities to promote learning as a research-like process of diagnosing problems, testing hypotheses and understandings, elaborating tentative solutions and checking their impact. In the school, CSMS had created disturbances and bugs. But these new characteristics of the situation were not consciously used as resources for learning and the development of social skills. Yet, in these repairs and breakdowns, we have observed that new relations between staff, students and machine were emerging, creating opportunities for knowledge building and retrieval (for example, bugs and other disturbances were creating new thinking spaces in order to de-bug the machine, adjust or fix it). But these were not thought of as moments of knowledge production and learning, nor were they acknowledged as central in the training: they were merely seen as a loss of time. The significance of these practices had to be made visible by the researchers.

Concluding comments

A technological change is not only a technical change. It induces other changes for the concerned individuals, groups and society. Human–artifact interdependencies are quite clear when observing such a learning scene. The arrival of a new artifact created notable changes in the budget of this small school, but also architecturally and socially. Quality norms as well as the curriculum, timetables and other organizational aspects were changed. The role of the expert and the challenges to the novices were new, in particular concerning social interactions in collaborative work and learning. And all the actors were under strain, trying to give meaning to the changes. They felt threats on their self-image and professional identity and insecure about their competencies.

Such a technological change doesn't come alone. Simultaneously, and by various routes, the global technical revolutions induced by computer-supported technologies were threatening as well the market and the local socio-economical practices and networks. It was very difficult for the actors of the educational field, when left alone, to attribute the changes and difficulties not only to the new machine and themselves, but also to parallel social and institutional changes. Anxiety and a feeling of helplessness were discouraging students and staff as insecurity grew without adequate meaning-making strategies. Transitions are difficult to manage when identity, competencies and meanings are threatened simultaneously (Zittoun, 2007).

Boundaries were being challenged: was it reasonable to fight to preserve traditional know-how? How much is it necessary to change habits and identities to develop (ill-identified) new skills? Is the school's autonomy, and in particular its economic autonomy, important? Will the contact with the local firms be lost and is this a problem? All these questions are still open for the individual learner and professor, but also for the school and its director, as well as for the cantonal and federal states that are reorganizing the dual vocational system.

In this study, the entry of a cumbersome new artifact (CSMS) into the school was considered by the researchers and analyzer (a "critical event"). It has opened a window on the complexity of the processes involved in the activity of teaching and learning micro-mechanics in the Jura Mountains. By following, week by week, the arrival of this new technology, it has been revealed how institutions, individuals and groups are affected. Representations, norms, practices and identities had been shaped by decades of activities with other artifacts. None seem to have made demands as complex as this one. The school had imagined that it was just a matter of "taming" one more new machine and adapt the curricula accordingly. But, in fact, training for CSMS was threatening the linear tradition of step-by-step teaching.

The school was in the course of being reorganized by state authorities (themselves looking for international recognition in Europe), in order to conform to the new state regulations. All the attention was laid on curriculum, teacher status (bringing them back to the norms of "normal" teachers and leaving no more space for entrepreneurship), timetables and evaluation. The goal of the school's activity was gradually becoming that of producing outcomes such as: numerous students with standardized diplomas, successful examination records, low costs, and so on. As a result, the enthusiasm around the CSMS or even the interest in it declined. The machine was not becoming the expected boundary object at the centre of an expanding process. The teacher in charge of the CSMS was left alone (alone, with the researchers). In spite of the tradition of engaging professors in development and students in real industrial tasks, this was abandoned in favor of a top-down new management mode. Students' desire to catch the train in time at the end of the day and other similar attitudes started prevailing over other dimensions of the activities in the practical training sessions devoted to computer-supported manufacturing. As a consequence, students seemed to restrict themselves to following instructions in order to get rid of the exercises on the CMCS as soon as possible – even developing tricks to "feed data" into the machine so that it would proceed (even if it was at the cost of poor performance and no learning).

A final consideration raised by this study is that the research process matters. For instance, what is meant behind the terms "student" or "teacher" cannot be taken for granted. An informed cooperation between researchers and the different actors of the activity systems is necessary. In the present case, our main task, as researchers, has been to describe the on-going activities, their changes as well as the adaptations and learning that have occurred; to contribute to the elaboration of thinking tools (micro-models and micro-theories) in order to retrieve the information linked to various events; and finally to develop communication that could help actors and researchers in the reflective and critical processes of knowledge building on what teaching and learning had meant and what it was becoming. Research thereby becomes a cooperative activity between "scientists" and "laymen," both groups reflecting on the impact of their actions on their social, natural and technical environments (Latour, 2005).

To some degree, the school has "absorbed" this jointly created knowledge. It has used it to communicate, adapt the teaching (in particular in the practical training sessions devoted to computer-supported manufacturing), save face, preserve its identity, understand changes and stakes. In the meantime the CMCS stopped being considered affordable by the technical school and the local enterprises. Some of the staff, building upon the lessons learned, moved out to undertake new jobs, such as consultants, experts for the teacher training centres, and so on. Others found that the newly acquired status of a state teacher was rewarding and the whole school merged with another technical school, but this is not the end of the story: the processes described are also at work in the enlarged teaching environment on a greater scale.

We would like to extend special thanks to Åsa Mäkitalo, David Middleton and the editors of this book for their useful and very stimulating comments on a draft version of this chapter. The fieldwork was made possible thanks to a grant of the Swiss National Science Foundation (contract FNS 4033-35846). The preparation of this chapter was rendered possible by KP-Lab (IST project of the 6th European Framework Program): http://www.kp-lab.org/

References

Delbos, G. and Jorion, P. (1984). *La Transmission des Savoirs*. Paris: Éditions de la Maison des Sciences de l'Homme (Collection Ethnologie de France).

Engeström, Y. and Middleton, D. (eds). (1996). *Cognition and Communication at Work*. Cambridge: Cambridge University Press.

Engeström, Y. and Mittienen, R. (eds). (1999). *Perspectives on Activity Theory*. Cambridge: Cambridge University Press.

Gilomen, H. (2002). *Indicateurs de l'éducation en Suisse: Stratégies pour l'avenir*. Neuchâtel (Suisse): Office Fédéral de la Statistique.

Golay Schilter, D., Perret, J.-F., Perret-Clermont, A.-N., and De Guglielmo, F. (1999). Sociocognitive Interactions in a Computerised Industrial Task: Are they productive for learning? In K. Littleton and P. Light (eds), *Learning with Computers: Analysing productive interaction* (pp. 118–143). London and New York: Routledge.

Golay Schilter, D., Perret-Clermont, A.-N., Perret, J.-F., De Guglielmo, F., and Chavey, J.-P. (1997). Aux Prises avec l'informatique Industrielle: Collaboration et démarches de travail chez des élèves techniciens. *Apprendre un Métier Technique Aujourd'hui No. 7*: Séminaire de Psychologie de l'Université de Neuchâtel (Suisse): http://doc.rero.ch/record/11828?ln=fr

Kaiser, C. A., Perret-Clermont, A.-N., and Perret, J.-F. (2000). Do I Choose? Attribution and control in students of a technical school. In W. J. Perrig and A. Grob (eds), *Control of Human Behavior, Mental Processes, and Consciousness: Essays in honor of the 60th birthday of August Flammer* (pp. 427–442). Mahwah, NJ, and London: Lawrence Erlbaum Associates.

Kaiser, C. A., Perret-Clermont, A.-N., Perret, J.-F. and Golay Schilter, D. (1999). Rapport au Savoir et à l'apprentissage dans une Ecole Technique. *Revue Suisse des Sciences de l'éducation* (Editions Universitaires Fribourg).

Latour, B. (2005). Une Vertu: La prudence. *La Croix*, August 22, 2005.

Latour, B. and Weibel, P. (eds). (2002). *Iconoclash: Beyond the image wars in science, religion and art*. Cambridge, MA: MIT Press.

Lave, J. (1988). *Cognition in Practice: Mind, mathematics and culture in everday life*. Cambridge: Cambridge University Press.

Ludvigsen, S. R., Havnes, A., and Lahn, L. C. (2003). Workplace Learning Across Activity Systems: A case study of sales engineers. In T. Tuomi-Gröhn and Y. Yrgö Engeström (eds), *Between School and Work: New perspectives on transfer and boundary-crossing* (pp. 291–310). Amsterdam: Pergamon.

Marro P. (1997). Résoudre à Deux un Problème de Fabrication Assistée par Ordinateur: Analyse interlocutoire d'une séquence de travail. *Apprendre un Métier Technique Aujourd'hui No. 11*. Séminaire de Psychologie de l'Université de Neuchâtel (Suisse). http://doc.rero.ch/record/11833?ln=fr

Marro, P. (2004). Résoudre un Problème de Fabrication Assistée par Ordinateur: Une analyse socio-cognitive. *Hermès, 39*, 160–169.

Marro Clément, P. and Perret-Clermont, A.-N. (2000). Collaborating and Learning in a Project of Regional Development Supported by New Information and Communication Technologies. In R. Joiner, K. Littleton, D. Faulkner, and D. Miel (eds), *Rethinking Collaborative Learning* (pp. 229–247). London: Free Association Books.

Martin, L. M. W. (1995). Linking Thought and Setting in the Study of Workplace Learning. In M. N. L. Martin and E. Tobach (eds), *Sociocultural Psychology: Theory and practice of doing and knowing*. Cambridge: Cambridge University Press.

Muller Mirza, N. (2005). *Psychologie Culturelle d'une Formation d'adultes : L'île aux savoir voyageurs*. Paris: L'Harmattan.

Perret, J.-F. (1985). *Comprendre l'écriture des Nombres*. Berne: Peter Lang, Collection Exploration.

Perret, J.-F. (1997). Logique d'équipement et Logique de Formation: Nouvelles technologies dans une ecole technique. *Apprendre un Métier Technique Aujourd'hui No. 6*: Séminaire de Psychologie de l'Université de Neuchâtel (Suisse). http://doc.rero.ch/record/11826?ln=fr

Perret, J.-F. (2001). Concevoir une Formation par Alternance: Points de repère. *Dossiers de Psychologie, 57*, 9. Séminaire de Psychologie de l'Université de Neuchâtel (Suisse): http://doc.rero.ch/record/6302?ln=fr

Perret, J.-F. and Perret-Clermont, A.-N. (2004). *Apprendre un Métier dans un Contexte de Mutations Technologiques*. Paris: L'Harmattan. (Translation in English in preparation: Learning a Technical Trade, IAP.)

Perret-Clermont, A.-N. (2004). Thinking Spaces of the Young. In A.-N. Perret-Clermont, C. Pontecorvo, L. B. Resnick, T. Zittoun and B. Burge (eds), *Joining Society: Social interaction and learning in adolescence and youth*. (pp. 3–10). Cambridge: Cambridge University Press.

Perret-Clermont, A. N., Muller Mirza, N., and Marro, P. (2000). Que Sommes Nous Sensés Apprendre? Et Cela Nous Convient-il? *Cahiers de Psychologie* (Université de Neuchâtel), *36*, 27–34. http://doc.rero.ch/record/6301?ln=fr

Perret-Clermont, A.-N. and Carugati, F. (2001). Learning and Instruction, Social-Cognitive Perspectives. In N. J. Smelser and P. B. Baltes (eds), *International Encyclopedia of the Social and Behavioral Sciences* (pp. 8586–8588). Oxford: Pergamon.

Perret-Clermont, A.-N., Pontecorvo, C., Resnick, L. B., Zittoun, T., and Burge, B. (eds). (2004). *Joining Society: Social interaction and learning in adolescence and youth*. Cambridge: Cambridge University Press.

Perret-Clermont, A.-N. and Iannaccone, A. (2005). Le Tensioni Delle Trasmissioni Culturali: C'è spazio per il pensiero nei luoghi istituzionali dove si apprende? In T. Mannarini, A. Perucca and S. Salvatore (eds), *Quale psicologia per la scuola del futuro?* (pp. 59–70). Rome: Edizioni Carlo Amore.

Resnick, L.-B., Säljö, R., Pontecorvo, C., and Burge, B. (1997). *Discourse, Tools, and Reasoning: Essays on situated cognition* (Vol. 160). Berlin and Heidelberg: Springer Verlag.

Säljö, R. (1999). Learning as the Use of Tools: A sociocultural perspective on the human-technology link. In K. Littleton and P. Light (eds), *Learning with Computers: Analysing productive interaction* (pp. 144–161). London and New York: Routledge.

Scribner, S. (ed.). (1984). Cognitive Studies of Work. *The Quarterly Newsletter of the Laboratory of Comparative Human Cognition, 6* (1–2) (whole issue).

Trier, U. P. (ed.). (2000). *Efficacité de la Formation Entre Recherche et Politique*. Zurich: Rüegger.

Trier, U. P. (2003). *Twelve Countries Contributing to DeSeCo: A summary report*. Neuchâtel: Office Fédéral de la Statistique.

Verillon, P. and Rabardel, P. (1995). Cognition and Artifacts: A contribution to the study of thought in relation to instrumented activity. *European Journal of Psychology of Education*, 10 (1), 77–101.

Willemin, S., Perret-Clermont, A.-N., and Schürch, D. (2006). Une Expérience d'e-learning pour des Adolescents Grisons: «Progetto Muratori». In L.-O. Pochon, E. Bruillard, and A. Maréchal (eds), *Apprendre (avec) les Progiciels: Entre apprentissages scolaires et pratiques professionnelles*. (pp. 289–295). Neuchâtel, IRDP, Lyon: INRP.

Yamazumi, K., Engeström, Y., and Daniels, H. (eds). (2005). *New Learning Challenges. Going beyond the industrial age system of school and work*. Osaka: Kansai University Press.

Zittoun, T. (2006). *Insertions: à quinze ans, entre échecs et apprentissage*. Berne: Peter Lang, Collection Exploration.

Zittoun, T. (2007). The Role of Symbolic Resources in Human Lives. In J. Valsiner and A. Rosa (eds), *Cambridge Handbook of Socio-cultural Psychology* (pp. 343–361). Cambridge: Cambridge University Press.

Unpacking collaboration and trajectories of participation

Chapter 7

Intersecting trajectories of participation

Temporality and learning

Sten Ludvigsen, Ingvill Rasmussen, Ingeborg Krange, Anne Moen and David Middleton

Introduction

Time is a key issue in learning. When communicating past experiences and in planning future events, we create events where learning can occur. In any setting, there are meeting points, or zones, where participants create common objects. In these zones different temporalities intersect. Time is also central in tool use and in our organisation of activities. The semiotic potential of new technologies carries types of knowledge and potentials for meaning-making. Our view is that such artifacts connect us to our past and to how knowledge has been socially organised and accumulated. In other words, the actions and activities in which we participate are part of a process of historical socio-genesis (Valsiner, 1998; Valsiner and van der Veer, 2000; Ludvigsen in press).

At the same time, introduction of new technologies can rupture current practices in unpredictable ways. Their introduction and use creates the basis for tensions and breakdowns in any ordering of practice. The creation of new stabilities in practices using new technologies is dependent upon the re-orderings and emergence of new knowledge and competence. Time is also a critical factor in such interactional ordering of knowledge and for competencies necessary for the creation of new stabilities of practice in the use of new technologies. What exactly lies in these tensions and gaps, and what the new knowledge and competencies are, needs to be investigated and articulated.

This chapter discusses the concept of time in learning with particular reference to its potential for understanding learning in and through intersecting trajectories of participation. The temporal-spatial aspects of trajectories of participation are generally overlooked within cognitive theories of learning, but they are accounted for in a variety of ways within sociocultural perspectives on cognition and learning.

Our aim in this chapter is to create such a theoretical account based on a sociocultural perspective. We will use empirical data to illustrate what we can achieve analytically when using a multiplicity of timescales and intersecting trajectories of participation as central concepts in the study of learning. The data are gathered from health- and school-based settings. The chapter is organised according to the following two questions:

- How is time and temporality accounted for in different theoretical traditions?
- How is time used by participants in social practices of learning to constitute common objects?

These questions form the basis for discussing how the creation and use of common objects bring together learners' diverse trajectories of participation.

Approaches to trajectories of participation

The turn towards social practice as a key concept represents the broader reframing in the social sciences (Schatzki *et al.*, 2001). Our engagement with social practice as a core concept in order to understand learning follows this turn, which for us entails taking interdependencies as a starting point. These interdependencies are subject to continuing debate and discussion in the social science (for example, see: Middleton and Brown, 2005; Perret-Clermont, 2005). We position the discussion of trajectories of participation in terms of the interdependency between the historical and the specific situation. We set out to develop an account that brings in the temporal aspects of learning, and in so doing developed a more advanced understanding of how the interdependency is constituted.

We start by taking a step back and trace some of the most significant contributions to the concept of trajectory. One of the first scholars to introduce trajectory as a concept was Anselm Strauss. In studies from hospitals in the 1960s Strauss and his colleagues developed the concept to understand and analyse how the ill person and their family at home manage to live as normal a life possible in the face of the present disease (Strauss, 1975). The trajectory can be seen as a process of connected phases where there are individual differences, but common features of what to expect. According to them, trajectory is gradual and non-linear, with phases, clusters and sequences of tasks that constitute their specific details. There is dynamism within and between the phases, reflected in complexity and diversity, uncertainty and unpredictability (Strauss, 1975; Strauss *et al.*, 1985).

Strauss and his colleagues gave an account of trajectories as *differences* in how participants work with diseases, as sequences of tasks and calculations of risk (intervention–non-intervention) given available resources. The temporal aspects in Strauss's account were connected to how *time unfolds.*

From a critical psychology perspective Dreier developed a systematic approach to the concept of trajectory (Dreier, 1997 and 1999). Dreier focuses attention on how people's participation across multiple contexts is at the core of individual development. An important premise in Dreier's work is that social practices are diverse, which means that social structures do not work in an undirectional way, but as open-situated practices, where the local interaction is what connects the multiple trajectories of the participants.

Dreier's framework distinguishes between personal locations, positions and stances. Personal location concerns where a person takes part in some activity, a physical place. The idea of positions includes the dynamic aspect that people change between different settings where they represent different roles (father, mother, teacher, sports coach, etc.). Finally, the concept of stances highlights the importance of a clear idea of how people think, reason and act in a particular situation, because without these stances, we only get an abstract theory of mind and human activity. Stances are, in Dreier's words: 'grounded in complex, heterogeneous, and contradictory character of personal social practices' (Dreier, 1999: p. 15).

In Strauss *et al.* (1985), as well Dreier's accounts of trajectory, there is less attention to the use of artifacts in interaction, or to the connection between historical processes and the interactions here and now. By contrast, in cultural historical activity theory (CHAT), the focus is artifacts, objects and tools when 'long-term cycles of activities' are studied. In Engeström's work from 1987, the notion of learning by expanding was developed, to offer a theoretical basis for a new way to understand learning. The question often used to illustrate what is commonly referred to as the 'learning paradox', is how two simple cognitive structures can become one more advanced structure (Bereiter, 1995). While Bereiter tries to solve the learning paradox from within cognitive science, Engeström takes a very different approach, and from a dialectical position he shows how the learning paradox can be solved at a social level. To do so, the conceptual system that Engeström develops has social diversity and multiplicity as a starting point. Through concepts such as disturbances, tensions, breakdowns, contradictions, rules, community, division of labour, we can analyse social practice as activity systems or interacting activity systems. Historical contradiction creates radical social expansions, and such expansions changes the activity system's direction through the relation to the object. Radical change is, in other words, emphasised and prioritised in the analytic endeavour in CHAT.

Trajectories are, within the CHAT perspective, used to conceptualise how activity systems changes their relationship towards the object, or what we will call emerging objects to emphasise its dynamic and shifting character. In recent CHAT studies the concept of trajectories are used both as a theoretical and methodological concept (Saari, 2003; Toiviainen, 2003; Kerosuo, 2006). We could say that, within CHAT, *time* is built into the analysis both as a chronological and as a historical feature through the focus on artifacts, tools and objects. The interactional analytical details serve the purpose of showing how structural conflicts at different levels create contradictions, which could lead to radical expansions, and expansive learning.

An interactional account of temporality has been developed in ethnomethodology (Garfinkel, 1984; Heritage, 1984; Sacks, 1992; Psathas, 1995). Garfinkel's position has been criticised for not dealing with time. However, Rawls argues that this is based on a misinterpretation. Although Garfinkel's approach aims to study situated practice, time is a constitutive feature in his analysis, or, as Rawls puts it: 'interaction that inhabits small bits of present time and local space' (2005: p. 164). Time is not some 'measure of a relationship to a completed act that occurred in some other place or time' (2005: p. 168). Rather, time in Garfinkel's approach offers an interactional analysis of time in the sequential organisation of enacted practices (Rawls, 2005: p. 170).

Garfinkel re-conceptualises what he called the problem with individual and historical time. Individual time becomes related to the inner state of a person while historical time is external to persons and situations, not something that is constituted within the actions and activities. To solve these problems Garfinkel argues that there are two types of signs. In interactions some signs are taken for granted and serve as background for the signs that are activated and used in the interactions. Of particular relevance for our discussion is from Garfinkel's s later work, where he developed the idea that instructions indicate a trajectory for actions (Rawls, 2005). This means that instructions suggest sequential orderings of future actions, and that instructions are a planned ordering of interaction before a specific event takes place. These orderings work at two levels. The first is that institutions and long-term activities carry the history of 'rules' and orderings with them. The second level is that such 'rules' and orderings become part of the actual interactional account. However, instructions need to be transformed in the trajectory of the participation in order to become part of participants' meaning-making. Hence, this approach brings in both the historical background of the 'rules' and orderings at stake, and how they work in the specific situation.

We will argue that in the ethnomethodological turn, the semiotic potential of artifacts is underplayed. The implication of this for our understanding of intersecting trajectories of participation is that the archival potential of artifacts in the emergent orderings of interaction is rendered invisible in such analysis. The implication is that the infrastructural properties of artifacts and the institutional organisation of interaction cannot be fully accounted for. In other words, the infrastructural properties of artifacts have semiotic potential in terms of their archival potential (see: Lynch, 1999, on 'archontic infrastructures').

Heterochrony a concept developed be Lemke (2000) allows us to take this point further in the context of developing our discussion of trajectories of learning in and through intersecting trajectories of participation. Lemke (2000) argues that some form of reductionism is unavoidable. The question we need to raise is, instead, what types of reductionism are reasonable and how do we bring different levels together? Lemke argues that one way to approach this problem is to understand change on different timescales. What is relevant when we study change in relation to here-and-now interactions is not necessarily relevant in the same way when we study change in relation to a practice over a period of, say, three years. Episodes and sequences along some trajectory of participation, that are widely separated in time and space, may still be closely related. This is what we can understand as when 'time itself becomes folded' (Lemke, 2000). Such a focus implies that the analyst asks in what ways a current event is linked to a past event and to future events (and indeed the future in the past) (Middleton and Brown, 2005).

A short event may have long-term consequences. However, Lemke's view is that a more common event in human social activity is: 'the case of *heterochrony*, in which a long timescale process produces an effect in a much shorter timescale activity' (2000: p. 280). Heterochrony is a way of understanding our use of artifacts – material and non-material. For example, computers, books and hammers are material artifacts that are the result of accumulated knowledge over history in a vertical perspective. Furthermore, concepts and classification systems are examples of non-material historically accumulated knowledge and show how history is taken into account, or perhaps more precisely the practical consequences of history and artifacts. Here we see how the infrastructural properties of artifacts becomes relevant in interaction through the concept of heterochrony.

Discussion of the notion of trajectory in its relevance for learning

The present review gives an overview of concepts that have been used to understand the temporal aspects of trajectories of participation in learning. Across the different accounts there are arguments for a combination of a *vertical* in-depth analysis of moment-to-moment interactions and a *horizontal* perspective to include more longitudinal timescales that are made relevant in the moment. This is because culture and artifacts have timescales other than those of immediate interaction. The concept of artifact draws attention to what can be called history in the present, or how cultural heritage is made sense of and used (Holland and Cole, 1995). This implies that an important analytical endeavour is to investigate the ways in which participants make use of historical and cultural knowledge represented in artifacts to understand what constitutes the content and processes of learning. This implies that multiple interpretations are possible, since temporal and spatial aspects both give constraints but also becomes invoked *in situ*.

Maximising vertical timescales means that the analyst focuses on how different trajectories intersect in specific interactions and how multiplicity is played out in these interactions. Discursive approaches to sociocultural analysis start with historical analysis of a social practice, followed by detailed studies of social interaction with a strong emphasis on how artifacts are used (Säljö, 2000). The analyst focuses on the interactional constitution of the object of the activity. Time as experience, as resource, and as historical feature becomes the foreground 'picture', while time as unfolding over longer periods is in the background (Eklund, Mäkitalo and Säljö, this volume).

Approaches maximising horizontal timescales take as a premise how time unfolds chronologically. In CHAT, time and space is, as we have argued, built into the concepts. Time is modelled through interacting activity systems. The CHAT analyst uses interactional data, that is, a vertical event, to analyse in depth the horizontal dimensions of learning. Although the analyst here follows emerging objects, the actors are seen as deeply connected to horizontal developments through the activity systems. In CHAT the analytic focus is shaped by concepts such as breakdowns, tensions and contradiction. These concepts become the analytic lenses to understand radical social expansions on both individual and collective levels, understood as expansive learning. Expansive learning is connected to change in relation to emerging objects. When giving priority to the horizontal aspects, time is brought into to the analysis in a chronological way as a historical feature through artifacts. Time as experience is here in the background.

Our view is that how time is accounted for in the sociocultural traditions – the distinction between vertical and horizontal timescales – creates a significant difference. We argue that these accounts offer two different interpretations, both valid, but depending on what we, as analysts, want to address. In both approaches we cannot take the knowledge given in a book or a tool as the premises, we need to understand learning as a social activity, where the participants are accountable for their use of knowledge *in situ*, over time and in multiple social practices.

With regard to the vertical and horizontal dimension we argue that ethnomethodological approaches prioritise vertical timescales. Time is here related to our experience as a resource for action. To understand a situated practice we need to understand how the social order is created in and through the sequential ordering of social interaction. Hence, we need to do detailed studies of how actors learn through taking stances, which at the same time create specific forms of social practices. Here objects needs to be understood as part of actions and activities, it is the specifics of the object as part the practice that is important, not the location and objects in themselves (Goodwin, 2000; Rawls, 2005). Time is a constitutive feature, which is inherent in the social practice. Time becomes sequential and is a property of an event (Rawls, 2005). However, one might say that the focus on the sequential ordering of interactions also brings in the horizontal aspects of time. Hence, our view is that any ethnomethodologically informed approach addresses vertical aspects of time, since the focus is micro-analytic, but the horizontal is also accounted for as an interactional resource. When detailed interactions are the premises, other timescales are accounted for theoretically by showing how these timescales intersect in the situated practices (Garfinkel 1984; Rawls 2005).

To summarise, we can now emphasise a set of analytic concepts that will guide the analysis of the empirical material to be discussed. Overall, we highlight that learning occurs when different timescales meet and intersect, and meaning potential becomes transformed to common objects (physical and discursive). The combination of such processes and objects is what constitutes learning. Here the vertical and horizontal dimension meets in the unfolding trajectories of participation. One might say that learning is motion shaped by different types of practices and stabilised by the stances that is taken by the actor and tools and artifacts (Nespor, 1987: p. 131; Krange, 2007). Hence, one way to conceptualise learning is to say that learning occurs when you get stabilising out of flux or what we can label gap-closing. This conception of learning brings to the fore that time is a critical factor in interactional ordering of different types of knowledge and competencies for creation of new stabilities.

Analysis of empirical setting

To illustrate the present review and theoretical argument, we have selected two sets of data from health- and school-based settings. These two datasets are chosen because they actualise aspects concerning time, temporality and sequential ordering in learning in different ways. Analysis of the empirical material will illustrate how different timescales are made relevant through the knowledge and the artifacts in use, and how this mediates learning. The first example, from a peer support group related to a health condition, introduces the topic of time in intersecting trajectories of participation and illustrates central aspects in the concept of heterochrony. In this case heterochrony concerns how patients reinterpret biomedical knowledge on the basis of different individual trajectories.

In the second dataset we follow a group of secondary school students (aged 14–15) and their teacher while solving a task in a 3D (three-dimensional) ICT application. This example shows how increased complexity in new learning environments creates disturbances that intensify the importance of the temporal-spatial ordering of the interactions. The data presents here-and-now interactions, which bring in longitudinal aspects of time in different ways. This case also illustrates central aspects heterochrony and multiplicity of timescales by studying how different artifacts intersect during students' interactions, and how their creation of common objects brings together different timescales.

Introducing intersecting trajectories of participation: biomedical knowledge and life experience

In the first empirical data set we illustrate the concept of trajectories of participation introduced through considerations related to challenges of 'living well' with a chronic condition. The case relates to the condition 'anal anomaly', a congenital anomaly with life-long challenges to physical functioning, psychosocial and emotional well-being of the person with the condition and also their family (Diseth et al., 1998; Senter for Sjeldne Diagnoser, 2006). The data is an excerpt from a corpus of interviews where researchers asked adolescent and adult patients, as well as parents, about their experiences and challenges to everyday living. The interviews were conducted where ICT-based resources were being designed to supplement existing healthcare services.

The chosen excerpt gives examples of how two adolescents share their experience and handle an important issue related to the condition 'constipation'. In the excerpt the discussion illustrates the intersections between the accumulated generalised bio-medical knowledge and personal everyday experiences, and how they experiment and try to find their own path to deal with their additional challenge to everyday life.[1]

Peder: Constipation is the main issue with the syndrome. I think it varies from person to person. I can recognize the symptoms easily. I become aware when I start to be constipated . . . lose my appetite, eat poorly, do not drink, become fatigued and such things . . . you try to prevent it as much as you can, with medicines and so

	forth, sometimes it works, and sometime it does not . . .
Hans:	I eat most things. Of course, the doctors that know most about the stomach, give you 'orders' or recommend you eat full-grain bread and drink one litre of water . . . You learn from the experiences . . . if you do something wrong . . . when you are constipated or wait a little too long [with the irrigation] just because you do not care, you learn very quickly that that is not the thing to do.
Peder:	When I am about to be constipated, I take a 'chock' dose of those medicines – and they start to work 12 hours after, the laxatives – Laksoperal – don't they? And then I irrigate when they start to work, and then I empty all, and am OK again . . .
Hans:	I use mineral oil . . . take 20 ml every morning and evening, and I irrigate with 1 litre water every single day. And I take Lasoperal if I am constipated, if I feel it approaching, and before surgery and such things . . . as prevention.
Peder:	I think you are worse off than me with the constipation stuff.
Hans:	Yes . . . But lately I have been quite lucky . . . about four to five constipation episodes a year. That is good, compared to before. Two years ago, I think, I was hospitalised . . . that was three busy days with enema, and water and all you can think of . . . so you lay there then, and think about whether it is going to be Easter vacation soon or not.
Peder:	. . . suggestion – what can you do? Well, for example, concentrated prune, for those who can take that . . . mineral oil too . . . I hate magnesium . . .
Hans:	Mum was with her girlfriends, and one of them brought another friend who believed in some aloe vera stuff . . . there is a lot of stuff, and suggestions, things that is supposed to work for body and soul, and everything actually. Mum never believed in these things really, they were laughing and stuff. But she had listened to this the entire evening, and when she came home, she said I had to try. Well, I tried it with the other medication . . . I did it for a year. And it was like a dream – no problems, everything worked!

In this excerpt we see how the intersection and negotiation of bio-medical knowledge and everyday knowledge is played out. Medical knowledge: 'Constipation is the main issue with this syndrome', and personal experience: 'I feel when I am about to get problems', their own trial-and-error experiences: 'wait a little too long just because you do not care, you learn quickly that that is not the thing to do', or suggestions from mother and persuasions from friends: 'try this aloe vera – it is so great'. These two types of knowledge become relevant as life experiences, and are articulated in a number of ways. It becomes evident that the persons are testing out how to master their lives given the malformation, exemplified in the interplay between intersecting trajectories of personal experiences and general recommendations generated from within the healthcare system. We also see how past, present and anticipated future experiences influence the life trajectory in terms of experiences related to mastery from accumulated experiences, issues of prevention or maintenance, and what needs to be done if prevention and maintenance fails.

The excerpt of their dialogue illustrates two aspects of how people living with this congenital malformation deal with their 'differentness'. They relate this different-ness largely to consequences following the malformation and treatment thereof, i.e. experiences with different medications and remedies, surgical intervention for a colon stoma or appendix stoma and their use of special tools for colonic irriga-tion to prevent constipation and faecal incontinence. The differentness becomes relevant depending on the severity of the malformation; in terms of severity of the problem, ability to prevent constipation, perceived constraints to participation and psychosocial and emotional well-being of the person with the condition or their family.

The intensity or importance in the intersection between the two types of knowledge changes with accumulated personal experiences. The intersections also exemplify how personal experience and family members' experiences influence the intersecting trajectories. They (patient and family members) take different stances during the trajectory (Dreier, 1999). These stances create both continuity and possible new stances in the mastery of their challenges to daily living. This can illus-trate a third vector that contributes to development of the trajectory: bio-medical knowledge as a resource and template rather than absolute recommendations to adhere to. In this perspective, knowledge is not a precise script of what to do, since members of a community represent a set of trajectories, where individual experiences and peer-support contributes to construct the trajectories.

The bio-medical knowledge represents a historical accumulated knowledge conveying a certain perspective on the health problem, and can be viewed as a knowledge infrastructure with certain properties (Lynch, 1999). The bio-medical knowledge largely suggests how to fix the malformation, required follow-up for optimal treatment results, when to perform different surgical procedures and their indications, and to some extent emotional burden and problems of psycho-social well-being. At the same time the patients and their families accumulate experience and knowledge through everyday dealing with this health problem. Such accu-mulated experiences and knowledge of everyday living focus more on prevention, early detection (avoiding manifest problems) and integration in daily living.

The bio-medical knowledge does not provide answers about the boundaries for each person with the specific disease, although this knowledge perspective provides some scripts for the patient and the family. The personal perspectives play crucial roles; because bio-medical knowledge seems interpreted from the perspective of the person's activities related to past, present and/or anticipated future experiences. Such actions and activities are typical gap-closing processes where the vertical and horizontal processes intersect. In such intersections the multiplicity of the knowl-edge types involved and the trajectories of participants, e.g. the person with the condition, family members and the healthcare providers, allows the identification of learning processes that transforms the person's knowledge and their creation of common objects over time.

Students' problem-solving interactions in a technology-rich science application

The second empirical example is from a design experiment (Brown, 1992; Collins, 1996) where a computer-based 3D model of the insulin gene and a supplemental website was designed to provide productive learning in distributed settings among lower secondary school students. We examine how the students' and the teacher's interactions were mediated by the knowledge domain and the technologies, how these were made relevant and became a theme, and how these intersect.

The 3D model may be understood as historical artifact representing a long developmental process in at least two different ways, as historical development in the knowledge domain about genes and DNA, and as historical development of design of computer tools for learning. In the 3D model these lines of development converge in a new type of representational tool. What the students are exposed to is just the tip of the iceberg of the accumulated knowledge in the artifact. The artifact understood as a product of multiple timescales exposes the students to this complexity. The students need to activate the meaning potential that is inscribed in computer-based models and make it relevant in their interaction here and now. This meaning potential is the foundation for learning to occur (Linell, 1998; Goodwin, 2000).

We followed four students and their teacher. They were located individually in different rooms at the school, but shared the application and a telecommunication system that enabled them to communicate verbally during the session.

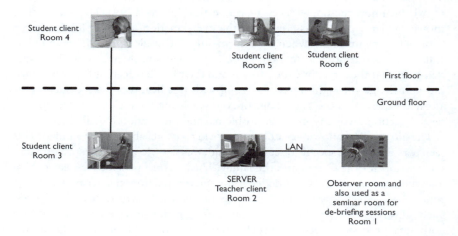

Figure 7.1 The distributed location of the students and their teacher in different rooms during problem-solving in the computer-based 3D models

The knowledge about DNA that the students are approaching has been developed in the biological sciences over an extensive period of time and is considered to be a complex problem area. The domain is presented for the students as given, and the task they are asked to solve is presented as a straightforward school task when they are requested to sequence a short part of the DNA molecule, the so-called insulin gene. The DNA molecule of insulin gene consists of pairs of bases. The bases are A (adenine) and T (thymine) that are always bound together, and C (cytosine) and G (guanine) that are also linked. Because there is a regular relationship between the base pairs, the scientific convention is that it is sufficient to mention only one of the sides of the molecule while sequencing.

Sequencing the insulin gene requires starting to read from the bottom of the gene and upwards to the top along one side. This entails that, according to Figure 7.2, the students are expected to read: 'ATG TTT . . .' That is the column on the right in Figure 7.2.

In the excerpt the students are expected to read the right-hand side of Figure 7.2. As we will see further down, this has to do with how the knowledge domain is inscribed in one of the technologies.

The insulin gene in Figure 7.2 has been made more authentic, when represented as a computer-based 3D model that has been rotated.

The 3D model has been designed and placed at a fixed point in the learning environment, and gives the students and their teacher the possibility to interact, and manipulate the objects by picking them up and putting them down by using the mouse. This allows the students and their teachers, represented by avatars, to move around it. The students and their teacher have different perspectives, just as in interactional settings of everyday life. The 3D model is supplemented by a website (see Figure 7.4). As part of the problem the students are asked to identify which one out of three sequences on the website resource (A, B and C) is similar to the 3D model of the insulin gene. The correct answer is A.

A	:	T
A	:	T
A	:	T
C	:	G
A	:	T
T	:	A

Figure 7.2 The beginning of the insulin gene. The first two codons "ATG" and "TTT" are taken down

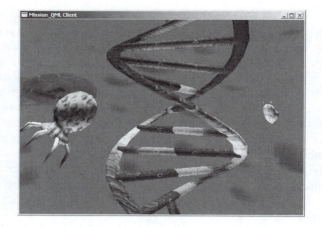

Figure 7.3 The computer-based 3D model of the insulin gene. Pairs of bases marked with 'base letters' and different colours. Two students are represented by avatars on each side of the molecule

Mission: Sequence the DNA molecule. Which of the three sequences, A, B, or C, is the right one?

Sequence A:

ATG TTT GTG AAC CAA CAC CTG TGC GGC TCA CAC CTG GTG GAA GCT
CTC TAC CTA GTG TGC GGG GAA CGA GGC TTC TTC TAC ACA CCC AAG
ACC GGC ATT GTG GAA CAA TGC TGT ACC AGC ATC TGC TCC CTC TAC
CAG CTG GAG AAC TAC TGC AAC

Sequence B:

ATG TTT GTG AAC CAA CAC CTG TGC GGC TCA CAC CTG GTG GAA GCT
CTC TAC CTA GTG TGC GGG GAA CGA GGC TTC TTC TAC ACA **CCC** AAG
ACC GGC ATT GTG GAA **CGT ACC AGC ATC TGC TCC CTC TAC CAG CTG
GAG ACT GCA** AAC TAC TGC AAC

Sequence C:

ATG TTT GTG AAC CAA CAC CTG TGC GGC TCA CAC CTG GTG GAA GCT
CTC TAC CTA GTG TGC GGG GAA CGA GGC TTC TTC TAC ACA CGC AAG
ACC GGC ATT GTG GAA **CAA TGC TGT ACC AGC ATC TGC TCC CTC TAC
CAG CTG GAG** AAC TAC TGC AAC

< The previous mission   Next mission >

Figure 7.4 The website – showing one correct (A) and two incorrect versions of the sequences (B and C). For the purpose of this article, the incorrect ones are given in bold to highlight where these differ from sequence A

The data excerpt illustrating students' interactions and how they try to adjust the procedure of sequencing to the inscribed characteristics of the 3D model and the information on the website. We enter the empirical setting in the 21st minute of an episode that lasted about 25 minutes, when the students have agreed to start reading at the bottom of the insulin gene and the teacher mobilises Fredric to be in charge of a second effort to sequence the 3D model of the insulin gene.

1	*Fredric:*	Do I start at T or do I start at A?
2	*Cornelia:*	You start . . .
3	*Pat:*	A. *Refers to the website.*
4	*Cornelia:*	Where are you then?
5	*Pat:*	We are in that . . .
6	*Fredric:*	Where do we explain?
7	*Fredric:*	There is the teacher (he, he).
8	*Mark:*	Come on, tell me . . .
9	*Fredric:*	OK.
10	*Mark:*	Yes.
11	*Fredric:*	AT . . . *Moves himself from side to side to handle the rotation in the computer-based 3D model of the insulin gene. The others are back at the web confirming and correcting Fredric's reading. The teacher withdraws from the scene. Immediately after they finish reading, the group agrees that sequence A is correct.*

We see that they continue to pursue the procedure built into the knowledge domain of how to sequence according to reading on one side from the bottom and upwards to the top of the insulin gene (1, 3, 11). The knowledge domain is made relevant as a theme through the students referencing (1, 2) and their way of manoeuvring in the 3D environment (11). Moreover, the technologies are mediating the students' interactions since they are not co-present. Concerning the website, the students are now clearly aware of the sequences on the website, and they make this information relevant as a theme (1, 3). According to the 3D rotation in the model, Fredric makes this relevant in the way he moves himself from side to side while sequencing the insulin gene (11). In so doing, the knowledge domain and the technologies in use are intersecting, and the technologies are made explicitly relevant as a theme and in their actions. The consequence is that they succeed in sequencing, and identify that sequence A on the website is the correct one.

The students make interpretation of the knowledge domain and of how this knowledge is presented within the frames of the computer-based 3D model. The students did not start questioning the intersection between the knowledge domain and the tools before their practices come to a breakdown in the sequencing of the computer-based 3D model of the insulin gene. The excerpt illustrates that they take the knowledge of how to sequence an insulin gene as given, and the premises for doing this are not included as a subject in their talk. This entails that they are reducing the complexity of the knowledge domain and its inherent history of science to a minimum (Lemke, 2000). In order to keep the activity going the students must come up with an account of the relationship between the task and tools at hand. As they search for some kind of a sequencing script, in order to solve the task at hand, the 3D model, and its relation to the website, became an issue in the students' talk. Here they needed to understand the logic connected to the 3D element of the model for sorting out how to sequence the insulin gene in this particular setting. Going beyond what was directly relevant for solving the problem was not discussed. Students often take certain aspects of schooling for granted. It was towards the end of the session that the students, or at least Fredric, understood how the artifacts mediated their problem-solving interactions that they could solve the task (see also Rasmussen, 2005; Krange, 2007).

This is how students are exposed to new knowledge areas and types, which is accumulated in different kinds of sciences, and then transformed into curriculum for students. In which ways, then, the accumulated knowledge becomes relevant, is dependent on the local interaction between students and teachers, and historical aspects in the setting. The actions that the students take could be seen as processes of gap-closing where, in order to be able to continue, they must take actions based on their interpretation of the artifacts and other students actions. In order to solve the problem the students must create an object that to a certain degree is shared. So, in the interaction between the 3D model and the students' different timescales, a short-term effect occurs based on a long-term development in sciences and technology, as one type of heterochrony.

Discussion and conclusions

We started this chapter by asking how time and temporality is accounted for in different theoretical traditions, and how time is used by participants in social practices of learning to constitute common objects. In the first empirical example we illustrate multiplicity and heterochrony as highlighted in how trajectories of personal experiences intersect with the bio-medical knowledge in different ways. The bio-medical knowledge represented a knowledge infrastructure. In this case, the patient makes use of bio-medical knowledge dependent upon how she/he has dealt with the health problem in the past and in the present, and how the future is perceived. In this perspective, time becomes a resource for action, and the mastery of the health condition in everyday life becomes the emerging and collective object. In the intersection of the institutional accumulated knowledge of health and patient experience, the involved participants need to take stances which have implication for their well-being (Dreier, 1999).

In the second example we illustrated other aspects of the concept of heterochrony and multiplicity of timescales by studying how different artifacts intersect during the students' interactions (Lemke, 2000). Both schooling in general and new representational tools such as 3D models, or other designed learning tools (Arnseth and Ludvigsen, 2006), expose students to accumulated knowledge that becomes transformed and used through student and teacher interaction. We can say that relevance of this becomes more crucial than the history of the knowledge domain in school.

Examining vertical and horizontal timescales gives dimensions that cut across the different traditions that we have discussed. The vertical aspects point towards what is often called the ontogenesis, which means how individuals develop over time. The horizontal aspects address how historical artifacts and social interaction together create the processes that over time becomes the sociogenesis. By using such concepts we can choose which analytical aspect we want to make a contribution. How the relation between vertical and horizontal aspects is taken into account will of course vary according to the research problem to be addressed. However, we would argue that it strengthens the study if both aspects become transparent through the analysis, as we have showed with our empirical illustrations. The implication is that different analytic concepts could be used.

The theories and analytic concepts that we have chosen to emphasize should not be seen as a unified perspective, position or stance, but as a set of resources to improve our understanding of learning as socially organised activities. The concepts of trajectories of participation or learning trajectories provides a unit of analysis and levels of description that cut across different traditions and make learning across sites more transparent. Multiplicity and diversity as premises for movement between sites, tools and practices is what characterises human learning. We have emphasised that the construction of common objects, physical and discursive, is crucial for learning to take place, and that construction of common objects connects historical aspects, and interaction here and now with future orientation. The construction of the common objects is necessary for coordination to take place and to create order for the participants so they can achieve both breakdowns and continuity in their social practice. This line of argument is what makes us conceptualise learning in terms of when activities get stabilised out of flux.

Acknowledgements

This chapter has been financially supported by the project at InterMedia, University of Oslo; the TRANSFORM project and CMC is funded by the Norwegian Research Council, and Kaleidoscope, a NoE, and KP-Lab is funded by the IST program, EU's Sixth Framework for research. We started our collaboration on this chapter in a workshop in Oslo in May 2006. Andreas Lund and Hans C. Arnseth also took part in this workshop and developed ideas we have used in the text. We would like to thank them for contributing to our work. We would also like to thank commentators on this chapter: Anne-Nelly Perret-Clermont, Hanna Toiviainen, Jorunn Møller and colleagues at InterMedia, for valuable feedback on earlier drafts.

Note

1 Both transcripts were originally in Norwegian. The level of detail in both transcripts is based upon the type of analysis performed. Our ambition is for the reader to understand

how the interactions unfolded. Indications of what the participants were doing are displayed in italics.

References

Arnseth, H. C. and Ludvigsen, S. (2006). Approaching Institutional Contexts: Systemic versus dialogic research in CSCL. *International Journal of Computer-Supported Collaborative Learning* 1: 167–185.

Bereiter, C. (1995). A Dispositional View of Transfer. In McKeough, A., Lupart, J. and Marini, A. (eds), *Teaching for Transfer: fostering generalization in learning*. Hillsdale, NJ: Lawrence Earlbaum Associates.

Brown, A. L. (1992). Design Experiments: Theoretical and methodological challenges in creating complex interventions in classroom settings. *The Journal of the Learning Sciences* 2(2): 141–178.

Collins, A. (1996). Design Issues for Learning Environments. In S. Vosniadou, E. De Corte, R. Glaser and H. Mandl (eds), *International Perspectives on the Design of Technology-supported Learning Environments*. Mahwah, NJ: Lawrence Earlbaum Associates.

Diseth, T. H., Egeland, T. and Emblem, R. (1998). Effects of Anal Invasive Treatment and Incontinence on Mental Health and Psychological Functioning of Adolescents with Hirschprung's Disease and Low Anorectal Anomalies. *Journal of Pediatric Surgery* 33(3): 468–475.

Dreier, O. (1999). Personal Trajectories of Participation across Contexts of Social Practice. *Outlines: Critical Social Studies* 1: 5–32.

Dreier, O. (1997). *Subjectivity and Social Practice*. Centre for Health, Humanity and Culture Aarhus, University of Aarhus, Denmark. PhD: 143.

Engeström, Y. (1987). *Learning by Expanding: An activity-theorical approach to developmental research*. Helsinki: Orienta-konsultit.

Garfinkel, H. (1984). *Studies in Ethnomethodology*. Malden, MA: Polity Press/Blackwell.

Goodwin, C. (2000). Action and Embodiment within Situated Human Interaction. *Journal of Pragmatics* 32: 1489–1522.

Heritage, J. (1984). *Garfinkel and Ethnomethodology*. Cambridge: Polity Press.

Holland, D. and Cole, M. (1995). Between Discourse and Schema: Reformulating a cultural-historical approach to culture and mind. *Anthropology and Education Quarterly* 26(4): 475–490.

Kerosuo, H. (2006). *Boundaries in Action: An activity-theoretical study of development, learning and change in health care for patients with multiple and chronic illnesses*. PhD thesis, University of Helsinki, Department of Education. Helsinki: Helsinki University Press.

Krange, I. (2007). Students' Conceptual Practices in Science Education: Productive disciplinary interactions in a participation trajectory. *Cultural Studies of Science Education*, 2(1): 171–203.

Lemke, J. L. (2000). Across the Scales of Time: Artifacts, activities, and meanings in ecosocial systems. *Mind, Culture, and Activity* 7(4): 273–290.

Linell, P. (1998). *Approaching dialogue: Talk, interaction and contexts in dialogical perspectives*. Amsterdam: John Benjamins.

Ludvigsen, S. R. (in press). What Counts as Knowledge: Learning to use categories in computer environments. In R. Säljö (ed.), *ICT and Transformation of Learning Practices*. Amsterdam: Pergamon Press.

Lynch, M. (1999). Archive in Formation. *History of the Human Sciences* 12 (2): 65–87.

Middleton, D. and Brown S. (2005). *The Social Psychology of Experience: Studies in remembering and forgetting*. London: Sage.

Nespor, J. (1987). Academic Tasks in a High School English Class. *Curriculum Inquiry* 17(2): 203–228.

Perret-Clermont, A. N. (ed.) (2005). *Thinking Time: A multidiciplinary perspective on time*. Göttingen: Hogrefe & Huber Publishers.

Psathas, G. (1995). 'Talk and Social Structure' and 'Studies of Work'. *Human Studies* 18: 139–155.

Rasmussen, I. (2005). Project work and ICT: A study of learning as trajectories of participation. Unpublished doctoral dissertation, University of Oslo, Oslo.

Rawls, A. W. (2005). Garfinkel's Conception of Time. *Time and Society* 14(2/3): 163–190.

Saari, E. (2003). *The Pulse of Change in Research Work*. Department of Education. Helsinki: University of Helsinki.

Sacks, H. (1992). *Lectures on Conversation*. 2 vols. Oxford: Blackwell.

Schatzki, T. R., Knorr Cetina, K. and von Savigney, E. (2001). *The Practice Turn in Contemporary Theory*. London: Routledge.

Senter for Sjeldne Diagnoser (2006). *Anorektale Misdannelser: Analatresi og andre endetarmsmisdannelser*. Oslo: Rikshospitalet – Radiumhospitalet HF: 36.

Strauss, A. (1975). *Chronic Illness and the Quality of Life*. St Louis, MO: C. V. Mosby.

Strauss, A., Fagerhaugh, S., Suczek, B. and Wiener, C. (1985). *Social Organization of Medical Work*. Chicago: University of Chicago Press.

Säljö, R. (2000). *Lärande i Praktiken. Ett sociokulturelt perspectiv* [*Learning in Practice. A sociocultural perspective*]. Stockholm: Prisma.

Toiviainen, H. (2003). *Learning Across Levels: Challenges of collaboration in a small-firm network*. Helsinki: Helsinki University Press.

Valsiner, J. (1998). *The Guided Mind: A socio-genetic approach to personality*. Cambridge, MA: Harvard University Press.

Valsiner, J. and van der Veer, R. (2000). *The Social Mind: Construction of the idea*. Cambridge: Cambridge University Press.

Chapter 8

Noticing the past to manage the future

On the organization of shared knowing in IT-support practices

Ann-Charlotte Eklund, Åsa Mäkitalo and Roger Säljö

> Understanding is like knowing how to go on.
>
> Wittgenstein (1980, § 875)

Introduction

At present digital technology is a generic element in the transformation of work practices through ways we communicate, administrative procedures, the organization of production processes, and so on. To be useful in specific practices, the technology has to be adapted to local needs in relevant manners. In healthcare, electronic patient records are introduced in order to make hospital practices more efficient; in retail stores databases allow efficient monitoring of the inflow and outflow of goods; in the car-manufacturing industry computer technology monitors production processes and customizes products according to buyers' specifications. As a result of this development, knowing and skills tend to become more specialized (for empirical analyses and illustrations of the interplay between technology and specialization of work practices, see Heath & Luff, 2000; Luff, Hindmarsh & Heath, 2000; Resnick, L., Säljö, R., Pontecorvo, C., & Burge, B., 1997; Zuboff, 1988). Such changes in the cultural tools we use in everyday life as well as in professional settings make it important to study how professional knowing and learning are organized in various practices.

One result of these transformations is that the implementation, maintenance and support of digital systems per se have become significant activities and fields in which knowing has become professionalized. IT helpdesk practices are obvious symptoms of this development. When digital technology was first introduced in working life, companies relied on experienced users of computers to handle troubleshooting and support tasks alongside their regular duties. But this is no longer viable. The support function emerged as a professional field in its own right when network systems and products became increasingly complex. Today, helpdesks provide support services that concern the technological systems as well as users' individual issues.

An interesting feature of the work of support units is that services such as troubleshooting, monitoring and repair of systems in many cases are possible to carry out at a distance. The physical localization of the support is thus not dependent on proximity to clients. Hence, technology becomes both the substance of professional knowing and skills, and the means through which services are delivered. For the operations of such units, problem-solving is at the core of the activities and such skills are decisive elements of the competence needed. The number of possible problems and disturbances are almost infinite in this environment. Members of helpdesk teams thus continuously have to be prepared for the unexpected.

The overall aim of the empirical study to be reported in the following is to document and analyze how an IT helpdesk team operates in its everyday practice, and how members develop and maintain collective and individual knowing. The kind of work they engage in requires not only that they learn how different tools and technologies function, but they must also learn how to use them flexibly in the practical course of coordinating communication and collective action to accomplish their tasks. New hardware and software are, as well as updates, also introduced at irregular intervals. Since problem-solving is the core activity in this kind of setting, continuous learning is a necessity for achieving continuity. To paraphrase Wittgenstein, the members of the team we have studied have to understand in order to know "how to go on." In the following we will present our theoretical premises and summarize some previous studies that focus on the organization of knowing in complex, high-technology work settings of this kind.

On the social organization of knowing   *individual*

From a sociocultural perspective, processes of learning and knowing are analyzed at the intersection of individual and collective action (Wenger, 1998; Säljö, 2005). Learning is seen as an emergent property of involvement in social practices. Collective knowing is embedded in, and mediated through, language and the artifacts used in a specific practice (Vygotsky, 1986; Vološinov, 1973; Wertsch, 1998). Knowing is thus dependent on familiarity with material semiotic tools (Olesen & Markussen, 2003) available in technologies, classification tools and administrative routines (Mäkitalo & Säljö, 2002).

In the helpdesk studied here, the kinds of queries and failures the team has to attend to are very diverse. The products they support are complex and a high degree of unpredictability characterizes the work. In such a situation, the building up of collective knowing is essential. Earlier incidents and interventions must be remembered and made available to team members, and new experiences have to be documented and kept within the system. Such collective organization of knowing in teamwork is the focus of the work by, for instance, Hutchins and his colleagues (Hutchins, 1993; Hutchins & Klausen, 1998). In these studies issues of how problems are solved collectively through mobilization and coordination of knowing in complex activities have been explored, such as when navigating on board naval ships and when flying an aircraft. In such settings, the functional system is made up by persons and tools acting together to solve tasks. These studies point to how distributed cognition extends the capability of the system to become greater than the sum of the individuals contributing to the activity. This implies that members draw upon much more information and meaning than what is explicitly communicated in the situated activity. Also Suchman's ethnomethodological analyses (1997; 1998) of joint action in an airline operations room focus on the local knowing of so-called centers of coordination. She stresses the situatedness of activities and the importance of participants' knowing of how to contribute *in situ*. Experience and conception of possible outcomes are found to be important for participants' understanding of how their actions interrelate with others' when engaged in a work task. Participants' coordination is described as a field "of perception and interaction, continuously maintained over the course of the day's work" (1997, p. 53).

From our analytical stance, participants need to master relevant semiotic tools in an activity in order to make sense of and act in an accountable manner (Mäkitalo, 2003). Studying situated knowing and understanding, thus, implies that the object of analysis must include a concrete activity where actors interact with each other through the use of mediating tools (Wertsch, 1998). Accordingly, knowing and understanding cannot be viewed as abstract mental activities from this perspective. As Wittgenstein makes clear in a very concise manner: "don't think of understanding as a 'mental process' at all. – For *that* is the way of speaking that is confusing you. Rather, ask yourself: in what kind of case, under what circumstances do we say: 'Now I can go on'" (1981, § 446).

As collective knowing is established within a social practice, local modes of communicating emerge which allow participants to take things for granted and smoothly coordinate their activities. According to Grice's (1989) cooperative principle, it is expected that "[you] make your conversational contribution such as is required, at the stage at which it occurs, by the accepted purpose or direction of the talk exchange in which you are engaged." (p. 26). Such coordination of talk and what information is relevant to ongoing practice, are local concerns. In a prestudy of the helpdesk (Eklund, 2003) it was found that the team shared information and coordinated their actions by means of a highly indexical local jargon. Minimal explanation was needed to accomplish rather complex joint action. Settings characterized by such implicit use of local semiotic tools present an interesting challenge to the study of learning and knowing. Next, we describe the adopted research strategy and continue with an ethnographic description of how work continuity is organized at the helpdesk. The challenges of analyzing learning and knowing in this kind of setting will be discussed in connection with the analyses of shift-change meetings.

Research strategy, methods and data

In a sociocultural tradition, artifacts and people are constitutive elements of the social activity in which they are engaged. For this reason, a research strategy was adopted in which participant observation was combined with the in-depth study of a core activity, resulting in ethnographic data, video-recordings and a collection of work documentations used in the activity. The general insights gained through the observations were used to select "hot spot" activities (Jordan & Henderson, 1995). In our case, the shift-change meetings were seen as such a core activity in the internal work of achieving continuity and collective knowing. In the following section, the ethnographic observations (field notes) have been used to make a description of the organizing aspects of work continuity. The video data and the documentation collected (covering the morning and day shift changes from one week) are used to give a concrete description of the actual work of shift changes. Each change of shifts consists of two meetings; one between incoming and outgoing shift leaders, and one shortly after between the starting shift leader and the engineers starting their shift. This arrangement resulted in 27 recordings, varying in length between a few minutes up to the twelve-minute time limit, which totals 160 minutes of video. Interaction analysis (Jordan & Henderson, 1995) was used when analyzing the video along verbatim transcriptions. The shift reports used by the participants in the activity were also used as a resource for the researchers in the analytical process. To ensure the anonymity of the participants and the company, fictive names of individuals and technological systems are used.

The helpdesk and the organizing of activities

The helpdesk team studied consists of 15 persons who operate around-the-clock at a Swedish site of a large multinational manufacturing company. The responsibilities of the team include surveillance, running and maintenance of global systems including expert support of user problems. Problem-solving at all hours requires the team to work in shifts. Job sharing of this sort implies that the support engineers are highly dependent on each other; they take over each other's tasks, and have to be familiar with the total range of activities the team is responsible for. Conditions like these stress the need for continuous access to the collective knowing of the team.

The helpdesk resides in one corner of a large open-plan office. On the wall there are clocks showing current time in countries around the world. Below, monitors show server statuses. There are sets of four desks where the support engineers work. Desks and computers are shared in ways that enable the shifts to sit together and not dispersed in the office area. This is an informal mechanism of significance for sharing knowing between support engineers circulating between shifts. Securing redundancy and overlap of both people and information is characteristic of this setting and achieved by means of several strategies; resources, and thus potentials, for work continuity are features built into the everyday practice.

Documentation and the doing of case work

Documentation is a vital aspect of support work. All troubleshooting tasks the team deals with are documented as cases in a web-based case-management software.

The software automatically time stamps all documentation of actions, and it is customary to sign entries with name and function. Through this documentation practice, it is possible to backtrack previous events of a case and continue the problem-solving process on later occasions, which allows for several people to work with the same task over time.

The documentation of cases constitutes the material basis for institutional remembering (Brown, Middleton & Lightfoot, 2001). The nature and diversity of problems that can be reported are almost infinite, and are what gives the work a troubleshooting and problem-solving character. The support engineers turn to different resources when needed, for example, troubleshooting pages or routine instructions on the intranet. These pages are created by the support engineers themselves and are continuously updated with information estimated to be of use for others. Our observations also suggest that need for help is expressed through verbal requests. This indicates that what is regarded as essential to know is a joint concern, and that talk during work not only supports the solving of current issues, it also has wider implications for building up a collective memory and for achieving redundancy of knowing.

Changing shifts

The workday and -night is divided into three shifts. Each shift is constituted by one (night and weekend shifts) to four engineers (morning and day shifts), of which one is assigned the role of shift leader. The engineers all assume the responsibility of serving as shift leader on a rotating basis, which is an indication of an important feature of this work environment: all support engineers are expected to be equally competent. The role of shift leader implies special responsibility to document and report ongoing tasks and relevant information to the next shift. To prepare for the shift change, the shift leader revises and produces the textual resource guiding this activity; the shift report. On the shift report, issues and problems in need of special attention, upcoming maintenances and other planned interruptions are documented. The report form is organized as a template with fixed headings for different categories of information. Relevant information from the support engineers is assembled and earlier information is erased, updated or complemented. The reports are saved to remember tasks, problems and actions taken. During the shift change, the report functions as a device for organizing the meeting and for remembering what needs to be shared within the twelve minutes at disposal.

From our observations of the continuous activities of the team, we see that several mechanisms have been introduced to avoid disturbances and gaps in work activities. The many strategies to achieve continuity, and an omnipresent focus on time constraints, reflect conditions formulated in written contracts with clients. The support engineers are collectively responsible and accountable for service delivery within time limits specified in the contracts with clients. This collective account-ability, as we refer to it, is an element that makes it necessary for team members to learn and share experiences. In this sense, learning how to evaluate, interpret and overcome problems in joint action is what work is about in this setting.

Accounting practices as situated knowing: analytical tools

we will now return to the question of how to analytically gain access to instances where collective knowing and accountability are articulated and thus observable in interaction. Lave (1988) has used the term "gap-closing" to describe the practices participants employ to overcome disturbances in situated activities. At an analytical level, such dilemmas and their way to resolution within an activity will give the analyst important insights into sharing of knowing in this specific social practice. In order to be able to continue with the activity at hand, situated knowing needs to be mobilized and explicitly elaborated by the participants. Gap-closing implies that the participants are able to draw upon their experiences of participation in such activities and make relevant use of cultural tools *in situ*. It thus points to the complexity of the situation. Knowing how to continue is, in this sense, an outcome of a dialectic process involving acting persons and their experiences, technical tools and the activity at hand.

Within the ethnomethodological tradition, gaps in the flow of mundane inter-action have been extensively studied empirically as a concern of participants and analyzed at a detailed level. Some results of these detailed empirical studies have proved useful for our analysis. Studies of participants' accounting practices (Garfinkel, 1967, p. vii; Antaki, 1994), for instance, reveal the significance of the obligation to act in a comprehensible and responsible manner in communicative activities (Buttny, 1993; Mäkitalo, 2006). If an action or utterance is incompre-hensible, irrelevant or unexpected, a gap will occur. This gap needs to be bridged in order for the participants to continue their activities. The presence of norms and routines is also visible to us as analysts if we look closer at what Schegloff (1996) calls "participants' noticing of negative events"[1] in interaction. If an interlocutor explicitly notices that something is missing, this does not only point to the fact that something is regarded as unanticipated, but also that it is of relevance in the specific situation. In both cases, the addressee needs to produce an account:

> An account is a linguistic device employed whenever an action is subjected to valuative inquiry. Such devices are a crucial element in the social order since they prevent conflicts from arising by verbally bridging the gap between action and expectation.
>
> (Scott & Lyman, 1968, p. 46)

Since accounts make explicit what is regarded as important and relevant from within a specific practice, it becomes possible to illuminate situated knowing at instances where such gaps are bridged. In line with a sociocultural perspective on situated activities, what the participants attend to is activity-bound and reflects their projects and local concerns (Mäkitalo, 2006; see also Buttny, 1993).

There are of course many disturbances in the communicative practices of the helpdesk team. In our analyses, however, the focus is limited to how gaps arise in the specific activity of the shift-change meetings, and how these gaps are bridged in the interaction in order for the activity to continue. It should be noted that the shift-change meetings take place under a strict time limit. This stresses the importance of adhering to the cooperative principle (Grice, 1989). It also requires that participants are well coordinated in their interaction. In what follows, we will point to such instances by giving examples where collective accountability is at stake and knowing is explicitly mobilized in order to be able to go on.

Knowing what is at stake: bridging gaps during shift-change meetings

We will illustrate our findings by means of two sets of examples. In the first example, the bridging is done as a gap occurs in the verbal interaction between participants. In the second set, we show instances in our material where gaps arise between participants and the artifact, the shift report.

Doing support: technical problems versus client frustrations

In order for the support engineers to know what to do, problems need to be framed in particular ways that transforms them into workable tasks. Such processes of defining and categorizing what should be done include knowing how problems are constituted, to whom they belong, and the significance they have in the practice. A core dilemma for the support engineers was balancing the infinite support side of work (the support engineers could spend virtually all their time supporting users) with the more strict technical side of problem-solving. A helpdesk team needs to be able to balance these two sides of their responsibilities to perform professional work, which is exemplified in our first example where conflicting perspectives emerge in a shift-change meeting. A gap appears between one of the support engineers and the shift leader as they discuss an error message a client has experienced. Their argumentation is focussed on whether or not this is to be regarded as a problem for the team. As we enter the conversation, the shift leader has finished a previous topic on the shift report and moves on to this one, under the heading "Major cases":

Major cases: Major cases towards e.g. Back Offices that need supervision

---

SE CBA 7–21778294, It is not possible to change PW on http://www.it.company.se/cba. Patrik Albinsson will contact link responsible and get back to us. Call him in the afternoon. / Aron

---

The support engineer (SE) orients towards the shift report and the text entry the shift leader (SL) points at as he proposes they should skip talking about it.

Excerpt 1

1	*SL:*	we can skip that because we've solved the CBA password (.) which they had problem with in the morning
2	*SE:*	okay
3	*SL:*	yes and we wait for an answer from Patrik Al- eh: no Ander- is his name
4	*SE:*	what [was the]
5	*SL:*	[Anderson]
6	*SE:*	problem then? I didn't work yesterday

The arriving shift leader informs the other support engineer that an earlier problem is no longer an issue even though it is on the report (turn 1). When claiming this, he does not provide any information about the problem and how it was solved. However, while first seeming to confirm the statement (turn 2) SE asks for additional information. What we see here is an explicit declaration of an expectation to share work-related issues; or, put differently, it can be seen as an element of a strategy for dissemination of knowing. SE points this out through the remark that she "didn't work yesterday" (turn 6) which is a legitimate account for her lack of knowing. As SL starts explaining the scenario to SE, he reformulates the description of the problem while hesitating whether or not to formulate the problem as a problem. SE now responds by laughing, but what is to be regarded as a problem becomes the topic of discussion and a gap in perspectives emerges.

Excerpt 2

7	*SL:*	the pro- no it was no problem, the problem was that [when they] changed password
8	*SE:*	[(((laughs)))]
9	*SL:*	(.) they got ▫error this eh: this userID cannot see the requested page▫
10	*SE:*	so you mean that's no problem?
11	*SL:*	no (.) you know why?
12	*SE:*	no:
13	*SL:*	if you change an CBA password it is just so that he can enter via the third way (.) but the page –
14	*SE:*	one shouldn't get that type of [message]
15	*SL:*	[yeah] because the *page* (.) is routed forward into the COMPANY's network. he has no rights in the COMPANY's network (.) so the userID has got no rights (.)
16	*SE:*	so something is wrong
17	*SL:*	so it's the wrong error message or that (xx) he [routes forward]
18	*SE:*	[(((laughter)))] *that is what I'm [say]ing*

19   *SL:*   [yes] yeah (.) but it is well it works for an internal user if you
                    go in and change then you'll fall back with you [but]
20   *SE:*   [◦yes◦]
21   *SL:*   he's external he's a consultant. works for eh: EDRIKS or what-
                    ever it was *that's* the reason

As described above, SE calls for a description of the problem and laughs (turn 8) as SL hesitates whether or not to refer to it as a problem. SL continues to account for this somewhat ambiguous statement by providing an explanation of the procedure of changing passwords and the effects of this on the system. SL's argumentation is that there was no problem by describing how the user received an error message (turn 9). SE's response (turn 10) is a challenge of SL's take on the issue and forces him to further explain himself. Our analysis is that SE regards the message appearing on the screen as a client problem and thus an issue of the team. A gap in the interaction is evident and an account is called for, as conflicting perspectives are emerging. SE's questioning shows that SL's account is not regarded as a reasonable explanation *in situ* (Scott & Lyman, 1968). There still is "a problem" to be attended to.

SL does not respond with a justification to meet this challenge. Instead he takes another perspective on the issue where he frames the subject as an issue of how the system works, technically (turn 13 and 15). According to this perspective, the error message appeared since the client did not have the necessary access rights. When responding to this, it becomes apparent how SE approaches the problem. Instead of aligning with the technical account where there is no problem, she insists on the client's perspective (turn 14). The difference in perspectives is now evident: SE refers to the user's problem, while SL is talking about the function of the system. From the user's perspective, the problem will still appear as a problem, since the user continuously will receive the error message. From a technical perspective, however, there is no problem since the system works in expected manners.

The point SE made by challenging the utterances of SL now seems to be clear to both parties. SE understands SL's point of view while still insisting: "so something is wrong" (turn 16). SL likewise acknowledges SE's take on the issue: "so it's the wrong error message" (turn 17). In his second explanation of how the error message is generated, the formulation "he [routes forward]"[2] is ambiguous in terms of the problem as caused by the user or the system (compare to the earlier "because the page (.) is routed forward," turn 15). SE laughs at this ambiguity, but it is now evident that SL manages to see the problem from both perspectives, so she acknowledges his account (turn 20). This coordination is enough to bridge the gap and to continue the activity. The accounting practice is then closed: "that's the reason" (turn 21).

The gap in this example indexes the responsibility and accountability of the team as a unit. Both engineers can see the problem with the user getting messages of restricted access, and both know that there is no technical error. The gap arises since they temporarily take different perspectives on what should be the priority of the team in this specific situation. The two perspectives are indicative of the team's situation and responsibilities toward the organization as well as toward clients. The team is a resource for clients who are in need of help and is in this sense a service team that ought to help people with whatever problems they have. At the same time, they need to establish the boundaries of where their responsibilities end, and where there are technical issues beyond their area of work. In that sense the support engineer addresses their responsibilities of providing users with support, while the shift leader's argument delimits the team's load of problems by strictly being concerned with the technical function of the systems.

Anticipating the future: strategies for dealing with uncertainty

In the next set of excerpts, taken from another meeting with three participants, collective accountability is again in focus, but actualized by a gap caused by a specific text on the shift report:

To do: Info & tasks to do **when possible**. e.g. we/night work. Important to do in red

ARUN:

-- (030316 N) If we receive mail concerning our accessibility to ME servers on Parent Compnay's X-net ... send this info to Nettan & Ragnar. This is to enable us to do text com through the FAULD Risley servers. Contact Nettan if something is unclear / Ragnar

---

The gap between the artifact and the participants is observable in the first lines of interaction below, where the text is treated as incomprehensible. The shift leader is not able to inform the support engineers about the implied task and needs to mobilize the team's collective knowing and engage the participants in the process of understanding it. As he points to the text entry he says:

Excerpt 3

1	SL:	eh: this (.) you need to shed light on cause I've got no idea of this (.) if we receive mail concerning
		—
5	SL:	if we receive mail concerning our accessibility to the ME servers on PARENT COMPANY'S X-net (.) it is to make it possible for us to ¤*testcom*¤ through FAULD RISLEY servers, contact Nettan if anything is unclear (.)
6	SE1:	[okay
7	SL:	[under*stand*] this? (1.5)
8	SE2:	((short laughter))
9	SL:	well. welcome to the club (.)

The reporting procedure is, on this occasion, a joint reading of the text, explicitly guided by SL and his finger moving along the text (turns 1 and 5). That the text entry is insufficient is suggested in turn 1 and 7 where SL's formulation and intonation communicate that the information is incomprehensible. It is met by a short yet noticeable pause followed by laughter (turn 8). SL concludes an agreement of the suggested vagueness of the text by "well, welcome to the club" (turn 9), which convey them all into the category of unaware persons. The issue of what is esteemed unclear is then elaborated:

Excerpt 4

10	SL:	so it will [we need a docu*ment*]
11	SE1:	[((laughs))]
12	SL:	cause when- they might just call and say (.) do this, just like that (.) [what will]
13	SE1:	[I thought] they would do that themselves (.) there [at]
14	SL:	[yes]
15	SE1:	RISLEY [but]
16	SL:	[yeah]
17	SE1:	well but if we should do [it then]
18	SL:	[but] this whole project is very enlightened in: dusk so I've got to say that I don't understand very much of all this (.) (xx) do ▫*test*com▫ but but hello (.) wha:t?
19	SE1:	no [me] neither-
20	SL:	[what eh:] what are the IP addresses [an:d all of that?]
21	SE1:	[yes exactly]
22	SL:	don't know anything
23	SE1:	I didn't even know we should do it
24	SL:	no

To SL, the problem seems to be an insufficiency in what the text entry implies in terms of action. After a few turns of coordination of the problem they jointly align against the text and the information. This starts out in turn 18, where SL says he does not understand the relevance of the information to which SE1 agrees (turn 19). This is further emphasized in the following two turns (20 and 21) that shows a similar pattern of questioning the lack of information in the text followed by an agreement. As they continue to elaborate on the issue, instead of moving on to the next issue on the shift report, they give an account of their willingness to deal with the situation, i.e. to act upon the unclear, but still in some sense available, information.

SL, for instance, notices the absence of a document for dealing with the potential task (turn 10) yet sticks to the expectation that the team has to be prepared for action (turn 12). The kind of document asked for, and information missing, is taken for granted. SL also notices an absence of "what are the IP addresses [and all of that?]" (turn 18). This would be necessary information for the participants when attempting to proceed with the implied task. It is thus evident that the text entry is read as the report heading suggests: as an action to be taken. This also seems to be the case if we consider SE1's utterance (turn 13 and 15) to which SL agrees. This reveals how the participants orient towards the entry: by appearing on the report and saying so in the text, it is treated as a potential task for which they are responsible.

Despite the gap that occurs as the interlocutors interact with the text in the shift report, it is worth noting that they do not only orient towards solving the problem of what is meant, they also prepare for taking on the task. The shift leader paves the way for dealing with the situation by drawing attention to work tools and information needed. It is evident that the shift report, as a powerful artifact of communication and coordination, mediates actions to be taken. It is also evident that the support engineers quickly mobilize their energies to find a strategy for dealing with the situation rather than just questioning it. The shift leader's orientation towards taking action is indicative of his role; if someone calls during his shift, he is responsible for taking appropriate action. The fact that the message is on the report, which means that someone in the team has added it, seems to make it relevant as a task and, accordingly, as a responsibility the team has to take into consideration. To close the information gap and continue with their activities, the participants align and prepare for preventive action with regard to the tasks and responsibilities that are, in fact, only implied in the text.

Discussion

The overall work climate of the setting we have studied seems to be characterized by a continuous readiness to prepare for the unexpected. The team members also take responsibility for what is brought to their attention. Being able to do so to a large extent implies learning at a meta-level, where aims and goals, and framing of events, are collectively formed and understood. As we have pointed out, such negotiation involves not only issues about how to solve problems, but also deciding on what problems to solve. The double responsibility of providing client-oriented support, while still being efficient in terms of resource management, presupposes different perspectives while working. Any one of the priorities may be invoked when defining and valuing issues to deal with.

Complex work settings rely on coordinating artifacts. The shift report permits intricate coordination of people, things and tasks that indicates the value of documenting techniques in this practice that are reliable and stable in terms of both content and procedure. Unclear pieces of text or missing information appear as gaps that must be bridged. At such instances, the headings, as a complementary tool, help the team to mobilize collective knowing in the work of anticipating future action. The mediating function this artifact has for coordination of activities is evident; the shift report not only provides participants with information, rather, any text entry implies that actions have to be taken. The shift report thus mediates the concerns of the team and structures collective action in a very concrete sense. It has a coordinating function not only in the situated activity of reporting itself, but also for the continuous work of the team that involves a wealth of information from other offices, units and persons.

Returning to the research on high-technology settings that we briefly reviewed, what can we add to our understanding of the organization of knowing in such complex settings? What distinguishes this helpdesk practice in terms of work practice and distribution of knowing? In the studies by Hutchins (1993; Hutchins & Klausen, 1998) the interplay and coordination of knowing is performed between individuals with different and complementary types of expertise and responsibility, the totality constituting performed activities. This implies that teamwork and joint action in their studies is seen as achieved between participants and tools in a system where cognition is distributed. In turn, it is implied that participants need to know how to smoothly draw on others' knowing and jointly orient to the overall task when acting as a team. In our empirical example, however, work continuity is instead entirely dependent on sharing everything worth knowing across the whole team.

The notion of sharing thus implies very different things and is approached differently if comparing our study to this earlier body of research. Shared knowledge (Hutchins & Klausen, 1998) refers to common experiences and pre-understandings of a situation. This kind of collective knowing is what makes coordination of individual activities in the functional system possible. In our study, we noticed how a shared body of knowledge is continuously oriented to. For example, we saw how a shift member asked to be updated about an event even though the shift leader writes this subject off in the first place. It seems that the matter is ascribed importance only by appearing on the shift report. Shared knowing in this setting, thus, is not about the operation of the system, rather, it *is* the system. Being left out of potentially useful information of the system is not accepted and shows us another side of the concept of sharing. That the shared body of knowledge is used as a resource in problem-solving situations was also illustrated by the shift leader's mobilization of the team's collective knowing in overcoming a gap of how to read and act upon an unclear text entry. Sharing and dissemination of knowing across the group, over time, is thus a critical feature in this kind of teamwork. Work in this setting is not only based and relies on collective knowing and shared understanding of the situation. Rather, the shared body of knowing constitutes a work tool, a way of reasoning that is continuously and actively produced and negotiated that implies that the meaning of sharing continuously needs expansion.

Negotiation of knowing becomes a prominent object of attention in itself in the helpdesk, which is not the case in all kinds of milieus we argue. Take the airline operations room (Suchman, 1997; 1998) for example. The structural division of work and responsibility is clearly assigned to different functions within the operation's staff group. Successful work is the result of coordinated tasks separated in time and space and dependent on individual member's expertise. Continuous reformulation of tasks or content would make it very hard to align in a flow of work activities that would no longer be predictable; negotiation of members' knowing would be time-consuming and, possibly, even risk people's lives. In the setting of the helpdesk, we see the opposite; such a division of expertise is not present, and the production and negotiation of shared knowing is focal in achieving work continuity. Conflicting perspectives on issues are dealt with through interaction, like in the example of the client's error message where negotiations of whether the subject constituted a problem with the team or not took place. Tasks and priorities that are considered focal thus need to be rationalized and shared in order for members to perform as a team. This implies that redundancy of knowing is an important feature of a functional system (Hutchins, 1993). Redundancy of knowing implies, in our sense, sharing of anything regarded as probably useful in future activities rather than an accumulated surplus of knowing.

In terms of accountability (Scott & Lyman, 1968), the team members have to show responsibility in all situations and take action, but not only for solving problems *in situ*. They also need to anticipate future uncertainties and problems, even when the reasons for doing so are not obvious. This stresses the need for learning, and responsibility is designated to all team members for both being updated and to continuously inform others about relevant details. To conclude, sharing of tasks in the helpdesk essentially implies that an equal level of expertise is expected from all support engineers. The accumulation of both collective and individual experiences, i.e. learning, thus becomes vital for success. Past experiences have to be remembered in the organizing of support, stressing the responsibility of each individual to both learn and share in order to function as resources in the concrete work with clients and network services.

Acknowledgements

The research reported here has been funded by the Swedish Research Council through a grant to the project "Learning to Support: Bridging educational knowledge traditions and situated knowing in technologically intensive work practices." The work has been carried out within the Linnaeus Centre for Research on Learning, Interaction and Mediated Communication in Contemporary Society (LinCS).

Notes

1   The term "negative" is used to signify the lack of something in particular, and should not be read as the antonym of positive.
2   In Swedish, SL says "han rotar vidare." This is difficult to translate as the meaning is likely intentionally ambiguous. SL uses the Swedish word "rotar" (roughly: poke around or search) but at the same time he plays with the similarity between the Swedish "rota" and the English technical term "rout." The ambiguity of this mode of talking is ratified by the laughter that SE responds with in turn 18.

References

Antaki, C. (1994). *Explaining and Arguing: The social organization of accounts.* London: Sage.

Brown, S., Middleton, D., and Lightfoot, G. (2001). Performing the Past in Electronic Archives: Interdependencies in the discursive and non-discursive ordering of institutional rememberings. *Culture and Psychology, 7*(2), 123–144.

Buttny, R. (1993). *Social Accountability in Communication.* London: Sage.

Eklund, A.-C. (2003). *Achieving Continuity: Reasoning and knowing in IT support practices.* Unpublished bachelor's thesis, Göteborg University, Göteborg.

Garfinkel, H. (1967). *Studies in Ethnomethodology.* Englewood Cliffs, NJ: Prentice-Hall.

Grice, H. P. (1989). *Studies in the Way of Words.* Cambridge, MA: Harvard University Press.

Heath, C. and Luff, P. (2000). *Technology in Action.* Cambridge: Cambridge University Press.

Hutchins, E. (1993). Learning to Navigate. In S. Chaiklin and J. Lave (eds), *Understanding Practice: Perspectives on activity and context* (pp. 35–63). Cambridge: Cambridge University Press.

Hutchins, E. and Klausen, T. (1998). Distributed Cognition in an Airline Cockpit. In Y. Engeström and D. Middleton (eds), *Cognition and Communication at Work* (pp. 15–34). Cambridge: Cambridge University Press.

Jordan, B. and Henderson, A. (1995). Interaction Analysis: Foundations and practice. *The Journal of the Learning Sciences, 4,* 39–103.

Lave, J. (1988). *Cognition in Practice: Mind, mathematics and culture in everyday life.* Cambridge, MA: Cambridge University Press.

Luff, P., Hindmarsh, J., and Heath, C. (eds). (2000). *Workplace Studies: Recovering work practice and informing system design.* Cambridge: Cambridge University Press.

Mäkitalo, Å. (2006). Effort on Display: Unemployment and the interactional management of moral accountability. *Symbolic Interaction, 29,* 531–556.

Mäkitalo, Å. (2003). Accounting Practices as Situated Knowing: Dilemmas and dynamics in institutional categorization. *Discourse Studies, 5,* 495–516.

Mäkitalo, Å. and Säljö, R. (2002). Invisible People: Institutional reasoning and reflexivity in the production of services and "social facts" in public employment agencies. *Mind, Culture, and Activity, 9,* 160–178.

Olesen, F. and Markussen, R. (2003). Reconfigured Medication: Writing medicine in a sociotechnical practice. *Configurations, 11,* 351–381.

Resnick, L., Säljö, R., Pontecorvo, C., and Burge, B. (eds). (1997). *Discourse, Tools, and Reasoning. Essays on situated cognition.* New York, NY: Springer.

Säljö, R. (2005). *Lärande och Kulturella Redskap. Om lärprocesser och det kollektiva minnet.* [Learning and Cultural Tools. On processes of learning and collective remembering]. Stockholm: Nordstedts Akademiska.

Schegloff, E. (1996). Goffman and the Analysis of Conversation. In P. Drew and A. Wootton (eds), *Exploring the Interaction Order* (pp. 89–135). Cambridge: Polity Press.

Scott, M. and Lyman, S. (1968). Accounts. *American Sociological Review, 33,* 46–62.

Suchman, L. (1998). Constituting Shared Workspaces. In Y. Engeström and D. Middleton (eds), *Cognition and Communication at Work* (pp. 35–60). Cambridge: Cambridge University Press.

Suchman, L. (1997). Centers of Coordination. In L. B. Resnick, R. Säljö, C. Pontecorvo and

B. Burge (eds), *Discourse, Tool and Reasoning: Essays on situated cognition* (pp. 41–62). New York, NY: Springer.

Vološinov, V. N. (1973). *Marxism and the Philosophy of Language.* New York, NY: Seminar Press. (Original work published in 1929.)

Vygotsky, L. S. (1986). *Thought and Language.* Cambridge, MA: MIT Press. (Original work published in 1934.)

Wenger, E. (1998). *Communities of Practice. Learning, meaning and identity.* Cambridge: Cambridge University Press.

Wertsch, J. V. (1998). *Mind as Action.* New York, NY: Oxford University Press.

Wittgenstein, L. (1981). *Zettel.* Oxford: Blackwell.

Wittgenstein, L. (1980). *Culture and Value.* Oxford: Blackwell.

Zuboff, S. (1988). *In the Age of the Smart Machine. The future of work and power.* New York, NY: Basic Books.

Transcript legend

(( ))	Transcriber's comments etc.
(.)	Untimed audible pause, longer noted in seconds, e.g. (1.5)
[]	Simultaneous utterances
,	Continuing intonation
?	Question intonation
:	Prolonged sound
-	Cut-off sound or word
Italics	Emphasized word or syllable
(xx)	Inaudible word/s
◻ ◻	English word used originally
. . .	Omitted parts of interaction
* *	Laughter in voice

Chapter 9

Design and use of an integrated work and learning system
Information seeking as critical function

Anders I. Mørch and Mari Ann Skaanes

Introduction

Since the introduction of the World Wide Web in the mid-1990s, online (web-based) learning has attracted a great deal of interest in the Norwegian service industries and many companies are now pursuing web-based training for their staff. We use the term "web-based learning portal" and "web portal," to refer to the technology that aims to *mediate* work and learning. We show that this form of technology can strengthen the integration of work and learning when part of the work is computer-based, which is increasingly becoming commonplace in many organizations.

We extend the previous research with a focus on *socio-technological contexts* within the service industry area. This includes a design approach of web portals and a conceptual framework for analysis of the adoption process. In such a dynamic context, as the service industry represents as a result of frequent customer interaction, it makes sense to distinguish among types of work: here, we make a distinction between *primary work* and *secondary work*. Primary work refers to the compulsory tasks to be accomplished during a workday. Secondary work is work that is focused on training and learning. This ranges from organization-wide knowledge-management practices on one end to that organization's individual employees and project groups on the other (see the introduction in this book about the social organization of learning). A contribution of this chapter is to treat learning as a form of work that is associated with gap-closing primary and secondary work, participate in the design and implementation of an integrated work and learning system, and study its adoption and use in terms of specific secondary work characteristics: adaptation (Gasser, 1986), articulation (Strauss, Fagerhaugh, Suczek & Weiner, 1985; Suchman, 1996), and information-seeking.

Background and context

This chapter presents and analyzes data from a three-year Norwegian project, Learning and Knowledge Building at Work, carried out between 2001 and 2004. This project was organized as a consortium of two companies in the service industry, the Federation of Norwegian Commercial and Service Enterprises, and three research institutes. A goal of the project was to introduce web-based learning technology in the two companies. A primary emphasis has been on using participatory design techniques during the planning stages and evolutionary application development during the system-development stages. One of the companies was the petrol station division of an oil company (hereafter called Service Company) and the other was an accounting company (Åsand & Mørch, 2006). We will report on the Service Company's case in this chapter. Preliminary findings were reported in (Mørch, Engen & Åsand, 2004). This chapter analyzes data six months after the portal was first put to use on a large scale (Skaanes, 2005).

From the Service Company's point of view, web-based learning is a way to organize work to help reduce the high turnover rate among its employees. The average worker at a petrol station stays in the company for about 12 months. Although the work at the petrol stations is, for the most part, manual labor, it is thought that the addition of web-based training could extend this time by giving employees more enjoyable conditions in which to work. It was estimated that this could be achieved in at least two different ways: (1) by improving the interaction between customers and attendants; and (2) by providing online access to product information in a uniform way (for all product categories). Both of these goals are challenging. First, the work is not computerized. Computers are integrated in the cash registry and through a single computer in the back office of the stations. Second, there are, to the best of our knowledge, no established theories of technology-enhanced workplace learning to guide our analytic efforts. In the analysis we draw on articulation work (Strauss et al., 1985), computerized work (Gasser, 1986), learning on demand (Fischer & Ostwald, 2001), situated action (Suchman, 1994), and situated learning (Lave & Wenger, 1991).

The rest of the chapter is organized as follows. We start by identifying the learning needs of modern organizations in their effort to define new ways of working and learning. Next we describe techniques for involving users in the design of technology (participatory design), and an approach to end-user development to incrementally deliver a web-based learning platform. Then, we present a conceptual framework for analyses of the adoption process in an organization, and we make use of this framework to analyze findings from a field trial of a web portal introduced into a national chain of petrol stations. Finally, we discuss our findings and compare our results to related research.

Technology-enhanced learning at work

The learning situations we discuss are different from most learning situations in educational institutions. Learning at work is, to a large extent, driven by situational demands, which means that employees' learning needs vary over time and depend on the goals of the company they work for. To address varying learning needs, multiple learning strategies have to be supported, ranging from just-in-time "fix-it" strategies to in-depth tutoring of domain-specific skills (Fischer et al., 1998), with and without computer support, and catering to both old and young employees. Furthermore, the mandated use of a learning platform, which is common in educational institutions, is not a viable option for most commercial organizations because teaching and learning is not their business goal. Where a teacher can require all students in his or her class to use a certain educational technology, we could not rely on that in our study because web-based learning is not high priority (mission critical) and it competes with other more established forms of training support (lectures, seminars, self-directed learning, etc.) organized by the human resources (HR) division of the company.

In the "office of the future." web-based learning has been envisioned as a tool that will assume a prominent role as a technology that can be tapped into at any time to provide information that is relevant to an employee's task. Bjerrum and Bødker (2003) have studied modern workplaces with institutionalized practices that promote learning and cooperation with new technology. In these environments, the physical and computational infrastructure is open and flexible (open offices, transparent walls, wireless LAN) so that the employees and managers can access the company's online knowledge-base at any time. The potential for legitimate peripheral participation (Lave & Wenger, 1991) is high in this kind of environment, supported by an improved awareness (over-hearing and over-seeing) of the activities of others (Bjerrum & Bødker, 2003). When this is supplemented with context-aware computer applications (Dey, Abowd & Salber, 2001) and computational awareness mechanisms (Mørch, Jondahl & Dolonen, 2005), it provides a technical framework for learning on demand (Fischer & Ostwald, 2001). However, the envisioned potential for increased learning was not realized in the companies studied by Bjerrum and Bødker, and they found patterns of conformity and anonymity rather than new forms of cooperation and creativity. The technology and new physical spaces, by themselves, did not promote learning.

By treating technology as *mediating artifact* rather than stand-alone innovation or discrete IT-solution, it takes on a different role that broadens the application context and integration with older technologies (Eklund, Mäkitalo & Säljö, this volume; Ludvigsen, Rasmussen, Krange, Moen & Middleton, this volume). Instead of "learning from computers" or "learning through computers" one can "learn with computers." By this it is meant that technology-enhanced learning should be treated as equal to and as an alternative for other learning approaches, such as textbooks, lectures and seminars. This approach to mediation might increase the acceptance of web-based training in organizations because it allows learners to choose their preferred learning approach from a range of alternatives (from computerized to conventional). This is more in line with company strategies and objectives for institutionalizing learning at work. In the context of educational technologies this is sometimes referred to as *blended learning*, which means to combine online and face-to-face approaches (Fjuk & Kristiansen, 2001). In the context of computer-supported cooperative work (CSCW) it has been associated with *discretionary use* of new technology, which has been identified as an important principle for successful introduction of groupware in working-life organizations

(Grudin & Palen, 1995). It means that employees should have the right to choose among alternative technologies to support their business goals. A shortcoming of this approach (as well as blended learning) is that older (alternative) technologies need to be maintained in parallel with the latest technological tools (books need to be printed, courses held, etc.). This is not always an attractive feature for a company that wishes to promote advanced learning technology, but costs will decrease if measures are taken to anticipate future use situations and to design for it in such a way that the older technologies are gradually phased out or continued for special needs and niche markets (printing on-demand, older technology as workarounds during repair of primary work support, etc.). Thus, in many companies web-based training will be introduced to cater to two needs: (1) to provide an alternative to existing competence initiatives and (2) to strengthen the company's technological image to the outside world. This means enriching and spearheading, rather than supplanting traditional human resources (HR)-based training programs.

Design and development of a web-based learning portal

To plan for the challenges associated with institutionalizing web-based learning in a large organization we opted for a design methodology that combined participatory design (PD) and end-user development (EUD).

Participatory design

One of the primary goals of the Learning and Knowledge Building at Work project was to involve the workers at the petrol stations in the design of their future workplace. By making the employees "owners of the problems" (Fischer, 1994), and "champions of the project" (Åsand & Mørch, 2006) they helped us: (1) to identify situations for which technology-enhanced learning could improve existing work practice and (2) to sustain the project after it was completed. This was accomplished using participatory design (PD) techniques (Bjerknes & Bratteteig, 1995). We made extensive use of PD techniques, including the exploration of design alternatives, and the design of learning scenarios. This broadened the design space and led to some degree of decentralized decision-making (empowering the actual users) as well as extending the time for reflection throughout the implementation process.

Mock-ups and design alternatives

The use of low-fidelity mock-ups for rapid prototyping has been an integral part of the PD tradition since it was pioneered in the UTOPIA project (Ehn & Kyng, 1991). It is widely recognized that communication with end users must be done through concrete representations of ideas, and that such representations nurture the creativity of both end users and researchers in cooperative design settings (Svanæs & Seland, 2004).

The mock-ups the employees created were not merely representations of their collective understanding of their workplace. The materials employed are inexpensive and readily available, which meant that the participants could create different versions in a brief period of time, thus empowering all those who wanted to take part, including those without the background for or interest in using computers. When the employees had modeled their ideas, the mock-ups needed some polishing before they could be presented to the developers in the IT department (who later developed solutions). The researchers made new mock-ups by varying the size and refining the interactive behavior of the user-generated models. This is what we refer to as design alternatives (Mørch & Solheim, 2005). Design alternatives are intermediate abstractions that have "family resemblance" (Ehn & Kyng, 1991; Mørch, 2003) to both workplace materials and computer interfaces. They can function as a platform for end-user development, which we illustrate by an example later in the chapter.

The mock-up that was chosen by the Service Company was a large-sized information display. The deciding factors in the selection process were the envisioned location in the store of this mock-up and its size; it was thought that the smaller sizes would more easily be misplaced by attendants or stolen by customers. Nevertheless, the employees definitely contributed to the decision-making process through their constructive participation in the workshop. They generated ideas, made clear what they wanted, and understood the consequences of intermediate abstractions.

Simulating the future with role-playing techniques

We employed a technique we called "learning scenarios," which are PD scenarios depicting future integrated work and learning situations at the petrol stations. We

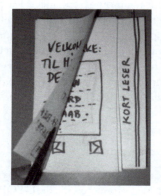

Figure 9.1 Alternative information displays: mock-up with Post-it notes and hand drawings to enable simulation of desired interaction with a handheld device

both created scenarios and we executed (played) them, similar to how role-playing is done in dramaturgy. We hired a professional theatre instructor to provide the participants with an introduction to dramaturgy for the purpose of creating convincing scenarios (to fuel interest and acceptance in the company at large). The participants (selected station attendants, regional managers and researchers) in collaboration created scripts that were later enacted in two situations. During the first simulated situation (current workplace) the audience (those participants that waited for their turn to play) was told to identify potential breakdowns that could occur (e.g. someone pumping gas and leaving without paying), and write them down on 4 × 6 inch index cards. The theatre instructor incorporated a selected set of these as prompts in the second round of role-playing.

The second situation was to simulate future work, which was dramatized in two acts. The second act incorporated and resolved the breakdowns identified in the first act. This was accomplished by a technique called "freeze spots," which stops the action and creates an interruption of the situation. The actors continue with a self-directed recovery that takes the situation in a different direction than originally planned (Brandt & Grunnet, 2000). When we dramatized the future work situation with the aid of recovery props (mock-ups, workarounds), the employees were able to see, in a semi-realistic way, the extent to which they were able to improve upon their current work situation with innovation.

End-user development

Transforming users' concrete ideas into software prototypes is not well supported in participatory design. The problem is related to the fact that software artifacts are abstract objects (Kramer, 2007). They are not easily learned and to modify them is even harder. We propose transitions to bridge PD representations (informal, inexpensive) and software representations (hardware platform, software design, program code) by end-user development (EUD). EUD consists of methods, techniques and tools for modifying software artifacts by non-professional software developers (for an overview, see Åsand & Mørch, 2006). We focused on supporting evolutionary application development (Mørch, 2003; Mørch, Dolonen & Nævdal, 2006).

Evolutionary application development (EAD) entails that ICT tools (software and hardware) can evolve along numerous paths, driven by user needs and end users' active participation. To design for EAD application, professional-systems developers must provide options (alternatives) or open points (hooks) for initiating further development. To the extent that users know about these options and open points, it provides them with various degrees of design opportunities. As well, to the extent that users can make use of them constructively, for example, when they are associated with domain-oriented design environments (Fischer, 1994), they will be able to contribute to the design process with (modifications to) designed artifacts. Furthermore, when domain-oriented design environments are aided by techniques for transforming informal (non-computerized) representations into formal (computational) representations, they are surprisingly useful. In sum, evolutionary application development suggests many small steps carried out by end-user developers in collaboration with professional developers, rather than a few big steps carried out by professional developers. This is demonstrated in the remainder of this chapter with an example.

The Service Company's IT department created the first computer-based prototype based on one of the refined mock-ups. This prototype was a touch-screen-mounted terminal facing the attendant and placed in a pilot station for a period of two months (Figure 9.2). The system contained product information about car batteries and windshield wipers. During the trial period, all employees at the petrol station explored the prototype's features at least once. They were eager to tell us what they thought of it and how it could be improved. The feedback we received gave us the impression that the employees had a real need for access to detailed information about automobile products due to the complexity of this type of information and the frequent request from customers. The employees were enthusiastic about having a web-based tool that could supply this information.

Although initially intrigued by the system, the attendants only sporadically used it. Its design was criticized for various reasons. For example, the information was organized from the perspective of the system's builder (IT department) and not from the perspective of the users' problem situation (i.e. several menus had to be traversed to retrieve the necessary information). Furthermore, the attendants mis-understood the use of color-coding to differentiate the various models and types of automobile products, and in some instances they found it difficult to understand the written explanation on the screen. Based on these findings (revealed during a

Figure 9.2 First prototype (touch screen) created by the IT department based on the mock-ups created in the design workshop. It is located next to the cash register, facing the attendant

usability test), we decided to improve the user interface by using a simpler navigation structure, more intuitive symbols and a uniform organization of information for all automobile products. The second prototype was created with the rapid application development platform ColdFusion (Mørch & Solheim, 2005).

In the next round, a third prototype was developed. The decision-makers of the company (the IT department in collaboration with the HR department) saw the potential of the previous prototypes and opted for a web portal developed on a laptop (Figure 9.3). In addition to automobile product information, hot food procedures, news and product campaigns from the central administration were incorporated. The rationale for the new information was to integrate the portal with the company's existing communication and information-sharing system. Finally, a bulletin board was added as an extra tool. The aim of the bulletin board was to support communication among employees at the three pilot stations with the option that the other stations would be able to use this feature at a later date. However, there was no mandated use of the system. After another usability test, the system was improved and its database increased by adding more information, eventually making it a pilot web portal, supporting realistic usage. The latest version (completed one year after the project ended) has been installed at 230 petrol stations, and outside Norway as well. It continues to exist after the project ended as of 2009.

Research questions and data collection

Before the portal was introduced nationwide, the employees at the petrol stations used non-computerized methods to support information-seeking. The research question we set out to address was: (1) how does the portal integrate with existing ways of seeking information, and (2) how can we conceptualize learning at work in terms of primary work?

Data was collected by observation, survey (online questionnaire) and interviews (Table 9.1 shows evaluation techniques for the various prototypes). The questionnaire was sent to 25 retail stations, representing the 230 stations. Interviews

Figure 9.3 The third prototype installed in a petrol station. The IT department developed it as a response to an evaluation of the second prototype

Table 9.1 The series of prototypes and corresponding evaluation techniques (HQ = headquarters)

Version	Installation	User interface	Data collection
Simulation	January 2003 (scenario at HQ)	Mock-up	Design workshop
Prototype 1	June 2003 (HQ pilot station)	Touch screen	Observation, walk-through
Prototype 2	July 2003 (HQ demonstration)	PC/horizontal prototype	Demonstration and feedback
Prototype 3	August 2003 (three pilot stations)	Laptop	Usability evaluation
Pilot web portal	November 2003 (25 retail stations)	Laptop (enhanced functionality)	Observation, interviews
Integrated web portal	January 2005 (230 stations)	Integrated in cash register	Questionnaire and interviews

were used to cross check (triangularize) the data. The majority of the respondents were attendants in the age group 20–29. (Three station managers and a regional manager were older.) The average number of years working for the company was three. The items in the questionnaire concerned information-seeking approaches employed during daily work as this was judged to be an important method for learning at work. Thirty-four respondents completed the survey. On average, one or two persons from each of the 25 retail stations filled out the form. This is about half of the total population. We did not notice any bias according to educational background or work responsibility among the respondents, but the age difference made an impact on the data.

Conceptual framework for analysis

We propose two basic concepts for learning at work, *primary work* and *secondary work* and we understand the integration of primary work and secondary work as a "gap-closing" activity in line with findings reported in other chapters in this book (e.g. Engeström & Toiviainen, this volume; Eklund, Mäkitalo & Säljö, this volume). We do not employ an activity-theoretical discussion; we focus instead on identifying the mechanisms at work and illustrate how they interact at a relatively detailed (meso) level. Primary work refers to the main tasks to be accomplished during a workday and these tasks are often written in a work description. Secondary work supports and augments primary work and comes to the foreground when complex work is analyzed in detail or is otherwise disrupted and becomes an object of reflection.

We draw on some early computer-supported work to identify concepts for analysis that relate to primary and secondary work. Gasser was the first to study computerized work as secondary work and defined it (without using the term) as composed of articulation work and adaptation work. *Articulation work*, first proposed by Strauss (e.g. Strauss, Fagerhaugh, Suczek, & Weiner, 1985), is the work involved in coordinating interactions between "social worlds" of people, technology and organizations, and, at a more detailed level, to "smooth out inconsistencies" in primary work tasks (Gasser, 1986). It applies to a wide range of application domains, ranging from interactive customer service (Hampson & Junor, 2005) to air traffic control (Suchman, 1996). Suchman describes the articulation work of air traffic controllers in their effort to coordinate the arrival and departure of planes at an airport. She found that many of the details of air traffic controllers' work were glossed over in job descriptions (Suchman, 1996).

Gasser identified three types of *adaptation work*: fitting, augmentation, and working around. *Fitting* is the strategy of modifying a computer system or changing the structure of work to accommodate a mismatch between worker and technology. In the context of modifying computer systems, this is referred to as end-user tailoring (Mackay, 1990; Mørch, 1996). *Augmentation* refers to undertaking additional work to make up for an inconsistency in primary work (Gasser, 1986). As such, it can be seen as an extension to primary work. *Working around* refers to using a computer system in ways it was not intended, or avoiding its use and relying instead on alternative, suboptimal means. One example is *backup systems* (Gasser, 1986). They are older technologies one relies on when the main work support fails or becomes temporarily unavailable. They can be manual or computerized and may even be redundant in functionality and duplicate data across systems. An example is the use of Post-it notes around a computer display in order to remember difficult operating system commands.

In addition to analyzing a special kind of secondary work (information-seeking), we discuss some issues related to the integration of primary work and secondary work in the case we report below.

Findings from early adoption and use of the portal

The portal adoption process lasted for about 14 months, and the data collected represents a three-month period during which the portal had been installed at 25 stations, three to six months after the first installation. The use of the system was not mandated, but the station managers encouraged the attendants to use it and the attendants were informed about its introduction well in advance. To support local use the portal had local champions (super users) (Åsand & Mørch, 2006) at selected stations, a training session for all station attendants, and several early adopters (Mørch & Solheim, 2005).

Primary work in petrol stations involves serving customers by using the cash register and periodically ordering out-of-stock items (automobile parts, food items, etc.). Secondary work is work that supports primary work, such as making sure that serving customers and ordering out-of-stock items can be carried out without major disruptions in workflow. Information-seeking was identified to be the main secondary work method. It was used to find required information to carry out primary work tasks. Secondary work is also in-depth learning about specific products and services periodically introduced by the Service Company. The HR division organized these initiatives.

Before the introduction of the portal, the attendants made use of a range of non-computerized (manual) methods for accessing information to support primary work. Figure 9.4 gives an overview of these methods, ranked according to frequency of use. In the questionnaire data we report below, the number of respondents is 34.

Results from the survey show that 81 per cent of the respondents reported that asking a colleague was the most useful approach to seeking information. This method would be used when an attendant received a difficult request from a customer. In addition, 38 per cent of the respondents said they would call a colleague at home if he or she encountered problems that no one present could answer. The station manager and the assistant manager were the two people most likely to be contacted in this way. They could be accessed by mobile phone any time of the day.

The other frequently used methods for information-seeking were paper

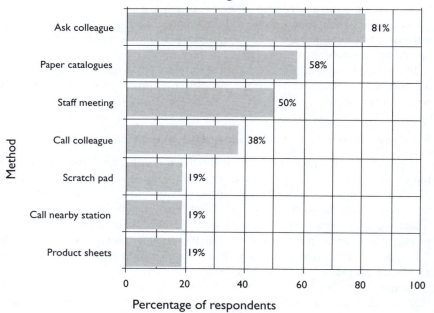

Figure 9.4 Information-seeking methods before the Portal (N = 34)

documentation (58 per cent) and staff meetings (50 per cent). Paper documentation refers to vendor-specific product catalogues containing automobile parts information. The catalogues were consulted when an attendant needed specific information about a product. The staff meeting was a weekly forum for information exchange where questions could be asked. When new products were introduced, the attendants would be informed about them at a staff meeting.

The HR division of the company periodically sent out product sheets that provided information concerning new products or service in the regular (snail) mail to the station attendants. In total, 19 per cent of the respondents said this information was useful. Finally, 19 per cent of the respondents relied on a scratch pad (Post-it notes) to jot down important reminders for interacting with customers and operating the cash register. These notes were placed on the side of the computer screen.

After the portal was introduced, 46 per cent of the respondents said they stopped using one or more of the older methods. We have no data that indicate which specific method(s) was replaced by the portal, but we have anecdotal evidence the "Post-it" notes and "calling colleagues" were seen to be redundant and no longer needed.

Regarding use of the portal, one of the respondents said: "It simplifies work to get rid of all the papers scattered around the cash register and to get all this information in one place" (respondent #23). Paper-based methods that are costly to produce (e.g. product sheets and automobile parts catalogues) or those that tend to mess up shared workplaces, like Post-it notes, may eventually disappear when web-based methods take on a more dominant position. New innovations tend to make older technologies obsolete (for example, the mobile phone has made coin-operated public phones obsolete in many parts of the world, and online yellow pages have replaced paper-based yellow pages, etc.).

The remaining 54 per cent said they continued to use the older methods despite the availability of the portal. In fact, several employees preferred to use the paper-based catalogues instead of the computerized information display in order to find product information. As one employee said in an interview: "I am not very good with computers. Most of the time it is much faster to use the paper catalogues."

The senior attendants and older employees were among those who preferred the older methods. They had less exposure to use of computers from other spheres of life (at home, previous jobs). Even though some of the employees were not skilled computer users, they were familiar with using paper-based catalogues to find information. We analyzed these findings in terms of the socio-technical conceptual framework we have outlined above (Suchman, 1994; 1996; Lave & Wenger, 1991; Fischer & Ostwald, 2001; Gasser 1986; Strauss *et al.*, 1985), which provides a theoretical account of two under-theorized areas of technology-enhanced learning, namely, blended learning and discretionary use of a learning technology.

Analysis of findings

Learning at work is a form of secondary work, which, as in the case we have presented here, means making sure customers are promptly serves and all other required activities are carried out without disruptions in workflow. Secondary work includes all the types and strategies that were identified by Gasser (1986): articulation (Strauss *et al.*, 1985) and adaptation (fitting, augmenting, working around). In this section, we discuss three implications of this: (1) Combining old and new methods for information-seeking, (2) integrating primary and secondary work, and (3) the distance principle for primary and secondary work support.

Combining old and new methods for information-seeking

The following dilemma was observed. On one hand, the management of the Service Company would like to make the work as efficient as possible. They plan to terminate the production of some of the older methods, which are costly (e.g. paper-based manuals). On the other hand, many employees at the petrol stations believe it is important to have alternative means for accomplishing work, even if some of the alternatives are sub-optimal.

Therefore, removing the sometimes sub-optimal alternatives may complicate recovery from a difficult situation and prevent work completion altogether. It seems that older methods have a well-defined role as back-up systems (Gasser, 1986) in the Service Company. There were plenty of back-up systems at the petrol stations and they provided recovery when the recommended method failed. Furthermore, the duplication of data across information systems did not cause any difficulties for the employees (as it did for management). Indeed, it may have helped them in certain situations.

We suggest a term introduced by Suchman to describe the situation as seen by the employees. She used the term "artful integration" to define a hybrid of technology and work practices where technology is comprized of multiple layers of heterogeneous devices, each associated with a specific generation of work support (Suchman, 1994). In our case, this would mean the coexistence of multiple technologies and practices associated with helping employees find information to help with the work at the petrol stations: cooperative problem-solving with customers, contacting colleagues, staff meetings, Post-it notes attached to computer, paper-based catalogues, and computerized information displays (web portal).

Integrating primary and secondary work

We do not have complete records in our data set to map out the tangled web of extraneous secondary work that was necessary to resolve problematic situations in primary work. Secondary work at the petrol stations include a combination of adaptation, articulation and information-seeking. For example, attendants used to adapt to customer-interaction situations and they worked around many problems by choosing back-up systems to gain access to required information (Gasser, 1986). The back-up system could be a non-computerized method, such as browsing a parts catalogue, contacting a colleague, using a map book (for finding travel routes), or jotting down a reminder on a Post-it note. The attendants would frequently find a way out of a difficult situation. Some of the alternatives would slow down work; others would require on-the-spot problem-solving.

We see a continual shift between primary work and secondary work. Seen from the perspective of the Service Company, primary work is periodically updated to reflect the demands of society in terms of increasing customer service and to provide a certain image to the outside world about its priorities. Secondary work is often the source for updates to primary work because it is more responsive to new innovations from the outside and less rigid than explicit work descriptions. Furthermore, access to information to answer everyday challenges has increased a result of the Service Company's continual effort to expand into other market segments. To stay abreast, employees must continually adopt the new methods and practices, mainly because they are more efficient, but also in case the older ones become unavailable for further use.

This can be seen as gap-closing activity, which for the employees means to gradually extend the scope of their repertoire of working methods while simultaneously evaluating the relevance of the existing methods. This was accomplished when reflecting on what methods to choose. Some of the employees were more skilled in this than others, mainly the younger attendants and the new employees. Learning in this context is seen as a form of work, which is associated with secondary work (adaptation, articulation, information-seeking). The relationship between primary work and secondary work is complex and characterized by tensions and contradictions. Further work ought to study this dynamic relationship in more detail.

Distance design principle for primary and secondary work support

As mentioned earlier, the portal had been through a series of iterations before it was integrated with the cash register. The version immediately preceding it was a laptop with a similar user interface, but placed at the end of the cash register counter. Based on an evaluation of this configuration, it was concluded that its adoption as combined work and learning support was unsuccessful (Mørch & Solheim, 2005). The portal was barely used and one reason for this was that it was located too far away from where the "action" (primary work) took place.

The developers of the latest (current) version of the portal learned from this and brought the portal closer to the cash register (see Figure 9.3). This resolved the problem, but with the unanticipated consequence of bringing the portal "too near" to where the action is. Based on observation and interviews, it became clear that some of the attendants avoided the portal because it could interfere with the operation of the cash register. They were concerned that the cash register would stop working if they crashed the portal. The two systems were running on the same computer (with separate screens and keyboards). This was an unacceptable solution for some of the attendants, since primary work is more important to accomplish, even though avoiding the portal could lead to sub-optimal customer experiences.

When secondary work interferes with primary work, the employees often switch to another secondary work strategy and resort to (sometimes sub-optimal) alternatives. All of the existing information-seeking seemed to follow the same pattern: "nearby without interfering." This is what we mean by the *distance principle* between primary and secondary work support. It is featured as a technology design principle for technology-enhanced workplace learning in its capacity to provide a heuristic for determining the relative positioning of two types of technological tools (for work and learning; primary and secondary work). The heuristic suggests they should be near enough to each other to allow for easy access from one to the other, but not too close in order not to infer with each other's internal workings.

Summary and conclusions

Over a three-year period, we have participated in the introduction of a web-based learning portal in a Norwegian service company, a petrol station division of an oil company, and analyzed the results. The overall aim has been to participate in the design process and help sustain the resulting system-building efforts beyond the project lifetime, and to conceptualize the results in terms that can improve the understanding of technology-enhanced workplace learning.

During the early phases of the project, we made extensive use of participatory design techniques to involve future users (employees) in the process of designing their future workplace. Learning scenarios were incorporated to envision the integration of primary and secondary work. It resulted in the creation, usability testing, and field deployment of a web portal.

The findings from the study are based on early use of the web portal. It focuses on situations that require learning on demand (Fischer & Ostwald, 2001), and it reports on the emergence of web-based information-seeking as a type of secondary work. Although information-seeking is already supported by existing (non-computerized) methods, the new web-based portal was preferred by half of the users we surveyed. In this regard, we provide new insight into the successful co-existence of old and new technologies and we provide an initial picture of the tangled web of multiple information-seeking strategies the employees make use of in their everyday work as they alternate between them and aim to bridge the gap between primary work and secondary work to accomplish required tasks.

This type of working shares characteristics with forms of learning associated with teaching communication (Wegerif, 2002), information-sharing (Netteland, Wasson & Mørch, 2007), and categorization (Ludvigsen & Mørch, 2005). Our tentative hypothesis is that it seems to be a convergence of working with large-scale information spaces (information-seeking) and the type of learning for the knowledge society presented by other authors in this volume and elsewhere. We plan to explore the conjecture in more detail in further work.

Acknowledgements

The authors thank the former InterMedia staff and students who participated in the LAP project and contributed to the research presented here: Camilla Brynhildsen, Bård Ketil Engen, Ida Tødenes, and Hege-René Hansen Åsand. Jiri Lallimo and Anne Moen provided constructive comments on a previous version of this chapter.

References

Åsand, H.-R. and Mørch, A. I. (2006). Super Users and Local Developers: The organization of end-user development in an accounting company. *Journal of Organizational and End User Computing*, 18, 1–21.

Bjerknes, G. and Bratteteig, T. (1995). User Participation and Democracy: A discussion of Scandinavian research on system development. *Scandinavian Journal of Information Systems*, 7, 73–98.

Bjerrum, E. and Bødker, S. (2003). Learning and Living in the "New Office." In K. Kuutti, E. H. Karsten, G. Fitzpatrick, P. Dourish and K. Schmidt (eds), *ECSCW 2003: Proceedings of the Eighth European Conference on Computer Supported Cooperative Work* (pp. 199–218). Dordrecht: Kluwer Academic.

Brandt, E. and Grunnet, C. (2000). Evoking the Future: Drama and props in user-centered design. In T. Cherkasky, J. Greenbaum, P. Mambrey, and J. K, Pors (eds), *PDC 2000: Proceedings of the Participatory Design Conference* (pp. 11–20). Palo Alto, CA: CPSR.

Dey, A. K., Abowd, G. D., and Salber, D. (2001). A Conceptual Framework and a Toolkit for Supporting the Rapid Prototyping of Context-Aware Applications. *Human-Computer Interaction*, 16, 97–166.

Ehn, P. and Kyng, M. (1991). Cardboard Computers: Mocking-it-up or hands-on the future. In J. Greenbaum and M. Kyng (eds), *Design at Work: Cooperative design of computer systems* (pp. 169–195). Hillsdale, NJ: Lawrence Erlbaum.

Fischer, G. (1994). Putting the Owners of Problems in Charge with Domain-Oriented Design Environments. In D. Gilmore, R. Winder and F. Detienne (eds), *User-Centered Requirements for Software Engineering Environments* (pp. 297–306). Heidelberg: Springer-Verlag.

Fischer, G., Nakakoji, K., Ostwald, J., Stahl, G., and Sumner, T. (1998). Embedding Critics in Design Environments. In M. T. Maybury and W. Wahlster (eds), *Readings in Intelligent User Interface* (pp. 537–561). San Francisco, CA: Morgan Kaufmann Publishers.

Fischer, G. and Ostwald, J. L. (2001). Knowledge Management: Problems, promises, realities, and challenges. *IEEE Intelligent Systems*, 16, 60–72.

Fjuk, A. and Kristiansen, T. (2001). Kombinerte Modeller for IKT-støttet Læring: Historie, praksis og utfordringer [Combined Models of Technology-enhanced Learning: History, current practice, and future challenges], Telenor FoU Repport 1/2001.

Gasser, L. (1986). The Integration of Computing and Routine Work. *ACM Transactions on Information Systems*, 4, 205–225.

Grudin, J. and Palen, L. (1995). Why Groupware Succeeds: Discretion or mandate? *ECSCW 1999: Proceedings of the European Conference on Computer Supported Cooperative Work* (pp. 263–278). Amsterdam: Kluwer Academic.

Hampson, I. and Junor, A. (2005). Invisible Work, Invisible Skills: Interactive customer service as articulation work. *New Technology, Work and Employment,* 20, 166–181.

Kramer, J. (2007). Is Abstraction the Key to Computing? *Communications of the ACM,* 50, 36–42.

Lave, J. and Wenger, E. (1991). *Situated Learning: Legitimate peripheral participation.* Cambridge: Cambridge University Press.

Ludvigsen, S. R. and Mørch, A. I. (2005). Situating Collaborative Learning: Educational technology in the wild. *Educational Technology Magazine,* 45, 39–43.

Mackay, W. E. (1990). *Users and Customizable Software: A co-adaptive phenomenon.* Unpublished doctoral dissertation, Sloan School of Management, Massachusetts Institute of Technology, Cambridge, MA.

Mørch, A. I. (1996). Adaptation Through End-user Tailoring. In M. Muhlhauser (ed.), *Special Issues in Object-Oriented Programming: Workshop reader of the 10th European Conference on Object-Oriented Programming* (pp. 43–52). Linz, Austria: Dpunkt Verlag.

Mørch, A. I. (2003). Evolutionary Growth and Control in User Tailorable Systems. In N. Patel (ed.), *Adaptive Evolutionary Information Systems* (pp. 30–58). Hershey, PA: Idea Group Publishing.

Mørch, A. I., Engen, B. K., and Åsand, H.-R. (2004). The Workplace as a Learning Laboratory: The winding road to e-learning in a Norwegian service company. In A. Clement, F. de Cindio, A.-M. Oostveen, D. Schuler, and P. van den Besselaar (eds), *PDC 2004: Proceedings of the Participatory Design Conference* (pp. 141–151). New York, NY: ACM Press.

Mørch, A. I., Jondahl, S., and Dolonen, J. (2005). Supporting Conceptual Awareness with Pedagogical Agents. *Information Systems Frontiers,* 7(1), 39–53.

Mørch, A. I. and Solheim, I. (eds). (2005). *Integrert E-Læring i Bedriften: Pedagogikk, teknologi og organisasjon.* Oslo: Unipub. (In Norwegian)

✳ Mørch, A.I., Dolonen, J., and Nævdal, J. E. (2006). An Evolutionary Approach to Prototyping Pedagogical Agents: From simulation to integrated system. *Journal of Network and Computer Applications,* 29(2–3), 177–199.

Netteland, G., Wasson, B., and Mørch, A. I. (2007). E-Learning in a Large Organization: A study of the critical role of information sharing. *Journal of Workplace Learning,* 19(6), 392–411.

Skaanes, M. A. (2005). *Innføring og Bruk av Arbeids – Og Kunnskapsstøttesystemer i Kundebetjening. Case: Statoil Detaljhandel,* master's thesis, Department of Informatics, University of Oslo, Norway. (In Norwegian)

Strauss, A., Fagerhaugh, S., Suczek, B., and Weiner, C. (1985). *Social Organization of Medical Work,* Chicago, IL: University of Chicago Press.

Suchman, L. (1994). Working Relations of Technology Production and Use. *Computer Supported Cooperative Work,* 2, 21–39.

Suchman, L. (1996). Supporting Articulation Work. In R. Kling (ed.), *Computerization and Controversy,* 2nd edition (pp. 407–423). San Diego, CA: Academic Press.

Svanæs, D. and Seland, G. (2004). Putting the Users Center Stage: Role playing and low-fi prototyping enable end users to design mobile systems. In E. Dykstra-Erickson and M. Tscheligi (eds), *CHI'2004: Proceedings of the Conference on Human Factors in Computing Systems* (pp. 479–486). New York, NY: ACM Press.

Wegerif, R. (2002). Literature Review in Thinking Skills, Technology and Learning: A report for NESTA, from Future Lab Series website: http://www.nestafuturelab.org/research/reviews/ts01.htm

Chapter 10

Versions of computer-supported collaborating in higher education

Charles Crook

When young people first started to make use of personal computers, social scientists observed their activity and issued warnings. They suggested that this was a compulsive technology and one that could cultivate a rather solitary style of engagement in the user (Turkle, 1984; Wiezenbaum, 1976). Accordingly, as computers began to migrate into classrooms, there was an inevitable fear that the experience of teaching and learning would change in ways that echoed this (Bliss, Chandra & Cox, 1986; Lichtman, 1979). Perhaps pupil–machine interactions would replace the congenial bustle of classroom talk and activity.

In fact, matters developed in the opposite direction. Classroom computers became the catalyst for pupils to do work together – not alone. One simple reason was that classrooms had very little of this technology, while pressure on teachers to use it was great. The natural solution was to have pupils share a single computer: in short, to work in small groups. Teachers then noticed that these groups were quite animated. Indeed, in the UK at least, this helped teachers with another professional pressure: namely, development of collaborative learning. Unsurprisingly, educational researchers began to notice what was happening in classrooms and, by the mid-1990s, the field of 'computer-supported collaborative learning' (CSCL) emerged (Crook, 1994; Koschmann, 1996; O'Malley, 1994).

Any new research field will want to build a relationship with some theoretical tradition. Then, if that field flourishes, it will – in its own way – inspire and progress the underlying theory. That has happened for CSCL and more will be said about it below. However, there is another relationship to consider. Any new educational research field will also want to influence mainstream *practice*: to influence events beyond the laboratory. Again, there is no doubt that this has occurred.

So, in the present chapter, I wish to coordinate around these three themes. I am concerned with CSCL's evolving synergy between theory, research method, and legacies to practice. However, this practice of education is inevitably lived out in a very wide range of settings for teaching and learning. Such 'sites for learning' have their own distinctive ecologies and it is important to reveal and understand them. Because, for innovators, learning sites may differ in ways that present a challenge to the design process. It follows that some settings may be more receptive than others to those interventions that are derived from new research and theory – such as CSCL. In particular, some settings may be more resilient than others. They may be more cautious in responding to any such implications for change.

Here I shall consider these matters as they relate to CSCL in typical higher education: that is, full-time, post-secondary students living in or around a campus. I shall argue that innovations associated with the emergence of CSCL have proved particularly challenging to implement in higher education. Yet more recent lines of thinking about the management of collaboration may now offer greater promise. I illustrate this promise with two modest interventions of my own: examples that suggest at least the *spirit* of what might be possible in supporting collaboration.

The chapter is organised as follows. The first section sketches theoretical influences that have consistently framed CSCL. This reminds us of the ambitions for successful CSCL-led innovation in universities. I then turn from theory to practice. The three following sections address contrasting designs for implementing computer-supported collaboration, considering the status and fate of each in higher education. I argue that the third of these designs represents the most useful way forward. However, promoting it needs to be properly theorised and this requires a final section of the chapter. This will consider more deeply the very nature of collaboration as an experience of learning. So, in effect, this fifth section comes full circle to revisit theory, considering again the psychological basis of collaborative configurations for learning.

Theoretical influences of and on CSCL research

Much research in CSCL continues to pitch its analyses at the level of individual learners: characterising their agency and outcomes, somewhat decoupled from broader social and institutional contexts. Yet a significant core of CSCL research has tracked a shifting conceptual climate in cognitive and developmental psychology that contrasts with this individuated approach. This shift might be termed an 'enculturing' of cognition (Cole, 1996; Shore, 1996; Shweder, 1991; Lave & Wenger, 1991; Wertsch, 1991). Partly, this requires seeing cognition as inherently shaped by the particular 'designs for living' – the culture – in which each individual finds themselves. More especially, it requires theorising cognition as 'distributed' across the material, symbolic, and social resources available in that specific cultural niche (Donald, 1993; Hutchins, 1991). Mind, being constituted through its relations with such resources, is no longer best studied by considering the individual actor in isolation. Cognition is not to be theorised as some processes circumscribed by the skull.

This implicit prescription about how we best *study* cognition is the important one for an enculturing perspective. By insisting that cognition is actually *constituted* within culture, this theoretical tradition requires that any occasion of thinking or learning is studied only and always with careful attention to its context. Problem-solving is studied as something realised through engagements with *particular* worlds at *particular* moments.

The practice of CSCL squares up nicely with a cultural theory of cognition.

This is because its practical focus always entails a human agent acting with another cultural member (a collaborator) and a cultural artifact (computer) in the (cognitive) interests of learning. As a research agenda, this is an almost canonical case for inviting the integration of culture with cognition.

As well as tracking evolving cognitive theory within psychology, CSCL has also emerged alongside shifts in our *everyday* conceptions of thinking and problem-solving. There is now a popular belief that the modern workplace demands from individuals a willingness and ability to coordinate mental effort with others (Schrage, 1990). In particular, working in the new digital economy requires a style of thinking that is comfortable with the social structures of networking and teamworking (Brown & Duguid, 2000). Faced with this changing societal and political context, educators have welcomed CSCL as a force for shaping classroom learning in work-relevant ways.

This resonance of CSCL with both cultural theories of cognition and with societal trends is captured within two quotations taken from seminal contributions to a recent handbook of learning science (Sawyer, 2006). The first reinforces the previous point about the corporate demands of thinking in workplace settings. It notes how a more cultural ('situative') approach to cognition is better adjusted to this reality than traditional theories: 'A situative approach, in contrast, begins by noting that problem-solving often occurs in group settings' (Greeno, 2006, p. 85). The second quote borrows this 'situative' term, builds upon Greeno's observation of the natural or everyday conditions for problem-solving, and thereby aligns CSCL with a *radical* tradition of theorists who

> aspired to construct a new view of learning and knowing, one that properly located it in the world of everyday affairs. CSCL embraces this more situated view of learning, thereby rejecting the foundations of conventional educational research. CSCL locates learning in meaning negotiation carried out in the social world rather than in individuals' heads.
>
> (Stahl, Koshmann & Suthers, 2006, p. 416)

This allusion to 'the world of everyday affairs' offers a useful reference point for relating the methods and theorising of CSCL to designs more intended for sites of formal learning. Insofar as locating learning and knowing in everyday affairs entails talking and tool use, then CSCL certainly offers a credible scenario. It positions learners to *negotiate* meaning while acing in a richly *mediated* environment. Yet there remains something to be scrutinised in the CSCL position articulated above: namely an insistence in this community that meaning-making is *inevitably* a (social) 'negotiation' and, thereby, a resistance to recognising any private forms of such achievement. This point will be returned to later.

From the outset, the almost exclusive empirical formula for CSCL researchers to pursue their concerns was through short episodes of pupil interaction around some computer-based problem. Such scenarios can be studied either through the lens of learning-as-acquisition or through the lens of learning-as-participation

(Sfard, 1998). An acquisition view might encourage framing these collaborating episodes with pre-testing and post-testing of learners' domain knowledge. In which case, the CSCL scenario becomes a kind of educational method or learning procedure through which individuals might be shown to *acquire* new knowledge. Alternatively, a more participative view on learning might invite analysis of the the discourse of collaboration itself. In which case, analysis of these episodes could reveal how far the interpersonal process of collaboration created a sense of learners *participating* in the construction of new knowledge.

So far, the following claims have been made. First, in terms of theory, CSCL prescribes learning to be strongly interpersonal, mediated, and active. Second, in terms of research method, an early strategy has been to analyse pairs or trios of pupils solving some problem around a computer. Finally, in terms of educational practice, CSCL has resonated with teachers' interest in using computers to facilitate small group work. This kind of group work is sometimes termed 'synchronous' collaboration. The collaborators are convened at a common time and place – within which their joint activity proceeds to completion. However, it was noted earlier that research-led designs for educational practice – such as synchronous collaborating – do not always fit neatly into the ecologies of particular educational settings. That tension will be explored next in two sections that evaluate CSCL designs within higher education. Two further sections then attempt to resolve the tension. In them we explore neglected aspects of CSCL in relation to first, practice and, second, theory.

Higher education and synchronous collaborating

Universities place learners in rather different settings to the school environments in which much CSCL research has been carried out. We may derive some sense of this from natural history research on how undergraduates actually spend their time as learners. Figure 10.1 provides data from one such study (Crook, 2002a) in which 45 students stratified across teaching faculties kept detailed activity diaries for a week. Across the day, they recorded engagement in a variety of study (and leisure) activities down to a resolution of 15-minute blocks.

The rather low probability of social study in the evenings (when no classes are timetabled) reminds us that collaborative study is not a very favoured way for students to organise their independent learning (cf. self-report data from undergraduates documented by Crook [2000, 2002b]). Sociometric data from one representative class suggests that *recreational* connections between peers were very well developed, yet convening outside of class for the sole purpose of *study* was rare (Crook, 2002c). This is the situation even though all these students were resident and studying on a large, geographically continuous university campus (with very high standing in teaching audits).

This pattern, characteristic of *self*-governed study, is reproduced for study governed by *classes*. Figure 10.1 shows that classroom time was infrequently experienced as a collaborative occasion of peer interaction. And when it was, it tended to be

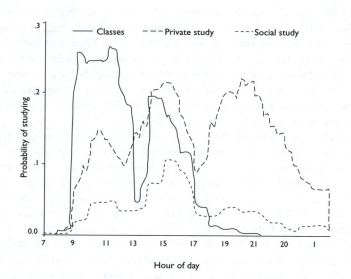

Figure 10.1 Average probability that an undergraduate will be engaged in various types of study as a function of time of day. Data from 45 students keeping diaries over one week

as rather tightly orchestrated (afternoon) lab work. Other data from this project revealed that computers were heavily used by these students, yet it seems that computer-supported collaboration was not a significant part of their learning – at least in the traditional format of CSCL research. For these students, co-present social studying remains an irregular experience (with our without computers).

It is necessary to reconcile the observation that 'problem solving often occurs in group settings' (Greeno, 2006, p. 85) with the observation that the problem-solving of undergraduate learning is most likely to be rather solitary. This in turn invites careful specification of what follows from the claim that 'CSCL locates learning in meaning negotiation carried out in the social world rather than in individuals' heads' (Stahl *et al.*, 2006, p. 416). Such claims can usefully stand, as long as we recognise that 'social' is not to be innocently equated with its everyday connotation of 'conversational'. A lecture (or even the reading of text) could be termed a 'group setting'. But this can be done only if we allow that there is an implicit dialogue between the learner and the lecturer/author. A lecture thereby becomes 'social' by virtue of the encultured modes of (private) conversation that are evoked by the (engaging) lecturer.

By the same token, commitment to social theories of learning should not suggest that there is simply no such useful thing as a process of solitary reasoning. Such processes take place – even outside the dialogues of reading, listening, or talking: going on, if you will, in 'individuals' heads'. The problem is not that this restriction of view about learning is what is actually being promoted in, for instance, the quotations discussed above. The problem is that the CSCL project in general may too easily get interpreted this way. What may then follow is an insistence that learning must, wherever possible, be optimised into a form of synchronous conversation, a kind of vigorously resourced group work. Such a view tends to be forever chasing the collaborative episode as the preferred scenario of learning: that is, a circumscribed problem-solving occasion, which is governed by live conversation.

The fieldwork observation above – that collaborative study of that sort is rather rare among undergraduates – does not, of course, imply that this is how things inevitably must be. Perhaps one message of the CSCL experience is that we should intervene to make collaborative study episodes simply more commonplace. Yet what has actually taken place in the CSCL research community is a different strategy. It involves a broadening in the understanding of 'collaboration' to allow that circumstances of joint activity need not be synchronous at all. This has not simply been a response to inertia in the rather solitary study practice among undergraduates. It has been a response to the emergence of a very different mode of configuring higher education: namely distance learning. It has stimulated visions of a more 'virtual' kind of university.

Higher education and asynchronous collaboration

Societies dependent on an information and communication technology (ICT) that evolves so rapidly need a workforce that adapts to these changes. In short, a workforce receptive to lifelong learning and the 'learning society' (Blair, 1999). In such a situation, access to university learning through the traditional age-governed route may not seem sufficiently flexible. Lifelong learners need to pace their studying according to individual needs and opportunities. What is certainly clear is that they may not appreciate being disciplined into periods of study that must occur at defined times and in set places. Yet if such 'personalising' entails not having to congregate in this manner, then learning through collaboration looks rather difficult to provide. At least it does if we persist with a sense of 'collaborating' that requires convening students into synchronous conversations.

The architects of virtualised distance teaching are sensitive to educational theorising that stresses social interaction for learning. Certainly, those designers have embraced the collaborative ideal. Indeed if ICT has proved a gift to lifelong and distance learning, it is not simply because ICT provides an effective delivery vehicle for course content – which it certainly does. It is also because networked computers provide a vehicle for distance learners to exercise a form of *conversation* and, hence, participate in a form of collaboration.

For the most part, such discussion will be text-based. Although, being geographically distributed does not mean that it cannot, therefore, sometimes be synchronous. 'Chat' systems can furnish that synchrony. However, for the formal designs of most distance learning, asynchronous communication is a better understood and more widely used medium. Such communication will, again, be largely text-based. Clearly, collaborating through an asynchronous text-based discussion is not going to feel the same as collaborating through synchronous verbal conversation. Achievements that arise from the fast pace and rhythm of talk will be lost. Achievements that depend upon visual contact with the paralinguistic correlates of talk will also be lost. On the other hand, new opportunities will arise from being able to measure and plan one's individual contributions more carefully. Or from being able to revisit and reflect on the (written) turns in an unfolding exchange. All of which variety reminds us that collaborating – as a format for learning – can never be mediated through any singular technical design. The manner in which contributions are given and received within joint activity can be made to vary considerably, depending on the tools that support such exchange.

The growth of e-learning inevitably stimulated CSCL researchers to shift their interests towards these new contexts for computer-supported collaboration. However, the concern for collaborative learning in this chapter is less with distance learners and more with traditional, campus-oriented university populations. In that context, there is little evidence that computer-based asynchronous designs are being widely adopted. The fact that these populations often furnish the participants for small-scale research on such communication does not mean that the practice is commonplace within their own experience as learners.

Again, the campus furnishing the data in Figure 10.1 provides a compelling example. Here, a locally designed virtual-learning environment (VLE) has been in operation for ten years (at the time of writing). It comprises a web-readable filespace that offers a hypermedia arena for every module taught. Moreover, the frame in which staff may store their course-related materials includes a prominent link to a user-friendly, threaded, text-based discussion forum for each module. This is visible to any student taking that module and any student may make entries from any internet-enabled computer. The maturity of this VLE means that it is extensively populated by staff (posting their course materials) and widely accessed by students. However, studying the use of the discussion boards on this system, reveals that, at the end of the year, less than half of the module boards have any postings on them at all. Moreover, the median number of postings on those that do is less than 10. These are short, frequently playful and, very often, they merely seek clarification on routine matters to do with coursework or examinations. Only very occasionally did one find an exchange that seemed to illustrate a real effort at collaborative meaning-making.

It is interesting that students do not find this mode of communication a very convivial prop for informal collaborative learning. Enthusiasts for asynchronous text collaboration will argue that its success on campus will depend on a more orchestrated effort of interaction *management*. In particular, that staff will probably need to actively prompt such an exchange – and actively to coordinate it. Again, it is interesting that this did not seem to be happening in this particular environment. It reminds us of other obstacles to be tackled. These will, for instance, concern the time and effort that such coordination demands of staff. Moreover, documented experience of doing such communication-management suggests there is as uncertainty which students still bring to the initiative (Tolmie & Boyle, 2000).

Of course networked computers can support collaboration that is not structured by the designed spaces of VLEs and which is not initiated by the encouragement of tutors. But again, in this representative campus we found that use of the medium in this spirit was scarce. For instance, when email content was tracked across a single week (by students' self-coding), it was found to include very little content that would pass for collaborative study-related discussion (Crook, 2002b). If computer-mediated collaborative exchange was going to occur among these students at all, it was rather more likely to do so in desktop chat systems than in the formalised (and more public) structures of the local VLE.

Once again, invoking fieldwork observations from higher education has been rather dispiriting to the promise of CSCL in this sector. Despite a rich infra-structure of personal and institutional computing, there is little evidence that the technology is routinely supporting learning that is collaborative. This judgement arises from reflection on the two major realisations of CSCL discussed above: first, organised occasions of synchronous interaction *at* computers and, second, more extended threads of asynchronous interaction *through* computers. Yet there is a third approach to design that is more far-reaching and, consequently, less well tested. I turn to this next in order to explore its potential.

Higher education and blended, progressive collaboration

Earlier, reference was made to Sfard's (1998) distinction between learning based upon the metaphor of acquisition versus the metaphor of participation. However, there is now encouragement to go beyond the acquisitive and the participative learner to consider the 'creative' learner. This proposal is based on the idea that human learning should have at its core the building of 'knowledge objects' (Bereiter, 2002). Such a proposal usefully foregrounds the material and conceptual 'objects' that – it is argued – should arise within any environment where learning is being stimulated. The proposal then supposes that the learner work of creating such objects is typically infused with collaboration. These objects exist within communities and learners must encounter them within community experience. This may seem merely to evoke again the 'participative' learner. Yet it is different. The 'participation' within this learner knowledge-building requires of us an environment for interaction that is carefully designed. In particular, the design must be one that reproduces some of the material resources and communicative structures that characterise knowledge-building in more authentic but non-educational contexts (studios, laboratories, workshops, marketplaces, and other sites of creative labour).

This formulation of collaborative learning is appealing for a number of reasons. First it involves theorising learning in terms of a broader culture of (collaborating) practice and less in terms of managing circumscribed episodes (or threads) of social interaction. A CSCL inquiry is thereby less about the construction of 'a' collaboration and more about the design of contexts in which knowledge-building interactions can flourish and evolve. If you will, it is more about cultures and less about episodes. As Lipponen, Hakkarainen and Paavola have commented in advocating this approach: 'Creative collaboration is . . . distributed across time and requires a relatively long timescale' (2004: p. 41).

Second, and related to this, the 'knowledge-building' perspective defines collaboration as unfolding. It involves an experience of progression: a trajectory of intellectual growth, upon which learners are moving forward. This suggests approaching collaboration as something that is 'progressive' in the temporal sense.

Third, although within these proposed systems of learning the collaborating is pervasive, it is not always rigidly managed and not strongly episodic, nor is it the only mode for learner activity. We might therefore say that the social engagement of knowledge building becomes 'blended'. The social experience of collaborating is integrated with strategies of *private* investigation – perhaps in a rhythm, pace, or pattern that suits the context, history, and needs of the individual learner. This suggests approaching collaboration as something that is 'blended' in the structural sense.

The viability of this context for learning and the central place of technology within it have been documented through secondary school interventions (Bereiter, 2002). One challenge is to consider how it might be imported into a higher-education context – through recruiting technology to the progressive and blended spirit of corporate knowledge-building. The attraction of the university context is that it already has in place much of the necessary networked computer infrastructure. But in what particular ways might this be made to happen?

The strategy may be to innovate first on a modest scale. That is, pursue interventions that could recruit existing technologies to re-mediate existing arenas of student learning. The outcome should *feel* like doing something that is familiar but doing it a little differently. Rather than doing something new. Moreover, the ideal intervention should be achieved at low financial cost and at low cost to staff time. If something useful was observed to arise from this, then the intervention might be scaled up. However, to earn a sympathetic response, this should probably happen without disturbing the existing curriculum or its regimes of assessment – only re-mediating the experience of learning within them. So, what are the existing 'arenas' of student learning that might be approached in this slightly subversive way? The ones that I have addressed are central to undergraduate experience. They are the practical class, the lecture, and the small group discussion. The two intervention examples sketched below refer, first, to the practical and, second, to the lecture-tutorial configuration. The academic context is a psychology degree programme.

The practical class is the easier challenge. The CSCL goal was to design conditions where students might derive a sense of creative knowledge-building through the class-wide coordination of investigative studies – although these may themselves be conducted in groups or alone. First, the practical activity was released from the traditional three-hour classroom session. Students took responsibility for pursuing the fieldwork in their own time. For example, one topic concerned cognitive interpretations of how children's drawing develops. A class of 100 students can encounter collaborative knowledge-building if they are each charged with recruiting a child participant, collecting materials, and composing field notes from their experience. These are emailed to a class assistant who organises and displays it in web-readable formats. Small student groups are then convened to build interpretations of this material from differing perspectives (see www.deveurope. com/research/drawing/).

The experience proves engaging and productive. It is collaborative but not in the strong sense of orchestrated episodes of group work. It requires a degree of coordination and collation that leaves the student alert to the knowledge-building opportunities and sensing participation in a community of shared research practice. In this way, the standard arena of practical work is re-mediated to be experienced in collaborative terms. As an isolated case, such a modest intervention must be limited in its impact. If there is promise here, it can only be properly be realised if such activity is scaled up to be more typical of *all* practical exercises associated with the study programme.

My second example develops the same technology (networked email and web servers) to achieve a similar sense of community knowledge-building but around the lecture and the tutorial. Traditionally, the university tutorial is an infrequent adjunct to the core (and probably weekly) experience of the lecture. However, in the present intervention, these occasions were to be integrated more closely. Students would take from this coordination a sense of both progression and construction. First, tutorials should occur weekly in order to complement the lectures. However, if this was to involve the same number of staff continuing to work one tutorial hour per week, then such expansion could only be achieved if the individual tutorials themselves were very short. Twenty-minute sessions would permit four staff to service three groups an hour, while keeping the groups intimately small.

Such 'speed tutoring' seemed only likely to work if two things could be achieved. First, students arrived on time and in the right place. Second, they arrived primed to have an intense and goal-oriented discussion. Technology looked after both needs. The mapping of groups onto times and tutors was constructed at the start of the semester as an Excel database. This tool generated personal emails that automatically constructed a reminder of time, place, and purpose. 'Purpose' was managed by having the email include a weblink to material that required students to do interpretative work – exercising the language of the discipline they were studying. As this happened to be child development, the material might include photographs of everyday interactions, diagrams of research findings, or other artifacts that demanded some analysis for closure. Individual interpretations were then aired in the tutorial discussion, which was required to converge on a set of psychological questions the students would like answered. Finally, the reminding emails would have nominated a scribe for each group. This student took notes of what was said and the questions derived. These notes they uploaded to a webpage for viewing by the class.

The discussion images were chosen to relate to the next topic in the course syllabus. This meant that the lecture following each tutorial could be grounded in the questions that came out of the tutorial discussion. In short, that lecture was built around the central task of answering those emerging questions and elaborating their concerns. In this way the participating students experienced the lecture series as meaningfully related to the evolving character of their own understanding – in part, collaboratively negotiated in tutorials. Moreover, such coordination seemed to cultivate a stronger sense of corporate involvement.

These two examples (and certain others like them, for example Arnseth & Ludvigson, 2006; Ivarsson, 2004) capture a looser sense of 'collaborative learning' than would normally be embraced by CSCL research. Yet they worked well and they do seem to illustrate the way in which the ecology of university teaching and learning can creatively adapt to the prescriptions of a more collaborative climate of study. As to *why* one should aspire to do these things: two general reasons need considering. First, arguments already rehearsed here suggest that confidence in practising collaborative knowledge-building will serve learners well in the wider world. The demands of intellectual work outside of school will require such coordination with others. Second, we should entertain the idea that the experience of collaborative learning is – at least at its most effective – a strongly *motivating* force within learning. This claim is more controversial. Yet it deserves reflection and I do so in the next section.

Theorising the collaborator: the cognition and affect of intersubjectivity

Typically, the case for cultivating CSCL will be argued from theoretical claims about the nature of learning and cognition – such as those sketched earlier. These claims certainly include a conception of learning as *social*. But I am arguing here that designing this social experience as *collaborating* is not straightforward. Moreover, neither is it a universal imperative. So, to justify this position, in the present section I return to theory and suggest considering collaboration in more motivational terms. Designing better interventions may depend on a firmer grip on two possibilities. First and put quite simply, collaborating can be difficult and unwelcome. Decisions about entering such arrangements need to be strategically made. So, learners may be best served by designs and ecologies that integrate social interaction with solitary reflection. Second, collaborating has an *affective* dimension and it not a purely cognitive matter. So we need to understand how the attractions of collaboration we *want* to take part in arise from the emotional quality of the experience.

All of these concerns can be anchored down to the consideration of a single observation: collaborative learning does not always 'work'. In promoting this way of supporting learning, some CSCL advocates will stress pre-test/post-test gains, showing that collaborating tends to benefit individual collaborators – compared with learning alone. However, fine-grained studies of interaction within such joint activity reveals great variation in how things are said and done. This can be so even when individuals convened into problem-solving groups are well matched in terms of domain knowledge (Barron, 2003).

Put simply: orchestrating a joint activity is not the same as orchestrating a collaboration. Variation in what happens – including disappointing products or outcomes – requires us to scrutinise and theorise the dynamics of the social interactions that take place. Edwards and MacKenzie (2005) develop similar ideas in theorising the 'relational agency' that defines an individual's 'learning trajectory'.

If we ask what interpersonal process directs the effort of constructing shared knowledge (that is, the effort of *collaboration*), the answer must be that peculiarly human striving for intersubjectivity (Rommetveit, 1979; Trevarthan, 1980). This refers to jointly acting partners exercising a capacity to read the mental states of the other (their beliefs, desires, expectations, etc.). To say knowledge becomes 'shared' is to say that you know what the other knows but, more especially, you know that they know you know this (and so on, in hall-of-mirrors fashion). Awareness of this reciprocity then offers a powerful platform on which to build yet newer understandings. It is 'powerful' not just because it resources an evolving conversation with the other (drawing on an archive of jointly established understanding) but also because of how it makes it increasingly *un*necessary to say certain things at all (drawing on a history of mutually monitoring each other).

Inevitably, psychologists have considered individual differences in how fluently this intersubjectivity is managed. So, faced with collaborative interactions that fail to deliver their promise, researchers are likely to explain such shortfalls in terms of individuals lacking intersubjective 'skills'. Such sorry collaborators may be poorly prepared to regulate the conversation within which shared understanding is constructed (e.g. Barron, 2003). This could be termed a 'cognitive' perspective on the varying fate of collaborations. However, collaborating involves emotion as well as cognition. We will all surely recognise the experience of being frustrated or irritated by the overheads of having to solve some problem as a team or in a group. Some of the earliest educational research in this area acknowledged such problems (Bos, 1937). More recently Salomon and Globerson (1989) have discussed teams that are 'not functioning as they ought to'. Finally, the possibility for a collaboration to have inhibiting effects on reasoning has long been acknowledged (and studied) in the social psychology of groups (e.g. Weldon, 2000) – a research tradition that seems rarely to intersect with CSCL.

Elsewhere, I describe collaborative exchanges among young learners that illustrate a shortfall in the intersubjective quality of the communication (Crook, 1994, ch. 7). However, there the analysis is of discourse-stressed troublesome *affect* rather than inadequate cognitive skill. In short, it highlighted a lack of participant engagement. So a collaborator might display a relative indifference to the task, effectively obstructing or distorting any effort to mobilise intersubjectivity. The character of that talk tended to imply participants had personal ambitions at odds with any useful commitment to collaborate. Perhaps they resented being put into this relationship, or they had independent motives to dominate it, or they wanted to complete it swiftly in order to move on. All such motives undermine exercising the intersubjective possibility – even though it was available to these partners as a cognitive skill.

I suggest we notice three psychological strands to the intersubjectivity that underpins collaborating. First, there is intersubjective *knowledge*: that is, a set of communication resources that individuals may call upon to manage shared problem-understanding. Second, we have what might be termed an 'intersubjective *attitude*': that is, the individual's willingness to recruit such resources and/or to direct them sympathetically towards constructing some desired product. But there is a third psychological dimension of intersubjectivity: that is, its status as an *outcome* of the collaboration – something sought and valued in its own right. If we regard collaboration as a kind of 'dance' (Argyle, 1991), then we must entertain the possibility that the achievement of such coordination is itself a satisfying endpoint (rather like fluent dancing) and may be strived for as something precious for itself.

This notion that collaborative achievements carry with them an affective quality has been neglected within CSCL (Crook, 2000). It is not that motivation and affect are missing in studies of learning more generally. These are often factored in as independent variables. However, where they are pursued, they are more likely to be treated as relatively stable trait variables rather than as more transient state variables – that are activated for and within particular occasions of joint problem-solving. The affective intensity of a given occasion of collaborative learning is not something that is typically evaluated by researchers. Yet everyday reflection must surely remind us that there is often a deep pleasure to be found in recognising the growth and achievement of jointly constructed shared knowledge (particularly, where the 'private-to-us' conditions of that construction impart to it a kind of *intimacy*).

How does this line of interpretation aid my earlier wish to justify the effort (and the outcome) of cultivating collaboratively 'progressive' knowledge-building in an undergraduate class? First, it may usefully enrich our conceptualisation of joint activity for learning – so as to accommodate my examples. This extending of the concept may, in turn, render institutions more receptive to certain forms of CSCL intervention.

Identifying motivational and affective aspects of collaborating serves to extend its psychological complexity. Previously, I have found it helpful to speak of the 'collaborative experience' of learning. To cast collaborating as a certain *experience* may be more helpful than thinking simply of 'a' collaboration – either as an episode or as a thread. It invites us to think of the activities of learning as variously infused with this collaborative *quality*. So, in my example, our university tutorial may be a collaboration not simply because it involves live (synchronous) discussion but because that discussion is fed out into the wider learning arena in which it is timetabled. The tutorial discussion is captured and made visible to the class beyond the classroom. In particular, it is used to ground and guide the content of lectures. This simple joining-up of the traditional occasions of teaching and learning is achieved by utilising technologies to make local perspectives and debates visible and shareable – and, ultimately, generative of new knowledge.

The joining-up allows students to understand learning as being about progression – a creative and corporate process of knowledge building. Moreover, my two case studies sketched in the previous section also respect the preferences that individual students may have as to how they participate in learning at particular times. Thus, the collaborative experience (as groupwork) is not strongly prescribed. Thinking alone or thinking in groups becomes a choice that students make as circumstances determine. Solitary and social periods of thinking are thereby 'blended'. The challenge is to engineer a course design that allows the products of those occasions to be integrated into an evolving process of knowledge building: something that becomes for the class a collaborative (and engaging) experience of learning.

Conclusion

I have converged on the vocabulary of collaborative experience in order to stress that solving problems with others is an arrangement that can be driven by emotion as well as cognition. So, particular occasions of joint activity may be more or less motivated and, thereby, more or less successful. But joint activity also *generates* emotion. The intersubjectivity that is characteristic of more motivated social interaction has an affective dimension. Research must confront the realities that orchestrated collaborative learning is not always adequately motivated in this sense and, moreover, its conduct may not always generate the affect that makes it attractive to learners.

It is surely important to persist in seeking opportunities for realising the learning designs so far inspired by CSCL in higher education: that is, episodes of communication *at* computers and threads of communication *through* computers. Yet if this is all we do, there is a danger that we are simply bolting on singular instances of a learning method to the bigger structure of a curriculum. That bigger structure needs itself to become more deeply collaborative. In particular, I have argued here, it needs to mobilise technology so as to coordinate for learners a stronger and pervasive sense of progressive knowledge-building. At the moment, higher education rarely does this. However, the direction of movement I have illustrated is one that admits and respects the complementary attractions of solitary thinking – while seeking ways to creatively blend such reflective occasions with group work. In short, universities need to evolve a better understanding of the collaborative *experience* of learning and thereby exploit the affect that successful social coordinations can inspire.

References

Argyle, M. (1991). *Cooperation: The basis of sociability*. London: Routledge.

Arnseth, H. C. and Ludvigsen, S. (2006). Approaching Institutional Contexts: Systemic versus dialogical research in CSCL. *International Journal of Computer-Supported Collaborative Learning*. 1 (2), 167–185.

Barron, B. (2003). When Smart Groups Fail. *The Journal of the Learning Sciences*, 12(3), 307–359.

Bereiter, C. (2002). *Education and Mind in the Knowledge Age*. Toronto: Lawrence Erlbaum Associates.

Blair, T. (1999). Oxford Romanes Lecture, Oxford University, 2 December 1999. http://www.number-10.gov.uk/output/Page1465.asp (accessed 30 August 2006).

Bliss, J., Chandra, P. and Cox, M. (1986). The Introduction of Computers into a School. *Computer Education*, 10, 49–54.

Bos, M. C. (1937). Experimental Study of Productive Collaboration. *Acta Psychologica*, 3, 315–426.

Brown, J. S. and Duguid P. (2000). *The Social Life of Information*. Boston, MA: Harvard Business School.

Cole, M. (1996). *Cultural Psychology*. Cambridge, MA: Harvard University Press.

Crook, C. K. (1994). *Computers and the Collaborative Experience of Learning*. London: Routledge.

Crook, C. K. (2000). Motivation and the Ecology of Collaborative Learning. In R. Joiner, K. Littleton, D. Faulkner, and D. Miell (eds), *Rethinking Collaborative Learning* (pp. 161–178). London: Free Association Press.

Crook, C. K. (2002a). Virtual University: The learner's perspective. In K. Robbins and F. Webster (eds). *The Virtual University?* (pp. 105–125) Oxford: Oxford University Press.

Crook, C. K. (2002b). The Campus Experience of Networked Learning. In C. Steeples, and C. Jones (eds), *Networked Learning: Perspectives and Issues* (pp. 293–308). Berlin: Springer-Verlag.

Crook, C. K. (2002c). Deferring to Resources: Student collaborative talk mediated by computer-based versus traditional notes. *Journal of Computer-Assisted Learning*, 18, 64–76.

Donald, M. (1993). *Origins of the Modern Mind: Three stages in the evolution of culture and cognition*. Cambridge, MA: Harvard University Press.

Edwards, A. and MacKenzie, L. (2005). Steps Towards Participation: The social support of learning trajectories. *International Journal of Lifelong Education*, 24, 287–302.

Greeno, J. J. (2006). Learning in Activity. In R. Sawyer (ed.), *The Cambridge Handbook of the Learning Sciences* (pp. 79–96). Cambridge: Cambridge University Press.

Hutchins, E. L. (1991). The Social Organization of Distributed Cognition. In L. Resnick, J. Levine and S. Teasley (eds), *Perspectives on Socially Shared Cognition*. Washington, DC: American Psychological Association.

Ivarsson, J. (2004). *Renderings and Reasoning: Studying artifacts in human knowing*. Göteborg: Acta Universitatis Gothoburgensis.

Koschmann, T. (1996). *CSCL: Theory and Practice of an Emerging Paradigm*. Mahwah, NJ: Lawrence Erlbaum Associates.

Lave, J. and Wenger, E. (1991). *Situated Learning: Legitimate peripheral participation*. Cambridge: Cambridge University Press.

Lipponen, L., Hakkarainen, K. and Paavola, S. (2004). Practices and Orientations of CSCL. In J.-W. Strijbos, P. A. Kirschner, and R. L. Martens (eds), *What we Know about CSCL and Implementing it in Higher Education* (pp. 34–50). Dordrecht: Kluwer Academic.

Lichtman, D. (1979). Survey of Educator's Attitudes Towards Computers. *Creative Computing*, 5(1), 48–50.

O'Malley, C. (1994). *Computer-supported Cooperative Learning*. Berlin: Springer-Verlag.

Rommetveit, R. (1979). On the Architecture of Intersubjectivity. In R. Rommetveit and R. Blakar (eds), *Studies of Language, Thought and Verbal Communication* (pp. 93–107). New York: Academic Press.

Salomon, G. and Globerson, T. (1989). When Teams do not Function the Way They Ought To. *International Journal of Educational Research*, 13, 89–99.

Sawyer, K. R. (2006). *The Cambridge Handbook of the Learning Sciences*. Cambridge: Cambridge University Press.

Schrage, M. (1990). *Shared Minds: The new technologies of collaboration*. New York: Random House.

Sfard, A. (1998). On Two Metaphors for Learning and the Dangers of Choosing Just One. *Educational Researcher*, 27, 4–13.

Shore, B. (1996). *Culture in Mind: Cognition, culture and the problem of meaning*. New York: Oxford University Press.

Shweder, R. (1991). *Thinking Through Cultures*. Cambridge, MA: Harvard University Press.

Stahl, G., Koschmann, T. and Suthers, D. D. (2006). Computer-supported Collaborative Learning. In R. Sawyer (ed.), *The Cambridge Handbook of the Learning Sciences* (pp. 409–425). Cambridge: Cambridge University Press.

Tolmie, A. and Boyle, J. (2000). Factors Influencing the Success of Computer Mediated Communication (CMC) Environments in University Teaching: A review and case study. *Computers and Education*, 34, 119–140.

Trevarthan, C. (1980). The Foundations of Intersubjectivity: Development of interpersonal and cooperative understanding. In D. Olson (ed.), *The Social Foundations of Language and Thought: Essays in honor of Jerome Bruner* (pp. 216–242). New York: Norton.

Turkle, S. (1984). *The Second Self*. New York: Simon & Schuster.

Weizenbaum, J. (1976). *Computer Power and Human Reason*. San Francisco: Freeman.

Weldon, M. S. (2000). Remembering as a Social Process. *The Psychology of Learning and Motivation*, 40, 67–120.

Wertsch, J. (1991). *Voices of the Mind: A sociocultural approach to mediated action*. Cambridge, MA: Harvard University Press.

Chapter 11

Promoting knowledge creation and object-oriented inquiry in university courses

Hanni Muukkonen, Minna Lakkala and Sami Paavola

Changing practices of work, especially those relating to knowledge work, have initiated novel research questions on what kinds of competencies higher education should provide for students. University teaching is claimed to have a special task to support students in adopting ways of thinking and producing new knowledge anchored in scientific inquiry practices (Geisler, 1994; Gellin, 2003; Resnick, 1987). What have been examined as cognitive (individualistic) or social (participatory) forms of expertise and learning (Sfard, 1998), are now complemented with knowledge-creating or networked dimensions of expertise and learning (Paavola, Lipponen & Hakkarainen, 2004; Hakkarainen, Palonen, Paavola, & Lehtinen, 2004).

The *knowledge-creation approach* on learning highlights those kinds of activities where people collaboratively develop new artifacts and products or commit themselves into long-term processes of working. It necessitates questions about what kind of pedagogical practices could facilitate this kind of learning (see also the introduction by Ludvigsen *et al.*, this volume), and in what sense are students and teachers able to realize a knowledge-creation approach in practice. How, for instance, can standard studying-for-an-exam practices be transformed towards engagement in open-ended, but focused, inquiry practices, where students are developing new ideas, designs, and products?

The development of technologies to support collaborative inquiry has provided new possibilities for the design of courses. The last decade has witnessed an increasing understanding of the aspects and benefits of technology-enhanced collaborative inquiry, including computer support for intersubjective meaning-making (Stahl, Koschmann & Suthers, 2006), dialogic interaction (Wegerif, 2006), and collaborative argumentation as a means to learn to think critically about contested issues (Andriessen, 2006). Technology, at its best, can provide moderation for knowledge-building (Bereiter, 2002) and endorsement of processes in which ideas are developed together (Scardamalia & Bereiter, 2005) by directing efforts towards advancement of common objects. However, as cumulating evidence on learning technologies suggests, socially established practices delineating, for example, how responsibility is distributed and why collaboration is deemed beneficial, are essential in defining if, or in which form, knowledge-creation will turn out eventually, quite independent of any particular technological solutions.

This chapter makes an exploratory investigation of *collaborative object-oriented inquiry processes* in two university courses. These two courses represent descriptive cases for how to redesign tertiary-level courses to expand beyond individual or social aspects of learning. We will first address the concept of object-oriented inquiry by drawing on both activity theoretical and learning-science conceptualizations, the first in terms of highlighting the concept of object-orientedness, and the latter by providing an analytical framework. Second, we will examine the pedagogical infrastructures of two university courses to evaluate how the implementation of the courses can be said to represent object-oriented inquiry practices. Third, we address the question of what kinds of shared objects were dealt with and what kinds of competencies the students found critical in these courses. This provides a perspective on what kinds of competencies, or "metaskills" students value in handling such inquiry processes.

Collaborative object-oriented inquiry

Our previous research has examined learning in university courses from various perspectives. Following the CSCL tradition, it has united the perspectives of collaborative technology-mediated learning, scaffolding expert-like inquiry practices, and designing technology to support these kinds of processes (Muukkonen, Lakkala, & Hakkarainen, 2005; Lakkala, Muukkonen, & Hakkarainen, 2005). The two courses in the present study were realized without an explicit emphasis on object-orientedness; hence, they were analyzed from the point of view of how existing practices in university course could be described to reflect object-oriented inquiry, in terms of analysis of pedagogical design and elaboration of shared objects, as well as depicted by students' self-reflections. The encompassing challenge is to understand these structures and their interdependencies in order to be able to support a more conscious emphasis on collaborative work on shared objects.

The notion "object of activity" has aroused fertile discussion lately, especially within cultural-historical activity theory (Kaptelinin & Miettinen, 2005; Engeström & Blackler, 2005; Miettinen, 1998). For us, object-orientedness gives an important perspective on learning and the design of educational settings also beyond the framework of activity theory. According to activity theory, all activity is object-oriented (Leontiev, 1978). In its most general sense, the "object of activity" is a collective "motive" for the whole activity system (e.g. finishing a certain project within certain social and cultural settings) but it is also those concrete objects which are outcomes of that activity (e.g. end-products of that project). Furthermore, object-orientedness has built-in tensions within itself; the object of activity is something concrete but simultaneously something which is in the process of development (Engeström & Blackler, 2005; Lund & Hauge, this volume); it "includes both a knowledge of its properties, and a desire to transform it" (Miettinen, 1998, p. 424); it is the motive behind individuals' activities but also something social (Kaptelinin, 2005; Stetsenko, 2005).

We are applying ideas of object-orientedness from activity theory more generally in order to build a framework where collaborative object-oriented inquiry is emphasized as a potential design principle of educational practice. A key characteristic present in various models describing knowledge creation appears to be that collaboration is organized around long-term efforts for developing shared, tangible objects such as articles, models, and practices. It can be maintained that all human activity is object-oriented, although this object may take very different forms when examined at different levels of activity (see also Kaptelinin, 2005). Accordingly, individual students' activities are also focused on some objects, for example, writing an essay for a course. Collective activity system have their own objects of activity, for example, in the educational system to produce educated students for professional life. We are, however, concentrating on those "trialogical" processes in deliberately arranged educational settings where students are collaboratively developing some shared artifacts or practices (Paavola & Hakkarainen, 2005). So, for us here, object-oriented inquiry means that students' work is organized for developing together some concrete outcomes during the course as a result of sustained inquiry process. We think that dialogical thinking skills, as well as individualistic working practices, are central elements of advanced learning paradigm (Wegerif, 2006), but inquiry-learning should also focus on those ways that students' activities are organized for collaboratively modifying and making something tangible together. Therefore, the notion of "shared object" (object basically in a thing-like sense) has a more prominent place than before. Further, the emphasis on modifying a shared object together can be distinguished from merely dealing with a common artifact which is shared (e.g. a presentation) by participants. We argue that this focus has not been explicit in most previous educational practices or studies concerning collaborative learning.

Taken back to educational practices, making such emphasis naturally leads to numerous questions about whether such practices are feasible or what the knowledge-creation approach actually gives to students and teachers, or demands from them. We suggest that by addressing together the aspects of individuals, small groups, and, thirdly, objects of activity in educational settings, we may gain novel understanding of students' and teachers' practices. In short, we are in search of educational practices that support the development of what we call *metaskills of collaborative object-oriented inquiry*, although we acknowledge that using the term "meta" is in many ways problematic. Metaskills of collaborative inquiry (Muukkonen & Lakkala, 2009) are proposed to address commitment to collective, object-oriented, and prolonged inquiry efforts, which are not reducible to individual productions. Furthermore, it means those skills that students must develop for monitoring, evaluating, and coordinating efforts of knowledge advancement. In a sense, these skills are triggered by practices where students are responsible for coordinating and directing their activities over different aspects of inquiry: own individual efforts, effective collaboration in a group, and the progression and high quality of the knowledge objects they are developing.

Designing educational settings that promote object-oriented inquiry

Educators face a demand of changing their traditional ways of designing teaching, if they are inclined to experiment with the pedagogical practices of object-oriented inquiry. Classic models of instructional design are not very applicable to collaborative object-oriented inquiry because they mainly concentrate on individual processes of learning and are based on the predefined structuring of content, activities, and outcomes. The pedagogical design of object-oriented inquiry is more indirect, focusing on organizing the preconditions for the inquiry culture but not aiming at causally determining the learning results. Building on such views and previous studies (e.g. Bielaczyc, 2006; Guribye, 2005; Lipponen & Lallimo, 2004; Paavola, Lipponen, & Hakkarainen, 2002), we have started to use the notion *pedagogical infrastructure* to illustrate how the pedagogical design of object-oriented inquiry practices resembles the construction of basic physical infrastructure to support as effective functioning of people's daily activities as possible (Star, 1999). By exploiting the idea of infrastructures, we argue that the functionality, implementation and use of inquiry practices in university courses are based on, and require the creation of, a set of interconnected structural elements into the learning setting. We have developed *the pedagogical infrastructure framework* for describing the implementations of object-oriented inquiry into actual educational settings, consisting of the following four dimensions:

- *Technical infrastructure* is shaped by tools provided, especially technology that enables and facilitates the co-construction of shared knowledge artifacts, and the organization of the use of technology and related guidance.
- *Social infrastructure* is shaped by such features as the explicit arrangements to advance collaboration; social interaction and activities around shared knowledge objects; sharing of the process and outcomes; and the integration of face-to-face and technology-mediated activity.
- *Epistemological infrastructure* is shaped by ways of operating with knowledge and knowledge-related things that the practices and tools reflect; the role of knowledge sources used; students', teachers', and knowledge artifacts' role while creating and sharing knowledge; and the emphasis on knowledge-creating inquiry and object-orientedness in the tasks and assignments.
- *Cognitive infrastructure* is shaped by features that support students' awareness, conscious understanding and independent mastery of the critical aspects in the desirable practices; such as explicit modelling of the strategies of inquiry and object-oriented knowledge work; timely guidance provided for the students; methods used to promote metalevel reflection of the inquiry process and object-oriented practices; and scaffolding functionalities embedded in technology to support the desirable practices.

The four infrastructures are overlapping and cannot, in reality, be totally separated.

However, they are proposed to represent some fundamental aspects that need to be taken into account in designing pedagogical settings promoting collaborative object-oriented inquiry.

The overall aim of the study is to extend a theory-based framework for developing pedagogical practices. The following research questions were addressed: (1) How does the implementation of the pedagogical design of the courses represent object-oriented inquiry practices? (2) What kinds of shared objects the students were creating and how was this carried out in a virtual learning environment? (3) How did the students evaluate their experience of participation in the inquiry processes?

Methods

General investigative approach

Two courses from university education were selected as cases for reflection on how object-oriented inquiry is implemented in existing educational practices. Both cases presented the students with open-ended tasks, a small group composition (3–5 students) for collaboration, and a final report that student groups were to create together in a timeframe of three months. Although these aspects of pedagogical design were similar, there were a number of aspects that made the courses different, and therefore interesting to compare. The first case tried to model research practices, which rely on deepening question-explanation processes, while the second case was focusing on modelling virtual distributed work.

The basic investigative approach can be characterized as exploratory case research (Yin, 2003). Typical for such research is that its problems are open-ended, it investigates complex social phenomena and holistic characteristics of real-life events, it is iterative in nature, and it aims at new theory-building of poorly recognized phenomena (Verschuren, 2003).

Two cases from university education

Case I: Progressive inquiry in cognitive psychology

The first case was an undergraduate course in cognitive psychology that was designed according to the pedagogical model of progressive inquiry (Hakkarainen, 2003; Muukkonen *et al.*, 2005). In progressive inquiry, students' work is organized with the aim of promoting a deepening process of creating challenging research questions collaboratively, formulating explanations, and producing elaborated explanations with the support of knowledge sources. Undergraduate students (N=13) from various faculties of the University of Helsinki took part in the course on psychology of modern learning environments. The students were guided to form their own questions about the phenomena and create their intuitive working theories as initial explanations to answer the questions. These stages were undertaken before using authoritative information sources, to challenge the students' own thinking. The students obtained new information by exploiting various information sources after having together evaluated the ideas and explanations. The process was repeated gradually with deepening cycles of formulating subordinate study questions and more elaborated theories and knowledge products.

The course consisted of six seminar meetings (3–4 hours each), collaborative work within a web-based environment, FLE3 (see http://fle3.uiah.fi), between the meetings and a final meeting at the end of the course to evaluate the experiences jointly. Based on the research problems created by the students, three sub-groups (including 4–5 students) were formed. A group of three tutors was responsible for organizing the activities and guiding the students.

Case II: Virtual project management

The second case was an undergraduate course on distributed project management (Marttiin, Nyman, Takatalo, & Lehto, 2004). The whole study process was organized to resemble a real virtual project-management process aiming at creating, in expert teams, innovative problem solutions for a genuine client. The goal of the course was to get students acquainted with the theories, methods, and practices of organizing distributed work by participating themselves in a virtual teamwork process and conducting a study for the customer organizations. The participants were undergraduate students from the Department of Psychology (University of Helsinki) and from two other institutions, Helsinki School of Economics and Helsinki University of Technology, 46 students altogether. The theme of the course was based on a customer's assignment: the future possibilities and challenges of a broadcasting company in offering digital-TV services for people as workers, learners, citizens, and consumers or "Digi-humans." One team's assignment was to produce a report and a presentation which together describe a solution for the customers' problems. Several teachers and tutors took part in the course as facilitators of students' work; metaphorically they were introduced as the board of directors, not directly involved in the execution of tasks.

The course was organized in a project model, including team structure, planning, reporting, shared tasks and web-based collaboration tools; the same phase structure was also in each team's shared virtual working space in Optima system (see www.discendum.com/). Team management responsibility was rotating; in turn, each student was the manager in their team. In addition to virtual project teams, one student group was a coordination team whose task was to coordinate virtual teams' work and mediate information between the teams, the teachers, and the customers. Another student group was a research team, which was responsible for evaluating other group's experiences.

The teams were multidisciplinary, approximately five students in each team. In the first phase of the project, the coordination team collected the other teams' "offers" about solving the customers' problems and negotiated with the customers about carrying out the tasks. The second phase consisted of the coordination team assigning the sub-problems to teams, after which the teams started planning how to conduct their study. In the third phase, based on the collected knowledge, the teams constructed a half-hour presentation to the clients and a more extensive hard copy version. Throughout the phases, the coordination team supervised the other teams, and the research team studied team awareness and project-management issues via questionnaires and interviews.

Data collection and analysis

The data examined included observation notes of the course meetings and lectures, all database materials from the two virtual-learning environments, self-reflective questionnaires with open-ended question the students were asked to reply to at the end of the course, and group interviews of the student groups and the teachers in the second case.

Pedagogical infrastructures

The pedagogical design of the courses was examined using multiple data sources, partially reconstructed from the teachers' descriptions, the database structures and materials, and observations, following a model from our previous study of implementing progressive inquiry in university courses (Lakkala, Muukkonen, Paavola, & Hakkarainen, 2008). Given the basic similarities of the design of the courses, a set of "how" and "what" questions where devised to examine the design features in general and from the point of view of object-orientedness, for example, "How does technology support object-oriented inquiry?" or "How is the work epistemologically organized around concrete knowledge objects?" Three researchers analyzed the data together in an explorative way to identify the infrastructures and to describe the actual implementation of technical, social, epistemological, and cognitive infrastructures in the course designs.

Shared objects

To examine students groups' collaboration on shared objects, we had to rely on the digital artifacts produced in or posted to the two virtual learning environments (VLEs). The categories were produced according to subtasks for generating knowledge that the groups were engaged with: in Case I, the categories closely follow the sub-steps during the progressive inquiry process, but are organized by types of products that were encountered in the database; in Case II, they are more directly the outcomes of the sub-tasks assigned to students. Hence, we embarked upon a categorization that deals with tangible objects. We counted the number of different types of objects and examined their role in the groups' collaboration. Particularly, we were interested in the revisions made to different documents and the versioning of reports, presentations, and conceptualizations. We considered these as indications of working on shared objects.

Participants' self-reflections

The teacher interview in Case II and the students' self-reflection at the end of both courses were analyzed qualitatively. In this chapter, the selected excerpts were chosen to present illustrative self-reflections that (a) the teachers expressed on the authentic problems, and (b) the students expressed on commitment to shared efforts, challenges of inquiry, coordination of teamwork, and the development of shared objects. We considered this analysis to expose some relevant aspects about what kind of new metaskills the collaborative, object-oriented inquiry practices appear to require, examined from the viewpoint of the participants' self-reflections.

Outcomes

Pedagogical infrastructures in the two courses

To discuss the pedagogical design of these two cases in relation to the goals of object-oriented inquiry, we shall address similarities and differences in the courses by classifying some of their design features according to the four pedagogical infrastructures: technical, social, epistemological, and cognitive.

Technical infrastructure

In Case I, access to technology and guidance for using it was provided in all seminar meetings; technology helped the sharing of the inquiry discourse and knowledge artifacts throughout the course, both during meetings and distance periods. In Case II, use of technical tools was demonstrated in one meeting, otherwise the students gained technical guidance only from a distance. In this case, technology tools were in a crucial role in sharing all activities and artifacts because the student teams worked mainly virtually. From the point of view of object-oriented inquiry, both cases were missing tools that would have concretely enabled the co-authoring of common digital artifacts in and through the VLE.

Social infrastructure

In both cases, the group formation was systematically organized so that students represented diverse domains: in Case I, based on voluntary choices of similar research questions; and in Case II, by teachers based on the students' background and expertise. In the latter, the assignment of roles and responsibilities were also explicitly structured.

Students were generally encouraged to share their ideas and report versions through VLE. In Case I, groups were arranged to work on their groups' problems and products during the seminar meetings, by drawing concept maps and working on the knowledge produced in the groups' discourse forums; also the final reports were produced in groups. In Case II, the virtual collaboration was organized through each team's shared working space; project plans, report drafts, presentations, and final reports were elaborated in teams. A circulating team leader was responsible for coordinating the production of objects in teams. Particular to this second case was that two client organizations were involved in the process, which intensified the efforts for developing quality outcomes and nurtured inter-organizational boundary crossing.

What was noteworthy in both cases was that there were no individual assignments to carry out, but all efforts were to be directed at advancing the group's knowledge products. Naturally, there were phases where either individual work was more central, for example, reading articles and writing drafts, or team interaction was emphasized, i.e. negotiation of group's activities. Groups were asked to reflect on the process in writing both individually and collectively during the last meeting.

Epistemological infrastructure

The task in both courses was based on "authentic" knowledge problems, in the first case defined by the students, in the second case by the real clients. In Case I, there was only one expert lecture from a professor in the field; the tutors provided background materials and the student groups searched information from various knowledge sources. In Case II, the customers presented the challenge of digital TV services. Three professors from different fields gave expert lectures introducing students to the problem areas and issues of virtual teamwork. The customer and the professors provided background materials and the student teams searched for information themselves.

In Case I, the main line of inquiry of the groups was a somewhat abstract research question, which was iteratively specified in seminars and virtual discourse. Further, the students were asked to outline the problem space by concept map drawings, written report drafts, slide presentations, and final reports. In Case II, the main object was based on an assignment from a real customer to be solved by project work. This was organized through tasks for producing concrete team productions: flyers, proposals, plans, presentations, and final reports. Probably the demand of producing a solution to the problem of real clients in Case II made the activity epistemologically more deeply object-oriented than groups' abstract research questions in Case I.

Cognitive infrastructure

In Case I, the students were very closely guided by a group of three tutors, meeting them weekly, in addition to communicating virtually, and discussing the next steps in the inquiry activity. The tutors provided the students with the heuristic model of progressive inquiry to support the conceptual understanding of the working strategies, but no clear templates or instructions for carrying the process out. However, tutors commented on the ideas and report versions thus focusing the work on the shared objects. In Case II, the teachers modelled the expert-like practices of virtual teamwork explicitly by providing students with concrete artifacts: the model for virtual project learning and research, templates, instructions and products from previous courses. Teams presented their research solutions to the clients and the teachers, receiving oral feedback from them. Finally, the evaluation and reflection of outcomes was more like self-assessment in Case I, whereas in Case II the most important evaluation was given by the clients and the teachers. In the latter case, students also answered to questionnaires twice during the course evaluating virtual teamwork; the research team analyzed the data and presented results in the last meeting.

Shared objects the students worked on

In Case I, students worked virtually principally by using a discussion forum-type tool, therefore, their productions were mainly notes to the forum. The groups had weekly face-to-face meetings during the seminars and several self-organized additional meetings in between. Therefore, only a small part of their discussions and negotiations can be traced back to the VLE. The numbers of different types of objects in Case I are presented in Table 11.1. In our analysis, the number of versions of plans or reports was considered indicative of the efforts put into developing a particular object. We found most notes defining research problems, theoretical concepts, and process reflection in Group C, and more report versioning in Groups B and C. Although there were considerable amounts of own explanations, they generally did not advance in explanation of some issue, but were more singular remarks. An analysis based on the self-reflections of the students and the database materials (presented in Muukkonen & Lakkala, 2009) further examined these groups and pointed to that Group C was most engaged in the development of shared objects, re-focusing their conceptual understanding in a question-explanation process, and editing in turns the report compared to the other two groups. Group A in particular, had split the task up into three subsections and basically combined them for the final report, without revising the report together.

In Case II, the VLE used was a project-management environment, where participants operated with files and the discussion-forum notes were used more to exchange managerial information. As shown in Table 11.2, there was large variation in the number of documents produced by teams. The coordination team (Team 9) and research team (Team 10) had different type of responsibilities in the project; therefore they lack a lot of the types of documents developed in Teams 1–8. Based on the versions of different documents, Teams 1, 5, 6, and 7 appear being especially focused on revising their productions, suggesting that team flyers, presentations, reports, and other materials (e.g. background materials, status reports, and diaries) were shared objects under development.

Table 11.1 Objects developed by students in Case I

Developed objects	Group A	Group B	Group C
Documents in VLE	8	3	13
Discussion forum notes	51	56	74
Introductions	3	5	4
Research problems	8	7	12
Own explanations	17	17	13
Notes defining theoretical concepts	3	9	13
Process organization	5	4	10
Report versions	1	4	4
Other	16	15	15
Discussion forum memos	1	0	1
Links	5	1	10

Table 11.2 Objects developed by students in Case II

Developed objects	Team

Developed objects	1	2	3	4	5	6	7	8	9	10
Documents in VLE	61	23	16	35	59	55	64	14	9	23
Team flyer	10	2	1	6	6	1	8	1	0	0
Team rules	1	2	1	0	2	2	0	2	3	0
Project proposal	6	4	2	6	1	2	0	0	0	0
Project plan	5	4	2	3	3	3	16	2	0	0
Presentation	1	1	1	2	2	7	4	3	1	1
Report versions	4	3	2	5	5	15	10	3	0	0
Other materials	34	7	7	13	40	25	26	3	5	22
Discussion forums	3	2	3	9	1	1	4	2	3	1
Discussion forum notes	198	90	14	71	14	41	180	1	62	25

Participants' self-reported experiences and challenges of object-oriented inquiry

What was common to the experiences reported by the students in both cases was that it was quite demanding to learn to take one's place in the multidisciplinary collaboration and to relate to the ill-defined quality of the task. In Case I, a lot of self-reflection was included in the seminar meetings, to discuss the challenges of advancing inquiry, academic practices of writing and referencing as well as issues of collaboration. An excerpt from a student's self-reflection written at the end of the course addresses the challenge of the process: "*The working felt enormously difficult and laborious, but afterwards I would say that the effort was worthwhile. The process was very instructive. I suppose that our course work was more than any one of us could have achieved alone*" (Group C).

Two other groups' work in Case I was more in the direction of fulfilling the reporting task by combining their individual efforts under one report: "*Our group's knowledge building started when we began to create the final report together. Everyone was well familiarized with own topic, which we combined for the final report*" (Group B).

Those students less successful in collaborative inquiry were, however, often explaining how – through their more active participation or by receiving more appropriate guidance – their inquiry could have made more progress, suggesting that they were considering the challenges of novel inquiry practices introduced by the course. The following excerpt provides an example of it:

> Now knowledge building was largely (luckily not entirely) a separate phase. It requires clearly a new type of approach to studying, to be able profit from knowledge building fully. One should change own learning strategies – but it is not so easy after having the last 18 years been doing it "the other way."
>
> (Group B)

In Case II, one of the teachers explained in an interview that one of the guiding objectives for organizing such type of course was "*to provide them with abilities to operate in a multi-professional environment; our study books do not help in that at all.*" Further, he was hoping to show about "*realities of management, self-organization, and knowledge management in an organization.*" All teachers in Case II mentioned the importance of solving authentic client's problems, by explaining that "*clients provide the motivation,* [. . .] *we have aimed at a client demand, which is answered by efforts of the coordination team by selling the package to the client, a type of real life activity involved.*" Further, a second teacher added that "*it is not clear at all to these students, and to a majority of our teachers, what types of problem solving takes place in business world.*" A third teacher continued by saying that "*it is also about teaching courage to dare to go with own professional expertise to meet people from different professions, and that they can go somewhere and solve problems*" for the client. Further, they had organized the whole working process, tasks, phases, and team structures very systematically according to a virtual project management model. However, their prior experiences had already showed them that despite their efforts to be as organized as possible, the feedback of students often contradicted this:

> but as one reads the essays and feedback, I've quite often noticed that the end gain has been more of the type of now we know how this team should

not be organized, and that it functions more in a bad general rehearsal style which generates later on much better results.

In this case, the advancement of the team's knowledge-creation (or, rather, the challenges related to it) was not in other ways monitored by the teachers besides their ability to meet deadlines, which all did. The monitoring responsibility had been delegated to the coordination team, which again undertook it from the project timeline angle. Hence, each team had to take, very concretely, the responsibility of advancing their work. In their self-reflections, students were addressing the challenges of coordinating virtual and multidisciplinary teamwork, naming it often the most central aspect in their learning experience, as can be seen from the following excerpt.

> The course was a very good tool for getting familiar with virtual working. The only weakness in the course was the general messiness, especially in the beginning. This was caused by changing expectations and partly by unclear tasks. On the other hand, this probably is a central feature in virtual work.
>
> (Team 7)

In the self-reflections, the open-ended assignments and the lack of teacher-regulation was often linked to experiences of confusion and initial insecurity of how to proceed.

> Although the virtual teams taking part in the course may have experienced bewilderment from feeling of too vague and free assignments, too unfamiliar team mates or clumsiness of virtual tools, this confusion probably was inevitably part of the chosen course implementation. The teams succeeded in the tasks and created good ideas.
>
> (Team 10)

Further, "we had to seek novel solutions" was also often mentioned, although not all students were satisfied in reaching this aim. The shared development of objects may be obstructed, if the views of how to proceed are controversial. In one team, this controversy was recognized and dealt with adeptly, which for us represent metaskills of advancing collaborative inquiry.

> [I]n the beginning we noticed that we, as students from different universities and of course with different personalities and working habits, had somewhat different views of how exactly should the documents be done. I like to take a long time in the beginning of a project, developing crazy ideas, and there's always dozens of different drafts, plans and "versions" before it develops into the final product; in other words I like to start from a big, somewhat vague, picture first and then gradually (and a bit disorganizedly . . .) condense "the mess" toward the final product. Whereas another [. . .] student told that she

likes to do thing very organized and finish one part of the final product first, then move on to the other parts and finally put the parts together. There was a short time of conflict in the beginning concerning this, but we discussed it over immediately and it never got into a personal conflict in our team.

(Team 10)

Summary

The examination of the two cases provided us perspectives on their pedagogical design, development of objects, and self-reflections of participants. They provide evidence for two different ways of facilitating object-oriented inquiry, examined in terms of technical, social, epistemological, and cognitive infrastructure. The overall pedagogical design of the cases appears to have been rather systematically in line with the goals of each course. In Case I, the goal was to model the knowledge practices of scientific inquiry resembling the work of a research group. The shared object the groups worked on were particularly the research problems, explication of theoretical concepts, process reflections, and partially the reports. In Case II, the goal was to simulate the activities and challenges of virtual project-management work, with authentic clients participating. The shared objects for the teams were the team flyers, project proposals and plans, and final reports with presentations. The analysis of the development of objects showed considerable variation between groups in both cases in regard of the revisions made to different documents and the versioning of reports, presentations, and conceptualizations. The way that Case II was organized appears to have endorsed a more concrete focus on creating versions of their documents as the students mainly collaborated virtually, together with the pressure of producing outcomes for the clients. Future research efforts are required to understanding the conditions for successful engagement in developing shared objects.

Seemingly the teachers had taken a number of efforts to provide structure and to model the advancement of the inquiry process or project. However, the analysis of the two cases suggested that being taken to a motivating, and yet highly ill-structured, course, was indeed a challenging situation for most students. It appears to have created a contradiction in terms of their expectations about a learning situation in a higher-education course; student teams were asked to define themselves a large part of the content to study, to manage the teamwork in collaboration, and to produce solutions on authentic problems, all within an ill-defined process. The students perceived it confusing and controversial to work initially, but generally acknowledged the importance of such experience towards the end of the course.

Discussion

In recent years, a wide range of research has expanded our understanding about the possibilities of collaborative inquiry and expert-like practices in learning. We are advocating object-orientedness, in addition to practices of individual activities, dialogic interaction, and reflection as aspects of collaborative inquiry. Such practices require new pedagogical models, different kind of curriculum design, and learning culture that values such competencies. The present article is one effort to integrate theoretical approaches for promoting object-oriented inquiry to those concrete solutions that educators have already applied in designing courses.

To synthesize our point of view, an emphasis on the object-orientedness of inquiry as a pedagogical approach entails that, first, activities within courses represent collaborative orchestration of individual efforts in relation to joint practices. Second, efforts are directed at advancing shared objects, rather than just individually carried out tasks or dialogic interaction. Third, reflection on learning – as well as evaluation of learning – is directed towards the examination of artifacts, social practices, and processes (i.e. shared objects) representing advancements in knowledge, rather than just the improvement of personal understanding or social interaction as such. Finally, the process of advancing ideas, explanations, and products of knowledge work is closely related to the use of technologies supporting collaborative activities.

We argue that metaskills are likely to emerge across sustained participation in inquiry practices focused on the advancement of knowledge. The time scale of developing such presumed skills may, however, be relatively long, taking several years to become fully articulated. Even so, we believe that the learning experiences from individual courses can also cumulatively support the development of metaskills of collaborative object-oriented inquiry. Knowledge-creation practices are at times extremely fuzzy and chaotic if there are many perspectives, interpretations, or objects emerging. However, being able to tolerate the confusion and have trust in finding the focus (with appropriate scaffolding and feedback) and to recognize that the quality of the shared objects should be constantly upheld are aspects pertinent to knowledge creation. The metaskills of collaborative object-oriented inquiry need to deal with the strategies and efforts that are helpful in getting the inquiry going and improving the object, despite difficulties and controversies.

One open question that has not been discussed in the present article is the demand for formal evaluation of learning in university settings. In general, it has been suggested that evaluation of learning should shift towards assessment *for* learning in addition to assessment *of* learning (Birenbaum *et al.*, 2006). In relation to inquiry, this could mean steps that would make evaluation itself a useful part of the learning process and not merely providing an end-score. It could include providing the participants process-based evaluation criteria in addition to content-based criteria. Further, the participants themselves should have a distinct role in reviewing the process and its products (see Lee, Chan, & van Aalst, 2006), and consider these efforts as part of their expertise and development of metaskills.

Focusing on the design of pedagogical practices for knowledge creation still leaves a lot of the institutional practices, that students are part of, unaccounted for. Possibilities of changing learning and evaluation practices are in multiple ways limited by the priorities of the entire educational system. Taking into account curricular constraints and limited resources in university teaching, it appears quite risky and even contradictory to general practices to initiate an ill-defined collaboration process without clearly defined content for outcomes. There is an obvious mismatch between those non-predefined and self-organizing processes of object-oriented inquiry we wish to emphasize, and the achievement of greater compatibility and comparability in the systems of higher education by implementation of standards for quality assurance, which is one of the emphases stressed by the Bologna process for the reform of European higher education (Bologna Declaration, 1999). Nonetheless, the two cases described were for us highly motivating examples of small-scale efforts of transforming educational practices towards knowledge creation and object-oriented inquiry.

References

Andriessen, J. (2006). Arguing to Learn. In K. Sawyer (ed.) *Handbook of the Learning Sciences* (pp. 443–459). Cambridge: Cambridge University Press.

Bereiter, C. (2002). *Education and Mind in the Knowledge Age*. Hillsdale, NJ: Erlbaum.

Bielaczyc, K. (2006) Designing Social Infrastructure: Critical issues in creating learning environments with technology. *Journal of the Learning Sciences, 15*, 301–329.

Birenbaum, M., Breuer, K., Cascallar, E., Dochy, F., Dori, Y., Ridgway, J., Wiesemes, R., and Nickmans, G. (2006). A learning Integrated Assessment System. *Educational Research Review, 1*, 61–67.

Bologna Declaration (1999). *The Bologna Declaration on the European Space for Higher Education: An explanation*. Retrieved January 11, 2007, from http://ec.europa.eu/education/policies/educ/bologna/bologna_en.html

Engeström, Y. and Blackler, F. (2005). On the Life of the Object. *Organization, 12*, 307–330.

Geisler, C. (1994). *Academic Literacy and the Nature of Expertise*. Hillsdale, NJ: Erlbaum.

Gellin, A. (2003). The Effect of Undergraduate Student Involvement on Critical Thinking: A meta-analysis of the literature 1991–2000. *Journal of College Student Development, 44*, 745–762.

Guribye, F. (2005). *Infrastructures for Learning: Ethnographic inquiries into the social and technical conditions of education and training*. Unpublished doctoral dissertation, University of Bergen, Norway. Retrieved April 3, 2006, from: http://hdl.handle.net/1956/859

Hakkarainen, K. (2003). Emergence of Progressive Inquiry Culture in Computer-supported Collaborative Learning. *Learning Environments Research, 6*, 199–220.

Hakkarainen, K., Palonen, T., Paavola, S., and Lehtinen, E. (2004). *Communities of Networked Expertise: Professional and educational perspectives*. Amsterdam: Elsevier.

Kaptelinin, V. (2005). The Object of Activity: Making sense of the sense-maker. *Mind, Culture, and Activity, 12*, 4–18.

Kaptelinin, V. and Miettinen, R. (2005). Perspectives on the Object of Activity. *Mind, Culture, and Activity, 12*, 1–3.

Lakkala, M., Muukkonen, H., and Hakkarainen, K. (2005). Patterns of Scaffolding in Computer-mediated Collaborative Inquiry. *Mentoring and Tutoring*, *13*, 283–302.

Lakkala, M., Muukkonen, H., Paavola, S., and Hakkarainen, K. (2008). Designing Pedagogical Infrastructures in University Courses for Technology-enhanced Collaborative Inquiry. *Research and Practice in Technology Enhanced Learning*, *3*(1), 33–64.

Lee, E. Y. C., Chan, C. K. K. and van Aalst, J. (2006). Students Assessing their Own Collaborative Knowledge Building. *Computer-Supported Collaborative Learning*, *1*, 278–307.

Leontiev, A. N. (1978). *Activity, Consciousness, and Personality*. Englewood Cliffs, NJ: Prentice Hall.

Lipponen, L. and Lallimo, J. (2004). From Collaborative Technology to Collaborative Use of Technology: Designing learning oriented infrastructures. *Educational Media International*, *41*, 111–116.

Marttiin, P., Nyman, G., Takatalo, J. and Lehto, J. A. (2004). Learning Virtual Project Work. In J. Cordeiro and J. Filipe (eds), *Computer Supported Activity Coordination: Proceedings of the 1st International Workshop on Computer Supported Activity Coordination*, CSAC 2004 (pp. 91–102). Portugal: Insticc Press.

Miettinen, R. (1998). Object Construction and Networks in Research Work: The case of research on cellulose-degrading enzymes. *Social Studies of Science*, *28*, 423–463.

Muukkonen, H. and Lakkala, M. (2009). Exploring Metaskills of Collaborative Object-oriented Inquiry in Higher Education. *International Journal of Computer-Supported Collaborative Learning*, *4*(2), 187–211.

Muukkonen, H., Lakkala, M., and Hakkarainen, K. (2005). Technology-mediation and Tutoring: How do they shape progressive inquiry discourse? *Journal of the Learning Sciences*, *14*, 527–565.

Paavola, S., Lipponen, L., and Hakkarainen, K. (2002). Epistemological Foundations for CSCL: A comparison of three models of innovative knowledge communities. In G. Stahl (ed.), *Computer Support for Collaborative Learning: Foundations for a CSCL community. Proceedings of the Computer-supported Collaborative Learning 2002 Conference* (pp. 24–32). Hillsdale, NJ: Erlbaum. Available: http://newmedia.colorado.edu/cscl/228.html

Paavola, S., Lipponen, L., and Hakkarainen, K. (2004). Models of Innovative Knowledge Communities and Three Metaphors of Learning. *Review of Educational Research*, *74*(4), 557–576.

Paavola, S. and Hakkarainen, K. (2005). The Knowledge Creation Metaphor – An Emergent Epistemological Approach to Learning. *Science and Education*, *14*, 535–557.

Resnick, L. (1987). *Education and Learning to Think*. Washington, DC: National Academy Press.

Scardamalia M. and Bereiter, C. (2005). Does Education for the Knowledge Age Need a New Science? *European Journal of School Psychology*, *3*, 21–39.

Sfard, A. (1998). On Two Metaphors for Learning and the Dangers of Choosing Just One. *Educational Researcher*, *27*, 4–13.

Stahl, G., Koschmann, T., and Suthers, D. (2006). Computer-supported Collaborative Learning: An historical perspective. In R. K. Sawyer (ed.), *Cambridge Handbook of the Learning Sciences* (pp. 409–426). New York: Cambridge University Press.

Star, S. L. (1999). The Ethnography of Infrastructure. *American Behavioral Scientist*, *43*, 377–391.

Stetsenko, A. (2005). Activity as Object-Related: Resolving the dichotomy of individual and collective planes of activity. *Mind, Culture, and Activity*, *12*, 70–88.

Verschuren, P. J. M. (2003). Case Study as a Research Strategy: Some ambiguities and opportunities. *International Journal of Social Research Methodology*, 6, 121–139.

Wegerif, R. (2006). A Dialogic Understanding of the Relationship Between CSCL and Teaching Thinking Skills. *International Journal of Computer-supported Collaborative Learning*, 1, 143–157.

Yin, R. K. (2003). *Case Study Research: Design and methods.* Third Edition. Thousand Oaks, CA: Sage.

Chapter 12

Social practices of group cognition in virtual match teams

Gerry Stahl

The Virtual Math Teams (VMT) project is an effort to promote interest in mathematics by teenagers around the world in a way that is not necessarily linked with formal schooling. It invites people to meet online in small groups of about three to six participants to chat about mathematics. The Math Forum, which hosts VMT, is a leading online site for math information and services, which has grown during the past 15 years to now serve several million visitors a month. While it offers a variety of math-related resources, the Math Forum had not featured a strong, ongoing collaborative learning service until VMT.

The VMT project (Stahl, 2009) explores a model for informal networked collaborative learning. As researchers in the VMT project, my colleagues and I are particularly interested in analyzing the way that learning takes place in a context like VMT; we focus on the group cognition (Stahl, 2006b) that can be observed in the logs of math chats (see next section). To support this analysis, the VMT project has developed a methodology for recording and analyzing practices that contribute to group cognitive accomplishments (third section). Our research using the VMT experimental platform and methodology has resulted in an increased understanding of group practices that are developed and used by participants in the online informal collaborative learning environment (fourth section). In particular, we will summarize in the last sections of this chapter the results of three case studies of VMT interactions that illustrate the variety of group practices that occur in this context.

The purpose of this chapter is to provide an overview of what has been learned to date from about a thousand student-hours of VMT sessions, as published in a number of more detailed analytic case studies (several reported in Stahl, 2009). In particular, it aims to describe how online text chat is carried on with the use of innovative group practices and how this enables teams of students to accomplish group cognitive results.

An online math discourse community outside of school

We are building the foundations for a global online community of people who are interested in mathematics. Our focus is on students, rather than professionals or graduate students, so we feature math problems that can be solved with basic knowledge of algebra and geometry. The math-education research community stresses the importance of math students discussing their reasoning (Lockhart, 2009; Moss & Beatty, 2006; Sfard, 2008), but school classrooms continue to be dominated by problem-solving by individuals. So we are creating a place where students can explore and discuss math with other students, either independent of or in parallel with classroom routines.

The VMT project is an ongoing effort to design an online math-discourse community. Starting very simply in 2003 from a successful online math problem-of-the-week service and taking advantage of popular off-the-shelf chat software to make it collaborative, we have since then gradually evolved a more sophisticated environment involving carefully scripted pedagogical interventions, open-ended math issues and custom software – guided by extensive analysis of student behaviors through cycles of trials.

While the ubiquity of networked computers connected through the Internet from homes and schools creates an exciting opportunity for students around the world to explore math together, the practical difficulties are enormous. We are interested in facilitating the development of high-level thinking skills and the deep understanding that comes from engaging in effective dialog (Wegerif & De Laat, this volume) and merging personal perspectives (Stahl, 2006b, ch. 4 & 6), but we find that students are accustomed to using text chat and the internet for superficial socializing. Furthermore, their habits of learning are overwhelmingly skewed toward passive acquisition of knowledge from authority sources like teachers and books, rather than from self-regulated or collaborative inquiry. Finally, attempts to invent technological solutions have failed for lack of regard for issues of social practice. Designers of online environments have too often been driven more by technological capabilities than by careful analysis of the needs of people trying to work or learn together. Moreover, they have assumed that online environments will be used as intended by the designers rather than as adapted by the users through creative social practices constrained by institutional contexts.

Our experience to date suggests three stubborn challenges that need to be addressed:

- How to deepen the learning that takes place, given that most current examples of social networking and learning in online communities remain shallow.
- How to introduce inquiry learning by student-centered informal online communities into social contexts dominated by formal schooling.
- How to integrate (a) pedagogical scaffolding, (b) technological affordances and (c) motivational sociability into a coherent service that fosters a growing community.

In order to address these needs, we have been using our emergent online community as a laboratory for studying the practices of group cognition "in the wild." Virtual math teams are small groups of students who meet in a chatroom to discuss mathematical topics. These are typically three to six teenage students who interact for about an hour at a time. The chatrooms are set up by staff of the Math Forum. New students are invited through Math Forum initiatives, although students can subsequently set up their own rooms and invite friends or the online public. These meetings may be encouraged by teachers, but they occur online while the students are at home, in a library or elsewhere. No teacher is present in the room, although a facilitator may be present to provide guidance in learning how to use the online environment. In the long run, these small, short-lived teams may evolve to become part of a global community of math discourse.

As designers of educational chat environments, we are particularly interested in how small groups of students construct their interactions in chat media with different possible configurations of technical features. How do they learn about the meanings that designers embed in the environment and how do they negotiate the practices that they will adopt to turn technological possibilities into practical means for mediating their interactions? How can we design with students the technologies, pedagogies and communities that will result in desirable collaborative experiences for them?

The analysis of group practices summarized in this chapter points to the potential of text-based chat to provide an effective medium for computer-supported collaborative learning outside of school settings. We have found that in many contexts chat is more engaging than the asynchronous media often used in education. However, text messaging and chat as normally practiced by teenagers is customarily a medium of informal socializing, not of group knowledge-building. Creating a virtual place, a technological infrastructure and a set of group practices to foster more serious group cognition requires coordinated design based on detailed analysis of usage in settings like virtual math teams. If the group experience is a positive one for the participants, they may want to return. Many chats end with people making plans to get together again. In some experiments, the same groups attended multiple sessions. Eventually, we would like to see a community of users form, with teams re-forming repeatedly and with old-timers helping new groups to form and to learn how to collaborate effectively.

As the researchers who build the VMT service, we are studying how students do mathematics collaboratively in online chat environments. We are particularly interested in the group practices that they develop to conduct their interactions in such an environment. Taken together, these practices define a culture, a shared set of ways to make sense together. The practices are subtly responsive to the chat medium, the pedagogical setting, the social atmosphere and the intellectual resources that are available to the participants. These practices define the ways in which chat groups interactively manage resources and conduct activities.

Group cognition in math chats

Through the use of the kinds of practices we have analyzed, small groups construct their collaborative experience. The chat takes on a flow of interrelated ideas for the group, analogous to an individual's stream of consciousness. The referential structure of this flow provides a basis for the group's experience of intersubjectivity, common ground and a shared world.

Our goal in the VMT project is to provide a service to students that will allow them to have a rewarding experience collaborating with their peers in online discussions of mathematics. We can never know exactly what kind of subjective experience they had, let alone predict how they will experience life under conditions that we design for them. Our primary access to information related to their group experiences comes from our chat logs. The logs capture most of what student members see of their group on their computer screens. We can even replay the logs so that we see how they unfolded sequentially in time. Of course, we are not engaged in the interaction the way the participants were and recorded experiences never quite live up to the live version because the engagement is missing. We do test out the environments ourselves and enjoy the experience, but we experience math and collaboration differently to middle-school students.

We also interview students and their teachers, but teenagers rarely reveal much of their life to adults. So we try to understand how collaborative experiences are structured as interpersonal interactions. Our focus is not on the individuals as subjective minds, but on the group as constituted by the interactions that take place within the group.

During VMT chats, students work on math problems and themes. In solving problems and exploring math worlds or phenomena, the groups construct sequences of mathematical reasoning that are analogous to proofs. Proofs in mathematics have an interesting and subtle structure. One must distinguish: (a) the problem situation; (b) the exploratory search for the solution; (c) the effort to reduce a haphazard solution path to an elegant, formalized proof; (d) the statement of the proof; and (e) the lived experience of following the proof (Livingston, 1986; 1987). Each of these has its own structures and practices. Each necessarily references the others. To engage in mathematics is to become ensnarled in the intricate connections among them. To the extent that these aspects of doing math have been distinguished and theorized, it has been done as though there is simply an individual mathematician at work. There has been virtually no research into how these could be accomplished and experienced collaboratively – despite the fact that talking about math has for some time been seen as a priority in math education.

More generally, we investigate how these groups construct and make sense of their shared experience of collaborating online (Stahl, 2007). While answers to many questions in computer-mediated interaction have been formulated largely in terms of *individual* psychology, questions of collaborative experience require consideration of the *group* as the unit of analysis. Naturally, groups include individuals as contributors and interpreters of content, but the group interactions have structures and elements of their own that call for special analytic approaches (see section on the group of individuals). When groups work well, they can succeed in accomplishing high-order cognitive tasks – like inquiry, problem-solving, generalization and insight – as a group. We call this *group cognition* (Stahl, 2006b).

Problem-solving by groups often takes place through interactions involving multiple people. Key ideas do not simply reflect mental representations of an individual, but arise through interactions in which people and groups respond to each other. Online, the sequentiality of chat messages can become confused without the turn-taking conventions of face-to-face communication. Both participants and analysts must learn how to reconstitute and represent the response structure that drives group interaction. At this level, we analyze a proposal-response pair that is typical in math chats, and look at the referencing patterns that determine chat threading when this pair is successfully completed and when it fails (see section on math proposals). Often, math proposals involve deictic references to math objects. Accomplishing such references without physical gestures can be challenging; they require support from special software functionality (see section on deictic referencing).

In the most successful VMT chats, meaning is created at the group unit of analysis rather than by particular individuals or isolated minds. The recognition that collaborative groups constitute themselves interactionally and that their sense-making takes place at the group unit of analysis has fundamental methodological implications for the study of collaboration. The field of computer-supported collaborative learning (CSCL) was founded a decade ago to pursue the analysis of group meaning-making (Stahl, Koschmann & Suthers, 2006). We view the research described here as a contribution to that CSCL tradition.

Research methodology for recording group practices and group cognition

The VMT service and its technological infrastructure have been systematically designed as an experimental test-bed for studying group cognition (Stahl, 2010). The chatroom is itself persistent and the drawings and text messaging can be replayed for researchers with their original sequentiality. There is no need to involve videotaping and transcription, with their methodological complexities, in order to capture what takes place and make it available for detailed study. While many things are not captured that may take place for individual participants at their distributed physical locations, most of what enters into the group interactions and is necessary for its analysis is readily available to researchers. For instance, the students know little about each other from outside of the chatroom. Communication cues that are hard to specify in face-to-face communication have been largely excluded from the text-based interaction.

In chat settings, participants exchange textual postings. This is the sole visible basis for interaction, communication, mutual understanding and collaborative knowledge-building within a simple chat environment. The VMT chat environment now supplements this with some social awareness features and with a shared whiteboard for drawing geometric figures, but for the moment let us consider a generic chatroom. In addition to the content of the typed postings, their order, sequentiality and timing typically play a significant role in how the postings are understood (O'Neill & Martin, 2003). The participants log in with a chat "handle" that is associated with their postings; the wording of this handle may imply something about the person so named. The postings by a given participant are linked together as his (or hers) via the handle. Furthermore, we assume that the participants come to the chatroom with specific expectations and motivations – in our case, because it is part of the Math Forum site and may be recommended by a teacher, parent or friend. Thus, there is an open-ended set of factors that may enter the chat from its sociocultural context. There is also more-or-less shared language (e.g. English and basic math terminology) and culture (e.g. contemporary teen subculture and classroom math practices) that can play a role in the chats.

The current VMT environment is quite complex. In addition to the chat window, there is a shared whiteboard for drawing diagrams, geometric figures, tables of numbers and text boxes (see Figure 12.1 in the section on referencing). The chat and text boxes support mathematical notation. Both the chat and the whiteboard are persistent and their history can be scrolled by the users. There are social awareness messages indicating who is typing and drawing at the moment or entering and leaving. Many students participate in multiple sessions, and in these cases Math Forum staff provide feedback in the chatroom between sessions, which the students can read later. Recently, we have added a wiki, where students from different teams can post results and respond to what others have discovered.

To support our research, we now have a replay facility in which we can view the whole interaction process in real time or fast-forward and step through the interaction with the display of the chat, drawing and awareness notices all coordinated. This gives us a tool for analysis that is analogous to digital video for face-to-face interaction, but without all the complications of lighting, camera angles, transcription and synchronization. Moreover, there is nothing going on "off camera" that affects the interaction because everything that was visually shared by the participants is replayed for us.

To study what takes place among students in chatrooms, we hold interaction analysis *data sessions* (Jordan & Henderson, 1995). These are meetings in which a number of researchers collaboratively take a careful look at chat logs and discuss what is taking place. Focus is directed toward brief extracts that present interactions of analytic interest to the research group. The chat log reveals to the researchers what was visible to the student participants. The researchers can take into account the institutional context in which the chat took place when it is made relevant within the chat. As members of the broader society to which the students also belong, the researchers share to a large extent a competent understanding of the culture and language of the chat. Thus, they are capable of making sense of the chat because they see the same things that the participants saw and can understand them in similar ways. Moreover, by repeatedly studying the persistent log of the chat and by bringing their analytic skills to it, researchers who have made themselves familiar with this genre can make explicit many aspects of the interaction that were taken for granted by participants in the flow of the moment. By working as a group, the researchers can minimize the likelihood of idiosyncratic analyses.

We also work individually, studying transcripts and writing about them, but we periodically bring our analyses to the group for feedback and confirmation.

We have adapted the scientific methodology of conversation analysis to the microanalysis of online, text-based, mathematical discourse (see next section). We adopt an ethnomethodological (Garfinkel, 1967) focus on the methods that participants use to make shared sense of what they are jointly doing. Later in this chapter, we summarize some of our preliminary findings about how small groups make sense collaboratively in settings like VMT.

Ethnomethodology provides a further theoretical justification for the ability of researchers to produce rigorous analyses of recorded interactions. This has to do with the notion of *accountability* (Garfinkel, 1967). When people interact, they typically construct social order (such as conducting a fun chat or developing a math solution) and may produce shared objects (like textual postings). These objects are accountable in the sense that they were tacitly designed to reveal their own significance. A brief text, for instance, is written to be read in a certain way; its choice of wording, syntax, references and placement in the larger chat are selected to show the reader how to read it (Livingston, 1995; Zemel & Çakir, 2009).

The account that a chat posting gives of itself for the other students in the chat can also be taken advantage of by the researchers. The researchers in a data session discuss the log in order to agree on the accounts of the postings, individually and in their interactive unity.

The social structure and the accountability of human interactions make it possible for researchers to draw generalized understandings from the analysis of unique case studies. Interactions in the VMT setting and elsewhere are extremely dependent upon the specific circumstances of the interactional context that they sequentially build and the physical or sociocultural context that they repeatedly index. So the data of student interactions is not reproducible and cannot be compared under conditions of experimental control. However, the social structures that people construct during their interactions necessarily have a generality. Otherwise, if every event had a completely unique significance, people would not be able to understand each other. Shared understanding is the basis for human interaction and it relies upon the generality of the structures that are interactionally created. These structures may vary within limits from culture to culture and in reaction to different mediational circumstances. Students in an English-language chat in Singapore might interact differently from adults in an asynchronous discussion forum in Scotland. But experienced researchers can make sense of events in both contexts by taking into account the differences. As the analyses of interactions in VMT have shown us, there are basic patterns that students repeatedly call upon to discuss math; at the same time, even minor changes in technology support may cause participants to invent new forms of meaning-making in reaction to the affordances and barriers that they enact in their online environments.

The VMT service is being developed through a design-based research approach to co-evolve the software, pedagogy, mathematics and service through an iterative process of trial, analysis and design modification. The software started with off-the-shelf chat systems and now involves development of a custom-research prototype. The pedagogy started with principles of mathematics education and computer-supported collaborative learning and is now incorporating efforts to build a user community engaged in discussing math and facilitating collaborative practices. The math problems started out using the same problems-of-the-week offered to individuals and are now providing opportunities for groups to explore open-ended mathematical worlds as well as to work on issues that the participants generate themselves. The service started as occasional offerings and is now gearing up for continuous availability supported by as-needed monitoring and feedback.

As the trials progress, we analyze the resultant logs in the ways indicated in this chapter and use our results to inform our redesign of the software, pedagogy, mathematics and service. Thereby, ethnomethodologically informed interaction analysis provides the analytic component of design research, a component that is not often specified in discussions of design-based research (Koschmann, Stahl & Zemel, 2006). In this sense, the usage of our insights into how students interact in chat is at odds with the usual practices of ethnomethodology and conversation analysis, which claim not to impose researcher or designer interests on their data. While we try to understand what the student participants are up to in their own terms and how they are making sense of the activity structure that we provide for them, we are doing this in order to motivate our subsequent design decisions. Our goal is not just to understand the student meaning-making processes, but to use that understanding to modify the VMT service to allow groups to engage more effectively in math discourse.

Group practices for discussing math online

In order to understand the experience of people and groups collaborating online in VMT, we look in detail at the captured interactions. We conceptualize the patterns of interaction that we observe as *member methods* or *group practices*. This is a concept that we take from ethnomethodology (Garfinkel, 1967). Ethnomethodology is a phenomenological approach to sociology that tries to describe the methods that members of a culture use to accomplish what they do, such as how they carry on conversations (Sacks, Schegloff & Jefferson, 1974) or how they "do" mathematics (Livingston, 1986). In particular, the branch of ethnomethodology known as conversation analysis (Sacks, 1992) has developed an extensive and detailed scientific literature about the methods that people deploy in everyday informal conversation and how to analyze what is going on in examples of verbal interaction.

Methods are seen as the ways that people produce social order and make sense of their shared world. For instance, conversation analysis has shown that there are well-defined procedures that people use to take turns at talk. There are ways that people use to determine when they can speak and how they can signal that others may take a turn at conversation (Sacks *et al.*, 1974).

We adopt the general approach of conversational analysis, but we must make many adaptations to it given the significant differences between our chat logs and informal conversation. Our data consists of chat logs of student messages about mathematics. The messages are typed, not spoken, so they lack intonation, verbal stress, accent, rhythm, personality. The participants are not face-to-face, so their bodily posture, gaze, facial expression and physical engagement are missing. Only completed messages are posted; the halting process of producing the messages is not observable by message recipients (Garcia & Jacobs, 1998). The messages are displayed in a particular software environment and the messages are designed by their posters to be read and responded to in that environment (Livingston, 1995). The textual messages are persistent and may be read or ignored at will, and may be re-read later – although they scroll off-screen after several other postings appear. Multiple participants may be typing messages at the same time, and the order of posting these messages may be unpredictable by the participants (Çakir *et al.*, 2005). Consequently, messages do not necessarily appear immediately following the messages to which they may be responding. In addition to these features of chat, our logs are concerned with mathematics and are created within educational institutional contexts – such as the Math Forum website and sometimes school-related activities or motivations. Thus, the chats may involve building mathematical knowledge, not just socializing and conversing about opinions or everyday affairs.

These differences between our chats and normal conversation mean that the rules of turn taking, etc. have all been transformed. What remains, however, is that people still develop methods for creating and sustaining social order and shared meaning-making. Chat participants are skilled at creating and adapting sophisticated methods that accomplish their tasks in these unique environments. It is the analyst's job to recognize and describe these methods, which are generally taken for granted by the participants.

Among the student chat methods of interest to us are the interactional means that the students use to:

- introduce each other
- adapt to institutional settings
- socialize; to have fun; to flirt
- get to know each other better
- establish personal relations or roles
- form themselves into groups
- define a problem to work on
- start working on a problem
- agree on how to proceed
- bring in math resources
- clarify a point
- make a proposal
- tell a story
- justify a claim

- negotiate a decision
- reference an object
- count items together
- step through an analysis
- agree on solutions
- stop problem-solving.

These various methods of interaction can be used in interactions that have a more or less collaborative nature. That is, the cognitive work being accomplished can be predominantly individual or it can emerge from the interaction in which participant contributions build on each other to produce results that cannot be attributed to specific participants but only to the group at large.

The group of individuals

A given math chat log can be ambiguous as to whether it should be analyzed as a set of contributions from individual thinkers or whether it should be analyzed as a group accomplishment. Often, it is helpful to view it both ways and to see an intertwining of these two perspectives at work (Stahl, 2006a).

We tried a session where we had students solve standard math problems individually and then had the same students solve the same problems in VMT chat groups. In the group that we tracked, the group not only correctly solved all the problems that were solved by any one member of their group individually, but also solved some that no one did by themselves.

When we first looked at the log of a complicated problem that no individual in the group had been able to solve, it appeared that one student, Mic, who seemed particularly weak in math was clowning around a lot and that another, Cosi, managed to solve the problem herself despite this distraction in the chatroom coming from Mic.

In thinking about why Cosi could solve this problem in the group context but not alone, we noticed that she was not simply solving the problem as one would in isolation (e.g. setting up algebraic equations), but was interacting with the group effort. In particular, Dan, Mic and Hal had set up a certain way of thinking about the problem and of exploring possible solutions, although none of them was able to carry out the approach. Cosi was reflecting on the group approach and repairing problems in its logic. The numbers, words and considerations that she used were supplied by the group and its context of on-going interactive activities and shared meanings.

If we combine the sequence of proposals from Mic, Dan, Hal and Cosi, they fit together much like the cognitive process of an individual problem-solver. Clearly, Cosi made some contributions to the group that were key to the group solution. They were acknowledged as such. Cosi was termed "very smart" – although this could equally well be said of the group as a whole. While no individual in the group could completely see how to solve the problem, everyone contributed to exploring it in a way that rather efficiently led to a solution. In particular, Mic used clowning around as an extremely effective way to facilitate the group process. By joking and laughing a lot, the group relieved some of the pressure to solve a problem that was beyond any individual's reach and to open a social space in which ideas could be put forward without fear of being harshly judged. Through non-threatening forms of critique and repair, the group solved the problem.

Attributing the solution to the group rather than to the sum of the individuals in the group can be motivated by seeing that the construction of mathematical meaning in the solution process was done *across* individuals. That is, meaning was created by means of interactions among individual contributions (postings) to the chat – such as through what are called *adjacency pairs* in conversation analysis – more than by individual postings construed as expressing personal mental representations.

Math proposal adjacency pairs

In an early chat of the VMT project, we observed a repeated pattern of interaction that we have since found to be common in math chats (Stahl, 2006d). Here is an excerpt from that chat (line numbers added; handles anonymized):

```
17   Avr (8:23:27 PM):   i think we have to figure out the height by ourselves
18   Avr (8:23:29 PM):   if possible
19   Pin (8:24:05 PM):   I know how
20   Pin (8:24:09 PM):   draw the altitude
21   Avr (8:24:09 PM):   how?
22   Avr (8:24:15 PM):   right
23   Sup (8:24:19 PM):   proportions?
24   Avr (8:24:19 PM):   this is frustrating
25   Avr (8:24:22 PM):   I don't have enough paper
```

In this log we see several examples of a three-step pattern:

- A proposal bid is made (by Avr in lines 17 and 18) for the group to work on: ("I think we have to . . .").
- The bid is taken up by someone else (Pin in line 19) on behalf of the group: ("I know how").
- There is an elaboration of the proposal by members of the group. The proposed work is begun, often with a secondary proposal for the first sub-step (such as Pin's new proposal bid in line 20).

The third step in this pattern initiates a repeat of the three-step process:

- A proposal bid is made (by Pin in line 20) for the group to work on: ("Draw the altitude").

- An acceptance is made by someone else (Avr in line 22) on behalf of the group: ("Right!").
- There is an elaboration of the proposal by members of the group. The proposed work is begun, often with a secondary proposal for the first sub-step (such as Sup's new proposal bid in line 23).

But here the pattern breaks down. It is unclear to us as analysts what Sup's proposal bid, "Proportions?" is proposing. Nor is it responded to or taken up by the other group members as a proposal. Avr's lines 24 and 25 ignore it and seem to be reporting on Avr's efforts to work on the previous proposal to draw the altitude.

Breakdown situations are often worth analyzing carefully, for they can expose in the breach practices that otherwise go unnoticed, taken for granted in their smooth execution. Our analysis of Sup's "failed proposal" (in Stahl, 2006d) helps to specify – by way of counter-example – conditions that promote successful proposals in math chats: (a) a clear semantic and syntactic structure, (b) careful timing within the sequence of postings, (c) a firm interruption of any other flow of discussion, (d) the elicitation of a response, (e) the specification of work to be done, and (f) a history of helpful contributions. In addition, there are other interaction characteristics and mathematical requirements. For instance, the level of mathematical background knowledge assumed in a proposal must be compatible with the expertise of the participants and the computational methods must correspond with their competencies. *[handwritten margin note: Successful proposals]*

We call the three-step pattern described above a *math proposal adjacency pair*. It seems to be a common interaction pattern in collaborative problem-solving of mathematics in our chats. We call this a form of "adjacency pair" in keeping with conversation-analysis terminology, even though in chat logs the two parts of the pair may not appear adjacent due to the complexities of chat postings: e.g. line 22 responds to line 20, with line 21 intervening as a delayed response to line 19. As we see in other chats, however, not all student groups adopt this method of making math proposals.

Deictic referencing and threading

The more we study chat logs, the more we see how interwoven the postings are with each other and with the holistic gestalt of the interactional context that they form. There are many ways in which a posting can reference elements of its context. The importance of such indexicality to creating shared meaning was stressed by Garfinkel (1967). Vygotsky also noted the central role of pointing for mediating intersubjectivity in his analysis of the genesis of the infant-and-mother's pointing gesture (1978, p. 56). Our past analysis of face-to-face collaboration emphasized that spoken utterances in collaborative settings tend to be elliptical, indexical and projective ways of referencing previous utterances, the conversational context and anticipated responses (Stahl, 2006b, ch. 12). So we provide support for pointing in chat.

We recently adapted VMT-Chat (Mühlpfordt & Stahl, 2007), a chat environment that not only includes a shared whiteboard, but has functionality for referencing areas of the whiteboard from chat postings and for referencing previous postings (see Figure 12.1). The shared whiteboard is necessary for supporting most geometry problems. Sharing drawings is not enough; students must be able to reference specific objects or areas in the drawing. The whiteboard also provides opportunities to post text where it will not scroll away. The graphical references (see the blue line from a selected posting to an area of the drawing) can also be used to reference one or more previous postings from a new posting, in order to make the threads of responses clearer in the midst of "chat confusion" (Herring, 1999).

In one of our first chats using VMT-Chat, the students engaged in a particularly complex interaction of referencing a figure in the whiteboard whose mathematics they wanted to explore (Stahl, 2006c). Here is the chat log from Figure 12.1:

1	*ImH:*	what is the area of this shape? [*REF TO WHITEBOARD*]
2	*Jas:*	which shape?
3	*ImH:*	whoops
4	*Imh:*	ahh!
5	*Jas:*	kinda like this one? [*REF TO WHITEBOARD*]

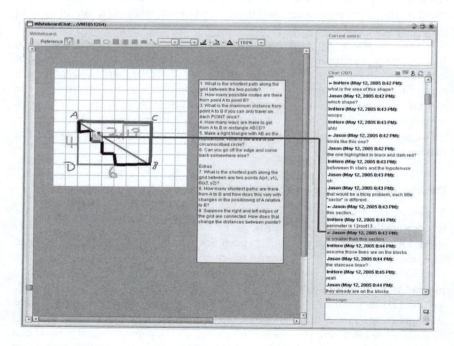

Figure 12.1 Screen view of VMT-Chat with referencing. Line 12 of the chat is selected

6	*Jas:*	the one highlighted in black and dark red?
7	*ImH:*	between the stairs and the hypotenuse
8	*Jas:*	oh
9	*Jas:*	that would be a tricky problem, each little "sector" is different
10	*Jas:*	this section [*REF TO WHITEBOARD*]
11	*ImH:*	perimeter is 12root3
12	*Jas:*	is smaller than this section [*REF TO WHITEBOARD*]
13	*ImH:*	assume those lines are on the blocks
14	*Jas:*	the staircase lines?
15	*ImH:*	yea
16	*Jas:*	they already are on the blocks

Line 1 of the chat textually references an abstract characteristic of a complex form in the whiteboard: "*the area* of *this* shape." The software function to support this reference failed, presumably because the student, ImH, was not experienced in using it and did not cause the graphical reference line to point to anything in the drawing. With line 5, Jas provides a demo of how to use the referencing tool. Using the tool's line, a definite textual reference ("*this* one") and the use of line color and thickness in the drawing, lines 5 and 6 propose an area to act as the topic of the chat. Line 7 makes explicit in text the definition of a sub-area of the proposed area. Line 8 accepts the new definition and line 9 starts to work on the problem concerning this area. Line 9 references the problem as "that" and notes that it is tricky because the area defined does not consist of standard forms whose area would be easy to compute and add up. It refers to the non-uniform sub-areas as little "sectors." Line 10 then uses the referencing tool to highlight (roughly) one of these little sectors or "sections." Line 12 continues line 10, but is interrupted in the chat log by line 11, a failed proposal bid by ImH. The chat excerpt continues to reference particular line segments using deictic pronouns and articles as well as a growing vocabulary of mathematical objects of concern: sectors, sections, lines, blocks.

Progress is made slowly in the collaborative exploration of mathematical relationships, but having a shared drawing helps considerably. The students use multiple textual and graphical means to reach a shared understanding of mathematical objects that they find interesting but hard to define. In this excerpt, we start to get a sense of the complex ways in which brief textual postings weave dense webs of relationships among each other and with other elements of the collaborative context in order to co-construct understanding of meaningful artifacts in a virtual social world.

Small groups and group practices

In order to accomplish their work and learning, people often form themselves into small groups and dyads oriented to a joint problem, group task or shared object (Engeström & Toiviainen, this volume; Wegerif & De Laat, this volume). In the VMT project, we look at the ways in which people form effective groups to accomplish the object of their activity. For instance, one person might engage in explanatory narrative and engage others as audience or might offer a proposal on how to proceed and elicit a group acceptance or challenge. One might joke or tease in order to engage and sustain others in a joint effort. Alternatively, one might point to an object and construe it as a problem to be understood and solved by a group. Once a group is constituted, similar group practices are used to make shared sense of the joint activities and available artifacts.

Group practices are typically established, shared and taken for granted within a culture. When innovative technologies and pedagogies open up new circumstances, participants in the new environments must often make sense of their unaccustomed situation and develop creative new or adapted practices, leading their fellow participants to adopt the proposed practices. In the VMT project, we put students into virtual worlds where the usual institutional practices of school, business or face-to-face sociality are largely missing. We observe how they manage and we respond to their difficulties with new designs to support their group activity and cognition.

Of course, our approach represents only one possible research perspective. It is also possible to focus on individual trajectories (psychology) or on larger social constructs (e.g. activity structures or communities of practice). In certain respects, group practices and group cognition provide a foundation upon which the other views can be built, for example, through internalization or structuralization. For the VMT project, this approach – concerned with the practices of group cognition – has proven useful in providing guidance and understanding for the iterative design process.

References

Çakir, M. P., Xhafa, F., Zhou, N., and Stahl, G. (2005). *Thread-based Analysis of Patterns of Collaborative Interaction in Chat*. Paper presented at the international conference on AI in Education (AIED 2005), Amsterdam, Netherlands.

Garcia, A. and Jacobs, J. B. (1998). The Interactional Organization of Computer Mediated Communication in the College Classroom. *Qualitative Sociology*, 21(3), 299–317.

Garfinkel, H. (1967). *Studies in Ethnomethodology*. Englewood Cliffs, NJ: Prentice-Hall.

Herring, S. (1999). Interactional Coherence in CMC. *Journal of Computer Mediated Communication*, 4(4).

Jordan, B. and Henderson, A. (1995). Interaction Analysis: Foundations and practice. *Journal of the Learning Sciences*, 4(1), 39–103.

Koschmann, T., Stahl, G., and Zemel, A. (2006). The Video Analyst's Manifesto (or the Implications of Garfinkel's Policies for Studying Instructional Practice in Design-based Research). In R. Goldman, R. Pea, B. Barron and S. Derry (eds), *Video Research in the Learning Sciences*.

Livingston, E. (1986). *The Ethnomethodological Foundations of Mathematics*. London: Routledge & Kegan Paul.

Livingston, E. (1987). *Making Sense of Ethnomethodology*. London: Routledge & Kegan Paul.

Livingston, E. (1995). *An Anthropology of Reading*. Bloomington, IN: Indiana University Press.

Lockhart, P. (2009). *A Mathematician's Lament: How school cheats us out of our most fascinating and imaginative art forms*. New York: Bellevue Literary Press.

Moss, J. and Beatty, R. A. (2006). Knowledge Building in Mathematics: Supporting collaborative learning in pattern problems. *International Journal of Computer-supported Collaborative Learning (ijCSCL)*, 1(4), 441–466.

Mühlpfordt, M. and Stahl, G. (2007). The Integration of Synchronous Communication Across Dual Interaction Spaces. In C. Chinn, G. Erkens and S. Puntambekar (eds), *The Proceedings of CSCL 2007: Of mice, minds, and society (CSCL 2007)*. New Brunswick, NJ.

O'Neill, J. and Martin, D. (2003). *Text Chat in Action*. Paper presented at the ACM Conference on Groupware (GROUP 2003), Sanibel Island, Florida.

Sacks, H. (1992). *Lectures on Conversation*. Oxford: Blackwell.

Sacks, H., Schegloff, E. A., and Jefferson, G. (1974). A Simplest Systematics for the Organization of Turn-taking for Conversation. *Language*, 50(4), 696–735.

Sfard, A. (2008). *Thinking as Communicating: Human development, the growth of discourses and mathematizing*. Cambridge: Cambridge University Press.

Stahl, G. (2006a). Analyzing and Designing the Group Cognitive Experience. *International Journal of Cooperative Information Systems (IJCIS)*, 15, 157–178.

Stahl, G. (2006b). *Group Cognition: Computer support for building collaborative knowledge*. Cambridge, MA: MIT Press.

Stahl, G. (2006c). Supporting Group Cognition in an Online Math Community: A cognitive tool for small-group referencing in text chat. *Journal of Educational Computing Research*, 35(2), 103–122.

Stahl, G. (2006d). Sustaining Group Cognition in a Math Chat Environment. *Research and Practice in Technology Enhanced Learning (RPTEL)*, 1(2), 85–113.

Stahl, G. (2007). *Meaning Making in CSCL: Conditions and preconditions for cognitive processes by groups*. Paper presented at the international conference on Computer-supported Collaborative Learning (CSCL '07), New Brunswick, NJ: ISLS.

Stahl, G. (2009). *Studying Virtual Math Teams*. New York: Springer.

Stahl, G. (2010). Group Cognition as a Foundation for the New Science of Learning. In M. S. Khine and I. M. Saleh (eds), *New Science of Learning: Computers, cognition and collaboration in education*. New York: Springer.

Stahl, G., Koschmann, T., and Suthers, D. (2006). Computer-supported Collaborative Learning: An historical perspective. In R. K. Sawyer (ed.), *Cambridge Handbook of the Learning Sciences* (pp. 409–426). Cambridge: Cambridge University Press.

Vygotsky, L. (1978 [1930]). *Mind in Society*. Cambridge, MA: Harvard University Press.

Zemel, A. and Çakir, M. P. (2009). Reading's Work in VMT. In G. Stahl (ed.), *Studying Virtual Math Teams* (pp. 261–276). New York: Springer.

Chapter 13

Changing objects in knowledge-creation practices

Andreas Lund and Trond Eiliv Hauge

Ours is a knowledge-creating civilization.

Scardamalia & Bereiter (2006, p. 97)

Introduction

In this chapter we examine how a small group of learners (aged 17) go beyond the limits of their previous and existing knowledge and how they engage in processes of collective knowledge creation. In this case, they seek to make sense of a tragic incident: the hostage situation and ensuing battle between Chechen rebels and Russian soldiers at School No. 1, in Beslan, where 344 people, 186 school children among them, died (September 2004). As Paavola and Hakkarainen (2005) point out, there is little or fragmentary empirical evidence of young learners engaging in knowledge creation. Our aim is therefore to contribute to this field of required research by examining the relations between knowledge-creation activity and its object. The rationale is that knowledge creation is seen as vital in responding to the challenges of the knowledge society and in increasing the overall intellectual capital of schools (Hargreaves, 2003; Scardamalia & Bereiter, 2006). Also, the notion of knowledge creation has recently been introduced as a third, main metaphor of learning (Hakkarainen, Palonen, Paavola, & Lehtinen, 2004; Paavola & Hakkarainen, 2005), the other two being the acquisition metaphor and the participation metaphor (Sfard, 1998).

However, knowledge creation does not necessarily mean historically new knowledge but may, for instance, be related to the position of learners in a school; how they go about developing insights that are new to *them* (Paavola & Hakkarainen, 2005). In the current study, we approach knowledge creation as emerging through interaction with social, semiotic and material resources. Within this framework, we argue that analyzing and understanding the relations between activity and its object(s) is of vital importance for pedagogic practice. In particular, we consider the object(s) of the activity as crucial in processes where learners face something new, where they have to make sense of a phenomenon that appears ill-defined, enigmatic, or impenetrable.

In order to examine such processes we first connect the concept of knowledge creation to object-oriented activity. The object is one of the most distinctive aspects of Cultural Historical Activity Theory (CHAT) (Stetsenko, 2005) or even the cornerstone of it (Kaptelinin, 2005b) since it provides direction to the collective activity. CHAT gives us conceptual tools to understand object-oriented processes (Engeström, 1987; Engeström, Miettinen, & Punamäki, 1999; Leont'ev, 1978; see also Hakkarainen, Lallimo, Toikka & White, this volume; Muukkonen, Lakkala & Paavola, this volume).

Activity Theory – conceptual tools

In the current study it is the notion of a shared object in particular that will be pursued. Objects are not stable or fixed but are culturally produced. Consequently, they may be perceived differently across individuals and groups and change as they become part of diverse learning activities. As this will affect the outcome of an activity, we ask – and examine – how the object of specific learning activities influences collective knowledge-creation practices. We do this by first elaborating on the notion of the object. The Beslan case is then used to address the role of the object at an empirical level. Finally, we discuss some implications of object-oriented activity that aims to capture new phenomena. In the discussion the object will be pursued in some detail in order to determine how we can conceptualize it as well as bridge the singular instance of the Beslan case with more general implications for educational practice. In particular, knowledge creation is sought conceptualized in terms of epistemic artifacts and epistemic agency; that is how cultural tools and participants' activities are responsible for or conducive to knowledge creation.

Shared object as important

The object

Institutional education revolves around curricula with their aims, goals, or targets. These are often formulated as levels to obtain, skills to master, or competencies to demonstrate. As such, they may appear somewhat abstract, fixed, and static and lend themselves to measurement in terms of grades. However, these notions do not necessarily tell us much about the activities that constitute such competencies. The object, on the other hand, is intrinsically linked to the activity and can, as a consequence, be used analytically to examine how learners seek to orient themselves towards demands that emerge. The object affords empirical analysis of how activity is structured over time and the human, institutional and material resources that delimit such activity.

object So What?

In CHAT the object has a dual nature; it is material as well as ideational. This dual but inseparable character becomes more explicit when translating from Russian and into other languages (English among them). Kaptelinin (2005a) captures this duality when he refers to one aspect as the material *object*; as projecting an external world on the mind. Another aspect is how the object is formed through and gives direction to activities – this latter quality referred to as (in Russian) *predmet*. Thus, *object* and *predmet* mutually constitute the theoretical construct that we here call object. The former is a realization (e.g. an equation, an essay, a building) while the latter embodies the direction and types of activities involved (e.g. exploration,

Product r Processes

negotiation, joint production); the former holds product features while the latter holds process features. Also, this latter aspect gives a collective, dynamic and non-finite quality to the object.

Object provides direction + focus

The object of an activity can thus be said to crystallize certain features of the activity and at the same time give direction to activity. It is constantly evolving and changing due to its partly material nature and partly social construction (Foot, 2002). Consequently, it may also appear slippery and may (at least temporarily) fade in and out of focus for the collective activity. As it is always embedded in and constructed by a cultural-historical activity, the object "determines the horizon of possible actions" (Engeström, 1999, p. 381).

In the case of the empirical study that follows we will now make use of the concept of the object to examine a group of learners' collective efforts at understanding and presenting a phenomenon that is beyond the limits of their existing knowledge. Their object, making sense of a complex ethical and political issue, is partly material in the form of different representations of the group's insights.

Shared object

Since the object of the group we follow is collectively constructed in their project work, it needs to be *shared* in order not to materialize as fragmented or self-contradictory. A shared object does not imply that it is identically perceived by participants in an activity but that it is the locus of common interests or motives and holds past experiences as well as future expectations (Matusov, 1996; 2001). Hakkarainen, Palonen, Paavola and Lehtinen (2004) place the shared object at the center of collective, knowledge-creating activities. Shared objects are developed collaboratively, they do not just exist as some common ground for communication. They do not just emerge from harmonious workflow but from disturbances, ruptures and breakdowns that force participants to reflect on the object of the activity. One type of disturbance may occur when the intended and the instantiated object (Kaptelinin & Nardi, 2006) do not conflate; the intended object may be threatened by substitute objects (e.g. artifacts) that take the center of attention. Object-oriented activity is mediated by cultural tools – mental and material – and the relations between such tools and the intended object can be problematic for learners to handle through enactment and representation (Wertsch, 1998).

Knowledge construction processes

In a knowledge-construction activity, the object is not yet "there"; that is, it must be created by those who engage in the object-oriented activity. In the case study that follows we see how a small group of learners (which also constitutes the unit of analysis) struggles to pursue and construct such an object in order to share it with the rest of the class.

Case: Beslan – School No. I

Background and method

As was noted in the introduction, there is only fragmentary empirical evidence of young learners engaging in collective knowledge-creation and innovation. This is somewhat surprising considering the fact that issues with such a "future" quality have been addressed in education as well as in working life (Cope & Kalantzis, 2000; Gee, Hull, & Lankshear, 1996; Hakkarainen *et al.*, 2004; Hargreaves, 1999; Scardamalia & Bereiter, 2006; Wells & Claxton, 2002). One common concern seems to be the need to align practices in schooling with practices in modern working life as well as in research.

One response to these challenges can be seen in the continued interest in and practicing of project work. In Norway, project work entered the national curriculum in 1987 as an approach to problem-solving. However, Rasmussen (2005) in her review of project work and ICT finds that problem-solving in schools tend to focus on "solving" the task at hand more than advancing knowledge that can prove useful in and across changing contexts and new situations that emerge. Also, few studies focus on the unfolding of learning activity where we can see the relationship between types of participation and the role of mediating artifacts.

Our study addresses the above concerns by analyzing a particular type of project work. Learners explore an ill-defined phenomenon that requires advanced cognitive integration and use of multiple resources in order for the phenomenon to be articulated and made into a shared object. It is important to note that teachers did not actively intervene in the project work after the initial phase but were mainly available for consulting. *[handwritten margin note: Knowledge Construction]*

Hillside Secondary School in Oslo has a tradition – albeit only a few years old – of involving learners in several aspects of teaching, from task construction to the use of wikis and peer-group assessment (Lund, 2006b; Lund & Smørdal, 2006). This policy is part of a larger (successful) school revitalization program for attracting learners. During the school year, learners in the foundation course (three classes, aged about 17) carry out two major interdisciplinary projects. During spring 2005 the point of departure for one project was ethics. Although the teachers decided on this general theme, it was very much left to the learners to give it shape and direction.

In the following we track the project trajectory of a group of four boys as they attempt to make sense of the tragedy in Beslan. We follow this object as it is constructed by and emerges through different activity types the group engages in, such as: information gathering, negotiating diverse views and opinions, and producing various representations of the initially enigmatic and complex phenomena they examine. The material instantiations of the object (poster, presentation, role play) are shared with the rest of the class. The project lasted two weeks and work was mostly done at school but also at home. *[handwritten margin note: learning goals]*

We (researchers) videotaped eight hours of work over the two weeks, audiotaped two sessions as well as short informal talks immediately after sessions, and collected notes, drawings, and material in development as the learners placed this on the school's Learning Management System (LMS). The videotaped material constitutes the primary data in the analysis. Selected sequences from the video recorded corpus were transcribed and analyzed in order to study situated, distributed, and multimodal communication in real time (Jordan & Henderson, 1995). *[handwritten margin note: Research process]*

The concept of the object in this study is used to bridge the gap between the lived situation (making sense of a seemingly inexplicable tragedy) and what can be said about it (the analytical account). The particular is not sought generalized or de-contextualized in a strict sense but indicates what is possible given certain cultural-historical affordances. This is why we argue that our analysis can be used not only to examine the object on a conceptual level but also to inform a discussion on implications for practice.

Approaching the object

At Hillside, a project is always kicked off by a so-called Planning, Integration, Evaluation (PIE) meeting. Such a meeting is attended by two learner representatives from each of the three classes (foundation courses) and one teacher from each class – altogether nine people. It is an institutionalized practice and one which can be seen as the first stage of negotiating a potentially shared object. The teachers first introduce the broad theme they have decided on, an ethical dilemma, and seek the learner representatives' approval. This is, as a rule, a straightforward procedure because the theme is typically open and lends itself to a wide variety of approaches from the learners.

In the PIE meeting the theme is first approached in a brainstorming session. Ideas are brought forward in the form of keywords on Post-it notes. These notes are placed on the table for all to see and in no particular system. It is a high-paced activity that usually goes on for 10–15 minutes or until the generation of ideas slows down. In this case about 60 ideas are jotted down and placed in front of all. The keywords span topics such as ethics in business life, personal consumption, animal testing, solidarity, and sex and violence in movies. From this diverse material topics are sought, extracted, bounded, and made more visible by organizing ideas in categories. In this phase the teachers actively help learners find a handful of logical categories with titles such as "medicine," "war," business life," and "personal responsibility," but mostly as discussion partners. Before the PIE meeting ends, the teachers check whether there are any doubts or ambiguities.

The six representatives bring the overall theme and the categories back to their three classes in order to "sell" the ideas and the categories that now have a series of keywords attached. In these three classes a number of small groups (3–5 learners) choose a category and use the keywords to articulate an ethical dilemma to be pursued. From this moment on the object is developed, negotiated and transformed over time and by collectives in the form of small groups but also on a larger collective level in the form of classes. Thus, the object accounts for how learners position themselves towards the task over time.

The object that so far is represented in the shape of categories consisting of collections of Post-it notes, now gradually takes on other forms and shapes within the horizon of possibilities afforded by the object. Across the various groups in the three foundation courses we see considerable variation as learners turn to various resources, from the production of a video film dramatizing the use of capital punishment to a documentary discussing the use of food additives. The object is gradually embedded in diverse material representations and productions (i.e. as *object*) while at the same time it emerges dialogically through the disciplinary discourse the learners engage in (i.e. as *predmet*).

During these activities there are certain guidelines at work. For example, all groups are to produce a poster introducing their particular topic. These posters add up to a poster session where all learners can get an idea about what is to follow in the form of a presentation from other groups. Another scaffolding feature is found in regular meetings between the groups and a teacher. These meetings are intended to spot difficulties and become aware of (lacking) progress.

In one of the groups we find Erik, John, Niels and Ole. They are engrossed in questions pertaining to the justification of war, violence, and terror. It is obvious that the attack on the World Trade Center on September 11, 2001 and the war in Iraq loom large in the background. However, they quickly agree that these issues are so well known that the group cannot add anything of substance – "everyone knows about this," as Erik puts it. John is reminded of another dramatic event in September 2004 when School No. 1 in Beslan was attacked by Chechens. After a tense hostage situation, a gunfight between Russian security forces and Chechen rebels resulted in 344 dead, among them 186 children. Everyone in the group has heard about the tragedy and knows that there is a historical conflict in the background, but they know nothing else. This means that from the outset the object for this group may appear to be somewhat vague.

The phenomenon, about to emerge as the object of their joint activity, appears enigmatic and blurred at this stage. They decide to examine the tragedy and present it in three different formats; first the mandatory poster, next a PowerPoint presentation for the rest of the class, which serves as an introduction to the main outcome – a role play in the form of a dramatized TV debate between representatives from Russia and the Chechen rebels. The group's intended outcome is for this staged debate to be followed by a real debate by the whole class. Ideally, the combination of the representations and the class debate would become the shared object for the whole class.

The group decides on a title for their project, "Chechnya – terrorism or struggle for liberation?" which serves as a first articulation of the object. The title is accompanied by an artifact in the shape of an organizational chart (Figure 13.1) that depicts how they aim to work out this approach in more detail.[1] The headline and the chart give the group a collective direction for the ensuing activities while at the same time the group works at giving the object material shape as they increasingly develop an understanding of it.

The object as activity

The process of transforming the object from a historical and complex phenomenon into current and manageable representations equals a process of knowledge creation for the learners. For example, the tragedy in Beslan has not made its way

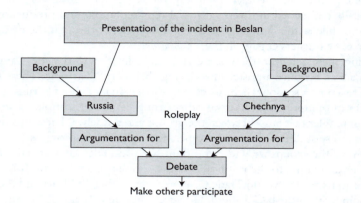

Figure 13.1 Organizational chart (translated) for the project made by learners in the initial phase of the project

into "authorized" accounts in, for example, encyclopedia or history books. The implication is that the construction of this object to greater extent relies on the group's capacity to navigate among unauthorized and often conflicting reports. In their efforts to give shape to the object, they choose cultural tools such as the search engine Google and the World Wide Web.

On the one hand these cultural tools facilitate the process and make the object visible; on the other hand they come with a price (Wertsch, 1998). A familiar experience for teachers is to witness how learners waste time online from faulty or poorly developed search algorithms. In the following short excerpt, Niels has failed to find the border countries of Chechnya due to a misspelling of the name. John seizes his keyboard and, incidentally, keys in the exact same algorithm that Niels now recognizes as unproductive:

John:	You just have to search for "Cheshnya" [sic], for . . .
Niels:	Nonono – no, no, no – noooo
John:	[(using keyboard while Niels speaks and uses mouse) Go to "Russia," errr . . . (pause)
Nils:	Yeah, there (both staring at screen)
John:	(surprised): Oh!
Niels:	Yes, here is "borders with" and then "no name"

The short excerpt shows a situation in which the learners end up with no information. It happens quite often and with the effect that the object slips away for the time it takes to repair a faulty search algorithm. At other times the object appears fragmented or blurred due to information overload or contradictory sources. Video recordings from the two project weeks reveal how the group struggle to make sense of bewildering and often contradictory information strive to keep to correct orthography. English as well as Norwegian (they use both languages) challenge our spelling competence with words such as Chechnya (No: Tsjetsjenia) and Shamil Basayev (the Chechen separatist leader who was mistakenly reported killed at the time of the project work but was later killed in an explosion on July 10, 2006).

As the group develops more precision in its pursuit and construction of the object and becomes more experienced in coordinating their actions they also develop a more comprehensive picture of the phenomenon under study. A few days into the project the following exchange takes place (the three boys watch the same web page):

Niels: Should I publish this one?
John: [What does *autonomous* mean?
Erik: [there you have pictures too
Nils: No, that's . . .
John: [Andreas (= researcher), what does *autonomous* mean? (all simultaneously turn their heads towards the researcher)

This is one example that their initial focus on facts such as borders and cities and repeated discussions on physical acts of terror has become broadened by a more conceptual framing of the object (Vygotsky, 1986). The concept of *autonomy* emerges as a central issue in the conflict between Russians and Chechen separatists, and one for which the learners need adult guidance in order to acknowledge its implications. In the group a lot of the ensuing work revolves around this concept, suggesting that it serves as a conceptual artifact that mediates a deeper understanding of what is at stake in the conflict.

Indication of knowledge creating processes can also be found in episodes where mediating artifacts are intimately linked to the group's dialogic approach (Bakhtin, 2000; Kostogriz, 2005; Wegerif, 2000). For example, it becomes increasingly apparent that the group members do not necessarily have identical interpretations of the object. When the following episode starts, all group members have been searching for background information on the conflict between Russia and Chechnya. The video recordings reveal that often learners together focus on one group member's screen, that they share or switch keyboards, and that they rapidly discuss each other's findings. Ole, however, has been working at a separate work station a few feet away from the three classmates. At one point, Niels brings up the website of the Norwegian Helsinki Committee (www.nhc.no/php/):

Niels: Yes! (points to screen) Here's the whole thing! The Norwegian Helsinki Committee, y'know.
Erik: (looks at the voluminous text, ironic voice) Yes, go through everything, Niels. I'm sure this will be a nice read.

All three learners intensely study Niels's screen. They discuss what would be relevant to include in their work. Opinions and views start to form:

John:	The Chechens have been oppressed and killed and abused and raped and . . . kidnapped
Erik:	I almost think it's easier to – hehe (nervous laughter) – sympathize with the Chechens
John:	Yes . . . so do I, in fact I think it's easy to sympathize with the Chechens now. Just think . . . look at all *that* . . . (studying screen, becomes excited) there, you see!
Ole:	(leaving his work station to join the three) John, John!
Niels:	(in response to John) Yes, that's just what I'm saying
Ole:	John!
John:	Yes
Ole:	This (referring to the Beslan tragedy) is not the only thing the Chechens have done, they blew up the headquarters used by Moscow in Chechnya, that Russia used in Chechnya
John:	When?
Ole:	In December 2002, they blew up (inaudible)
John:	We have found an *insanely* good page here (Ole moves to watch the screen, all four study intensely)

In the dialogue and the activity that constitute this episode we see how the shared object holds a potential for multiple interpretations. To the learners, it presents a horizon of possible understandings, not a fixed point of "truth" or "plain facts." The dual nature of the object, its materiality and its activity-oriented qualities, can be located in John's exclamation "there you see!"; it indexes the website that serves as a temporarily shared artifact and mediates his emerging acknowledgement of Chechen suffering. On the other hand, Ole's critical comments serve to illustrate the complex character of the object. In this short episode of dialogue and artifact-mediated knowledge-advancement we see how the group seeks to coordinate their interpretations by drawing on one particular resource at the end of the above excerpt. During the project many such episodes and situations arise. The group meticulously aggregates, discusses and develops material to be converted into the various representations of the object; the poster, the PowerPoint presentation, and the staged TV debate.

By following the group's efforts we have so far seen how the group first approached the larger assignment and identified their object and, in this section, how the object is further constructed through dialogue and exploratory and artifact-mediated activity. Through material and social mediation the object is transformed from a historical, enigmatic phenomenon into a contemporary representation that the learners can handle and make sense of. To grasp what happened at School No. 1 in Beslan, and why, gradually emerges as an object that exists beyond a fragmented, provoking, and seemingly irrational incident. In the final stage of the project this process now materializes in different products.

The object as product

At the end of the two-week project period the object materializes in three distinctive shapes. First there is the poster, which serves as an introduction to the topic. The group is quite satisfied with its poster; it shows the tragedy in Beslan but focuses on essentials and background information and without unnecessary gory detail. Next, the group has produced a PowerPoint presentation with Niels giving the spoken commentary. This is also factual and non-speculative, but does not pose questions or challenge views that might provoke discussion. Finally, there is the role play in the form of the TV debate. The debate is built around a meeting between the Russian Minister of the Interior (Niels) and the Chechen rebel leader Shamil Basayev (John). Erik serves as a political commentator while Ole has the role of the Russian TV anchorman, guiding the discussion. For about 15 minutes the discussion is performed in front of the rest of the class.

In this final and most ambitious representation of the object the participants struggle to give direction and continuity to the debate. The program host favors provocation and polarization to fact-seeking and informed questioning. Basayev (John) appears in camouflage outfit complete with balaclava, gun belt, and pistol in the studio. The minister (Erik) is dressed in suit and tie, as is the host (Ole). Copying a particular form of tabloid TV debate, four-letter words, provocations, and exclamations dominate. Finally, the whole show comes to an unresolved end. The format (the TV debate) and the artifacts (stage props) dominate and threaten to replace the original object in this most important and conclusive phase.

This indecisive finale makes its mark on the ensuing plenary debate. The group is met by aggressive questioning by their peers; and classmates are harsh in their criticism. They believe that instead of conveying insight on a special ethical dilemma, the group's televised debate degenerated into a tabloid squabble and cheap effects. Only sporadically the group needs to answer questions that pertain to the intended object.

After the presentation the group withdraws to a corner of the classroom, disappointed by the performance as well as the outcome of the debate. Niels (the Russian minister of the interior) blames himself for turning the debate into a disconnected show dominated by verbal abuse, only to be followed by similarly critical self-assessment by other group members. When questioned by the researcher how they assess their contribution, the group unanimously states that the content they intended to present was lost to the audience. They go on at some length analyzing what they ought to have done differently.

Implications for practice: objects, artifacts, and activity

In the introduction we raised the issue of the relations between the object of activity and collective knowledge-creation. The boys in the group faced a demanding and seemingly contradictory phenomenon. In making this the object of their activity they also were forced to go beyond everyday ethical contemplation, emotionally as well as intellectually. They did so by developing dialogue and multiple perspectives as well as drawing on available resources. However, this proved to be a demanding process. There are several implications, which we discuss in the following.

For pedagogical practice the case shows how important it is to be aware of the many aspects of the object; how it can be instantiated and how it is intrinsically linked to the type of ongoing activity. Throughout the assignment the object shifts as the type of activity shifts. In the exploratory first phase it appears as slippery and nearly impossible to pin down. By searching and compiling information, learners gradually come to acknowledge the object's multifarious character but it is represented in only loosely connected bits and pieces gleaned from multiple and often contradictory sources.

In the next phase, the object is developed as learners engage in negotiations as to what it means for those involved in the conflict as well as for themselves, as external investigators. Conceptual development and dialogic approaches do not reduce the compound object to a "fact" that learners agree on, but challenge their understanding of it and its implications. Occasionally such progress can be seen as qualitative leaps as when an artifact such as the Helsinki Committee's website mediates their acknowledgement of the conflict's historical roots.

In the final phase we see how the activity type moves from exploration and negotiation to presentation. Consequently the object is also affected. The activity reveals that it is just as important to identify the impact of non-productive interactions and strategies; how objects may become blurred by information overload, how artifacts intended to mediate object orientation in fact threaten to substitute the object. For example, the content of the role play was corrupted by the learners' fixation with costumes, props, and abusive language that did not serve knowledge-advancement purposes. Thus, during this phase of the project the object changed for the group and slipped away for the rest of the class. We see a contradiction in the activity system, a conflict at the object level where the result is that it ceases to structure the activity of the group in its attempt to realize a shared object. Such problems may disturb or even destroy the original object-oriented activity. But reflection on such disruptions can also bring about renewed activity of knowledge-creation; they represent opportunities for knowledge-advancement. When the role-play features threatened to replace the intended object of conveying insight in an ethical dilemma we witnessed a breakdown. However, this breakdown also resulted in response from peers that called for a return to the intended object. Within the group it led to reflection, self-criticism – indications of such a reorientation.

Together, the above activity types prompt the question as to what kind of object that emerges as learners cross boundaries from the known to the unknown. Hakkarainen (2006) analyzes various types of objects and in activity-theoretical terms. He lists several types of objects such as technical objects, network objects (e.g. Wikipedia, www.wikipedia.org), fluid or virtual objects (e.g. 3D-design environments), "fire" objects (messy and constantly changing), and epistemic objects. Typical of epistemic objects is that the focus is "on issues that are currently beyond the agents' knowledge and understanding and at the edge of the epistemic horizon" *epistemic objects* (Hakkarainen, 2006, p. 17) and that they are "open-ended projections oriented to something that does not yet exist, or to what we do not yet know for sure" (Miettinen & Virkkunen, 2005, p. 438). Thus, the notion of an epistemic object dovetails with the knowledge-creation metaphor. We argue that the object in the Beslan case study belongs to the epistemic object category, since it involves understanding a phenomenon on the edge of the learners' horizon. However, as the case study indicates, there are also "fire" aspects at play as the object changes with the activity types that construct it.

But the activity oriented towards the epistemic object also involves mediating artifacts. When such artifacts are employed in the purpose of knowledge creation they take on the attributes of epistemic artifacts, "tools that serve in the further advancement of knowledge" (Scardamalia & Bereiter, 2006, p. 99). These arti-facts can be conceptual (notions, models, theories) or material (representations, enactments). Both have a "feedforward effect" (ibid.), which implies that new knowledge enables the creation of yet newer knowledge, i.e. a spiraling process of emergentism. For example, in the Beslan case study the concept of *autonomy* served as an epistemic artifact that advanced the group's knowledge of what was at the heart of the conflict while the Helsinki Committee website served to mediate its broader historical-political context.

When learners do succeed in knowledge-creation practices it is, of course, not just a result of appropriating epistemic artifacts but as a consequence of taking on responsibility for knowledge advancement. Scardamalia and Bereiter (2006) also point to the control participants have over "the whole range of components of knowledge building" (p. 106). A mediated knowledge-creation process is also a process of tensions and contradictions between agents and cultural tools (Wertsch, 1991, 1998). Thus, artifacts will only serve epistemic purposes when appropriated through learners' epistemic agency.

Our case shows that epistemic agency is extremely demanding when facing a new and bewildering phenomenon. We have in previous sections pointed to the fact that teachers after the initial PIE meeting played a modest role in the knowledge-creation activity and only in a consulting role at agreed intervals. After the partly failed debate, one of the teachers sought out the group while they contemplated their missed opportunity, gave words of comfort and encouragement, and pointed to the fact that what they set out to do was very difficult and ambitious; making sense of and conveying to their peers complex, disputed, and (for the majority) new knowledge. He also reminded them that during one of the consultations he pointed out the difficulties inherent in representing the topic in the form of a televised debate. The teacher concluded by suggesting that their collective effort counted as an average performance and achievement. None of the participants objected to or complained about this preliminary assessment.

While these types of teacher scaffolding are valuable, we also see that learners were very much left to their own resources in crucial stages and moments in their efforts to construct a shared, epistemic object. Thus, we can label the Beslan case

A
Need for
guidance

as one of discovery or exploration with minimal guidance. In a survey article Kirschner, Sweller and Clark (2006) have shown that more emphasis on guidance and instruction is conducive to learning outcomes. Although they do not explicitly address knowledge-creation, and their position is more cognitive than sociocultural, we find their argument to be very much relevant for us. For instance, conflicting objects would stand a better chance of being discovered and resources that function as epistemic and object-oriented artifacts might be put to better use. To spot

"teachable
moments"

the "teachable moments" for knowledge construction emerges as one type of pedagogical expertise to be enacted in offline as well as offline learning environments (for some approaches, see Edwards, Gilroy, & Hartley, 2002; Lakkala *et al.*, 2001; Lankshear, Snyder & Green, 2000; Lund, 2004, 2006a; Lund & Smørdal, 2006; Rasmussen, 2005).

This does not mean that the object in the project work on Beslan was lost. Despite the unproductive role play and debate, the object lived on in the group's reflective talk after the presentation. The empirical data reveals how learners gradually make important distinctions and develop a conceptual orientation towards the phenomenon they have set out to understand and make visible. However, to what extent the learners become carriers of new insights and new knowledge of the historical and current forces that may explode into the kind of violence witnessed in Beslan remains unanswered and would need a more longitudinal study that would relate this project work to subsequent ones. Similarly, Foot (2002) concludes that we need to study objects over time, from different perspectives and different types of data. She encapsulates this approach by suggesting that, "Perhaps the most illuminating questions a researcher in pursuit of object understanding

Research
question

can ask are toward what is the collective activity oriented, and what is energizing it?" (p. 148). Our study has been intended to evoke one type of response to these questions.

Conclusion

In this chapter we have addressed what we take to be a crucial competence in the knowledge age; the capacity to take on challenges that involve going beyond existing knowledge and that, due to their complexity, require collective efforts. Consequently, we have analyzed a situation where given knowledge and the canon of representation (cf. the introduction to this volume) are challenged. In a case study involving ethics and terror we have analyzed classroom interactions; how a group of young learners sought to develop a shared epistemic object through dialogue, use of artifacts and epistemic agency. We also saw how this involved going beyond the primary site of learning, the classroom, and venturing into complex online information sources and genres from popular media culture. In such processes, the notion of the object in CHAT has emerged as a key concept in order to understand and support knowledge-creation. In particular, the object's dual character – it holds material as well as activity aspects – has served to examine how learners construct and advance their knowledge.

However, the study has also shown that objects change as the activity changes and can be threatened by intruding artifacts that replace the original and intended object. Since there are, to the best of our knowledge, few empirical studies of collective knowledge-creation in schooling, we argue that our findings reveal the need to develop theory as well as practice to foster and sustain collective object-orientation in school settings. How teachers can prepare for and participate in collective-knowledge advancement emerges as one particularly crucial challenge.

Note

1   The organizational chart is a reproduction of a handwritten drawing with Norwegian text. Except for a minor typographical error in the original, it is an exact copy.

References

Bakhtin, M. M. (2000). *The Dialogic Imagination: Four essays by M. M. Bakhtin*. Austin, TX: University of Texas Press.

Cope, B. and Kalantzis, M. (eds). (2000). *Multiliteracies: Literacy learning and the design of social futures*. London and New York: Routledge.

Edwards, A., Gilroy, P., and Hartley, D. (2002). *Rethinking Teacher Education: Collaborative responses to uncertainty*. London: Routledge Falmer.

Engeström, Y. (1987). *Learning by Expanding: An activity – theoretical approach to developmental research*. Helsinki: Orienta-konsultit.

Engeström, Y. (1999). Innovative Learning in Work Teams: Analyzing cycles of knowledge creation in practice. In Y. Engeström, R. Miettinen and R. Punamäki (eds), *Perspectives on Activity Theory* (pp. 377–404). Cambridge and New York: Cambridge University Press.

Engeström, Y., Miettinen, R., and Punamäki, R. (eds). (1999). *Perspectives on Activity Theory*. Cambridge: Cambridge University Press.

Foot, K. A. (2002). Pursuing an Evolving Object: A case study in object formation and identification. *Mind, Culture and Activity*, 9, 132–149.

Gee, J. P., Hull, G., and Lankshear, C. (1996). *The New Work Order: Behind the language of the new capitalism*. Sydney: Allen and Unwin.

Hakkarainen, K. (2006). *Scientific Challenges of Knowledge-Practices Laboratory (KP-Lab)* (Working paper). Helsinki: University of Helsinki.

Hakkarainen, K., Palonen, T., Paavola, S., and Lehtinen, E. (2004). *Communities of Networked Expertise*. Amsterdam: Elsevier/Earli.

Hargreaves, A. (2003). *Teaching in the Knowledge Society: Education in the age of insecurity*. Maidenhead and Philadelphia, PA: Open University Press.

Hargreaves, D. (1999). The Knowledge Creating School. *British Journal of Educational Studies*, 47, 122–144.

Jordan, B. and Henderson, A. (1995). Interaction Analysis: Foundation and practice. *Journal of the Learning Sciences*, 4, 39–103.

Kaptelinin, V. (2005a). The Object of Activity: Making sense of the sense-maker. *Mind, Culture and Activity*, 12, 4–18.

Kaptelinin, V. (2005b). Perspectives on the Object of Activity. *Mind, Culture and Activity*, 12, 1–3.

Kaptelinin, V. and Nardi, B. A. (2006). *Acting with Technology: Activity theory and interaction design*. Cambridge, MA, and London: MIT Press.

Kirschner, P. A., Sweller, J., and Clark, R. E. (2006). Why Minimal Guidance During Instruction Does Not Work: An analysis of the failure of constructivist, dicovery, problem-based, experiential, and inquiry-based teaching. *Educational Psychologist*, 41, 75–86.

Kostogriz, A. (2005). Dialogical Imagination of (Inter)cultural Space: Rethinking the semi-otic ecology of second language and literacy learning. In J. K. Hall, G. Vitanova and L. Marchenkova (eds), *Dialogue with Bakhtin on Second and Foreign Language Learning* (pp. 189–210). Mahwah, N.J. and London: Lawrence Erlbaum Associates.

Kvale, S. (1996). *InterViews*. Thousand Oaks, CA: Sage.

Lakkala, M., Muukkonen, H., Ilomäki, L., Lallimo, J., Niemivirta, M., and Hakkarainen, K. (2001). Approaches for Analyzing Tutor's Role in a Networked Inquiry Discourse. In P. Dillenbourg and A. Eurelings (eds), *First European Conference on CSCL* (pp. 389–396). Maastricht: Maastricht McLuhan Institute.

Lankshear, C., Snyder, I., and Green, B. (2000). *Teachers and Technoliteracy: Managing literacy, technology and learning in schools*. St Leonards, NSW: Allen and Unwin.

Leont'ev, A. N. (1978). *Activity, Consciousness and Personality*. Englewood Cliffs, NJ: Prentice Hall.

Lund, A. (2004). Teachers as Agents of Change: ICTs and a reconsideration of teacher expertise. In T. Fitzpatrick (ed.), *Information and Communication Technologies in the Teaching and Learning of Foreign Languages: State-of-the-art, needs and perspectives. Analytical survey* (pp. 27–37). Moscow: UNESCO Institute for Information Technologies in Education.

Lund, A. (2006a). The Multiple Contexts of Online Language Teaching. *Language Teaching Research*, 10, 181–204.

Lund, A. (2006b). WIKI i Klasserommet: Individuelle og kollektive praksiser [WIKI in the Classroom: Individual and collective practices]. *Norsk pedagogisk tidsskrift*, 90, 274–288.

Lund, A. (forthcoming 2008). Assessment Made Visible: Individual and collective practices. *Mind, Culture, and Activity*, 14.

Lund, A. and Smørdal, O. (2006). Is There a Space for the Teacher in a Wiki? In *Proceedings of the 2006 International Symposium on Wikis* (*WikiSym '06*) (pp. 37–46). Odense, Denmark: ACM Press.

Matusov, E. (1996). Intersubjectivity Without Agreement. *Mind, Culture and Activity*, 3, 25–45.

Matusov, E. (2001). Intersubjectivity as a Way of Informing Teaching Design for a Community of Learners' Classroom. *Teaching and Teacher Education*, 17, 383–402.

Miettinen, R. and Virkkunen, J. (2005). Epistemic Objects, Artefacts and Organizational Change. *Organization*, 12, 437–456.

Paavola, S. and Hakkarainen, K. (2005). The Knowledge Creation Metaphor – An Emergent Epistemological Approach to Learning. *Science and Education*, 14, 535–557.

Rasmussen, I. (2005). *Project Work and ICT. A study of learning as trajectories of participation*. Unpublished doctoral dissertation, University of Oslo, Oslo.

Scardamalia, M. and Bereiter, C. (2006). Knowledge Building: Theory, pedagogy, and technology. In R. K. Sawyer (ed.), *The Cambridge Handbook of the Learning Sciences* (pp. 97–115). Cambridge: Cambridge University Press.

Sfard, A. (1998). On Two Metaphors for Learning and the Dangers of Choosing Just One. *Educational Researcher*, 27, 4–13.

" Learning as trajectories of participation "

Stetsenko, A. (2005). Activity as Object-Related: Resolving the dichotomy of individual and collective planes of activity. *Mind, Culture, and Activity, 12*, 70–88.

Vygotsky, L. S. (1986). *Thought and Language* (A. Kozulin, Trans.). Cambridge, MA: MIT Press.

Wegerif, R. (2000). Applying a Dialogical Model of Reason in the Classroom. In R. Joiner, K. Littleton, D. Faulkner and D. Miell (eds), *Rethinking Collaborative Learning* (pp. 119–136). London: Free Association Books.

Wells, G. and Claxton, G. (eds). (2002). *Learning for Life in the 21st Century: Sociocultural perspectives on the future of education*. Oxford: Blackwell Publishing.

Wertsch, J. V. (1991). *Voices of the Mind: A sociocultural approach to mediated action*. Cambridge, MA: Harvard University Press.

Wertsch, J. V. (1998). *Mind As Action*. Oxford: Oxford University Press.

Learning trajectories as a foundation for learning design.

Taxonomies
Development   Processes ⎡ cognitive
Identity   ⎢ Social / Emotional
                         ⎣ Novice / Expert

Chapter 14

Socio-cognitive tension in collaborative working relations

Jerry Andriessen, Michael Baker and Chiel van der Puil

Introduction

In this book, learning is studied in relation to the (institutional) context in which it is taking place, examining the tensions occurring when something new is introduced into a learning environment, as well as their potential for learning (Yamazumi, Engeström & Daniels, 2005). At the dialogic level, one can observe participants confronting each other, in a more or less rational manner, by means of argumentation. Elsewhere (Andriessen, Baker & Suthers, 2003) we stated that participants confront 'each other', rather than, for example, being confronted with 'a societal question to be debated', as a means of insisting on the primacy of interpersonal confrontation over so-called 'cognitive confrontation'. Such a postulate turns, nevertheless, on a view of the microsocial and cognitive dimensions of interaction as two faces of the same coin of sociocognition. In this chapter we propose to explore confrontations at the socio-cognitive level by looking at the role of argumentation in collaborative interaction in learning settings. We choose to consider the specific case of argumentative interaction for two main and related reasons. First, it is perhaps the most salient place to study the interplay of socio- and cognitive dimensions of collective activity, since confrontation of ideas can lead to making views explicit, and this can be associated with confrontation of persons and identities. Everyone knows that a difference of ideas and opinions can 'degrade' into an emotionally charged dispute where mutual respect, self- and other-images are at stake; and also, that if arguers can deal successfully with the interpersonal aspect, they may in fact develop their ideas. Second, some progress has been made over the last ten years on understanding how argumentative interaction leads to cognitive change during cooperative learning (see several contributions in Andriessen, Baker & Suthers, 2003). One particular form of such learning is termed 'broadening and deepening a space of debate', whereby the result is a richer representation of ideas (Baker, Quignard, Lund & Séjourné, 2003; van Amelsvoort, 2006). This last description of learning is what we have in mind when we study the learning effects of argumentation (Andriessen, 2005).

We do not want to claim that these micro-conflicts are the atoms of community progress; but they can be important ingredients of it. Such progress can take place along radically different timescales, from seconds to weeks, months and years. The relationship between socio-cognitive confrontation and progress is also not necessarily contiguous in time: a particular confrontation may be the source of an intrapersonal dialogue taking place over a time interval that goes well beyond the source interpersonal dialogue.

When two students work together in an educational context, they characteristically work on assignments selected by their teacher, with partners that they may know as persons, but not necessarily as collaborators. Under such conditions, the students will be uncertain concerning the way they are going to work together. The issue at stake is that collaborating students, whether they are arguing or not, have at least two interdependent 'jobs' to do: solving the problem, including resolving cognitive conflicts, and maintaining a workable interpersonal relationship. If an appropriate interpersonal relationship is not maintained, students may not collaborate effectively on the cognitive level. If maintaining the interpersonal relationship requires too much effort (whether agreeable or problematic), then the other job will not get done.

interpersonal work and problem work

While precise theories and models of cognitive change are becoming more developed, this is less true with respect to the 'socio' side of sociocognition, in the case of argumentation. We would like to focus on the socio-cognitive dimension of what we call the *collaborative working relationship* (van der Puil, Andriessen & Kanselaar, 2004). The collaborative working relationship (CWR) is a notion we propose in order to characterize the manner and degree of maturity in which people collaborate in an educational context.

Collaborative Working Relationship

We examine a case of collaborative interaction between two 17-year-old students,[1] with the goal of presenting an illustration of the socio-cognitive tensions that emerge during that interaction, discussing how such tensions relate to learning in a particular educational setting and context. In particular, we elaborate on the idea of argumentative interactions leading to a type of learning called 'broadening and deepening a space of debate'. We show that the computer interface covers direct social emotional communication, which now takes place mainly through the argumentative interactions about the domain. This means that the learning experience can be seen as a game of tension/relaxation.[2]

Socio-cognitive tensions

In what follows, we discuss argumentation and collaborative learning, leading up to a presentation of work in progress that aims to develop an interaction-analysis method for understanding the interplay of socio- and cognitive dimensions of computer-mediated argumentative interaction in an educational setting. Our concluding discussion attempts to propose perspectives for our largely programmatic work.

Argumentation and collaborative learning in context

Collaboration and educational practice

Collaboration between individuals can serve numerous purposes, including learning contexts. What is seen as successful collaborative learning in such contexts is very particular to each specific situation. Neither in educational practice, nor in the research community, has a shared notion of successful collaboration been established (Dillenbourg, 1999). In addition, ideas about what kinds of knowledge can be considered valuable targets for learning are changing, in theory (Lipponen, Hakkarainen & Paavola, 2004), and in practice (Kollias, Mamalougos, Vamvakoussi, Lakkala & Vosniadu, 2005). For evaluating collaboration in educational practice this means that not only do desired outcomes in a specific situation (and the ways they are supposed to be achieved) have to be clear, but also the significance of such outcomes in the learning context, for researchers and educational practitioners.

To illustrate how a learning context affects the goals for collaborative learning we use the scenario concept, proposed by Andriessen and Sandberg (1999). The educational context for collaborative learning can be arranged or interpreted in a manner corresponding with a specific pedagogical scenario, which represents a basic set of values, beliefs, goals, and assumptions about learning. Within a scenario, these basic reference points are 'translated' into pedagogical models, guidelines, and practices. Andriessen and Sandberg (1999) identify three distinct learning scenarios for collaborative learning, namely transmission, studio, and negotiation. The identification of different scenarios assumes that a group of learners can study a similar knowledge domain along different dimensions.

The most important differences between the scenarios concern their conceptions of the purpose of education. In the transmission scenario, education should strive for the acquisition of knowledge and skills that are generalizable across domains. The main source of knowledge is the teacher (authority), and negotiation mainly involves dealing with the norms and values of this teacher. The studio scenario upholds crucially different conceptions concerning the goals of education. Students here acquire metacognitive knowledge and skills requiring (among other things) the social and practical skills to collaborate with peers as well as with coaches. In the negotiation scenario, students, in groups, are involved in activities that characterize and transform their practices. In the negotiation scenario, transformation involves careful negotiation, being absorbed in the process of co-elaboration of knowledge, by mindful and responsible use of discourse. The following table[3] shows the pedagogical dimensions of the scenarios.

Whereas learners' collaboration may evolve with each experience, learning itself also evolves, from transmission-reception towards learner management of knowledge and progress (Andriessen, Baker, & Suthers, 2003). Evaluation of collaboration at the individual level is insufficient; collaboration is a characteristic of the group, and it is to this that the notion 'collaborative relation' applies. In

Table 14.1 Different scenarios and different learning goals

Mission	Transmission	Studio	Negotiation
Acquisition of knowledge and skills	Drill & practice, lectures and reading	Collaborative, project-based learning	Knowledge transformation
Learning to learn	Generalization	Metacognition & reflection	Discursive practice
Learning to participate	Acquiring expertise	Social & practical skills	Negotiate and be responsible

this chapter, we mainly examine the minimal group: the dyad.

By introducing collaborative learning tasks that focus on knowledge elaboration and transformation in the regular classroom environment (based on knowledge transmission), a discrepancy between two cultures is created, namely: the traditional perception of learning and the interactive culture of collaborative learning. Because of this discrepancy, learners need to adapt to this different culture (van der Puil & Andriessen, in press). Contrary to the traditional learning situation in which a teacher dominates and structures the practice of learning, and where all participants know what is expected of them, there is often no tradition of collaborative learning that can be observed in the everyday classroom. In other words, participants, when brought into a collaborative situation, do not have a clear idea about what their role is, and thus about how to behave. This perspective means that when students are placed in a collaborative situation, they do not by definition engage in collaborative learning.

Very divergent situations appear to be termed collaborative learning (e.g. 'knowledge-building community', Bereiter 2003, 'negotiation scenario', Andriessen, Baker & Suthers, 2003; Andriessen & Sandberg, 1999). Some are closely related to the traditional situation by, for instance, attributing a central role to the teacher (cf. Stahl, 2005), while others diverge so much that collaboration per se is rarely achieved. What generally binds these perspectives together is that learning is in one way or another perceived of as a shared active construction of knowledge that depends on the interaction between participants. Collaborative learning is used in this chapter as a qualification of a peer relation, rather than as an attribute of a situation or an electronic environment. The purpose of collaborative learning, in a long-term perspective, is the development of a professional culture of collaboration, that is, collaboration embedded in practices fostering negotiation of knowledge (cf. Allwood, Traum, & Jokinen, 2001). The extent to which collaboration is successful from a shorter perspective is contingent on the particular demands of the situation.

Argumentation and regulation of collaboration

While argumentation in interaction can enable knowledge co-construction (Baker, 1999), it should rather be seen as a process that primarily favours knowledge 'tuning' or restructuring, such as in the case of conceptual differentiation (Baker, 2002). Our working hypothesis in the current paper is that in addition to this cognitive tuning, we suppose, at the socio-cognitive level, a related process of 'relationship tuning'. A study reported by van der Puil, Andriessen and Kanselaar (2004) shows that after an argumentative exchange in a collaborative learning task, social repair was necessary, possibly to reinstate the collaborative working relationship. Hence, tuning at the cognitive level (conceptual differentiation) may be related to tuning at the socio-cognitive level (maintaining the working relationship).

To explain the complex processes happening during collaboration, a framework was developed that identified four regulatory forces acting upon the interaction: (a) self-regulation, or participants reflecting and acting upon achieving personal goals; (b) task regulation, where participants are conforming to task and contextual constraints; (c) mutual regulation, where participants are pressed to share and explain in a social context (Bunt, 1995; Baker, 1999) auto-regulation, or the regulatory force determining contributions coming forth from relational and interactional conventions and collaborative history. The manner in which these regulatory forces operate depends on the educational context in a broader sense, setting the objectives, norms and sanctions for the collaborative work, and providing the possibilities (scaffolds, rewards) for collaboration and building up relationships.

Van der Puil *et al.* (2004) distinguished progressive and conservative directions that regulation may take. The progressive force aims at working towards achieving the task goal, while the conservative regulatory forces primarily pay attention to what has happened before, especially (small) conflicts and misunderstandings. In a learning context in which collaboration still has to mature, at the relational level, the regulatory forces mutual regulation and auto-regulation could be described as conservative; self-regulation and task regulation as progressive. The latter two relational forces can be manipulated by instruction, to achieve certain pedagogical goals, thereby changing the development of the interaction (van der Puil *et al.*, 2004, p. 183).

Within such an approach, argumentation can have a deregulating effect on the collaboration, which needs to be regulated in order for collaboration to proceed. Regulation can be conceived as a multifaceted process during which several objectives are at stake at the same time: learning, communication, interaction, efficient time-management, and so on. It can be assumed that regulatory forces achieve equilibrium in mature collaboration, or that several levels of equilibrium may exist during the development of collaboration.

A proposal for a tension/relaxation analysis

In order to get a different understanding about the relation between argumentation and learning, from a socio-cognitive point of view, we propose to take up the issue of the collaborative working relationship. Two students, brought together into a new learning situation, have to establish a working relationship in order to be able to effectively collaborate and communicate by interaction. In the initial stages, such a relationship is characterized by understanding of the situation, knowledge of the subject matter, and, most importantly, their image of the other's estimation and respect. We suppose that the greater the difference in knowledge, intentions, ways of communication, and so on, the greater is the tension created in the working relationship, but also, the more potential mutual gain is present in the situation. On the other hand, when too much tension predominates the collaboration, this is at the cost of attention to the domain of reference. Tension should be released during collaboration, in order to focus attention on learning and problem-solving. Although there are personality characteristics involved in tension/relaxation management, our focus is on the interaction itself, and how potential tension is dealt with by the participants.

Initial stage of CWR

We suppose that in a dialogue, utterances have potential tension-raising or relaxing qualities, depending on various contextual characteristics (see also Bales, 1950). In addition, such qualities may have an effect on the context itself: it can become more tense or relaxed. Supposedly, participants in a collaborative learning situation create a working relationship which functions according to some desired level of tension. At the level of interaction, one may suppose that participants contribute to this process by their utterances. In the context of computer-mediated communication, there are no other means for conveying intentions or communicating meaning than through written text. Van der Puil, Andriessen and Kanselaar (2004) report some evidence that shows that the social dimension of communication gets lost when students communicate through chat. We do not suppose that negotiation at the social plane gets lost, but it may take place at a level that has not yet been captured in descriptive analyses (cf. Stahl, this volume).

As a first step, also inspired by previously discussed readings, we can look at the potential tension/relaxing of utterances likely to occur in argumentative interactions. First, the argumentative utterances, as described by Muntigl and Turnbull (1998), fall into the aggravation category, with different degrees of intensity: irrelevancy claims (so what?), challenges (why?), contradictions (no, I don't), and counterclaims (yes, but . . .). One may propose counterparts that reduce tension, but not necessarily as opposite pairs. Concessions, constructive contributions that build on what the other has said, or arriving at a compromise may count as tension-reducing contributions. Explicit tension can be raised by personal attacks and sarcasm, while humour and polite consideration might serve as tension reducers. At the level of reactions, one may suppose that interrupting (if the CMC system allows that), ignoring what the other says, raise tension, while giving the floor or explicitly reacting to the other may relax tension. On the other hand, persisting with a 'tense topic' aggravates that tension. Table 14.2 provides an overview of these tentative, probably highly content- and context-sensitive, tension/relaxation potentials of utterances in a learning dialogue.

Tension creating + tension reducing utterances

Table 14.2 A proposal for tension/relaxation analysis criteria

Tension	Relaxation	Confirmation of CWR
Irrelevancy claims	Concession	Self/other disclosure
Challenges	Building	Dyadic pronouns
Counterclaims	Compromise	Motivating the other
Claim against doxa (contentious)		Joint purpose
Taking stance		
Questions		
Requests (for justification or clarification)		
Personal attacks	Humour	Conversational equality
Sarcasm	Consideration	
Interrupting	Giving a turn/time	Future orientation
Ignoring	Focusing	
Persisting	Change of focus	

In order to test the feasibility of these ideas, we examine an example of a collaboration interaction on these terms.

An analysis of the socio-cognitive dimension in electronic argumentative interactions

Our initial question was to examine the relationship between the face-threatening quality of argumentative contributions and the depth of argumentation. To that goal, we examined a case of a collaborative learning dialogue between two students, which is part of an existing set of dialogues, a corpus assembled in the SCALE project by the French partner in Lyon (Baker, Quignard, Lund, & Séjourné, 2003). This project was about using collaborative graphs to support computer-mediated argumentation (see, for example, van Amelsvoort, Andriessen & Kanselaar, 2007). We take this specific dyad, because it has been extensively analyzed as an interesting case of broadening and deepening by collaborative argumentation (Baker & Séjourné, 2007), and is also saliently interesting along the socio-relational dimension.

Task sequence

The task sequence that the students followed has four phases:

- Instruction: students are introduced to the notions used in argumentation (opinion, claim, argument, argumentative relation . . .) and experiment with the computer environment (a simple chat tool in this case).
- Preparation for debate: the students are requested to read a number of texts

about genetically modified organisms (GMO), which include the opinions of various participants in the debate. They are asked to fill in a table in order to represent (the space of debate) these opinions in terms of their argumentative characteristics. Then, they individually produce a text answering the question: 'Should we allow production of GMO?'

- Debate phase: the teacher pairs students which each other and they have to chat (by synchronous computer interface) in order to deepen their understanding of the domain for improving their texts. At the end of the session they are asked to summarize the main points of agreement and difference.
- Consolidation phase: the students are asked to improve their texts written during phase two, in the light of what was discussed.

The interaction case revisited

We will present the complete debate between Carla and Betty. Baker and Séjourné (2007) conclude that globally, Betty won the debate in the sense that she was able to counter the different arguments in favour of GMOs, raised by her partner. Carla mainly reacted to what Betty proposed, instead of defending her position. Only Betty raised counter arguments. Nevertheless, Carla changed the opinion expressed in her text afterwards to 'in favour'. This seems in opposition to her conceding to Betty's argumentation during the debate, and also against her including a number of those counterarguments in her own revised text. This leaves us with a question: why does Carla change her opinion in the opposite direction of her concessions during the debate? To what extent was she really expressing her own opinions? Or to what extent did she do that in the revised text? One possible answer is to be found in our subsequent analysis of the socio-cognitive dimension. In our analysis, followed through sequentially from the beginning to the end of the interaction, we shall attempt to be predictive, i.e. to state whether tension needs to be released or increased, given the state of T/R so far. These predictions can then be validated in the ensuing analysis.

Sequence I

The collaboration starts with a focus on interaction and social relation, showing that these participants know each other quite well, since we see personal, playful jokes. When Carla hesitates to clarify her opinion (which is that she is unclear), Betty teases her (31).

From the point of view of the cognitive dimension of argumentation, there is no tension increase, there is no opposition of opinion: only Carla has stated her opinion, and it is an open 'neither for nor against' one.

In terms of relaxation, this is playful humour. The only small cloud on the horizon is Betty's slight sarcasm (31, 40). Now it is time to get down to the task, which is a debate, so we expect tension to rise . . .

	Speaker	Utterance	Argumentation	CWR
10	Betty	Hi		
11	Carla	Hiya		
12	Betty	how's it goin?		R: conventional/ politeness
13	Carla	good and you?		
14	Betty	ok, so what about GMOs?		T: question
Q	Carla	and you?		R: giving a turn
16	Betty	no, you first		
17	Carla	you little rascal		R: humour
18	Betty	why?		
19	Carla	you're vicious		R: humour
20	Betty	oh don't get excited		
21	Carla	i'm just kidding		R: consideration
22	Betty	of course i know		R: self disclosure
23	Betty	Ouououou		
24	Carla	no but seriously i'm half fig half grape	opinion	R: focusing
25	Carla	no but seriously i'm half fig half grape		
26	Betty	what?		
27	Betty	,,,		
28	Betty	????????		
29	Carla	i'm not for and I'm not against	opinion	
30	Carla	i have a shared opinion		
31	Betty	that's a good argument		T: mild sarcasm
32	Carla	what i really think is . . .;		
33	Betty	it's		
34	Carla	just a second I'm thinking		
35	Betty	take your time		R: giving time
36	Carla	Thanks		R: politeness
37	Betty	no problem		
38	Carla	i'm sick of this		Self disclosure
39	Carla	There		
40	Betty	of what to think?		T: question

Sequence 2

	Speaker	Utterance	Argumentation	T/R
41	Carla	there'll be a better production thus less famine	Argument	T: taking stance
42	Betty	yeah but if it's bad for the organism, then it comes down to the same thing	Counterargument	T: challenge
43	Carla	it will maybe permit us to create vaccinations against mucovicidose and i think that that is maybe a good thing	Argument	
44	Carla	there'll be – pollution and this is essential if we don't want to die	Argument	
45	Betty	yeah but they can create it without making all food and the rest genetically modified	Counterargument	T: challenge

After some hesitation, Carla comes up with an argument (41: GMO → better production → less hunger). Betty immediately replies with a counterclaim (42: yes, but . . .), but it is a very forceful counterclaim, suggesting that Carla did not produce a serious argument. This is supposed to raise the tension of the relationship: Betty suggests Carla has produced an irrelevant argument. Muntigl and Turnbull suggest now that Carla is supposed to react with aggressive support for her own claim when she feels threatened, while she could counter Betty's argument when she feels less aggravated. In this case she comes up with another argument for her own claim (43: maybe, maybe we can develop new vaccinations), which may support the face-losing character of Betty's counterclaim which suggests irrelevancy.

Note that we interpret arguments from the point of view of the social dimension, i.e. we do not infer from explicit acknowledgements of loss of face, or increased tension, but rather from the type of contribution, its content as a possible irrelevancy claim. Our storyline reads that Carla tries another argument, in order to avoid further embarrassment. Betty brushes it aside, as she had done previously. It is the style that counts. She does not seem to require much effort, but, then again, what she says is also not very constructive.

Carla has lost; Betty demolished her arguments without much further ado; we predict that Carla must 'get her own back'. Tension has built up, it must be released; but before it can be, Carla must re-establish equilibrium in terms of her self-image as competent and intelligent, and present herself as such. She needs to 'score some points' now.

Sequence 3

	Speaker	Utterance	Argumentation	T/R
46	Carla	but tell me i think you're against so explain why to me will you?	Request for challenge (changing burden of proof)	T: Request (for clarification/ justification)
47	Betty	because it's bad for the human organisms	Counterargument	T: challenge
48	Carla	answer me		T: time constraint
49	Betty	and if we start with plants, in 10 years at least it will be human beings' turn	Counterargument	T: challenge
50	Carla	to be modified?	Request (clarification)	T: Request (clarification)
51	Betty	yeah sure, maybe we'll even be cloned	Counterargument	T: challenge
52	Carla	yes it's true but ya know i am totally against cloning any individual	Concession	R: Concession
53	Betty	so am i of course	Concession	R: Concession

Then, in line 46, Carla tries a different approach: reversing the burden of proof. Quite positively, she asks Betty to explain herself and her position against GMOs. We may suppose that she asks this because Betty needs to explain to her why she considers her arguments as irrelevant, and by explaining she would have reduced the tension, because Carla would have been granted some attention by Betty reacting to her topic. Betty expresses her fear that one day humans will be cloned, but she does not really support that idea. Carla nevertheless concedes.

The previous prediction, that Carla must 'get her own back' is not validated (at least not yet). Here, again, she has had to concede, and this is the second consecutive sequence that she has lost! So in terms of facework, things have got worse for Carla; but in terms of tension/relaxation, this is a sequence that lowers tension, since Carla concedes everything.

We therefore need to make a clear distinction between face loss/preservation and tension/relaxation: it is possible to lose (more) face and yet for tension – as it is manifested in the interaction itself – to remain on a reasonable level: here, tension seems to be balanced by relaxation (concession). This seems to be an early indication for a CWR that appears to be adequate. Despite the fact that Carla lost the last sequence, she is nevertheless able (and forced) to concede this sequence 'gracefully' and reasonably.

We predict that since two sequences have been lost by Carla, yet tension is at a reasonable degree, she must and will get even, but not by a very violent outburst.

Sequence 4

	Speaker	Utterance	Argumentation	T/R
54	Carla	why are you against GMOs? Isn't there a single positive argument in your opinion?	Request (clarification/ justification)	T: request
55	Betty	phhh maybe but nothing has been proved	Counter-argument	T: challenge
56	Betty	for the vaccinations nothing has been proved	Counter-argument	T: persisting
57	Carla	it's obvious that these are nothing but hypotheses at the moment but imagine just one instant if it worked don't you think that it would be a great step for mankind?	Request (clarification/ justification)	T: request
58	Betty	yeah but they can succeed otherwise until now how have we done	Counter-argument	T: counterclaim
59	Carla	if gmos can help in many different domains i can totally for but suggestion: just, domains, but	Argument	R: focusing
60	Betty	but?	Request	T: challenge
61	Carla	just a sec		
62	Betty	and then the flavour and the savour of food could be lost!	Counter-argument	T: challenge
63	Carla	you can't be sure of that!!!!!!!!!	Counter-argument	T: challenge
64	Betty	you can't be either for the vaccines!!!!!!!!!!!!!!!!!!!!	Counter-argument	T: challenge
65	Carla	ok even score	Concession	R: concession

Carla now changes strategy (54): she asks Betty if she is so completely against that she cannot produce a single argument in favour. This is a clever strategy, it would give Carla ammunition to support her own point of view, which then becomes stronger. Betty bluntly refuses: cloning has not been proved. Carla insists, up to the point where she risks tension rising too high on Betty's side as well, which does happen, as indicated by the signals of tension – exclamation marks in 63 and 64. Carla concedes after this, without a similar sign from Betty, but it may be the start of a new strategy.

Betty would only concede when Carla shows some actual proof, of some achievement that would require GMOs. In order to come up with this, Carla has to be knowledgeable in the area, maybe she needs to consult her data sources. This extra effort (because that's what it is) may need some positive motivation on Carla's part, probably the possibility that it may get Betty out of her trench. But is may also be the case that the tension that is building up prevents some clear strategic thinking.

Carla's strategy to get some arguments in favour if GMO from her partner has failed. Tension has risen, but still seems under control. For the next sequence we predict that Carla will try again, or else has to concede again, thereby confirming Betty's domination.

Sequence 5

	Speaker	Utterance	Argumentation	T/R
66	Betty	and after the genes in the human organisms could also be modified	Argument	T: counterclaim
67	Carla	that's not for sure	Counter-argument	T: challenge
68	Betty	if they eat genetically modified food	Counter-argument	
69	Betty	So		T: challenge
70	Carla	it's true that nothing has been proved but if it turned out to be true, and that no problems came of it then the utility would be multiplied by 100000000 . . .	Argumentation	T: counterclaim
71	Betty	and then what about the farmers what's going to happen to them???	Question	T: challenge
72	Betty	and nature what do you with her nothing is stronger than nature herself	Argumentation	T: challenge
73	Carla	every solution begins from hypotheses so why are you closing yourself up in this opinion??????	Counter-argumentation	T: challenge

(continued on next page)

Sequence 5 (continued)

	Speaker	Utterance	Argumentation	T/R
74	Betty	Which opinion?	Question	T: request
75	Carla	it's true that nature is the work of Madam super nature	Concession	R: concession T: sarcasm
76	Betty	oh oh that's so beautiful		T: sarcasm
77	Carla	that you are against but it would be good if you would still admit that if it worked then it would be beneficial for everybody	Argumentation	T: counterclaim
78	Betty	if it worked on what*	Question	T: challenge
79	Betty	i'm telling you that if man starts with the plants, after they going to want to do more and it's going to degenerate and soon we ourselves are going to be genetically modified and after it'll get worse as time goes on . . .	Counter-argumentation	T: contradiction
80	Carla	in the medical domain, in the environment, public health, food, economy	Argumentation	
81	Carla	but I completely agree with you	Concession	R: concession
82	Betty	as far as medicine goes i agree with you but	Concession	R: concession

Some argumentation takes place during this process, which we claim is triggered by Carla's attempts to get recognition for her point of view, without necessarily trying to prove that she is right. Carla is tense, as is shown by the question marks in 73: 'Why are you closing yourself up in this opinion?????' Betty will not move from her stance, and Carla has somewhat saved face by telling her that.

Most arguments are produced by Betty, but she repeats herself a lot. There are some slight concessions in 79 and 80, but the most important contribution to tension/relaxation is in 86, where Carla changes the subject and Betty immediately goes along. In this case, no one's face is threatened, and the neutral state is immediately taken.

Carla is challenging Betty's reasonableness; she is implicitly accusing her of having a rigid point of view: she can say nothing in favour of GMOs, she concedes nothing to Carla, whereas Carla has conceded much, and presented her opinion initially as 'open'.

Sequence 6

	Speaker	Utterance	Argumentation	T/R
83	Carla	c'mon now we have to resume our discussion		R: focusing
84	Betty	for the environment and for food, i would really be surprised	Counter-argumentation	T: persisting
85	Betty	the synthesis is that you are for and i'm against	Conclusion	
86	Carla	(my throat hurts)		R: change of focus
87	Betty	are you sick?		
88	Betty	i wanna sleep!!		
89	Carla	you'll see that this system is put into work all the benefits that it will bring	Argumentation	T: taking a stance
90	Carla	did you know that the prof is going to read our discussion the researcher just told me		R: change of focus
91	Betty	no i'm not as sure as you and for the moment most everybody is against so it's not going to happen right away	Argumentation	T: challenge
92	Betty	no that's not true	Counter-argumentation	T: contradiction
93	Betty	so are you for or against??????	Question	
94	Carla	look it's like piercing in the beginning everybody was against it but then people changed their minds	Argumentation	T: challenge
95	Betty	yes that's a fashion it's not the same this is nature that's on the line and the human organism	Counter-argumentation	T: challenge
96	Carla	i am for j300% in the only case that it doesn't cause any problems but they have to be sure 600%	Conclusion	R: concession
97	Betty	no i'm against 1000	Counter-argumentation	T: contradiction

(*continued on next page*)

Sequence 6 (continued)

	Speaker	Utterance	Argumentation	T/R
98	Betty	%		
99	Carla	you put make-up on though so that's not natural it's more or less the same	Counter-argumentation	T: challenge
100	Betty	i am for		
101	Betty	no it doesn't go into the organism*	Counter-argumentation	T: contradiction
102	Carla	we gotta stop so see ya big kisses bye		R: change focus
103	Betty	ok bye kisses		
104	Carla	Garden~doa~		
105		Carla is no longer with us		
106	Betty	you're gone?		

The previous sequence ended with Carla's concessions – it is Carla all the time who concedes, and by this in fact she is regulating the relationship. Although she is fair to developing her own point of view, she is not able to make Betty change her role as opposing every argument in favour of GMO. When tension gets too high because of that, Carla concedes. Nevertheless, we see that she develops her point of view, perhaps because she is not impressed by the repetitive nature of the opposition. Both contestants are able to adequately grasp their own point of view in a summary statement.

Note the change of strategy of relaxing the tension in 86, a complete change of focus, and Betty immediately follows that lead. After that, although the contenders firmly state their opinions, tension remains released and the debate ends cheerfully, although there is no compromise, and many issues remain unresolved.

Discussion

The girls had a good starting point: a fun, friendly interpersonal relationship. This enabled them to quite frequently disagree (it is known that students commonly avoid this) and to be able to 'live with' a relatively high degree of social tension.

At the beginning of the interaction, they rehearsed standard school arguments, but that were quickly refuted. It was only when the interaction 'got off the ground', and some degree of social tension arose, that they touched on, but did not manage to deepen, two crucial issues for conceptual learning: the nature of scientific proof and the concept of Nature.

Why were they not able to deepen their understanding, despite the good general relationship? There are at least two possibilities: these students do not commonly collaborate in school; they are friends, but have not developed a CWR. Second, a reason may lie in the educational setting; they did not have enough prior knowledge of the GMO topic to be able to collaboratively refine that knowledge. In addition, there is the notion of the efforts invested: why bother if no one is going to rate this?

In this chapter, a related possibility is put forward: they do not deepen because their working relationship does not allow it. That is, they go as deep as the participant with the least motivation decides, because their individual regulation is stronger than their mutual regulation. From an institutional viewpoint, his conception fits within a transmission of knowledge scenario, where individual cognition is preferred over collaborative elaboration. We return to this idea in the concluding section.

Summary of the analysis

When we look at the tension/relaxation pattern, quantified[4] as the number of tension statements minus the number of relaxation statements and argumentation (in the same way quantified as the number of argumentative contributions) over time (Figure 14.1), we seem to observe a complicated pattern.

One can picture this relationship as interweaved, tension increase sometimes seems to follow deepening in argumentation, and on other occasions, since tension takes time to 'die out', it can 'linger on' to the next argumentative deepening and interfere with it. Alternatively, we could say that the argumentation is deepened precisely because of such a high degree of socio-relational tension. Social tension sometimes precedes cognitive conflict: Carla is driven by the desire not to lose face, and therefore generates challenges in argumentation.

There can be a great distance between cognitive conflict and social tension. In a proper collaborative working relationship there should be a harmony between the

Table 14.3 An overview of the main characteristics of the six sequences

Sequence 1	Carla expresses open opinion	Low tension, playful fun
Sequence 2	Betty demolishes all of Carla's arguments	High tension
Sequence 3	Betty argues against, and Carla concedes	Lowered tension
Sequence 4	Carla asks Betty to clarify her ideas, but Betty refuses	High tension
Sequence 5	Carla challenges Betty's reasonableness but has to concede again	High tension
Sequence 6	Change of focus, summary statements	Low tension

two dimensions, which seem separate, but actually depend on each other. Instability is the default situation, and it can go in any direction. In a way we are talking about two separate dimensions: relating to each other (learning to collaborate) and performing a task. In a CWR, people know how to deal with both.

Some conjectures

Within current institutional contexts, often characterized by knowledge transmission, collaborative learning can be seen as two individuals trying to solve a problem, leading to (sometimes unresolved) tensions. We aim to develop a more systematic approach to the tension/relaxation analysis in order to investigate the following claims:

- In some problem-solving interactions, the production of arguments is not driven by participants actively looking for elaboration and better understanding of a domain, but rather by socio-cognitive tensions.
- Some tensions are the result of participants failing to arrive at a common understanding of the assignment and its procedures, or from other major differences between participants that manifest themselves via a different understanding of collaboration and the working relationship.
- The negotiation of the working relationship as it unfolds during electronic interaction, can be described as a narrative, whereby the end is characterized either by tension/relaxation or by explosion.
- Argumentation in most traditional learning situations is interpreted by participants at the socio-cognitive level, and not at the rational cognitive level.

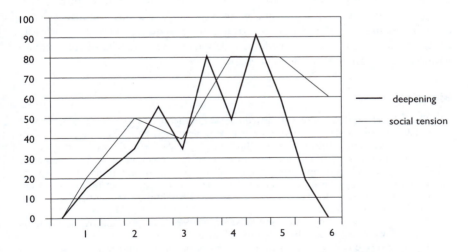

Figure 14.1 Depicting social tension and deepening by argumentation in the six sequences

- Most emotion in these dialogues is manifested in the arguments themselves: in their capacity as tension-aggravation objects.

Conclusion

What about learning in collaboration? We conceived it here as learning in inter-action, under the form of broadening and deepening understanding of a space of debate. This involves increasing cognitive conflict, and thus associated socio-relational conflict, and the other way round. We argued that inappropriate ways of dealing with or managing socio-relational tension will prevent this type of collaborative learning, and perhaps others. Also, we assume that the occurrence and inappropriate dealing with socio-relational tension is characteristic of educational systems focusing on individuals rather than on groups.

In a good CWR participants have learnt to manage the interplay between social and cognitive tensions; such knowledge can have a general aspect (there are some people who are 'good at working in teams'), and it may have an aspect that is specific to the collaborative partner(s) (how can tension be reconciled with that person?).

What constitutes the appropriate level of tension is in part the result of the his-tory of the specific CWR, as part of the educational context and shared personal experience of the participants. Developing a good CWR takes time.

You cannot have collaborative learning without having developed a collaborative relationship. Much collaboration requires establishing a CWR with (un)known partners, trying to understand each other, having to negotiate appropriate roles in specific learning contexts, requiring effort in establishing a shared history.

Our exploratory work presented above can be seen as concrete illustrations of the inseparability of socio-relational and cognitive dimensions of interactions between persons. After all, a person can not be reduced to a pure cognitive proces-sor, whether in interaction with others or not: we all require, and so must provide, consideration as and to persons, within a collaborative working relation, blossoming within an appropriate educational scenario.

Notes

1 The research reported here was carried out within the SCALE project (Internet-based intelligent tool to Support Collaborative Argumentation-based Learning in second-ary schools, March 2001–February 2004, http://www.euroscale.net) funded by the European Community under the 'Information Societies Technology' (IST) Programme. The project studied computer-supported collaborative argumentation-based learning.

2 This notion is in part inspired from work on narrative tension/relaxation structures in Western tonal music, for example, as they are described in the seminal work of Lerdahl and Jackendoff (1983).

3 In comparison with Andriessen and Sandberg (1999), this table and the descriptions of the goals of negotiation have slightly changed.

4 This means of quantifying is, of course, purely notional and illustrative of our analysis approach, at its present state of development. A more satisfying approach would involve estimating the degree of tension increase or decrease of specific types of moves.

References

Andriessen, J. (2005). Arguing to Learn. In: K. Sawyer (ed.) *Handbook of the Learning Sciences* (pp. 443–459). Cambridge: Cambridge University Press.

Andriessen, J., Baker, M. and Suthers, D. (eds). (2003). *Arguing to Learn: Confronting cognitions in computer-supported collaborative learning environments.* Dordrecht: Kluwer Academic Publishers.

Andriessen, J. and Sandberg, J. (1999). Where is Education Heading and How about AI? *International Journal of Artificial Intelligence in Education, 10*, 130–150.

Baker, M. J. (1999). Argumentation and Constructive Interaction. In P. Coirier and J. Andriessen (eds), *Studies in Writing: Vol. 5. Foundations of argumentative text processing* (p. 179 – 202). Amsterdam: University of Amsterdam Press.

Baker, M. J. (2002). Argumentative Interactions, Discursive Operations and Learning to Model in Science. In P. Brna, M. Baker, K. Stenning and A. Tiberghien (eds), *The Role of Communication in Learning to Model* (pp. 303–324). Mahwah, NJ: Lawrence Erlbaum Associates.

Baker, M. J. and Séjourné, A. (2007). L'élaboration de Connaissances chez les Élèves dans un Débat Médiatisé par Ordinateur [Students' Knowledge Elaboration in a Computer-mediated Debate]. In A. Specogna (ed.), *Enseigner dans l'interaction* [Teaching in Interaction], pp. 81–111. Nancy: Presses Universitaires de Nancy.

Baker, M. J., Quignard, M., Lund, K. and Séjourné, A. (2003). Computer-supported Collaborative Learning in the Space of Debate. In B. Wasson, S. Ludvigsen and U. Hoppe (eds), *Designing for Change in Networked Learning Environments: Proceedings of the International Conference on Computer Support for Collaborative Learning, 2003* (pp. 11–20). Dordrecht: Kluwer Academic Publishers.

Bales, R. F. (1950). A Set of Categories for the Analysis of Small Group Interaction. *American Sociological Review, 15*, 257–263.

Bereiter, C. (2003). *Education and Mind in the Knowledge Age.* Mahwah, NJ: Erlbaum.

Brown, P. and Levinson, S. (1987). *Politeness: Some universals in language usage.* Cambridge: Cambridge University Press.

Bunt, H. C. (1955). Dialogical Control Functions and Information Design. In R. J. Beun, M. Baker and M. Reiner (eds), *Dialogue and Instruction: Modeling interaction in intelligent tutoring systems* (pp. 197–214). New York: Springer-Verlag.

Dillenbourg, P. (1999). *Collaborative Learning: Cognitive and computational approaches.* Amsterdam: Pergamon / Elsevier Science.

Kollias, V., Mamalougos, N., Vamvakoussi, X., Lakkala, M. and Vosniadu, S. (2005). Teachers' Attitudes to and Beliefs about Web-based Collaborative Learning Environments in the Context of an International Implementation. *Computers and Education, 45*, 295–315.

Lerdahl, F. and Jackendoff, R. (1983). *A Generative Theory of Tonal Music.* Cambridge, MA: MIT Press.

Lipponen, L., Hakkarainen, K. and Paavola, S. (2004). Practices and Orientations of CSCL. In J.-W. Strijbos, P. A. Kirschner and R. Martens (eds), *What we Know about CSCL and Implementing it in Higher Education* (pp. 31–50). Amsterdam: Kluwer Academic Publishers.

Muntigl, P. and Turnbull, W. (1998). Conversational Structure and Facework in Arguing. *Journal of Pragmatics, 29*, 225–256.

Stahl, G. (2005). *Collaborating with Technology: Mediation of group cognition.* Mahwah, NJ: Lawrence Erlbaum Associates.

Van der Puil, C. Andriessen, J. and Kanselaar, G. (2004). Exploring Relational Regulation in Computer-mediated (Collaborative) Learning Interaction: A developmental perspective. *Cyberpsychology and Behavior, 7*(2), 183–195.

Van der Puil, C. and Andriessen, J. (in press). The Collaborative Relation as the Basis for Learning Interaction. In R. Säljö (ed.), *ICT and the Transformation of Learning Practices.* London: Pergamon/Elsevier.

Van Amelsvoort, M. A. A. (2006) *A Space for Debate: How diagrams support collaborative argumentation-based learning.* Doctoral dissertation, Utrecht University.

Van Amelsvoort, M. andriessen, J. and Kanselaar, G. (2007). Representational Tools in Computer-supported Collaborative Argumentation-based Learning: How dyads work with constructed and inspected argumentative diagrams. *Journal of the Learning Sciences, 16*(4), 485–521.

Yamazumi, K., Engeström, Y. and Daniels, H. (eds). (2005). *New Learning Challenges. Going beyond the industrial age system of school and work.* Osaka: Kansai University Press.

Chapter 15

Productive e-feedback in higher education

Two models and some critical issues

Olga Dysthe, Sølvi Lillejord, Barbara Wasson and Arne Vines

Introduction

In this chapter we investigate one element in the complex web of student learning experiences in higher education that has been shown to be a very important part of the learning process, namely feedback or formative assessment.[1] The introduction of an artifact in a social process, such as technology in education, challenges traditional and unquestioned structural and organisational pedagogical habits (Popkewitz, 1998). Not only must educators learn new ways of communicating with their students; technology itself opens for a re-evaluation of taken-for-granted practices. In this chapter we show how different e-feedback practices may influence student learning.

Several comprehensive meta-reviews of research on feedback have concluded that feedback greatly impacts the quality of student performance and effectively promotes student learning across disciplinary areas, types of outcomes and levels. (Black and Wiliam, 1998; Hattie & Timperley, 2007; Shute, 2008). Feedback, as an integral part of the students' learning process, has the potential to make the process more productive. Summative assessment in the form of a grade is feedback in the sense that it gives information about the 'closeness of fit' between the standard required and the actual student performance, but is inadequate for student improvement.

Traditionally, feedback on student work in progress has either been given orally by face-to-face communication between the teacher and the student(s) or as written comments on student drafts. E-feedback is emerging as a new literacy practice and *how* e-feedback is conducted may have great implications for learning. While a number of basic questions of what constitutes good feedback practices remain the same regardless of technology, the introduction of new information and communication technology into the teaching and learning ecology in higher education raises a plethora of new issues relating to feedback.

We analyse 'productive e-feedback' from a sociocultural perspective with the ambition to show how it ties into a cluster of concepts on activity and transformation. Drawing on examples from the relational process of giving, receiving and utilising feedback in virtual learning environments (VLEs), we will highlight certain critical aspects of this complex relation. The triadic relationship (Fjuk, Sorensen & Wasson, 1999) between pedagogy, technology and institutional issues has inherent opportunities for renewal that may or may not be seized by teachers and students. We use the term 'e-feedback' when ICT is used to provide or organise feedback on student work, by e-mail or through VLEs.[2] Our aim is not only to contribute to the rather sparse theoretical discussion of this new pedagogical genre,[3] but particularly to discuss how different ways of structuring e-feedback lead to different practices and outcomes.

In our perspective, e-feedback must be regarded as a *joint* activity, presupposing interactions between actively participating students and teachers. We use feedback in a broad sense, not only about the formal response-giving activity, but about the whole process, including how students receive and utilise the feedback. The term 'productive' implies a value judgement. In this chapter we discuss what characterises feedback processes that are 'productive' in the sense that they are likely to improve the quality of the material object (the product), for instance, a student text.

Another important question is how feedback processes influence the subject (the students), for instance, their disciplinary understanding, their ability to self-assess, their motivation and agency. We do not aim at causal explanations of, or normative statements about, the relation between process and product. We have performed a theoretically informed re-analysis of two previous case studies at the University of Bergen, one at the Faculty of Law; the second the Department of Education. The theoretical basis for our discussion is sociocultural theory in general and dialogue theory in particular. The re-analysis was conducted by reiterative readings of the empirical material, i.e. interviews with students and teachers, small-scale surveys, evaluation data and student logs.[4] We chose to focus on the meso level, that is, the pedagogical design of the feedback systems and how the sites utilise the potentials of technology. We are concerned with feedback to tasks that require multidimensional and complex answers, not about correct grammar and spelling. In both our sites the students are asked to write quite advanced texts.

Our re-analysis generated two analytic models of dealing with the practice of e-feedback, an 'authoritative model' and a 'dialogic model'.[5] The authoritative model emerges from a transmission view of education, where the teacher 'owns' the knowledge and the student receives it. The authoritative model is vertical, based on the *authority* of the expert, and on the conduit metaphor of communication (Reddy, 1979), and focuses on informing the student of the gap between expectations and performance. The dialogic model is predominantly horizontal, based on a different epistemology where new understandings are created through joint or participatory activities (Lillejord & Dysthe, 2008). It is therefore regarded as important that students gain access to different and even conflicting 'voices', and at the same time develop a sense of ownership and agency of the product. Quality criteria are not communicated as a top-down given, but determined through a negotiating process. A crucial question is what it takes to reduce the 'guessing game' of revision by creating an ongoing dialogue about quality criteria.

In this chapter we address what these two models look like in practice, what part is played by technology, how different epistemological perceptions influence the different practices, and what are 'productive' and 'unproductive' aspects of each model. Because e-feedback is an emerging pedagogical phenomenon, we place it in a wider perspective of theory and research.

A glimpse into the research field of feedback and a brief literature review of e-feedback

Research on feedback exists in several fields: in writing research, where response to student drafts is regarded as a crucial aspect of the writing process (Freedman & Sperling, 1985); in assessment research where the importance of formative assessment has been foregrounded over the last two decades (Sadler, 1989; 1998); in education research on student learning processes; and in linguistics where the interest is predominantly on comments as a text genre. Second-language research has had a strong interest in effective feedback, because foreign language students are particularly dependent on teacher comments and correction of errors (Hyland & Hyland, 2006). Most recently, e-feedback practices have emerged in the research field of technology-enhanced learning (Crook, Gross, & Dymott, 2006). In order to provide background for our two models a glimpse of these research fields is given.

Early theories of feedback in the assessment literature were grounded in behaviouristic stimulus–response theories. The tacit or explicit understanding of feedback in much practice-oriented literature is based on Ramaprasad's (1983) definition: 'Feedback is information about the gap between the actual level and the reference level of a system parameter which is used to alter the gap in some way' (p. 4). From the 1980s, however, writing research was based on cognitive theories of higher mental functions, including models of the feedback process. This research relied heavily on protocol-analysis methods of expert and novice writers to provide data for constructing mental models (Hayes & Flowers, 1980). Bereiter and Scardamalia's (1987) research established the transition from 'knowledge telling' to 'knowledge transformation' as a major goal for feedback and revision. The 'process approach to writing' was initially strongly influenced by the extensive cognitive research on writing, feedback and revision processes (Anson, 1989). The social turn in writing research, particularly influenced by Vygotsky's (1986) theories, changed the focus from the individual writer to sociocultural processes and the contexts of writing (Nystrand, 1992). This also had consequences for how feedback was conceptualised, and the interest of practitioners as well as researchers changed from individual comments on student papers to response groups and peer feedback.

The recent interest in feedback seems to have three different theoretical foundations. The first is predominantly behavioural and focuses on the teacher's or the automated feedback system's (e.g. Mørch et al., 2005) effective delivery of feedback to students. The second is based on constructivism, and emphasises student autonomy and self-regulation as its main goal (Nicol & Macfarlane-Dick, 2006). The third is based on sociocultural perspectives and the importance of dialogic interaction and joint activity (Tannacito, 2004).

While there is a considerable amount of research on traditional feedback practices, there is still relatively little research on e-feedback. Many issues are the same regardless of technology and need to be taken into consideration when introducing a new artifact in a familiar process. A recent meta-study on the effect of feedback on second-language (L2) students' writing, states that changes in writing pedagogy and insights from research studies have transformed feedback practices in general, 'with teachers' written comments now often combined with peer feedback, writing workshops, oral conferences, or computer-delivered feedback' (Hyland & Hyland, 2006, p. 83). If feedback primarily focuses on formal aspects of language, as is often the case in second-language writing, an authoritative model of feedback may be most effective, but when content issues are at stake, a dialogic model is useful for all kinds of learners, as it makes the writer reflect on alternatives.

Advantages of e-feedback reported in research studies

Both synchronous and asynchronous writing networks allow students to take a more active role by asking for feedback when needed instead of waiting for the teachers to find time to provide it. Hyland and Hyland's review summarises many of the known advantages of e-feedback. E-feedback positions itself between oral and written feedback in the sense that it retains much of the informality and immediacy of oral communication, while it has the permanency of written communication that makes it available at any time. There are, however, more studies of feedback as part of online conferencing than about one-to-one e-feedback. This indicates an interest in e-feedback construed to serve the larger purposes of fostering overall communicative competence and language development (Hyland & Hyland, 2006).[6] Student participation in online conferencing was found to foster a sense of community, encourage group knowledge and student participation (Ware & Warschauer, 2006) and offer alternative spaces for academic student involvement because of more democratic power structures and a reduced risk environment (Selfe, 1992). Web-based discussions made student writing transparent, more widely available and thus created audience awareness (Ware, 2004). A case study by Tannacito (2004) of electronic peer response in a composition course showed that students built very close and supportive communities in their electronic peer response groups and good processes resulted in better products. While peer response often mirrors teacher response, Nicol and Milligan, 2006, report on a comprehensive e-feedback project designed to support *alternative* feedback practices in large classes with the use of technology. A major goal of the project was to foster student self-regulation and self-assessment. Considerable gains were found in students' grades.

Some critical issues emerging from the literature

Most of the research studies on e-feedback report advantages over traditional feedback, particularly related to peer involvement. There are, however, a number of critical issues arising from the literature. Peer feedback has long been seen as a way of introducing a dialogic model of feedback, giving more control and agency to students, instead of passive reliance on teacher feedback to fix their writing (Freedman & Sperling, 1985). Several studies show, however, that students are selective about using peer feedback. Connor and Asenavage (1994) claimed that peer feedback made only a marginal difference to student writing. Zhang's (1995) study showed that 75 per cent of 81 college freshmen preferred teacher feedback, and that they trusted teachers as experts but were reluctant to trust their peers. Hyland (2000) also found that students had problems providing quality feedback. Jacobs *et al.* (1998) argue, however, that asking students to choose between teacher and peer feedback is misleading, as they supplement one another. Research also indicates that careful preparation and training in peer response increases the quality and usefulness of peer comments (Sluijsmans, 2002; Zhang, 1995). Training is also likely to benefit student reviewers and make them more critical evaluators of their own texts (Ferris, 2004). Crook, Gross and Dymott (2006) found that students were very vulnerable to e-feedback. Written feedback, given electronically is sensitive to the possibility of misinterpretation due to the lack of synchrony that allows one to modulate and moderate what is said and this must be conveyed in any training.

Concerns have also been raised about the disadvantage of relying on e-feedback for less technologically savvy students. Lindblom-Ylänne and Pihlajamäki (2003) found, for instance, that Finnish students did not like to share drafts with peers in this way. This is confirmed in a study by Blignaut and Lillejord (2006) of students in the South African region. Not surprisingly, a series of studies have shown that e-feedback works best when integrated into the curriculum (Hyland & Hyland, 2006, p. 94). In our own study we document *how* e-feedback is integrated into the whole teaching-learning environment.

Theoretical perspectives

Our two university sites exhibit varying degrees of online community building and varying degrees of student ownership of texts, issues identified in the literature as crucial to feedback processes. We introduce, however, new issues that so far have received little attention, such as how students are enculturated into diverse disciplinary communities and the importance of disagreement in productive learning. Our theoretical perspective is particularly relevant for these issues. In light of sociocultural theory, feedback can only be understood in its cultural context. The theoretical basis of the teaching-learning regime needs to be explored as well as the implications of disciplinary cultures. We will therefore look at the epistemological foundation of the 'authoritative' and the 'dialogic' model of feedback.

A Vygotskyan understanding of intersubjectivity in joint activity is particularly relevant for our discussion of the Law and Education cases.[7] It is based on his theory about interpsychological communication being transformed through processes of participatory appropriation (Rogoff, 1995). Matusov (1998) has pointed out that 'unlike intersubjectivity as sharing, the participatory notion of intersubjectivity is joint-activity oriented rather than individual-oriented' (p. 32). He claims that 'The traditional concept of intersubjectivity as sharing stresses reproductive aspects of learning and culture as a whole at the expense of their productive, creative aspects. This notion of sharing is designed to describe stable, preservative trends in the culture' (p. 33). Rommetveit (1974) theoretised intersubjectivity as a reciprocal perspective focused on the importance of the participants building a 'temporarily shared social reality' (TSSR). As the discourse continues, this shared reality is progressively modified and expanded. His point is not that TSSR is a goal in itself but that it provides a point of departure for the negotiation of meaning when multiple interpretations collide. This is in our view relevant for feedback conceptualised as joint activity, because it involves sharing, but needs to transcend this in order to create new meaning.

Bakhtin's concepts of 'authoritative and inner persuasive word' are particularly useful for understanding our two models of feedback. Bakhtin's dialogism (1981, 1986) represents an alternative analytical perspective and epistemology to monologism, which is still the dominant perspective in many fields (Linell, 2009). Where monologism is concerned with transmission of knowledge, dialogism sees knowledge as emerging from the interaction of voices and is concerned with transformation of understandings (Nystrand, 1992). While feedback has traditionally been conceptualised as the teacher's transmission of the correct standard or norm (authoritative model), in a dialogic model it is a process of gradual, participatory appropriation of the words of others to make them our own:

> The word in language is half someone else's. It becomes 'one's own' only when the speaker populates it with his own intention, his own accent, when he appropriates the word, adapting it to his own semantic and expressive intentions.
>
> (Bakhtin, 1981, p. 293)

In a dialogic perspective, students' revision processes can thus be understood as adapting the words of others to their own intentions, ascribing it their own accent. Obviously, the two perspectives on learning underlying our two models entail different ontologies and will support different practices. Particularly relevant to our discussion is Bakhtin's distinction between 'the authoritative and the inner persuasive word'. The authoritative word demands that the listener acknowledges it as 'the truth'. Because it is hierarchical and distanced, bearing a previous authority, it binds the listener regardless of any power it may have to persuade him or her internally. It does not demand free reflection about its content, but 'our unconditional allegiance' (Bakhtin, 1981, p. 343). Internally persuasive discourse is, in contrast, supported by the power of its argument 'as it is affirmed through assimilation, tightly interwoven with "one's own word"' (p. 345). Central to Bakhtin's notion of the 'internally persuasive word', however, is the tension and struggle between conflicting views and interpretations. This is why the 'dialogic model' becomes particularly important in academic disciplines where truths are contested and where critical thinking and the ability to argue are more important than giving a 'correct' answer.

E-feedback in the learning ecology of two higher educational sites

At the Faculty of Law the teaching-learning practices have been radically reformed during the last six years. Law is an 'argumentative science' and students must be proficient in the oral and written genres used by the professional community of lawyers. Writing and talking are thus not only tools for acquiring disciplinary knowledge, but crucial to the practice of the discipline. 'Law students need to learn how to produce knowledge, not just reproduce set opinions from authorities such as textbooks authors, professors, statutory provisions, and legislators' (Vines & Dysthe, 2009). How students' knowledge-production is put into practice is therefore important. When the Quality Reform of Norwegian higher education[8] was implemented in 2003, the Faculty of Law scaled up a promising model of a technology-enhanced, problem-based teaching and learning environment, where technology is an integral part of the learning architecture and not an add-on.

Our second site is a web-based master's programme at the Department of Education where students learn the genres of the research article and thesis. The master's programme is developed for students who want a part-time study or, for other reasons, do not wish to follow a campus-based programme. As the students only see each other (and the teachers) 1–2 times a year, they interact and learn through a meticulously structured network of assignments, feedback and discussions. The programme is built on sociocultural and dialogical perspectives on learning. A central idea is that the students use peer-feedback to build their own academic self-confidence.

In both sites technology is an indispensable part of the infrastructure for learning (Guribye, 2005) and acts as an artifact for interaction in students' writing processes. Because law has more students than education, the difference in the number of students in the two programmes has consequences for the infrastructural design needed to serve the students. A strictly structured system is indispensable in the Faculty of Law and the space for extensive teacher response is much less than in a programme with 20 master's students. In both our sites a seemingly dialogic model of feedback is established, but our case studies show that there is no automatic relationship between the implementation of new processes and the ensuing product. This has to be considered very carefully in each context. While we have chosen to focus on the overarching aspects of the writing–feedback–revision activities, an analysis of the sub-processes will be the next stage of the research.[9]

Law: strict structuring of the study activities and spaces for dialogues

The study activities of law students in the undergraduate courses are structured in weekly cycles of lectures, individual writing of drafts, group discussions of drafts published in a VLE, peer and TA feedback and posting of final papers (Vines & Dysthe, 2009). Groups of ten students are led by a teacher assistant (TA) who is an advanced student. When the writing assignments are posted in the VLE, students prepare individually for group meetings where the assignment is discussed and possible outlines are negotiated. Each group is divided into three 'commentator teams' to ensure student feedback on all assignments. Because the teams alternate, a student receives feedback from different peers. The mandatory process is strictly regulated: student drafts are due at 5 p.m. on Wednesday, peer comments must be posted at 5 p.m. on Thursday, and each TA comments on half of the texts every week, within Monday at 2 p.m. The group assignments are case-based, i.e. authentic legal problems constructed by experienced law teachers. Student papers are not graded. The final exam consists of a take-home group exam that is a prerequisite for the individual, traditional sit-down exam, where students write essays similar to the kind they have been practising.

The change from the earlier study system is radical. Organised activities used to be restricted to lectures and seminars, individual study was the norm, writing was voluntary and assessment was postponed until the end of the third semester, when not surprisingly the failure rate was high. In our re-analysis of the empirical data we looked for activity-types and patterns. We found the new study regime 'dialogic' in the sense that there are rich opportunities for discussion and exchange of views among peers and with the tutor. However, we detected a contradiction between an underlying authoritative view of teaching and learning and the dialogic elements. Our interpretation is that this inhibits students in developing their own 'voices' and their 'inner persuasive word'. The dialogic potentials seem to be overridden by an implicit authoritarian understanding of knowledge and learning.

Discussion of findings at the law faculty

At the Faculty of Law, compulsory group attendance, writing assignments, feedback system and frequent assessment have paid off in terms of a dramatic reduction of students who fail. In this respect there is no doubt that the regime, including the feedback model, has been 'productive'. It is difficult to isolate the effect of feedback as such from the system in which it is embedded, but the fact that comments to student texts in one group amounted to approximately 15,000 words testifies to its importance. Student evaluations also ascribe the good exam results to the structured writing and feedback processes. The expectations and the criteria are no longer a guessing game for the students (Sadler, 1998).

There are, however, signs that the system has some counterproductive effects. First, in the interviews students talked about losing motivation because of the repetitive nature of the teaching–learning sequences week after week for three years. The consequence may be less discussion, perfunctory peer comments and more free-riders, all aspects mentioned by students in the interviews. Second, the empirical material shows that teacher's and TA's textual comments are interpreted and treated as 'authoritative' in Bakhtin's sense. Even though the group discussions provide opportunities for dialogue, doubt and resistance, the word of the teacher or TA has social authority. There is evidence that students take the oral or written comments just as corrections and then just try to align their text and 'make it right'. Textual comments, as any authority's word needs to be questioned or even resisted, according to Bakhtin, in order to become productive and internally persuasive. Third, some students report that they do not take part in discussions because they are afraid of giving wrong answers and appearing ignorant. These are, in our view, indications of a learning culture where the authoritative word prevails and where there is not enough space for disagreements, conflicts and diverging views. There may be different reasons for this, for instance that law is a discipline where there is a large body of authoritative texts that cannot be ignored by future lawyers. On the other hand students know they need to develop interpretative and argumentative skills, and it could be expected that they would welcome the dialogic spaces to develop critical and independent thinking. Another explanation is that the TAs, who lack experience, may be more authoritative than professors would have been in their feedback. Our point here is not to make any final judgement, but to show the complexity one has to deal with when designing a 'productive' e-feedback system.

Education: fostering productive learning through divergent voices and disagreement?

The web-based Master of Philosophy in Education programme is also strictly structured, but here, the students receive assignments every second or third week. Except for an annual face-to-face seminar, all communication in this study programme is web-based, also the feedback. Anchored in problems from their own practice, the students discuss practice-related problem statements in light of educational theory. Based on the fundamental sociocultural idea that students should be active participants in their own learning process, the focus for this group of students is therefore on their own and fellow students' texts. Through a meticulously structured system of assignments and e-feedback procedures they learn to improve their text. The students first answer the assignments in collaboration with fellow students before later receiving feedback from the supervisor. For the work not to become too trivial, the procedure is changed for every assignment. The supervisor may give traditional individual feedback or focus on the group's product and even on the peer students' previous peer-feedback. There are, however, also some stable elements in each new assignment, in order to assure a certain degree of predictability and thereby reduce the level of stress

Discussion of findings in education

For this peer-learning network to function, the students must learn how to ask good questions about the other students' texts. Master's students are balancing the predominantly reproductive coursework with the productive work on their individual thesis. For many of them it is a new experience to actively use feedback formatively to improve their own texts. Therefore, early in the programme, some of the students request the 'correct answer' from their supervisors, a tendency also reported in the research literature (Cuthell, 2002). When they discover that the supervisor asks them to argue for their own perspectives instead of giving them the answer, they worry that they are not learning enough (Lillejord, 2006). They want the authoritative 'truth', but education (like law) is an argumentative science, with few 'truths'. Instead of building their own argumentative competence, they seek refuge in a traditionally passive or reproducing student role. In order to break this cycle, the students have to write two versions of their own texts. As this process is open in the VLE for all the students, they are in a position to evaluate improvements influenced by the feedback process.

Interviews with students as well as comments in their regular course evaluations give interesting insights. Many students insist that while support may be (emotionally) important, text criticism is more productive for their own learning process and the final product. They soon realise that being too lenient in their feedback on the peer students' texts takes them nowhere, and that feedback as constructive criticism is needed to further their own learning process (Lillejord & Dysthe, 2008). The divergent voices from the peer students represented a challenge for all the students, but in particular for those who expected the authoritative 'correct answer' from the supervisor. The process of establishing an internally persuasive discourse by making the words of others their own (Bakhtin, 1981) obviously takes more time for some students than for others. As soon as they began to perceive the other students' feedback as a resource and a productive contribution to their own learning process, they could not imagine working differently.

Discussion of findings from both case studies

The transparency afforded by technology has provided new learning potential

A crucial feature at both sites was the open access to other students' papers and comments given by both peers and teachers, involving a move from the private spaces of writing and feedback to public spaces. ICT facilitates feedback as a joint activity making interactive processes transparent for those who have access to the technology. Hence, they see suggestions for improvements as well as revisions and learn from the actual process of producing a product. Many students in the empirical material from both sites appreciate this as an important way of learning how to write. They see a variety of models of how to solve an assignment. Writing apprehension is reduced when seeing that peers also struggle. Sharing comments gives a rich source of understanding course content and what constitutes good argumentation. Some students, however, find the demand of publishing unfinished texts very stressful.

A crucial factor in our two cases is that technology facilitates feedback as a joint activity; thus making interactive processes transparent. One significant difference between the two sites is that while several revisions may be posted in the master's programme, only first drafts and comments are posted in law. Thus law students have less opportunities of seeing how texts are being improved by revision. In the blended learning system in law the initial discussion groups provide a 'temporarily shared social reality' (Rommetveit, 1974) as they negotiate the interpretation of the assignment. Students then produce individual texts before getting comments from students and TAs. They do not, however, go that extra step and improve their products.

The quality of commenting

The quality of teacher/TA feedback improves in e-feedback practice because written comments are publicly available not just to the students but also to colleagues. Students, however, are not consistent in their evaluation of the effect on peer commenting. Tannacito (2004) found that students preferred e-response to face-to-face response primarily because they actively used the written record of suggestions in revision. This is also the case at our two sites. Education students use their e-stored sequences of feedback when working on their thesis and law students when preparing for exams. The importance of training students in giving feedback is brought out in a number of research studies (Sljuismans, 2002; Tannacito, 2004) and our study confirms this. It may be argued, however, that the chances of students learning how to give feedback by imitating good models, is an advantage of an open-access system, and may substitute or at least supplement training sessions.

Enculturation: does it mean productive learning?

The learning cycle of reading, writing, getting and giving feedback, revising and rewriting is, to a large extent, about enculturation and appropriating the words of others. The fact that law students are doing better in exams indicates that the study cycle, with the massive commenting on student texts, has been successful in enculturating students into legal genres and ways of arguing, and has in this sense been productive. This also seems to be the case in the master's programme in Education, but the final material product here is a master's thesis, and quality assessment only comes at the end of the year-long process. Nevertheless, in our view, enculturation is more than a neat, one-way process. Enculturation is a dynamic process, and whenever a new person is introduced in a context, the culture changes. A profound understanding of dialogue, reciprocity and co-production of meaning is vitally needed in order to achieve the double goal of enculturation and independence, of learning the trade as well as developing a critical stance towards it. This is why we see 'productive' learning as Janus-faced. While one of the faces is that students learn how to communicate and argue in ways recognized and accepted by the discipline, the other face has to do with developing intellectual autonomy, creativity and critical thinking. For feedback to be productive, it must go beyond helping students to learn academic genre conventions and develop the ability to self-assess their own work, which are the major goals in most feedback literature. Productive feedback must also aim at developing the student's identity as an independent critical thinker and writer in the discipline. The latter is at the centre of Bakhtin's insistence of the importance of the 'inner persuasive word'.

Bakhtin's inner persuasive discourse

Bakhtin's texts reveal that internally persuasive discourse involved questioning the authoritative word and taking a critical stance. He talks about experimenting with the text, questioning the author, imagining alternatives, evaluating diverse discourses, and challenging the text. From this perspective it is necessary for those who give feedback to insist on a position as dialogue partner in order to reach the double goal of enculturation and independence. Through transition from authoritative to internally persuasive discourse, the teacher lets go of his/her authority – unilateral control over students – so that the internally persuasive discourse can establish a shared collaborative control in the classroom. Under a regime of internally persuasive critical discourse, the teacher is an equal partner of discourse (but may be more skilful or knowledgeable) without extra authority beyond the persuasive power of his or her critical argument in the discourse (Matusov, 1998). This may be frustrating for those who seek the 'correct' answer, as the education students did initially, but necessary for students to develop their own voices and strengthen their own agency.

Concluding remarks

The two case studies clearly indicate the challenges of structuring a productive network of intersubjective, multivoiced learning processes that are conducive for the learning outcomes. Participants' contributions must be coordinated in joint activity that incorporates both agreement and disagreement. Matusov (1998) has argued that a traditional definition of intersubjectivity has overemphasised agreement and de-emphasised disagreement, and we ask if educationalists – trapped in the rationality of education – are too preoccupied with either presenting their authoritative answers or with establishing harmonious learning environments and therefore underestimate the learning potential in conflict and disruption. With reference to Bakhtin (1981, 1986), our conclusion is that students in higher education benefit from being exposed to the divergent voices and conflicting perspectives of the research community. Students learning to write academic texts and develop argumentative competency in a networked learning community have provided us with concrete examples of the importance of this perspective.

If we are to understand the multiple literacies of the 21st century, electronic response – both the process and its result – are aspects of a new literacy practice that needs to be better understood. One of the most compelling advantages of e-feedback in a networked environment is the support it provides for the transition from one to many voices, thus enabling conflict and disruption, that is disagreement together with agreement, to be visible for the participants.

Acknowledgements

This research has been conducted as part of the TRANSFORM project funded by the Norwegian Research Council. The authors would thank Anders Mørch and Charles Crook for insightful comments on an earlier draft of this chapter.

Notes

1 Formative assessment refers to assessment that is specifically intended to generate feedback on performance to improve and accelerate learning (Sadler, 1989). Students are more likely to use the term 'feedback' and we treat the two terms as synonyms.
2 Automated feedback systems are not discussed in this chapter.
3 By 'pedagogical genre' we mean a specific, structured activity or practice aimed at improving students' learning. 'Textual feedback', 'comments to drafts' and 'teacher and peer response' are used as synonymous concepts.
4 For further information about the methodological aspects of the research studies to which we refer, see Lillejord, 2006; Lillejord and Westrheim, 2006; Vines and Dysthe, 2009.
5 'Dialogic' is used both in a strong and weak version. The weak, instrumental version is sometimes synonymous with 'discursive', emphasising turn-taking, verbal interaction and discussion. The strong version is about the nature of knowledge as contested and about fostering learner agency.
6 For an extensive review of e-feedback as online interaction in second-language learning, see (Liu, Moore, Graham, and Lee, 2002).
7 Vygotsky's conception of intersubjectivity in relation to the theory developed by Piaget and his followers on the productive role of disagreement in socio-cognitive conflicts, is based on the idea of cognitive decentring through perspective taking (Piaget, 1932; 1969). A student in a response group, for instance, who has to deal with the diverging perspectives of other participants, may experience a socio-cognitive conflict (disequilibrium) that can lead to new and more advanced understandings, which ultimately might benefit the revision process and the text quality. In the 1970s and 1980s several studies explored Piaget's theory (Doise, Mugny, and Perret-Clemont, 1975; Perret-Clermont, 1980).
8 This reform, strongly linked to the Bologna process, introduced a new grading structure, closer follow-up of students, new forms of assessment, a new financial support system and increased internationalisation.
9 Sub-processes of the feedback-revision activity from a student's point of view: Submit draft; Read peer draft(s) and evaluate strengths and weaknesses; Give feedback (written and posted in VLE or face-to-face in groups); Read feedback from peers and teacher/TA; Self-evaluate own text on the basis of comments; Make decisions on which comments

to attend to in revision; Revise text and resubmit. This cycle may be iterated several
times depending on the study design and which text version is summatively assessed.
10 Student essays in the same group counted in total 17,000 words.

References

Anson, C. M. (1989). *Writing and Response. Theory, practice, and research.* Urbana. IL:
    NCTE.
Bakhtin, M. M. (1981). Discourse in the Novel. In M. Holquist (ed.), *The Dialogic
    Imagination: Four essays by M. M. Bakhtin.* Austin: University of Texas Press (C. Emerson
    and M. Holquist, trans).
Bakhtin, M. M. (1986). C. Emerson and M. Holquist (eds), *Speech Genres and Other Late
    Essays.* Austin: University of Texas Press (V. W. McGee, Trans.).
Bereiter, C. and Scardamalia, M. (1987). *The Psychology of Written Composition.* Hillsdale,
    NJ: Lawrence Erlbaum.
Black, P. J. and Wiliam, D. (1998). Assessment and Classroom Learning. *Assessment in
    Education, 5*, 7–77.
Blignaut, A. S. and Lillejord, S. (2006). Lessons from a Cross-cultural Learning Community.
    South African Journal of Higher Education, 19, 168–185.
Connor, U. and Asenavage, K. (1994). Peer Response Groups in ESL Writing Classes: How
    much impact on revision? *Journal of Second Language Writing, 3*, 257–276.
Crook, C. K., Gross, H. and Dymott, R. (2006). Assessment Relationships in Higher
    Education: The tension of process and practice. *British Educational Research Journal,
    32*, 95–114.
Cuthell, J. (2002). MirandaNet: A Learning Community – A Community of Learners.
    Journal of Interactive Learning Research, 13, 167–186.
Doise, W. G., Mugny, A. N. and Perret-Clemont, A. (1975). Social Interaction and
    the Development of Cognitive Operations. *European Journal of Social Psychology, 5*,
    367–382.
Ferris, D. (2004). The *'Grammar Correction' Debate in L2 Writing*: Where are we, and
    where do we go from here? (And what do we do in the meantime . . .) *Journal of Second
    Language Writing, 13*, 49–62.
Freedman, S. W. and Sperling, M. (1985). Written Language Acquisition: The role of
    response and the writing conference. In S. W. Freedman (ed.) *The Acquisition of Written
    Knowledge: Response and revision* (pp. 106–130). Norwood: Ablex.
Fjuk, A., Sorensen, E. K. and Wasson, B. (1999). Incorporating Collaborative Learning,
    Networked Computers and Organisational Issues into Theoretical Frameworks. *Proceedings
    of the 19th ICDE World Conference on Open Learning and Distance Education*, Vienna,
    20–24 June, pp. 35–45.
Guribye, F. (2005). *Infrastructures for Learning: Ethnographic Inquiries into the Social
    and Technical Conditions of Education and Training.* PhD dissertation, Department of
    Information Science and Media Studies, University of Bergen, Norway.
Hattie, J. and Timperley, H. (2007). The Power of Feedback. *Review of Educational
    Research, 77*(1), 81–112.
Hayes, J. and Flowers, L. (1980). The Cognition of Discovery: Defining a rhetorical prob-
    lem. *College Composition and Communication, 31*, 21–32.
Hyland, F. (2000). ESL Writers and Feedback: Giving more autonomy to students. *Language
    Teaching Research, 4*, 33–54.

Hyland, K. and Hyland, F. (2006). *Feedback in Second Language*. Cambridge: Cambridge University Press.

Jacobs, G., Curtis, A., Braine, G. and Huang, S. (1998). Feedback on Student Writing: Taking the middle path. *Journal of Second Language Writing*, 7, 307.

Lillejord, S. and Dysthe, O. (2009). Productive Horizontal Learning and Digital Tools Epilogue. In R. Krumsvik (ed.) *Learning in the Network Society and the Digitized School*, 311–313. New York: Nova Science Publishers.

Lillejord, S. (2006). Dialogen tar Aldri Slutt. Sosial læring i nettbasert undervisning. In H. Bjørnsrud, L., Monsen. and B. Overland (eds) *Utdanning for Utvikling av Skolen*, 120–144, Oslo: Cappelen Akademisk.

Lillejord, S. and Dysthe, O. (2008). Productive Learning Practice. A theoretical discussion based on two cases. *Journal of Education and Work*, 21 (1), 75–89.

Lillejord, S. and Westrheim, K. (2006). På Nett? Veiledning i en IKT-basert master i pedagogikk. In O. Dysthe and A. Samara (eds) *Veiledning i Høyere Utdanning*. Oslo: Abstrakt Forlag.

Lindblom-Ylänne, S. and Pihlajamäki, H. (2003). Can a Collaborative Network Environment Enhance Essay-writing Processes? *British Journal of Educational Technology*, 34, 17–30.

Linell, P. (2009) *Rethinking Language, Mind, and the World Dialogically*. Charlotte, NC: Information Age Publishing.

Liu, M., Moore, Z., Graham, L. and Lee, S. (2002). A Look at the Research on Computer-based Technology Use in Second Language Learning: A review of the literature from 1990–2000. *Journal of Research on Technology in Education*, 34(3), 250–273.

Matusov, E. (1998). When Solo Activity Is Not Privileged: Participation and internalization: Models of development. *Human Development*, 326–349.

Mørch, A. I., Cheung, W. K., Wong, K. C., Liu, J., Lee, C., Lam, M. H. and Tang, J. P. (2005). Grounding Collaborative Knowledge Building in Semantics-based Critiquing. Lecture Notes in Computer Science, 3583, 244–255. Berlin: Springer-Verlag.

Nicol, D. J. and Macfarlane-Dick. (2006). Formative Assessment and Self-regulated Learning: A model and seven principles of good feedback practice. *Studies in Higher Education*, 31, 199–216.

Nicol, D. J. and Milligan, C. (2006). Rethinking Technology-supported Assessment in Terms of the Seven Principles of Good Feedback Practice. In C. Bryan and K. Clegg (eds) *Innovative Assessment in Higher Education*. London: Routledge.

Nystrand, M. (1992). Social Interactionism Versus Social Constructionism: Bakhtin, Rommetveit, and the semiotics of written text. In A. H. Wold (ed.) *The Dialogical Alternative: Toward a theory of language and mind*. Oslo: Scandinavian University Press.

Perret-Clermont, A.-N. (1980). *Social Interaction and Cognitive Development in Children*. London: Academic Press.

Piaget, J. (1932). *The Moral Judgement of the Child*. London: Routledge & Kegan Paul.

Piaget, J. (1969). *Judgement and Reasoning in the Child*. London: Routledge & Kegan Paul.

Popkewitz, T. S. (1998). Dewey, Vygotsky and the Social Administration of the Individual: Constructivist pedagogy as systems of ideas in historical spaces. *American Educational Research Journal*, 35, 535–570.

Ramaprasad, A. (1983). On the Definition of Feedback. *Behavioral Science*, 28, 4–13.

Reddy, M. (1979). The Conduit Metaphor: A case of frame conflict in our language about language. In A. Ortony (ed.) *Metaphor and Thought*. Cambridge: Cambridge University Press.

Rogoff, B. (1995). Observing Sociocultural Activity on Three Planes, Participatory Appropriation, Guided Participation, and Apprenticeship. In J. W. Wertch, P. del Rio and A. Alvarez (eds) *Sociocultural Studies of Mind* (pp. 125–139). Cambridge: Cambridge University Press.

Rommetveit, R. (1974). *On Message Structure: A framework for the study of language and communication*. London: Wiley.

Sadler, R. (1998). Formative Assessment: Revising the territory. *Assessment in Education*, 5, 77–84.

Sadler, R. (1989). Formative Assessment and the Design of Instructional Systems. *Instructional Science*, *18*, 119–144.

Selfe, C. L. (1992). Computer-based Conversations and the Changing Nature of Collaboration. In J. Forman (ed.) *New Visions of Collaborative Writing*. Portsmouth: Boynton/Cook.

Shute, V. (2008). Focus on Formative Feedback. *Review of Educational Research*, 1, 153–189.

Sljuismans, D. (2002). *Student Involvement in Assessment: The training of peer assessment skills*. Doctoral dissertation, Open University of the Netherlands.

Tannacito, T. (2004). The Literacy of Electronic Peer Response. In B. Huot, B. Stroble and C. Bazerman (ed.) *Multiple Literacies for the 21st Century*. New Jersey: Hampton Press.

Vines, A. and Dysthe, O. (2009). Productive Learning in the Study of Law: The role of technology in the learning ecology of a law faculty. In L. Dirckinck-Holmfeld, C. Jones and B. Lindström (eds) *Analysing Networked Learning Practices. Technology-Enhanced Learning Series*. London: Sense.

Vygotsky, L. (1986). *Thought and Language*. Cambridge, MA: MIT Press.

Ware, P. (2004). Confidence and Competition Online: ESL student perspectives on web-based discussions in the classroom. *Computers and Composition*, *21*, 451–468.

Ware, P. D. and Warschauer, M. (2006). Electronic Feedback and Second Language Writing. In K. Hyland and F. Hyland (eds) *Feedback in Second Language Writing: Contexts and issues* (pp. 105–123). Cambridge: Cambridge University Press.

Zhang, S. (1995). Re-examining the Affective Advantage of Peer Feedback in the ESL Writing Class. *Journal of Second Language Writing*, *4*, 209–222.

Section 3

Institutional development

Breakdowns between teachers, educators and designers in elaborating new technologies as precursors of change in education to dialogic thinking

Baruch Schwarz and Reuma de Groot

The involvement of researchers, designers, and instructors in finding new ways for enhancing learning processes as self-organizing through collaborative practices is now a recognized paradigm in design research. In this context, instructors aim to function as agents of change. The case of teachers as agents of self-organizational change is special since institutional constraints imposed on teachers are enormous. To bring forth change, teachers are involved in two contexts: in design research meetings (with designers, developers and researchers) and in their classrooms. This collaterality of relatively simultaneous participation in two related activities is at the focus of the present paper. We observe teachers dedicated to fostering dialogic thinking in their classes. Shifts in practices and epistemological beliefs concerning teaching and learning are mandatory for such a purpose. To ease these shifts, a design research team developed DIGALO, a tool representing graphically collective argumentation. We observe here shifts in practices and in beliefs. Comparison between teachers' behavior in the research design team and in the classroom led us to discern several breakdowns. Since the design research team negotiated new ways to guide talk that challenged old practices rooted in their epistemological beliefs, we consider whether these breakdowns evidence processes of identity development.

The obstacles in changing teaching practices: the case of education to dialogical thinking

There are numerous constraints to collaborative self-organizing learning in schools. The socio-spatial structure of classrooms leads teachers to function as isolated individual practitioners. Another bureaucratic constraint concerns the temporal structure of discrete lessons punctuated by tests (Engeström, Engeström and Suntio, 2002). A third constraint is institutional and motivational: attaining grades is a main motive for schoolwork which leads to classification of students into categories such as weak, competent, passive, and so on. As a consequence, the redesign of the teacher's practices may encounter obstacles if it challenges these constraints.

Several initiatives have challenged the socio-spatial, bureaucratic, institutional and motivational character of formal education. Freire's *Critical Education* (Freire,

262   B. Schwarz and R. de Groot

1973) pledges for radical opposition to authority and for a reorganization of education in which educators are dissidents against the system. Other programs inspired by a philosophy of dialogue have proposed to negotiate responsibilities, structures, topics to be learned, and evaluation at all levels. Programs aimed at fostering dialogic thinking by opening perspectives and deepening them belong to this category (Schwarz & de Groot, 2007; Wegerif, 2006). In these programs, dialogic thinking is both an educational goal and a tool for negotiating with institutions and authority. Such programs seem realizable since teachers as well as students are fluent at participating in collective argumentation, one of the main vehicles for enhancing dialogic thinking. However, contrary to intuition, the familiarity people have about argumentation in informal settings cannot be capitalized on in classes as well as in coping with institutional issues. The know-hows that teachers have about dialogic thinking in natural settings (e.g. guidance as parents to learn basic skills, or dinner talks in which children learn to participate in conversations) are rich. They include eliciting explanations, answering questions, helping children facing contradictions or challenges. However, they are implicit and embedded in these contexts. In schools – places aimed at eliciting the elaboration of "scientific" knowledge, these argumentative know-hows are generally replaced by other types of talk in which the teacher functions as an authority that initiates most of the questions, provides many explanations and socially validates some answers over other answers without providing sufficient explanations. These strategies were already experienced by teachers at the time they were students in schools, in colleges and in pre-service programs, so that they impinge on the beliefs teachers have on valuable practices, norms of interactions, and norms of argumentation. "Knowledge acquisition" is then not only the overt goal of the teachers but is carved, interwoven, in school talk.

We hypothesized that tools that make salient argumentative moves embedded in informal settings in formal education would lead teachers to modify their pedagogical practices and that reflecting on how they function in school talk as mediators of knowledge construction and how with the new tools at disposal, they envisage new practices and norms would trigger change in their development. However, the promotion of dialogical thinking in schools was hypothesized to challenge the organizational constraints with which teachers had learned to comply.

The dunes project for fostering dialogical thinking

The Argumentation Group at the Hebrew University is dedicated to fostering dialogic thinking (Schwarz & de Groot, 2007). We integrate critical thinking and communication practices in which the self is identified and constructed through respect of the other and rationality. Collective argumentation gathers such practices with diverse educational goals (understanding, convincing, reaching consensus, accommodating divergent views, etc.). To be valuable according to dialogic thinking norms, collective argumentation should be productive, that is, (1) several arguments are raised, and (2) discussants capitalize on the arguments that emerged during the discussion in subsequent activities (Schwarz, 2009). In order to help teachers in promoting productive collective argumentation we developed the Digalo tool in the EC-funded DUNES project (IST-2001-34153) for facilitating (a-)synchronous discussions by graphically representing argumentative moves and structures. Typically, discussants would communicate through the progressive construction of an argumentative map. This map includes boxes with different shapes that represent argumentation functions (e.g. explanation, question, claim, argument, etc.) and arrows that help discussants make visible their reference to previous interventions (agreement, opposition or simple reference). After the first version of the tool was experienced, which showed the potential of the tool for deepening and broadening the space of debate, a group of teachers began designing argumentative activities in classrooms with technological tools. These teachers met regularly with the researchers, designers and educators of our group to discuss and reflect on their practices in their classes. These meetings can be considered as a setting of a cross-boundary lab (Engeström, 2001) for the further development of the Digalo graphical tool and for defining the appropriate way to actually introduce these tools in classrooms. Collective reflection helped the design research team make argumentative knowhows explicit. We highlight in this chapter the *bilateral consequential transitions* (Beach, 1999) teachers underwent to cope with the ongoing demands of their peers. The design research meetings focused on the following issues:

1   The evaluation of arguments written by students
2   The evaluation of e-discussions
3   The appropriateness of synchronous e-discussions in classroom activities
4   The role of the teacher in synchronous discussions
5   The introduction of the notion of "argument" in classes and its implication for the way knowledge is considered by students.

For these issues, we could trace the evolution of teachers' norms and beliefs underlying new argumentative practices through discussions in the design research team. It appeared though that collective work was far from being smooth and led to several serious breakdowns. We limit ourselves to the description of the breakdowns that occurred when discussing how to evaluate written arguments.

How to trace changes in teachers' beliefs and actions

Teachers are in charge of instilling societal norms, values, and knowledge. By elaborating exams and evaluating performance according to agreed tools, they convey the norms and values. By leading discussions in lessons, evaluating and validating explanations produced by students, they decide whether "knowledge is correct or not." Pre-service and in-service teacher programs are generally aimed at reproducing the norms, values, and knowledge agreed upon by society. Programs aimed at challenging and changing these agreed constructs induce two layers, the layer of action in which the teacher functions in class according to inherited norms and values, and the layer of ideology that involves reflection on this inheritance and instruments for modifying it. In our effort to promote dialogic thinking, we seek to harmonize these two layers. The two systems in which the teachers in our program were involved, meetings in the design research team and lessons in classrooms were intended to enable this harmonization. Many researchers traced change by observing activities in which new practices and tools are developed (e.g. Engeström, 2001; Hakkarainen, 2003), and new taken-as-shared under-standings (Cobb, Sophian, Whitenack & Gravemeijer, 2001). Since the teachers in our program are involved in two bilateral systems, it is crucial to compare these developments in the two systems, especially by identifying breakdowns to identify the consequential transitions between them (Beach, 1999). The breakdowns show that difficulties accepting new ways of evaluating or interacting with students are bigger in discussions in the design research team than in classrooms. We will also consider to what extent the harmonization sought between the two layers is actually reached.

Description of the research

In our endeavor to promote dialogic thinking in classrooms, we decided to join with a group of teachers and developers to function as a design research team. The first objective of this team was to follow up the development of the Digalo tool. The teachers were committed to engaging in dialogical thinking in their regular teaching. Two of the teachers were asked to design and implement a case in physics with Grade 7 students, while the other four teachers were invited to implement the argumentative tool in their regular teaching without being asked to design a specific case. The design research team met every two weeks for two-hour-long meetings. It included up to six teachers, three research students, two designers, two educators, and one researcher. It was clear from the beginning that any change in classroom activity would be negotiated in the design research team and that this discussion would be fed by actual experiences the teachers would undergo in their classes during the year. Altogether the group met 14 times. All meetings were video-taped; most of the lessons during this period were also video-taped.

The first issue we focus on concerns the elaboration of a tool for evaluating written arguments. This issue was discussed after the group considered the impor-tance of argumentative activities for learning, then demonstrated and experienced the use of Digalo in their classes to discuss moral dilemmas. The experience with Digalo led teachers to choose in advance discursive categories for the design of discussions. These categories – claim, argument, explanation, support, opposi-tion, question, information, and so on, inspired the teachers and the designers when they developed the tool for evaluation of written argumentation. In one of the group's meetings, the researchers explained first what they considered to be a good argument. This general suggestion was followed (in another meeting) by the presentation of a tool for evaluating the quality of written arguments by the designer. The group engaged in a discussion to react on whether, how and when to use this tool in the classroom. Participants proposed a new revised version of the tool. The participants discussed again how and when to use such a tool. This last discussion led to the common elaboration of a final revised tool especially in light of the experience teachers acquire in their classroom activities.

We considered these successive activities around the evaluation of written arguments as opportunities for: (1) eliciting externalization of dialogical know-hows in teachers; (2) identifying discrepancies between externalized know-hows and their enactment in practice; (3) developing new argumentative practices; (4) imagining new practices based on a new design to help elaborate scientific knowledge; (5) reflecting on the evolving role of the teacher in helping students construct knowledge. We will observe breakdowns and changes in teachers committed to fostering dialogic thinking who realized their goal by participating in parallel in the design research-team meetings and in lessons in their classes through the use of Digalo.

Discussing the evaluation of written arguments in successive activities

First breakdown: elaborating an evaluation tool or challenging epistemological beliefs?

After experiencing Digalo synchronous discussions, the teachers requested that the designers and the researcher create a didactical tool for evaluating written arguments. They claimed that in order to involve their students in these activities they should evaluate their students' achievements and give them grades which would appear in their final records by the end of the year. But, of course, the issue of quality of e-discussions (like Digalo maps) is a huge scientific challenge. Therefore, the designers and the educators adapted a tool for evaluating written arguments in science so that it could be used by the teachers for their present purpose. The first step was to use the scientific definitions of an argument, in order to instil a terminology and norms in classrooms. Although no clear exhaustive list of criteria was agreed upon by researchers, we proposed a partial list of criteria for the goodness of arguments based on criteria proposed by scientists who analyzed written arguments (Kuhn, 1991; Means & Voss, 1996; to some extent, Toulmin, 1958). We proposed arguments to be considered as good if (a) they include a claim and relevant reasons supporting it, (b) the reasons are rooted in evidential data and explanations, and (c) alternative conflicting claim and reasons are considered and rejected, based on a rational judgment. One of the educators successfully used the typology suggested by Kuhn (2001) to evaluate written arguments in science classrooms: absolutist (one-sided), relativist (two-sided but undecided), and evaluative (two-sided and decided) arguments. The educators and designers in the design-research team knew that the quality of arguments should be evaluated with respect to the goal to be attained, and the kind of issue on which arguments are constructed. However, the teachers were interested in a fixed and universal evaluation tool. The designer then proposed the following evaluation tool and suggested the teachers discuss whether, when and how to use it:

Tool 1

1   Identification of the type of argument

    a   *Claim*: An opinion is raised without any reason supporting it

    b   *Absolutist argument*: One claim with one reason invoked

    c   *Relativist argument*: Different reasoned claims are invoked. No clear opinion is brought forward

    d   *Evaluative argument*: Different reasoned claims are invoked as well as a reasoned preference for one claim

  b   Number of reasons invoked

  c   Number of perspectives covered

  d   Extent of relevance (for each of the reasons): not relevant, partially relevant, relevant and fully relevant

  e   Relevance of the warrant to the reason invoked: not relevant, partially relevant, relevant and fully relevant

  f   Type of reason: personal (not supported), non-professional authority, professional authority and scientific theory or empirical data.

Before he presented his tool to the teachers, the designer who elaborated Tool 1 was interviewed to understand why he chose such criteria:

> In my opinion, the primary goal is to say what we see in the text: Could we see a claim, a reason, whether there are perspectives that have been identified? It's worthy constructing a minimal evaluation tool that can give us the possibility to define what's there in the text and that will fit any argumentative text. An argumentative text is a text in which there is a claim and a reason (even when the text consists of one sentence only). The instrument must be usable to analyze texts whoever the students are and whichever the context is (what they already read, and what they use to support their arguments). I think that one should look at any text as a whole unit and one should identify argumentative instances (claim, reason, warrant, perspective, and so on). In my opinion, that's the minimum. I tried to refer to sufficiency, relevance, taking into consideration of challenging views and the acceptability of the reasons. I didn't use the concepts of evidence and explanations and rather used the term "reason" because I wanted the tool to be friendly for use in classes.

This excerpt shows that the designer was aware of the criteria suggested in research, but was first of all interested in a tool that could be used by teachers. So, she opted for simplicity. For example, she decided not to differentiate between explanatory and evidential reasons. The teachers were presented the tool after they experienced discussions using Digalo in which their students coped with a moral dilemma. We present here an excerpt of a discussion of the design-research team on Tool 1 (Ts are teachers; Ds, designers; and Es educators):

D1: Can an argument be good although it is scientifically unacceptable?

T1: For me, it is important that argumentation serves science.

T2: Is it possible to say that there is an argument when its components in the text are implicit?

D2: For me a high level of explicitness of the content is missing.

E1: Maybe we should be pragmatic and see whether it's clear.

T1: There is here the issue of the implicit. Often students don't articulate, although what they mean is clear.

D2: I want to define two concepts: consistency and coherency. Consistency is when something results from something else in a logical way; coherency means keeping everything together – an inner common sense. A text may be good if we look at the arguments, but that doesn't necessarily mean it is consistent or coherent.

This excerpt shows that D1 raises first the issue of correctness of scientific arguments. T1 seems to react in the same direction, but T3 pushes the discussion in the direction of the explicitness of the arguments. D1, who created Tool 1, concedes that a level of explicitness is missing. E1 attempts to show that this issue should not appear in the tool but rather, a demand for explicitness should be replaced by a simple request for clarity. She is echoed by T1. D1 tries to give a more scientific definition of clarity by evoking the concepts of consistency and coherency.

As a result of this discussion, the design-research team conjectured that the opposition of the teachers originated from the fact that the tool mixed argumentative and non-argumentative aspects. D2 decided then to split between the correctness of the text and its argumentativeness. As for explicitness, the team thought that, in spite of the importance in general of being explicit, proposing a tool with precise criteria for goodness should not deny students the right to be explicit when their intention is clear. More than that, it should guide the teachers to carefully trace this implicitness and to elicit more explicit explanations. The design-research team then put together the following new evaluation tool:

Tool 2

1   Evaluation of learning: extent of scientific acceptability of the text

   a   The text is mostly incorrect
   b   The text is partly incorrect
   c   The text is correct but incomplete
   d   The text is correct and complete

2   Evaluation of the argumentative skills in the text

    a   Claim without reason supporting it
    b   Simple one-sided argument: one claim + one reason
    c   Multiple argument: one claim + several reasons
    d   Complex argument: one can identify reference to different reasoned opinions but no clear decision is made
    e   Complex evaluative argument: one can identify reference to different reasoned opinions and a reasoned preference between them

3   Number of reasons invoked
4   Number of perspectives invoked (optional)
5   Type of reason

    a   Personal (not supported)
    b   Non-professional authority
    c   Professional authority
    d   Scientific theory or empirical data

Grade/Evaluation for correctness: _____
Grade/Evaluation for argumentativeness: _____

This tool was also presented to the teachers and discussed. We report here some of the reactions the teachers expressed:

T1:   Since this is an evaluation tool, should we tend to always reach one type of good argument?

D1:   This depends on the context. You should be aware of the context.

T2:   To check knowledge and argumentativeness at the same time, that bothers me.

T4:   That's important to know that if I give a text, I want to know the criteria. This tool . . . I can use it according to my goal. For example, one argument with two reasons may be perfect. Another thing: When I see a text, which is incorrect from a scientific point of view, it's difficult to evaluate, it's not right from an educational point of view.

T5:   It's important to check first to what extent the text is readable.

E2:   Concerning knowledge, you should have a cognitive empathy. Perhaps the student wants to say something the teacher didn't expect. Perhaps, tracing what the student argues helps understanding what the student knows.

This short excerpt shows that teachers question the generality of the tool (T1 and T4) and the fact that the tool checks content and argumentativeness even though separately: T4 claims that content and argumentativeness should be separated but that when arguments are incorrect, it is difficult to evaluate the quality of its argumentativeness. E2 frames the usefulness of the evaluation tool as what she calls "cognitive empathy": The tool helps understanding what the student means or knows. At the end of the meeting, the teachers rejected the evaluation tool in its proposed form for use in their classes. We interpret this rejection as well as the interventions of the teachers in the design-research team on the elaboration of the tool for evaluating written arguments as a way of preserving their epistemological belief that knowledge is valuable only when it can be clearly expressed and when it is correct. They discard the value of a rhetorical perspective of knowledge as something *justifiable* in the eyes of their students.

Second breakdown: discuss the quality of arguments as an indicator of a conflict between conformity to literacy skills, and commitment to promoting understanding

The discussions between teachers and the rest of the design-research team were generally practical. They were intertwined with classroom activities in which the teachers implemented argumentative activities. Designers often collected some good examples from the students' work. During one of the design-team meetings, they brought an essay written by a student in the class of the teacher T6 after he participated in a discussion on a moral dilemma, a tattle-tale story, in which students had to decide whether one should tell the truth to the teacher about an incident in which eight pupils threw chairs through a window (which would result in at least two of them being expelled from the school), or should not tell and have a collective punishment – not to go on the annual school trip. The design-research team was asked to evaluate the following student's essay with Tool 2:

> I think that one shouldn't tell because the pupils that threw the chairs didn't hurt anybody (except for the chairs they broke) and this action will remain on their conscience. This is their problem only.
>
> If we tell about the guilty pupils, we'll be considered as informers and as a consequence everybody will hate us and will refuse to get close to us, and the issue of our social status is at stake. In my opinion, according to what I just said before, there is a very subtle limit that separates between informing and reporting, so that if somebody gets hurts as a result of the other's actions, one should report in order to avoid future prejudice for others. In our specific case, reporting to the teacher on the guilty will be considered as informing since it is not necessary. For example, if I am a witness for a murder, I will call the police right away and this act will be a report because the police will come and put in jail the murderer who hurt somebody and can hurt others so that the series of crimes will be stopped. An opposite example: once my friend and myself laughed at each other and I gave him a blow just for joke, and he took it very seriously and complained to the teacher. In my opinion, this case is a tattle-tale since I didn't intend to hurt him but he understood what I did in a different way from what I did.

> In summary, I gave my opinion above concerning reporting and inform-
> ing, I gave examples, and in my opinion I proved my argument in the best
> way I could.

This report triggered a vivid discussion in the design research team:

D1:   There is here an evaluative argument. It takes into consideration other opinions.

T2:   This is not the problem. When you relate to another opinion, you are evaluative by definition.

D1:   Well. I have news for you. This is not true! A paragraph like this one, if only college students could write it! If only . . .

D2:   Be serious! Don't exaggerate! They don't know what a counterargument is?

T1:   Well, why are you so excited with this paragraph? Look at how many times he writes the same thing. I think that the opinion is not correct because . . . in my opinion . . . You know, I would have thrown this away!

D2:   But we focus on his argumentative skills.

E2:   Let's look at what we taught children. He did a great job! Classical! He wrote a claim and a reason, he referred to the opinion of others, he explained them then he rebutted them . . . This is a great job!

D1:   According to Kuhn's categories, this text is perfect from an argumentative perspective. Not only an argument, but also a counterargument, he explains the opinion of others.

T1:   But his explanations are minimal, they are very poor.

In this discussion, the teachers are not impressed by the quality of the written argument because, in their view, it is (a) incorrect (T1), (b) replete with repetitions (T1), and (c) contains poor explanations (T1). The rest of the research-design team appreciates the paragraph for its argumentative quality. The discussion between researchers and teachers uncovers a conflict which, we think, stems from the different points of view assumed by each group. The designers are interested in the principle that there are different opinions (D1), and the designer, to see argumentative skills (D2); the teachers are more interested in the student's performance from an institutional point of view, to how the student reacts to what he was asked (or expected) to do. The teacher T1 claims that she would have thrown the essay away because the student repeated the same thing so many times. When her opinion is challenged by the group, she turns to another critique stating that the student's explanations were minimal. Again, she brings her pre-defined expectation from the student – to elaborate his explanations. When the designer D2 claims that "the students don't know what a counterargument is," she uses the same notion of pre-defined expected categories in order to judge the students. We claim that the conflict between teachers and the rest of the design-research team is rooted in their different roles and perspectives towards the definition of the student's knowledge. The researchers recognize several argumentative components, such as "claim," "reason," "(counter-)argument," whose presence is important for learning through argumentation. Although one of the designers uses the term "argumentative skill," they do not look for skills but for meaning as expressed through argumentative components. The teachers, on the other hand, use their teaching practice, where the students' work is evaluated in relation to their overall performance in school. Since school favors literacy skills, poorly written essays are valueless even if they include relevant arguments and counterarguments.

Third breakdown: teachers' attitude toward the Digalo tool as an indicator of a conflict between reasoning as a cognitive activity and a communicative activity

The attitude of the teachers towards Digalo uncovers other phenomena. Digalo leads students to use an argumentative ontology: different geometrical shapes embody argumentative components or moves such as "claim," "explanation," "argument," "support," "opposition," or "question." Using this tool for synchronous e-discussion puts the teachers in a difficult position. Where should they concentrate when observing their student's performance: on the "right use" of the shape, which would elicit argumentative/communicative competencies, or on the content of the discussion, which would elicit understanding as a cognitive activity? These decisions led teachers to be often unable to express an articulated attitude towards the tool. In a further publication, we will show the role of designers and educators in the design-research team in helping teachers clarify their attitude. The teachers seemed quite perplexed about how they function in Digalo discussions and could not reflect on their actions.

However, for one of the teachers, T6, the situation was different. He decided to integrate Digalo in a seven-month-long history course. He also tried to convince his colleagues of the importance and the feasibility of programs to promote dialogic thinking based on the Dunes environment. We report here on one of the arguments he expressed in the design-research team:

> Yes, I do think so [I think there is an added value of the tool-based (written) discussion over the oral discussion]. First, in terms of thinking, the issue of how the students use the shapes is important. Often, they're uncertain as for what shape to use, which makes them reflect on what they are going to "say." And there's also the issue of how to put things in words. When they need to write something, it makes them think more rationally. There are two students who also take part in my history classes. I can tell you that in history lessons they don't participate at all; if I give them exams in the class – these two students usually hand me an empty paper. These kids have learning difficulties and here [in the Digalo class] they express themselves quite well. I

finally got a real essay from them, and this is something I couldn't achieve in the regular class. Now I taught them [in the Digalo class] a history case and they wrote serious essays. For them this is a great progress. There are a few parallel processes here. But one of the important things that are responsible for this is that I made them write during the lesson, something they seldom have to do in their classes.

T6 stated the two advantages he sees for the use of the Digalo tool. It is interesting to note that he first mentioned the "expected" argumentative approach, while he elaborated with much more detail on the social direction when he brought the example of his two students. No doubt that his appreciation of his students' use of Digalo – and, we guess, also grading their performance accordingly – is based on their unexpected act of submitting an essay rather than on their actual performance regarding the use of Digalo in the "right" argumentative way.

Breakdowns overcome? Introducing the notion of "argument" in a "Digalo Classroom"

What really happened in the classes? We show now a short example of classroom activity in which one teacher, T4, who was one of the most critical concerning the tool for evaluating written arguments, is engaged in argumentative activity. This example is taken from an English (second-language) lesson, in which T4 tries to instil in Grade 8 students the concepts of "turning point" and "climax" in short stories. The teacher gave a story to her students in which a hunter asks his 12-year-old son to hunt a deer in the forest for him. The son feels proud to "represent" his prestigious father, who he admires. But when he finds the deer, he feels he cannot shoot him. T4 asked the students to discuss what the turning point of the story is through Digalo. She then initiates a reflection on the e-discussion. T4 and the students communicated in English (often broken, though) so that we restitute the protocol verbatim:

T4:   Now let's go back to Digalo. Why do you think it is better to say something in writing more than it is in saying?

S1:   It is a lot of fun to write . . . and to see others' opinions.

T4:   Shahar, did you enjoy also writing with Digalo? Let's talk about it. Not only from the fun side, why it is better to write your opinion than to say it? Does writing allow you to do something that speaking doesn't allow you to do?

S2:   Yes, you can erase things, you can correct.

S3:   You can learn how to spell.

T4:   Why do you think it is important to erase things?

S4:   If you have a mistake . . .

T4:   And therefore, if you can fix something in a conversation, what does it mean?

S1:   In a discussion you can't erase, here I can see and correct . . . I can look at it again.

T4:   To summarize, I like what you say, because in Digalo you can think on what you say! You can put more thoughts into your ideas and into your reasons. I want to see now what you have done last week. Do you all remember what I'm talking about? Claims, arguments and reasons? Yeah? Could you tell us whether discussing with three is good or you would like more in the group . . .

The teacher turns to the classwork from the previous week and discusses, with Digalo, the turning-point of the story, which was the boy who didn't kill the deer. Students were asked to discuss, in triads, why they thought that the boy didn't kill the deer. Students were asked to give claims and reasons in their discussions. The teacher exported the Digalo map into a text and gave it to the students for reflection. A discussion then develops between the teacher and the students about the quality of the story. Many of the students claim that the story was boring. But T4 concludes:

T4:   I personally don't understand how you can say that it is a boring story . . . I think that it is wonderful story but you have your opinion, you are entitled to your opinions.

In the design-research team T4 was always reluctant to participate in the program and always played the role of the devil's advocate. The contrast between T4's attitude in the class and her attitude in the design-research meetings is compelling. Here, argument writing is identified as a way to express an opinion and to be accepted (as in the last of her interventions). She identifies also the use of the tools "claim," "reason," and "argument" as a way to be understood by others. For this reason, she completes (or, in fact) transforms Yuval's ideas so that they are understandable. She is here an agent of participation in dialogical thinking. The role of the Digalo map (which is not displayed here) is crucial: The students use the ontology proposed to express their opinions. Also, as mentioned by S1, they can look at others' opinions and reflect on them. In other activities, students expressed that with the help of arrows they can refer to others' opinions through support, opposition, or in a neutral way.

Crossing boundaries or cohabitating epistemological beliefs?

In spite of such an active engagement in argumentative activities, which was typical to the teachers, when these teachers met in design-research meetings, they turned back to their need to have a defined and simple evaluation tool. We present here the final revised evaluation tools, agreed upon by teachers. Teachers criticized the previous tool and raised the issue of the difficulty of checking so many variables.

One teacher proposed a much simpler tool:

A claim – 30 points
One reason – 40 points (and if it's incorrect or not precise, 30 points)
More reasons – 20 points
References to conflicting views – 10 points

This tool was not retained since it did not mention the correctness of knowledge, which remained crucial for them. Rather they agreed about the following "final tool":

Criteria			
1 **Correctness of content knowledge**	Correct and complete // **code: 3**	Partial or partially wrong // **code: 2**	Wrong // **code: 1**
2 **Claim**	Clear // **code: 3**	Unclear // **code: 2**	Doesn't exist // **code: 1**
3 **Number of reasons**	Number of reasons and their type:		evidence/explanation
4 **Number of aspects**	Number of aspects		
5 **Reference to different viewpoints**	Reference to and evaluation of and different opinions // **code: 3**	Reference to different opinions // **code: 2**	No reference // **code: 1**
6 **Source of knowledge**		Certified/verified // **code: 2**	Uncertified/ unverified // **code: 1**

To some extent, the final tool proposed reflected the teachers' wavering between the two activity systems in which they evolved, between the layers of ideology and of action; as compared to their opposition to the first tool proposed by the designer, they accept the value of pondering different viewpoints and acknowledge the importance of the source of knowledge. They insist on the centrality of correctness but contrarily to their attitude in their first meetings, they separate it from the argumentative rubrics and do not condition their use to evaluate written arguments to correctness. But this is not the end of the story of the harmonization between belief and action. The teachers rarely used the evaluation tools they agreed upon in the design-research team, in their classes. In interviews not reported here, teachers expressed concerns about the obstacles foreseen in their day-to-day work, with instilling argumentative activities while using the Digalo tool with their students (some of the obstacles were merely technical and organizational – how to handle a class with 40 students in such activities). In spite of suggestions of the rest of the design-research team, the teachers groped in the dark concerning how to interact and to evaluate in successive activities according to their new epistemological beliefs.

Discussion

Our aim in the present study was to observe teachers dedicated to fostering dialogic thinking in two activity systems and to compare their behavior in order to infer shifts in their epistemological beliefs and in their actions. As shown in the series of discussions we presented, the teachers behaved differently in the design-research team and in their classes. In the design-research team, they underwent several breakdowns: when they requested a list of precise criteria for evaluating arguments but rejected the suggestions to distinguish between argumentative components such as evidence and explanations, or when they rejected the suggestion to evaluate independently content and argumentativeness, and rather subordinated argumentative aspects to content ones; when they discussed the quality of a written argument brought from one of the classes (this activity challenged their bureaucratic–institutional view of learning outcomes); when they were perplexed concerning the communicative function of reasoning provided by Digalo. This perplexity contrasted with the propensity they showed in Digalo discussions, and with the innovative ways in which they animated the discussions according to dialogic principles in their work with their students. They helped students identify collective argumentation as a central vehicle of dialogical thinking: taking care of others' opinions, expressing opinions as a way to express an identity to the other, but also being committed to quality of reasoning as a way to convince and to be convinced. They capitalized on the very criteria they rejected when elaborating an evaluation tool. The sophisticated argument about the story of the hunter's son that one teacher presented suggests that she put a special stress on argumentative skills. However, this stress was put into action, not as a coercive way of labelling argumentative levels in students.

There are two possible interpretations to these discrepancies. The first one is that the breakdowns in the design-research team suggested a real resistance to change. In the Digalo discussions, the teachers were aware of the fact that they played a different role in a different system and intentionally instilled argumentative norms in their classes according to the principles they discussed in the design-research team. In contrast, in the design-research team, their status was at stake: they thought about how their institution would judge activities that promote dialogic thinking, and concepts such as "correctness," "content to be taught," and "criteria for evaluation" turned out to be central. The breakdowns we detected were signs of change in professionals ready to change their practices but anxious to preserve the infrastructure in which they continue to evolve.

The second interpretation is that in their classes, teachers *improvised* their interventions (see the notion of *improvisation* developed by Ludvigsen, Rasmussen, Ingeborg Krange,

Moen and Middleton in this volume). They could do so because the Digalo tool functioned as a *dual simulation* in both activity systems. They used terms and principles pertaining to dialogic thinking and argumentation that they heard in the design-research meetings. Also, the representational guidance of the Digalo tool afforded their fostering of dialogic thinking as the ontology provided enabled teachers to externalize their actions and to request from students to collectively discuss their opinions. The design-research team was a totally different activity system in which other values were at stake. They do not feel there are conflicts between the two very different activity systems.

We cannot decide between the two alternatives, but they are not mutually exclusive: teachers in their classes may improvize their teaching actions with a handy tool that affords collective dialogic argumentation and at the same time, they may oppose their own changing practices in the design-research team. Anyway, the important finding is that the teachers' actions witness a split in the two activity systems that convey the two layers in which teachers operate, the layer of dynamic action in their class, and the layer of reflection about their profession in a huge institutional constraining context. The ideas raised in the design-research team about arguments, claims and reasons, and even those to which they were opposed, were picked up and turned to prompts in action such as "state your opinion" and "clarify it" in the class context. By doing so, teachers became agents of change and leaders, rather than objects in the context of their in-service programs. This interplay between epistemology and ontology may evidence their developing identity (Packer & Goicoechea, 2001). And all the teachers that were reluctant to use Digalo in their classes followed T6 in his enthusiasm, and currently use Digalo in their classes. We currently keep on tracing changes in teachers' practices and possible consistency between the two activity systems. But change is everywhere: the collaborative work of teachers, researchers and designers yielded the elaboration of new tools and activities and of new pedagogical ideas that none of the participants envisaged beforehand to promote dialogical thinking.

References

Beach, K. D. (1999). Consequential Transitions: A sociocultural expedition beyond transfer in education. *Review of Research in Education, 24*, 101–139.

Cobb, P., Stephan, M., McClain, K. and Gravemeijer, K. (2001). Participating in Classroom Mathematical Practices. *The Journal of the Learning Sciences, 10*, 113–164.

Engeström, Y (2001). Expansive Learning at Work: Toward an activity theoretical reconceptualization. *Journal of Education and Work, 14*, 133–156.

Engeström, Y., Engeström, R. and Suntio, A. (2002). Can a School Community Learn to Master its Own Future? An activity theoretical study of expansive learning among middle school teachers. In G. Wells and G. Claxton (eds) *Learning for Life in the 21st Century: Sociocultural perspectives on the future of education*. Oxford: Blackwell.

Freire, P. (1973). *Education for Critical Consciousness*. New York: Seabury.

Hakkarainen, K (2003). Can Cognitive Explanation be Eliminated? *Science and Education, 12*, 671–689.

Kuhn, D. (1991). *The Skills of Argument*. New York: Cambridge University Press.

Kuhn, D. (2001). How Do People Know? *Psychological Science, 12*, 1–8.

Means, M. L. and Voss, J. F. (1996). Who Reasons Well? Two studies of informal reasoning among children of different grade, ability and knowledge levels. *Cognition and Instruction, 14*, 139–179.

Packer, M. J. and Goicoechea, J. (2001). Sociocultural and Constructivist Theories of Learning: Ontology, not just epistemology. *Educational Psychologist, 35*, 227–241.

Schwarz, B. B. (2009). Argumentation and Learning. In N. Muller-Mirza and A.-N. Perret-Clermont (eds) *Argumentation and Education – Theoretical Foundations and Practices* (pp. 91–126). New York and London: Springer.

Schwarz, B. B. and De Groot, R. (2007). Argumentation in a Changing World. *International Journal of Computer-Supported Collaborative Learning, 2*(2–3), 297–313.

Toulmin, S. E. (1958). *The Uses of Argument*. Cambridge: Cambridge University Press.

Wegerif, R. (2006). Towards a Dialogic Understanding of the Relationship Between CSCL and Teaching Thinking. *International Journal of Computer-Supported Collaborative Learning, 1*, 143–157.

Chapter 17

Researching classroom interactions

A methodology for teachers and researchers

Sally Barnes and Rosamund Sutherland

Introduction

Teaching and learning in schools is a complex social process which involves both the teacher and students in distributed knowledge-building activities. Research into this process includes researchers exploring from the outside and teachers exploring from the inside (Bassey, 1995). Jaworski (2003) draws on the work of Wagner (1997) to elaborate a form of research which she calls co-learning, in which research on classroom learning is 'conducted jointly by outsiders and insiders' (p. 250). The work we present in this chapter fits very much into this co-learning paradigm, and our emphasis here is on presenting a methodology for engaging in such co-learning. In this respect we present an approach to investigating classroom interactions which incorporates the perspectives of both classroom teachers and educational researchers, drawing on their different cultural backgrounds and particular areas of expertise. We explain how we use digital video to enable these researchers and teachers to distil the complexities of teaching and learning through creating video-linked commentaries of classroom practice.

Teachers are the main agents of change in the use of technology-enhanced learning in the classroom. As such they are often required to adopt technologies that involve transforming their teaching, with little scope for developing understanding about the relationship between the use of digital technology and the learning activities (Lankshear, Snyder & Green, 2000; Lim & Barnes, 2002). This expectation to both understand the potential of a new technology and at the same time to incorporate it into classroom practice is clearly difficult. The work we discuss in this chapter presents a way forward in that the active engagement and perspectives of teachers are combined through collaborative work with researchers, to make sense of unfolding classroom interactions. We describe our evolving approach through presenting and analysing the work of three teachers, all involved in developing understanding of how they could use interactive whiteboards to enhance learning in their classrooms.

Theoretical considerations

Technology in the classroom

The work discussed in this chapter develops and theorises the interrelationship between technology, learning and classroom interactions, with a particular focus on the ways in which technology changes the classroom dynamics.

The underlying assumptions for this research are derived from sociocultural theory, that learning occurs through interaction – both with people and with tools. The idea of 'tools' includes a wide range of artifacts and semiotic systems, where 'cultural artefacts are both material and symbolic; they regulate interactions with one's environment and oneself. In this respect they are "tools" broadly conceived, and the master tool is language' (Cole & Engeström, 1993, p. 9). The interactions we focus on are the communications that take place between people, in this case between teachers and pupils and between the pupils themselves, as they occur in the classroom.

In a discussion on distributed cognition, Pea extends this notion of tool use to include the idea that knowledge, or intelligence, can be thought of as residing within a tool's function (Pea, 1993). For example, in using a calculator to find the square root of a number you only need to press the square-root function key. The knowledge of how to perform the square-root calculation may not be known by the person pressing the key, however it is through interacting with the tool that the calculator takes over some of the knowledge processing. We consider classrooms to be 'distributed cognition' environments. In such situations pupils learn through their interactions with the teacher, and each other, and these are mediated through their use of tools (including language).

Edwards, Gilroy and Hartley (2002) argue that the skills teachers need today have changed and that trainee teachers need to develop reflective and interpretive practices that foster interactive and collaborative approaches to learning. This requires teachers to be able to 'assist learners' participation in communities where knowledge is used and constructed' (Edwards, Gilroy & Hartley, 2002, p. 108). Teachers also need to develop skills in their use of tools, in particular the pedagogical skills of incorporating technologies into their teaching and learning practices. Edwards *et al.* argue that because the use of technological tools in the classroom is related to an interactive style of learning, teachers need to shift from a transmission model of teaching to a model which facilitates the construction of knowledge. To do this requires not only a different set of skills but also a different conception of knowledge. 'Training for this interactive interpretative pedagogy cannot be based simply on sending novice practitioners into classrooms with lesson plans and seeing how well they deliver them' (Edwards, Gilroy & Hartley, 2002, p. 113). We would argue that similar shifts are needed for experienced teachers who may have a strong repertoire of teaching approaches but lack the experience of working with digital technologies. For both novice and experienced teachers, being part of a community which encourages the use of mediational tools, the sharing of experiences, of risk-taking, and of reflective practice can support the development and consolidation of skills to teach with digital technologies (Sutherland, John & Robertson, 2009).

The work reported here is based on studies which investigated how teachers create classroom environments which support the use of technology through interaction and the exchange of ideas (cf. Mercer, Wegerif & Dawes, 1999; Rogoff, 1998), so that students are more likely to become 'engaged in learning by participating in communities where learning is valued' (Greeno, Collins & Resnick, 1996, p. 26). The teacher plays a crucial role in orchestrating the way in which learning is mediated by language, other semiotic systems, tools and activities. In this sense, learning is inextricably linked to tool use (Säljö, 1999).

Collaborative research

To develop a collaborative research approach we are attempting to create a 'community of practice' (Wenger, 1998) of teachers, teacher educators and educational researchers who have an investment in understanding how digital technologies may be used to enhance learning, with a particular focus on the role of interactive whiteboards. By participating in joint-research activities the aim is to build new relationships and links between the participants, in which they develop common understandings and ways of working. It is not clear whether the general cohesion which builds within a long-standing group (e.g. primary teachers in one school) is a 'community of practice' but it is probable that as a stable cultural group they may have 'standard' ways of looking at the world. However, when temporary communities come together there may be disjunctions, confusions or clashes when the group begins to work together (Lindkvist, 2005; Sutherland, Claxton & Pollard, 2003). These tensions can provoke an imbalance within the group resulting in problems that need to be resolved (Engeström, 1987; Engeström, Miettinen & Punamäki, 1999). For example, as exemplified later in this chapter, when teachers and researchers work together to analyse classroom interactions it is likely that teachers will interpret the data differently from researchers. These different perspectives relate to a person's implicit and explicit theories of teaching and learning.

Sutherland, Claxton and Pollard (2003) suggest that points of disjunction are where learning and boundary crossings become possible, if not inevitable. The process of engaging with points of disjunction can lead to new ways of working and to the development of new understandings. In this respect a more open and collaborative way of working allows for multiple perspectives to be made explicit, providing the basis for changing practice. Within a community of practice, knowledge and know-how is distributed across the participants, and it is through the process of interaction between participants that individuals begin to develop, use and build on the knowledge and skills of each other.

In the projects reported here, each classroom teacher brought their knowledge and experiences of the classroom cultures within which they worked, which included knowledge of curriculum and assessment constraints, of their students, about subject matter and about teaching and learning. The researchers brought knowledge of research methodologies, and analytic practices and knowledge about teaching and learning. Each brought a culture and way of working which was possibly alien, certainly unknown, to the others, and it was through the process of paying attention to differences that these (often implicit) perspectives were made explicit. For example, a primary school teacher, Sarah Curran (discussed below), did this through the questions other teachers and researchers asked of her. As she said:

> The collaboration between researchers and teachers I feel is important. As a teacher you do some things instinctively and when talking to colleagues you do not justify these. But by talking with an outsider and explaining what you have done and what you think is happening means you have to really unpick what is going on. Also by using the video tapes allows you to replay incidences and each time you hear different things.
>
> (Armstrong & Curran, 2006)

An evolving collaborative approach

Through two research projects,[1] we have evolved a partnership model of research to explore the use and conceptualisation of technologies in classroom settings, incorporating the different perspectives of classroom teachers and educational researchers. In this work, the merging of cultures provides a space and sounding board for teachers to systematically consider the impact their actions have on teaching and learning in the classroom.

i) The interactive education project

The first project, the 'Interactive Education Project' (Sutherland, 2008; Sutherland, John & Robertson, 2009) was designed from the outset to bridge the divide between research and practice. At its heart was a partnership between university researchers, teacher educators and teachers. The project operated as a multilevelled set of overlapping communities of practice (John & Triggs, 2004). At the meso-level, the project was organised around Subject Design Teams (SDTs) in the areas of English, mathematics, science, modern foreign languages, music, history and geography. Much of the working through of these design initiatives was further developed at a local micro-level, where a teacher and researcher worked intensively together on the design, realisation and evaluation of a Subject Design Initiative (SDI). Design was informed by theory, research-based evidence on the use of ICT for learning, teacher's craft knowledge, curriculum knowledge, policy and management constraints and possibilities. The design initiatives started out as relatively simple ideas which exploited the use of the available technologies in a classroom. Over time and with iteration SDTs transformed SDIs into powerful new uses of ICT for learning.

Each design team (SDT) developed a common language which all participants could understand and work with. Through the analysis of video recordings, teacher interviews with different subject teams, and pupil interviews of different age groups, it was apparent that each participating teacher, teacher educator and researcher had different perspectives on what was unfolding in the classrooms (Gall & Breeze, 2005; Taylor, Lazarus & Cole, 2005; Sutherland, Armstrong, Barnes, Brawn, Breeze, Gall, Matthewman, Olivero, Taylor, Triggs, Wishart and John, 2004).

Through working together, members of the team were challenged on their beliefs about classrooms, pedagogy, pupils, and even their own roles. Each participant had to be thoughtful and reflective about their own practice and to find a form of words to explain it to the others in their group. These open reflective discussions gave participants of an SDT a glimpse of the world through another person's perspective as illustrated by the following quote from one of the partner teachers:

> Working closely with my university partner and the whole team was without doubt the biggest influence on my learning. I was introduced to new subject knowledge and new theories of teaching and learning. I was reading new things on language and research on language learning, as well as discussing ideas.
>
> (Partner Teacher)

Within this project 16 researchers and 59 teachers worked together over a period of two years. Where all teachers were actively involved in the process of developing and evaluating Subject Design Initiatives, only a minority became involved in the research process of analysing data and writing up the research.

ii) Distilling the complexity of teaching and learning

We developed a follow-on project from the InterActive Education project, 'Distilling the complexity of teaching and learning', in which four practising teachers worked with researchers to investigate the holistic impact of technology on teaching and learning (Armstrong, Barnes, Sutherland, Curran, Mills and Tahompson, 2005). In this project we worked as a collaborative team to analyse and interpret the video data. The participating teachers developed their own questions about the interrelationships between teaching, learning and the use of digital technology and then tested these out through analysis of video recordings of their classrooms. The papers and reports which have emerged from this project could only have been achieved through the multiple perspectives of teachers and researchers (see Armstrong, Barnes, Sutherland, Curran, Mills and Tahompson, 2005; Armstrong & Curran, 2006).

This follow-on project differed from the InterActive Education project in that the overall objectives were methodological. However, in order to work in partnership with teachers, it was decided to centre the classroom-based research around the use of interactive whiteboards for teaching and learning, because this was of major interest to both the researchers and teachers in the team (Armstrong & Curran, 2006; Armstrong, Barnes, Sutherland, Curran, Mills and Tahompson, 2005). At the time of the start of the project, IWBs were being promoted and installed in schools around the country through a government initiative (see also Mercer, Gillen, Kleine Staarman,

Littleton & Twiner, this volume). The project teachers were all beginning to use IWBs and were interested in learning more about how they could impact on their teaching activities. However, it has been noted that IWBs are not necessarily used interactively and may reinforce transmission approaches to teaching (Levy, 2002; Kennewell, 2004; Knight, Pennant & Piggot, 2004). Glover and Miller (2001) suggest that rather than transforming teachers' pedagogy, the interactive white-board can be relatively easily assimilated into existing ways of working. One aim of the study, therefore, was to explore further the ways in which teachers think that their use of IWBs has transformed their practice.

We worked in partnership with four teachers: Simon Mills[2] and Ian Thompson[3] who worked with us on the InterActive Education project, Adam Williams[4] who was introduced to us by another teacher who had been involved in the same project, and Sarah Curran[5] who approached us after a presentation we gave in Bristol about our work.

Roles for collaboration

The approach developed within the 'Distilling the Complexity' project-support teams to collaborate openly through every phase of the research from the development of research questions all the way through the final dissemination practices. Each participant has a role to play in this classroom-based research. The teacher carries out his or her regular professional role of teaching as well as reflecting on the decisions they make concerning curriculum choices, the role of technology, and so on. The researchers are responsible for recording classroom interactions, interviews with teachers and pupils and observing the lesson as it unfolds. What is important to note is that the design of the learning initiatives and the research design are worked out in joint discussions, although the teacher makes the moment-to-moment decisions about teaching and the researcher decides on the way the information is collected.

Teachers' inside knowledge of the classroom and school cultures were critical elements in making sense of classroom interactions. For example, in Ian's class (discussed below) it was not apparent to the researchers why one boy was allowed to be working at the IWB for much of the lesson. Through the group discussions it emerged that Ian encouraged this as a way of ensuring that this particular boy's behaviour problems did not impinge on the other pupils' work.

All the teachers were working full time as well as collaborating with us on this project. Their interest and motivation about the research was evident in their willingness to come into the university in the evening after teaching all day at school; giving up parts of their holidays to attend research conferences and willingness to code and record the video data in order to address the specific questions they posed. They were engaged in making sense of their classrooms and as part of this process they began to read and theorise about what they thought might be occurring in their classrooms. Initially, they seemed to be self-conscious about watching themselves on the recordings, hearing their own language and seeing their behaviour.

However, as committed professionals they became more interested in looking for connections between the things they observed they had done, as teachers, and the impact this may have had on the language and learning of pupils.

The role of digital video

Digital video was used to record spontaneous and naturalistic classroom interactions. The approach is an adaptation of that developed by Clarke (2001; 2002) and used in the Learner Perspective Study (LPS) of mathematics classrooms in nine countries. We used two digital video recorders over a sequence of related lessons, typically, three one-hour sessions. During the whole-class portions of a lesson, one camera was focused on the IWB to capture screen displays and interaction with the IWB by teachers or pupils. The other camera was focussed on the class as they faced the IWB. In this way we were able to track, to some extent, the pupils' focus of attention and their interactions with the teacher and other pupils. When pupils worked at computers, each camera typically focussed on a pair of pupils with the computer screen between them. Ideally, the same pupils were filmed over three lessons. This allowed us to explore their interactions and communication trajectories over the three lessons.

The first stage of processing the recordings involved making a composite time-linked video with a synchronised image from both cameras.

The resulting composite video was burned on to CDs, which meant the total class session became available for viewing. Crucially, we did not edit the videos in any way so each teacher received the unedited CD of their three classes. In a group session the teachers asked for some guidance about the focus the selected videos might cover. Collectively, we settled for 'interactivity' but did not narrow down the focus to any specific type of interaction. The teachers viewed the CDs of their class sessions and selected clips of approximately 10–15 minutes in length that they found particularly interesting. These clips could have been of part of the lesson that they felt had gone particularly well, or where they felt students had not been engaged in learning. Sometimes they selected clips in which a pupil had done something unexpected. We believed that in choosing the video clips, it was more likely that the teachers would invest time in analysing their classroom data. In addition we believed that the teachers were in a better position than the researchers to notice and ask questions and hypothesise about what had taken place in their classrooms. The clips which had been selected for further analysis were edited using FinalCut Pro. The teachers and researchers then worked together to make a transcription of the language used within the video clips.

Developing interpretative frameworks

The team of researchers and teachers held a day-long research seminar to begin the process of analysing data, by viewing and discussing the video clips. Each teacher presented their clips in half-hour sessions by first providing the situational context:

lesson objectives, ways of working, participants, and so on. Each clip was then viewed several times, focussing on different aspects of the emerging activity. At times the teacher's focus might be on the language used in the classroom; or the way the IWB was being used; or the way the pupils interacted with computers, the software or each other. Discussions of the video clips typically flowed freely around issues of curriculum, time management, the characteristics of the particular group of pupils, resources, and so forth. Always the goal was to try to make sense of the roles of the IWB, the teacher, learning activity, and so on. Multiple interpretations emerged which were tested against our own reflections and perspectives. We were able to develop an overview of classroom interactions on the basis of these viewings and the in-depth discussions surrounding each teacher's chosen video clip. However, each participant also had different questions they were asking about the video recordings and so these questions, too, were developed and refined over the course of the group discussion.

The resulting research questions became the focus of the next stage of the analysis. For instance, Ian Thompson wanted to investigate how use of the IWB may have supported his students in learning to write. Rather than presenting one pupil's work and then commenting on it, Ian and the pupils developed a narrative on the IWB using suggestions coming from all the pupils in the class. The pupils had a lively debate about what to write in the 'dual' narrative and Ian wanted to explore whether these skills extended to the narratives pupils developed when working individually.

During the research workshop a number of potential coding categories were generated which, we thought, would help to explore, more deeply, the teaching and learning interactions which occurred across the different classrooms. The initial focus was on categorising language. The group developed a simple coding frame, which enabled us to begin to analyse different forms of interaction in language (e.g. pupils' use of questions and subject-specific vocabulary; teacher instructional talk; or talk about use of tools such as the IWB).

Each teacher, together with the researchers, began to code their own video data using the coding frame developed jointly in the research seminar. The coding was carried out using Studiocode:[6] a bespoke software package developed in Australia through Clarke's Learner Perspective Study. Codes are entered and displayed through a multi-layered timeline beneath the video image.

The video can be started and stopped by clicking on a coded section on the timeline. Watching examples of coded language helped increase the reliability of the overall coding. We found that the main advantages of using Studiocode and its multi-layers of code are that:

- The layers have a visual impact on, in our case, the teachers and researchers. This visual image proved crucially important for teachers to begin to make sense of what was occurring in their classrooms.
- It was obvious from the representation, what codes were most used and the period of time a particular code was active.

- The participants found Studiocode easy and intuitive to use.
- Codes and sub-codes could be added at different times providing a flexible environment and the possibility of trying multiple coding systems, which addressed different aspects of the teachers' questions.

What became clear was that the language-coding frame devised in the joint session did not always cover the specific types of questions which the teachers were interested in exploring within their own classrooms. In this respect, the language analysis was not able to provide sufficient insights into the activity of any particular classroom setting. For example, in Simon's class seeing the non-verbal behaviour of the pupils became critical to his understanding of the language they were using. Each teacher, therefore, needed a coding frame specific to their research questions as well as being suitable for their particular classroom situations and teaching and learning interactions. The following case summaries highlight the way three[7] of the teachers developed theories and methods of exploring questions about their own teaching practices.

Sarah Curran

Sarah Curran was a Year 6 teacher in an inner-city primary school. She was using a web-based resource (Vitual FishTank[8]) in a science lesson to develop pupils' investigative skills. The pupils could adjust certain physical attributes of fish (e.g. the size of their eyes) then by logging the selected attributes they could investigate the survival rates of the fish when they were put into the Vitual FishTank. Based on her use of this software in a previous class, Sarah, assumed that the pupils would

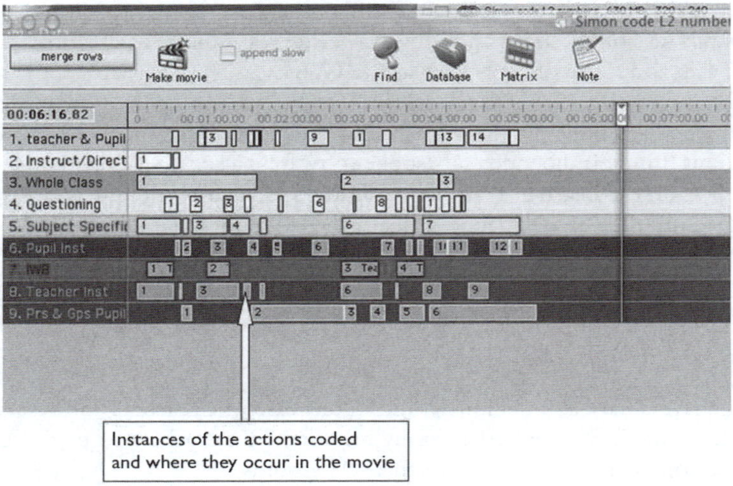

Figure 17.1 Coding categories as displayed through Studiocode

have time to design and log the outcomes of several fish. Her main purpose, then, was for the pupils to design several fish logging the attributes they chose (the size of their mouths, eyes and fins). She wanted the pupils to predict about how long a fish would live given the attributes the pupils chose. The pupils would then record the length of time a fish did live and then design a new fish based on their previous findings. The plan was that the pupils would do this three times and then find the average and see if the choices they made had been consistent over time.

Sarah introduced the lesson and, using the interactive whiteboard, demonstrated how to change the size of the fish's mouths, eyes and fins. She called on different pupils to come up and help design a fish and then the whole class watched to see what happened when the fish was 'put in the fishtank'. During the demonstrations there was a general discussion about what were desirable characteristics for fish to have to live long 'lives'. Sarah's impression was that during this period the pupils were engaged in the lesson and impatient to work on designing their own fish. The pupils then worked in groups of twos and threes on computers in the room.

Unfortunately, some of the fish the pupils designed lived for unusually long periods of time, up to 25 minutes. During this period the pupils could only act as spectators and some began to 'compete' with other groups to see whose fish would live longest. Sarah was unhappy with the way this lesson had gone and chose to analyse the lesson to understand what went wrong and how to change her teaching practice to ensure the objectives of the lesson would be met in future. One of the main objectives of this lesson had been for the pupils to systematically record their activities and then be able to reflect on which fish design would live longest and why. However, because the fish didn't die and the pupils had not recorded their actions they couldn't carry out the lesson as planned.

In the project's day-long research seminar questions were asked about how the pupils might have engaged with the software to develop understandings related to primary science.

Through viewing and interpreting the video as a group, Sarah became aware that the lesson had shifted from her original science objectives to becoming like a game. We decided that the next step was to explore the gaming element, in depth, to see if pupils became preoccupied with designing fish that lived as long as possible, or were other things happening?

To explore this aspect, Sarah coded the language following the original coding scheme developed by the group. However, the results did not help Sarah understand the gaming aspect as the coding focused mostly on questioning and response patterns. She therefore modified the original coding scheme to include the dialogue and activities in terms of science-specific, ICT-specific or other kinds of language. From this she realised that there were large tracks of dialogue and activities that she was not able to code with these categories. She then watched these sections more carefully and discovered that rather than science being the focus of their talk what she and the pupils had done in this class was to use language in a way that treated the episode as a game. In a fourth round of coding, she added 'gaming' as a new language category and found this became the most frequent type of talk.

These results suggest that the gaming language used by Sarah and the pupils contributed to the lack of emphasis on science in the lesson (Armstrong & Curran, 2006; Sutherland *et al.*, 2009). From a learning perspective the joint analytic session followed by her more in-depth work with the video and analysis of the language used by herself and the pupils allowed Sarah to reflect, learn and then develop a more effective teaching practice.

Simon Mills

Simon Mills is a very experienced Year 4 teacher in an inner-city primary school. He was involved in the InterActive Education Project and became interested in the connections between language, learning and the use of technology to the extent that he began a master's degree to explore the theories and methods which underlie his teaching practices. In our second project Simon again participated. This time we recorded sessions when he was teaching a series of lessons on data-handling to Year 4 children.[9] In the first lesson Simon introduced elements of frequency distributions by giving each child a packet of different-coloured chocolate sweets. During the lesson, the children worked in pairs at the computer to explore the frequency of different colours from both of their packets of sweets, and entered the results into the spreadsheet Excel. Later in the lesson the results were displayed on an interactive whiteboard to be discussed by the whole class. Over the next three lessons, the pupils continued their investigations and were introduced to concepts such as fractions, decimals and percentages.[10] In the group analytic session Simon introduced a whole class segment when Simon and the pupils were working with the interactive whiteboard. He selected this segment because he thought it showed how the children were developing very sophisticated language to talk about the results they had produced using Excel. In the course of the open discussion, Simon became aware that he might have been over interpreting some of the pupils behaviour. At times the language occurring in the classroom did not fit with the behaviour of the children; it wasn't always clear what the link was between the terms used and the meaning the pupils attached to them. As such the evidence was not as clear-cut as he originally thought. Also, for his master's degree, Simon had been introduced to sociocultural theories and felt considerable resonance with Neil Mercer's work. He developed a coding scheme based on Mercer's language codes which he applied to portions of his classroom's videos. What is interesting here is that when Simon applied Mercer's categories, they didn't work well and he found that he couldn't use them to explain what occurred in his classroom. However, by reading Mercer in greater depth and exploring other theories as well, Simon asked more questions and has since developed a coding scheme which explores non-verbal behaviour which, when analysed in conjunction with the language coding, provides a much clearer picture of classroom interactions

I had become increasingly interested in the work of Neil Mercer (1995; 2000) particularly his idea that classroom talk can be viewed as the 'social mode of thinking' and the primary vehicle by which shared understanding is negotiated and developed within learning situations. This 'Thinking Together', or 'Reasoning Together' idea had become a key element in my thinking when 'designing' teaching and learning contexts in the numeracy hour. The interactive whiteboard, as an interface, alongside selected software environments, had come to play a central role in facilitating, scaffolding, supporting and recording the outcomes of these classroom-based mathematical conversations, developed within my interpretations of the National Numeracy Strategy objectives (DFES, 1999).

This model of teaching and learning, led me to form very specific ideas about what I thought was happening in the teaching and learning spaces I created within my classroom, and to a belief that since my classroom practice had evolved from my understanding of Mercer, then I might be able to identify discursive practices within the data which coincided with the analytical categories devised and presented in the work I had read. However applying these categories, using the analytical tool, Studiocode™ proved problematic. The complexity of activity, which emerged during the shared data analysis process [between researcher and teacher] within the whole class context, revealed overlapping discourses between students and students, and students and teacher (Mills, 2007).

For Simon, his involvement in both projects has led him to theorise more widely about classroom interactions as they relate to the pupils' engagement with the subject through their conversations and use of technology. By developing his understandings of a range of theoretical perspectives he is developing sophisticated reflective and analytic skills which is evidenced in the quote above.

Ian Thompson

Ian is an experienced English teacher at secondary level. Unlike Simon, he had not embraced the use of technology in his teaching before joining the project. He was involved in the InterActive Education project and wanted to participate in the follow-on project as a way of investigating, for himself, the potential of different technological tools for teaching English. Ian believed that because the process of writing by hand is so different from the process of using a word processor that the experience results in very different writing outcomes. Over the course of three sessions, we recorded Ian teaching a low-attaining group of 12–13-year-old pupils in the computer room. In the first session, Ian created a whole-class activity for pupils to start the process of constructing a story using different narrative techniques. The pupils then worked in pairs to write their own stories. Within each session one pair's work was discussed by the whole class. Ian had been very concerned about how this particular class of pupils would behave when working in pairs and whether there would be classroom-management issues which could disrupt the lesson. However, through the analysis, the videos and discussions in the university, alternative explanations emerged.

In one session, for example, Ian reflected on his intervention in the class of what appeared to be off-task behaviour and how this radically affected the final writing produced by two boys.

. . . frequently pupils begin their talk with a social question such as 'Did you go out last night?' that appears to be a necessary precursor to their on task writing. It appears that pupils need the space to explore an idea through shared experience and shared talk and the best writing occurred after pupils had been encouraged to discuss the process before they began writing. Video clips which focussed on the pupils allowed us to see the practical outcome of teacher intervention as well as to glimpse some of the thought processes. What was clear from this short interaction was that, as a teacher, I often discouraged the sort of activity such as socially mediated talk that was in fact critical to the development of the writing process. A simple focus on the written outcome would not have allowed me the opportunity to observe and analyse this process.

(Thompson, 2006)

The theoretical explanations which Ian arrived at to make sense of this classroom work developed over time from the joint analytical sessions, with members of the English team within the InterActive Education project and from his reading and understanding of Vygotsky. He also drew from theories of discourse and multi-modality. His PhD investigates the impact of writing with a word processor on different writing genres among secondary school pupils.[11]

Discussion and concluding remarks

The examples presented in this chapter show how in-depth knowledge of class-rooms and an understanding of research methodologies and methods can be combined to produce more holistic and realistic understandings of classroom interactions. For Sarah, the co-learning of the group enabled her to become aware of how she had unintentionally encouraged the use of the science simulation software as a game. Simon's initial interpretations of his class were based on his own thoughts as a reflective practitioner. The video evidence, together with other members of the group, suggested that he had not been aware of key interactions between students that contributed to the whole class learning. His use of Mercer's language categories was only able to partially explain the results. By expanding his analytical categories to include non-verbal interactions he gained new insight into the way in which the IWB enhanced learning in his classroom. Ian's insights into the preparatory process his pupils' went through before they engaged in the process of collaboratively constructing a dual narrative grew out of his reading of the research literature and careful analysis of the video data.

From a methodological position collaborative partnerships, as discussed in this chapter, highlight how the blending of research and teaching cultures can potentially lead to more insightful notions of the inner workings of a classroom. Bringing together teacher and researcher perspectives can illuminate classroom interactions in ways that may not be visible by one group working on their own. Teachers of different subjects, and researchers from different disciplines are able to work through points of disjunction and develop ways of working which could eventually lead to building a community of practice where all participants have a voice in the analysis and interpretation of classroom interactions.

There are two key elements to the work we have presented here. First, the use of multiple research methods, which combine in-depth observational techniques with quantitative coding systems. The flexibility of digital video allows researchers to view films, repeating segments, and to import them into analytic tools, such as Studiocode. The use of qualitative interpretative techniques coupled with the in-depth systematic analyses of language and behaviour provide a basis for understanding classroom-based teaching and learning.

Second, when teachers and researchers collaborate on research activities they create distributed knowledge research systems (cf. Pea, 1993) which can feed into and support the creation and development of theories of classroom interactions. Elements of a distributed-knowledge research system can be seen in the reflective and interpretative activities of the teachers and researchers reported here. We suggest that the skills and practices which Edwards, Gilroy and Hartley (2002) argue are needed for teachers to teach with technology are the same skills which teachers and researchers need to adopt to be able to engage with the inevitable points of disjunction in carrying out and interpreting research outcomes (Sutherland, Claxton and Pollard, 2003).

One area where this research leads is to address the known difficulty for research theories and findings to have an impact on teachers and classroom practices. Sutherland (2006) highlighted that teachers do not typically read the research literature about teaching and learning. Nor do researchers typically read applied education journals, which might have a bearing on their research interpretations. Rather, these two different cultures continue to look at teaching and learning from quite different points of view. The collaborative and co-learning work reported here may contribute to the development of new representational techniques which support the dissemination of research results to different communities. For example, videopapers which are hyperlinked documents with three screen areas for text, video clips and scanned images. As such they can provide multiple texts to accompany a video clip. A videopaper could incorporate video of the classroom, together with text which relates to the teacher's perspective, the researcher's perspective and also the students' perspectives. This type of dissemination practice is being used with initial teacher trainees to develop dissemination practices which build on collaborative reflective practices (Beardsley & Cogan-Drew, 2007; Olivero, Sutherland & John, 2004).

Notes

1 The Interactive Education Project was funded through the UK's Economic and Social Science Research Council, Teaching and Learning Programme (2001–2004) Sutherland, Robinson and John. Ref: L-139-25–1060. See http://www.interactiveeducation.ac.uk

Distilling the complexity of teaching and learning was funded by the ESRC through the REISS (Research Equipment in the Social Sciences) Initiative (2004–2005) Sutherland, Barnes and John. RES-474-25–0008.

2   Teaching at Teyfant Community School and in the dissertation phase of MSc in Education, Technology and Society at the University of Bristol.

3   Teaching at Sheldon Secondary School and studying for a PhD at the University of Bristol.

4   Teaching at John Cabot City Technology College.

5   Teaching at Whitehall Primary School and studying for an MEd at the University of the West of England.

6   Studiocode was originally developed by SportsTec for use in the training of Olympic Athletes. Information about Studicode is available at: http://www.studiocodegroup.com/index.html

7   Adam Williams' position within his school changed during the course of the project and he was unable to take part in all our collaborations.

8   http://www.virtualfishtank.com/

9   This sequence of lessons was a reworking of his Subject Design Initiative for the InterActive Education Project.

10 For further discussion of this see Mills (2004) and Sutherland (2006).

11 The PhD thesis 'The Process of pupils', written using ICT, will be submitted in 2008.

References

Armstrong, V., Barnes, S. B., Sutherland, R. J., Curran, S., Mills, S., and Tahompson, I. (2005). Collaborative Research Methodology for Investigating Teaching and Learning: The use of interactive whiteboard technology. *Educational Review*, 57(4), 457–469.

Armstrong, V. and Curran, S. (2006). Developing a Collaborative Model of Research Using Digital Video. *Computers and Education*, 46, 336–347.

Bassey M. (1995). *Creating Education Through Research*. Edinburgh: British Educational Research Association.

Beardsley, L. and Cogan-Drew, D. (2007). Videopaper: Bridging research and practice for pre-service and experienced teachers. In R. Goldman, R. D. Pea, B. Barron, and S. J. Derry, (eds) *Video Research in the Learning Sciences*. Hillsdale, NJ: Lawrence Erlbaum Associates.

Clarke, D. (ed.). (2001). *Perspectives on Practice and Meaning in Mathematics and Science Classrooms*. Dordrecht: Kluwer Academic Press.

Clarke, D. (2002). The Learner's Perspective Study: Methodology as the enactment of theory of practice. Paper presented at the interactive symposium, International Perspectives on Mathematics Classrooms, at the *Annual Meeting of the American Educational Research Association*, New Orleans, April 1–5.

Cole, M. and Engeström, Y. (1993). A Cultural-historical Approach to Distributed Cognition. In Salomon, G. (ed.) *Distributed Cognition*, Cambridge: Cambridge University Press.

Edwards, A., Gilroy, P. and Hartley, D. (2002). *Rethinking Teacher Education: Collaborative responses to uncertainty*. London: Routledge.

Engeström, Y. (1987). *Learning by Expanding: An Activity-theoretical Approach to Developmental Research*. Helsinki: Orienta-Konsultit.

Engeström, Y., Miettinen, R. and Punamäki, R.-L. (eds). (1999) *Perspectives on Activity Theory*. New York: Cambridge University Press.

Gall, M. and Breeze, N. (2005). Music Composition Lessons: The multimodal affordances of technology. *Educational Review*, 57, 415–434.

Glover, D. and Miller, D. (2001). Running with Technology: The pedagogic impact of the large-scale introduction of interactive whiteboards in one secondary school. *Journal of Information Technology for Teacher Education*, 10, 257–277.

Greeno, J. Collins, A. and Resnick, L. (1996). Cognition and Learning. In D. C. Berliner and P. C. Calfee (eds) *Handbook of Educational Psychology*. New York: Simon & Schuster.

Jaworski, B. (2003). Research Practice Into/Influencing Mathematics Teaching and Learning Development: Towards a theoretical framework based on co-learning partnerships, *Educational Studies in Mathematics*, 54, 249–282.

John, P. and Triggs, P. (2004). From Transaction to Transformation: Information and communication technology, professional development and the formation of communities of practice. *Journal of Computer Assisted Learning*, 20, 426–439.

Kennewell, S. (2004). *Researching the Influence of Interactive Presentation Tools on Teacher Pedagogy*, paper presented at the British Educational Research Association (BERA) Conference, Manchester, 2004.

Knight, P., Pennant, J. and Piggott, J. (2004). What Does it Mean to 'Use the Interactive Whiteboard' in the Daily Mathematics Lesson? *MicroMath*, 20, 14–16.

Lankshear, C., Snyder, I. and Green, B. (2000). *Teachers and Technoliteracy: Managing literacy, technology and learning in schools*. St. Leonards, NSW: Allen and Unwin.

Levy, P. (2002). *Interactive Whiteboards in Learning and Teaching in Two Sheffield Schools: A developmental study*, Department of Information Studies, University of Sheffield. http://dis.shef.ac.uk/eirg/projects/wboards.htm (last accessed 15 November 2003).

Lim, C. P. and Barnes, S. B. (2002). 'Those Who Can, Teach' – The Pivotal Roles of the Teacher in the Information and Communication Technologies (ICT) Learning Environment. *Journal of Educational Media*, 27(1&2), 19–40.

Lindkvist, L. (2005). Knowledge Communities and Knowledge Collectives: A typology of knowledge work in groups. *Journal of Management Studies*, 42, 1189–1210.

Mercer, N. (1995). *The Guided Construction of Knowledge: Talk amongst teachers and learners*. Clevedon: Multilingual Matters.

Mercer, N. (2000). *Words and Minds. How we use language to think together*. London: Routledge.

Mercer, N., Wegerif, N. and Dawes, L. (1999). Children's Talk and the Development of Reasoning in the Classroom, *British Educational Research Journal*, 25(1), 95–111.

Mills, S. (2004). Who's a Smartie? *Micromath*, 20, 17–23.

Mills, S. (2007). *Technology, Classroom Spaces and Lesson Structure*. Unpublished MSc dissertation for Education, Technology and Society, University of Bristol.

Olivero, F., Sutherland, R. and John, P. (2004). Learning Lessons with ICT: Using videopapers to transform teachers' professional knowledge, *Cambridge Journal of Education*, 34, 179–191.

Pea, R. (1993). Practices of distributed intelligence and designs for education. In Salomon, G. (ed.) *Distributed Cognition*. Cambridge: Cambridge University Press.

Rogoff, B. (1998). *Cognition as a Collaborative Process*, Vol. 2, 5th edition. New York: John Wiley & Sons.

Säljö, R. (1999). Learning as the Use of Tools: A sociocultural perspective on the human-technology link. In Littleton, K. and Light, P. (eds) *Learning with Computers: Analysing productive interaction*. London: Routledge.

Sutherland, R. (2006). *Teaching for Learning Mathematics.* Milton Keynes: Open University Press.

Sutherland, R., John, P. and Robertson, S. (eds). (2009). *Improving Classroom Learning with ICT.* London: RoutledgeFalmer.

Sutherland, R., Armstrong, V., Barnes, S., Brawn, R., Breeze, N., Gall, M., Matthewman, S., Olivero, F., Taylor, A., Triggs, P., Wishart, J. and John, P. (2004). Transforming Teaching and Learning: Embedding ICT into everyday classroom practices. *Journal of Computer Assisted Learning, 20,* 413–425.

Sutherland, R. J., Claxton, G. and Pollard, A. (eds). (2003). *Learning and Teaching where World Views Meet.* London: Trentham Books.

Sutherland, R., Robertson, S. and John, P. (2004). Interactive Eduation: Teaching and learning in the information age. *Journal of Computer Assisted Learning, 20,* 410–412.

Taylor, A., Lazarus, E. and Cole, R. (2005). Putting Languages on the (Drop Down) Menu: Innovative writing frames in modern foreign language teaching. *Educational Review, 57,* 435–456.

Thompson, I. (2006). *The Process of Pupils' Writing Using ICT.* Unpublished PhD upgrade proposal, University of Bristol.

Vygotsky, L. S. (1978). *Mind in Society.* Cambridge, MA: Harvard University Press.

Wagner, J. (1997). The Unavoidable Intervention of Educational Research: A framework for reconsidering research-practitioner cooperation. *Educational Researcher, 26,* 13–22.

Wenger, E. (1998). *Communities of Practice: Learning, meaning and identity.* Cambridge: Cambridge University Press.

Chapter 18

Weaving the context of digital literacy

- Nice summary of activity theory (p.297)
- Literacies as socio-cultural
- Tools + meaning (p. 297)

Ola Erstad

Introduction

A broad range of work in psychology (Wertsch, 1998; Säljö, 2005), sociology (Castells *et al.*, 1999; Mattelart, 2003) and education (Wells & Claxton, 2002; Bereiter, 2002) has shown the impact of information and communication technologies on our culture and social life in general and on our conceptions of learning especially. As a frame of reference, these cultural developments raise some key issues concerning literacy, both how the new digital technologies change conceptions about what literacy is and how literate practices in schools change as a consequence of such developments.

'New literacy studies', as a field of research, is multifaceted. This is mainly because literacy constitutes, simultaneously, a social, an ideological, a cultural and an educational practice (Rassool, 1999). When information and communication technologies are introduced, additional issues of change are related to available systems of representation, cognitive aspects and social dimensions of literacy (DiSessa, 2001). As some researchers have highlighted (Gee, 2003) new media, like computer games, also challenge where literacy practices are taking place in our culture.

A lot of focus has traditionally been directed towards the technology itself, and which skills are needed in order to operate computers and software. I believe this is a restricted focus. Literacy is not in itself related to a specific technology (Lemke, 1998), but rather the competencies and skills needed in order to take advantage of different technologies in order to learn, framed within certain social and institutional settings like schools.

My aim in this chapter is not to present a definition of digital literacy per se, but rather to outline an approach towards digital literacy, especially as seen in school-based settings. The discussion raises a critique of most present-day perspectives on digital literacy related to formal learning in schools, seeing it as a skill in handling technological tools. My main point is that we need to grasp the wider contextual dimensions of school-based learning in order to fully understand how digital literacy might be developed. Context in this sense implies that we need to look beyond skills in operating hardware and software, towards a multilevel analysis including both institutional effects and educational practices (Daniels, 2005).

The theoretical assumptions on digital literacy and schooling will be based on an activity-theoretical framework, focusing on the concepts of activity and context, and also mastery and appropriation as discussed by Wertsch (1998). This chapter includes a review of relevant international research and empirical data on ICT in Norwegian schools. The introduction of digital literacy as an area of competence in schools is a new 'object of activity' that might create change in the relationship between learning, activity settings and social institutions. This, of course, involves increased complexity in the way we study such developments and understand its implications.

Digital literacy – a research agenda

The conceptual development of digital literacy goes back to the 'New Literacy Studies' in the 1970s and 1980s. Several researchers at that time (see, for example, Heath, 1983; Street, 1984, Graff, 1987) were critical to the conception of literacy as a neutral set of skills, what Brian Street (1984) describes as 'the autonomous model of literacy', where literacy, as a set of neutral skills, can be used in different contexts and for different purposes to complete a set of tasks. The New Literacy Studies expanded this limited notion of literacy to take account of sociocultural influences. (See, for example, Scribner & Cole, 1981.) The term 'literacies' emerged to signal the different ways people use language and different systems of representation in social practices. As stated by Pahl and Rowsell: 'Literacy as decoding and encoding without consideration of context belies the complex nature of reading and writing. When we read and write, we are always doing it in a certain place for a certain purpose.' (2005: 3). The consequence was that the concept of literacy was opened up to include interaction with different text forms and studying them in different social practices (Barton, 1994). In addition there has been an influence from studies of how children and youth use different media, and from media education in schools, focusing on the need to teach children about the social and cultural influences of different media in our society (Buckingham 2003). The term 'digital literacy' builds on these conceptions and is then linked to the development of digital technologies and media forms.

As a research agenda, Lankshear and Knobel (2006) describe the traditional conception of digital literacy as 'the IT thing', implying that it is about handling the technology itself. Lankshear and Knobel instead argue for focusing on digital literacies as social practices of reading and writing (keying, imaging, etc.) that can be seen in blogging, online fanfiction and recent developments of social software like MySpace and YouTube.

During the mid-1990s a group of researchers from different parts of the world, what has been called the New London Group (Cope & Kalantzis, 2000), gathered to make a statement on the research agenda on literacy and technologies. They argued for the use of 'multiliteracies' as an overall term. Their research perspective implies that literacy is a many-faceted thing, from James Paul Gee's (2003) work on computer games to Günter Kress on 'multimodal literacy' (2003). In a way this points back to what Freire and Macedo (1987) described as 'reading the word and the world', implying that literacy is linked to a critical analysis of the social framework in which men exist, and embedded in social practices that are important for people. It is not only about how we use specific artifacts, but also the social implications of such artifacts (Säljö, 2005).

In her book *Literacy for Sustainable Development in the Age of Information* (1999), Naz Rassool presents an overview of different debates on literacy during the last decades. Her point is that research perspectives on technology and literacy also need to reconceptualize power structures within the information society and an emphasis on 'communicative competence' in relation to democratic citizenship. ICT gives students a possibility to act upon their social contexts. The points made above indicate the importance of studying how new technologies represent new cultural tools that create new meaning structures. These tools create new possibilities for how people relate to each other, how knowledge is defined in negotiation between actors and also how it changes our conception of learning environments in which actors negotiate meaning. Empowerment, in this sense, is related to the active use of different tools, with actors that have the competence and critical perspective on how to use them for learning.

When we look at the existing research literature on digital literacy it is evident that there is not a lot to build on for establishing a broader research agenda for studying digital literacies in schools. There is a lot of research on how children and youth use digital media in their everyday culture, but much less on linking digital literacy to schooling and classroom practices (Ba *et al.*, 2002; Lankshear & Knobel, 2003; Buckingham, 2003). On the other hand there have been, for more than a decade, several studies on the impact of new technologies on learning activities in schools (Perkins *et al.*, 1995; Kozma, 2003). However, these have to a small extent been linked to broader issues of literacy developments. At the moment there are several policy-driven initiatives in the European community, the US and several Asian countries on developing digital literacy as part of school-based learning (the European Charter for Media Literacy, 2006; New Media Consortium, 2005). The rhetoric surrounding these issues is dominated by educational debates and policy on how to get teachers and students to use information and communication technologies to a larger extent as part of school practices. This review indicates that the research field on digital literacy is in need of a conceptual framework and theoretical approach that can grasp the complexities of these issues. I perceive activity theory as a possible answer to these challenges.

The shaping of activities in context

Activity theory, as developed by Engeström (1987), represents a holistic approach to studying change processes on different levels. Digital literacy, in this sense, has to be studied both in its implications for how human activity is mediated by tool use and the community within which the activity takes place; that is, the rules that hold within that community and the way in which work is organized to achieve its

(handwritten margin note top: Layers of activity - Context)

objective, what is described as 'division of labor'. The basic unit of analysis within activity theory is not the individual subject or a tool, but a system that considers intentional tool use within a cultural context. At the same time it is possible to interpret an inherent epistemic bias within activity systems, where subjects have agency in a way that tools, rules and even communities do not (Nardi, 1996; Oliver & Pelletier, 2006).

(handwritten margin note: Three levels of activity -)

The concept of activity is a core element in the way we study digital literacy in schools. It relates to how humans use tools in different settings. Within activity theory, three levels at which activity can be analysed have been identified (Kuutti, 1996). The most general level is called the level of activity, as an expression of collective activities, which describe high-level plans such as digital literacy defined within school curricula. The second level is more specific, focusing on the individual actions that contribute to the activity, such as teachers and students using computers as part of learning processes in specific subject domains. The third is more specific still, consisting of operations that contribute to each action, such as using specific software programs to work on specific assignments. Operations are usually routine or automatic, rarely being the focus of conscious attention unless something goes wrong (Oliver & Pelletier, 2006).

(handwritten margin note: Cole on Context)

Context, as an analytic perspective, becomes important by studying how activities and actions are embedded within activity systems in specific circumstances and situations. An important division in our understanding of context is presented by Michael Cole (1996: 132–137) in what he calls 'context as that which surrounds' and 'context as that which weaves together'. The first implies a common notion of context as all that lies around the activities performed and which influence these activities in different ways. These are studies of different layers with the learner, the task and the activity in the centre and organizations and communities as broader contextual factors. The point is that 'what surrounds' is interpreted as influencing the activities at the centre.

(handwritten margin note: Activity can not be understood separate from Context)

Another way of looking at context is through what Cole describes as 'that which weaves together'. He writes about this as: 'When context is thought of in this way, it cannot be reduced to that which surrounds. It is, rather, a qualitative relation between a minimum of two analytical entities (threads), which are two moments in a single process. The boundaries between "task and its context" are not clear-cut and static but ambiguous and dynamic' (1996: 135). This is also related to the goals, tools and setting that the act is part of. Cole refers to Bateson's example of the blind man and the stick to illustrate this point. One cannot just analyse the man and his stick, and the limitations of human perception and cognition, but needs to include the purposes and the environment in which this man finds himself.

Social context also relates to the way people need to develop an understanding of what forms of verbal and nonverbal behaviour are appropriate in which social context. As stated by Erickson and Schultz: 'This requires knowing what context one is in and when context changes. We think that the capacity for monitoring contexts must be an essential feature of social competence' (1997: 22). This raises questions about how digital literacy is to be understood in school-based settings, and how students and teachers interpret such a literacy compared to out-of-school usage of digital technologies.

The importance of integrating individual, social and institutional processes when studying context is further stressed by Minick, Stone and Forman (1993). They write that:

> It has become increasingly clear that the development of a sociocultural theory of mind demands careful attention to the institutional context of social interaction. Culturally specific institutions such as schools, homes, and libraries systematically structure the interactions that occur among people or between people and cultural artifacts such as books or computers. One cannot develop a viable sociocultural conception of human development without looking carefully at the way these institutions develop, the way they are linked with one another, and the way human social life is organized within them.
>
> (1993: 6)

Digital literacy, therefore, cannot only be conceptualized as a neutral skill that will be learned in school, but as a social practice which influences different aspects of the institutional context of schools.

As part of these developments we have seen an increasing number of studies on how ICT influences developments of learning environments (Bliss *et al.*, 1999; De Corte, Verschaffel *et al.*, 2003). It is being used to describe changes in the way we organize learning activities, both in real-life settings in classrooms and virtual environments. An important issue has been a transition from learning environments where the teacher and the textbook structure, define and control the learning process, towards student-centred learning environments (Land & Hannafin, 2000) where the students themselves are the main frame of reference for defining the learning process. Student-centred learning environments are designed to support individual efforts to negotiate multiple points of view, while engaging in authentic activities. Important assumptions in these environments are that learning is highly tuned to the situation in which it takes place.

The concept of 'mediated action' elaborated on by James Wertsch (1998) is linked to discussions of context in the way human action is mediated through the use of tools within social practices. One of his questions on mediated action is 'how the introduction of novel cultural tools transforms the action' (ibid.: 42). The point to infer is that modern technologies are important cultural tools to take into consideration, and that they have broad cultural and social implications on different levels. In this sense new technologies cannot only be seen as a continuation of old technologies like the typewriter or a calculating machine, but rather as something transforming the way we create knowledge and meaning, communicate and interact.

This also points to the relationship between 'mastery' and 'appropriation' as part of 'mediated action' (Wertsch, 1998). One might, for example, master the use of the technology without having appropriated it in the sense that it becomes a part of one's identity as a learner. This can easily be the situation when introducing digital technologies in schools without considering the broader social issues of how children and young people use such technologies outside of schools (Buckingham, 2003). The danger is that the teacher might try to use the technology in ways that are not seen as relevant by the students, but which are defined as part of the institutionalized practice in schools by the teachers.

My argument above has been that we need to grasp the interrelationship between activities, actions and operations and the wider contextual dimensions of school-based learning in order to fully understand the impact of ICT on learning, and not narrow down the educational use of ICT to certain skills in operating the computer or specific software. I will now turn to some empirical data that illustrate this point of looking at different aspects of school communities so that we better grasp how digital literacy works as new practices and is embedded in systems of activities.

The PILOT project

The research review mentioned before has direct implications for present developments in schools. This can be seen in curriculum developments in several countries during the last couple of years. In Norway, for example, 'digital competence/literacy' has been written into the new national curriculum as a key area for learning practices in schools for the years to come (White paper, 2004). However, the term used in the curriculum, defining it as one of five basic skills alongside the ability to read, write, numeracy and oral skills, is 'the ability to use digital tools', which imply a narrow conception of digital literacy as directly linked to operating a specific technology.

The research reported on below has been developed in order to study the educational use of ICT in Norwegian schools. The ultimate aim of studying such practices has been to understand the wider implication of using ICT in educational settings, what I have defined as digital literacies.

I will concentrate my discussion on one large-scale intervention study in Norway from 2000 until the end of 2003. PILOT (Project: Innovation in Learning, Organization and Technology) has been the largest and most extensive project in Norway related to the educational use of ICT in schools. The project consisted of 120 primary and secondary schools that worked on the extensive use of ICT in education during a four-year period. The project schools were spread across the country, in nine different regions, and with control schools in each region that did not take part in the project, but were part of ordinary strategies for implementation of ICT in schools. The methods used were a combination of quantitative and qualitative research. I was leading a team of 16 researchers from different District University Colleges in each region. A pre–post survey (spring 2001–spring 2003) was used to trace changes on certain indicators in school development and educational use of ICT. This was done with about 2000 students, 500 teachers and 60 principals at both times. It was also the foundation for planning the intervention study. In a smaller sample of schools, teachers and researchers in different regions worked closely together to create certain interventions within the school culture. Documentation was done by interviewing teachers, students and principals, doing observations and document analysis.

Three levels of analysis were identified. The first focused on norms and regulations in the way schools organized their activities and how ICT was used to change organizational practices. The second was directed towards the interrelationships between and among teachers and students (actions). And the third was focusing on the use of specific ICT-tools in certain subject domains and levels of schooling (operations). All together these inform us about broader issues of digital literacy in schools. In the following I will not discuss specific operations using specific digital tools, but focus more on the interrelationship between context and activities when using digital technologies in schools.

Institutional mechanisms

One of the main conclusions from the pre–post survey in the PILOT project was the connection between a holistic perspective on change and the educational use of ICT at these schools compared to control schools in each region (Erstad, 2004). This conclusion shows the importance of a broader contextual understanding across different school activities such as reorganizing time-schedules, tearing down walls to make more flexible learning environments and rooms, school leadership more involved in meetings on school development together with teachers, ways of processing and distributing information using 'learning managements systems' within the school community, and so forth. Thereby, creating a new institutional practice linked to the use of ICT, as a framework for digital literacy.

Students at PILOT schools reported significantly more often that they used ICT for subject-oriented activities towards the end of the project than in the beginning, while students at control schools used ICT mostly for entertainment, surfing and less goal-directed activities at both times. Students at PILOT schools experienced that their schools had a positive orientation towards school development and the educational use of ICT, while students at the control schools did not. The survey also showed that both principals and teachers at PILOT schools experienced that their school had moved beyond a focus on implementing ICT towards working on changes in school organization, debates about learning, more flexible methods of learning, increased team orientation and collaboration among teachers, where ICT was an important element in both initiating such activities and supporting change. These results support what was earlier discussed with reference to the different components of activity systems and the different levels for studying activity. Such results on ICT and school development also show how digital literacy, as the way digital technologies influence learning processes in schools, is related to how the school as a whole organize its activities.

In this project one strategic step several schools had taken in their reorganization of their practices was to create networks between schools and among teachers. In one of the Northern regions of Norway they started what was called 'dialogue conferences', where teachers met and discussed their own change processes, and related these to others. One teacher describes his experiences of this in the following way:

> To be able to look at yourself at a distance makes it clearer what you are actually doing. When you at the same time get comments, questions and ideas from others in the same situation, it forces you to reflect on your own everyday experiences in the classroom, and through that process you get more conscious about what, why and how.

Many of these discussions are about the teacher's own conception of their own roles and the changes they go through. This relates to many aspects of the institution of school, where new technologies is one aspect. However, we see that schools that do not look into their institutional practices have more problems of how they define the educational purposes of using ICT in their teaching, and thereby not creating a space for digital literacy to develop, because it is not seen as embedded in their social practices and then easily becomes just a technology they try to master.

Teachers and ICT in educational practice

From these overall considerations and results I now turn to how the teachers relate to the changing circumstances of technology-rich learning environments. This has been an important part of the project since how the teachers relate to ICT is a key element for the implications ICT might have on literacy and learning. As with many other change processes in schools we see that groups of teachers handle change processes related to the introduction of ICT in different ways. It is an 'object' that brings something new into the school culture. Almost all schools experience a divide within their school community as a consequence of this. As one teacher states:

> PILOT has created negative consequences internally in the community of teachers because some teachers have huge problems in managing using ICT. We have sort of two parts of the teacher community, those who can master the machines in a reasonable way and those who cannot . . . It is a sore feeling among some and I think they feel more unsuccessful after the project than before.

The expectations in the project, of increased educational use of ICT among teachers in their practices, created situations like this teacher describes. As we see from this school there is an increase in the division between the ones that master the technology and the ones that do not, which creates different feelings about their own success. The intervention made in the school community and the stated objective of looking more closely at the educational use of ICT in the classrooms, made it evident that teachers defined their own situation in this context in different ways.

Some see possibilities and affordances, while other see restrictions and constraints, which restricts the possibilities of using the technology more strategically for learning and the way teachers conceive of digital literacy as a change in educational practice.

When working with teachers it often becomes evident that their attitudes and convictions towards their own practice within school settings are hard to change. As one teacher told us in an interview at the beginning of the project:

> My students learned much more before these new technologies were introduced. I have long experience with teaching and know what works. New teaching methods create chaos.
>
> (Teacher, 2000)

But towards the end of the project the teacher reported on a different situation at this school, as the quote below indicates. One interesting aspect we see in many schools through the four-year period is a growing climate of discussion and debate about learning activities in the social setting of school. This is important because it implies a process of reflection about the social circumstances of their own practice with increased use of digital technologies.

> The PILOT project is finished, but I feel we are not yet 'there'. We have dug into our roots. What have become much clearer are the attitudes of different teachers towards the school and about learning. Here we have started a debate. There have been some small conflicts because of this. Using different concepts creates confusion.
>
> (Teacher, 2003)

Obviously at this school something has happened in the contextual setting. From a situation of being strongly convinced about their traditional role as teachers they have changed towards a more open situation where they debate different issues about schooling and their own and others' conception of learning. In this sense they have started a process. This is related to making the everyday processes of schools more open for debate and reflection. One quote from a teacher illustrates this:

> It is only after we joined PILOT that I understand what they are working on in the subjects of English and German at this school. That is quite amazing. And consider – I have been a teacher at this school for more than ten years!
>
> (Teacher, 2001)

These aspects of change are not directly related to the introduction of ICT, but where the technology is a catalyst for change across the school community because it is a new object of activity for most teachers.

However, in many schools the teachers struggled in their appropriation of new technologies into their everyday practices. It was mostly seen as a tool they had to master, without really incorporating it into the educational context in the schools and thereby not making it part of a digital-literacy practice in the classroom. One example is how many teachers conceive using Learning Management Systems (LMS) as part of their practices.

> We have used FirstClass, but we have not really gotten anything worthwhile out of it. There were technical problems in the beginning. After Christmas I think we have changed to ClassFronter.
>
> (Teacher, 2003)

> I am struggling a bit to find out what I can use it for.
>
> (Teacher, 2003)

> We use LMS on Wednesdays.
>
> (Teacher, 2003)

These quotes illustrate that many teachers have problems defining how best to use LMS and how it is woven into their own educational context. The schools have not had a debate about why they want to use these technologies and how they should be implemented to meet the needs of the teachers and students.

This is of course something that the students are very aware of and often complain about when we interview them about how their teachers use ICT in their teaching. As some students in the PILOT project expressed:

Student 1:   And many teachers are not so good at using a PC, so the teaching does not relate to that.
Student 2:   They continue with the traditional methods even though . . .
Interviewer: What do you mean with traditional methods?
Student 2:   Using the blackboard and . . .
Interviewer: Can you describe typical traditional teaching?
Student 2:   When the teacher enters he says, 'close all the computers and get your note-books'. Writes everything on the blackboard. Writes assignments with pen and pencil.
Student 1:   Our teacher in religion is about 70 years old. She does not know much about using the PC.

How the teachers conceive of using ICT in learning activities and how they think they organize student-centred learning environments is often very different from what the students experience and how they conceive of using ICT for learning. In that way teachers and students express different conceptions of how digital literacy might develop in schools. For example, about student involvement, or increased participation in their own learning, one student comments that:

Student: They (the teachers) say 'responsibility for one's own learning', but I am not sure if that is correct.

Interviewer: What do they mean then?

Student: I don't know, and I am not sure if they know themselves. In one instance it is 'responsibility for one's own learning', and in the next it refers to attendance register and follow up of homework. I don't know how much 'responsibility for one's own learning' that is. It is just like before. You get a mark if you have not done your homework. The thing with 'responsibility for one's own learning' is just nonsense.

(Student, PILOT, 2003)

However, we also see examples where there are changes going on in the way the learning environment has developed and how the role of the student is redefined. In one project the teachers focused on how they could change different situations in the school setting by using digital portfolios. One aspect of this was the meeting with the parents where the students traditionally were passive, but where they now became the centre of the discussions.

> I experienced that this created a whole new situation for the traditional parents-conference, where the teacher is the active part and student and parents often become passive listeners. Now it was the student who started the whole situation by presenting his work and starting a conversation based on this presentation. I experienced that it became a much more natural communication between equal partners. The parents became very impressed by what they were shown. The conversation flowed much easier and we could really sit much longer than the 45 minutes.
>
> (Teacher, 2003)

In this way a familiar practice, that is, parent conferences, has changed due to increased use of ICT and involving digital literacy among the students. We also see that a few schools report on how using ICT changes specific literacy practices. As part of the international SITES M2 study (Kozma, 2003; Erstad, 2005), we studied project work using ICT in twelve Norwegian schools. At one of these schools a mother made the following statement concerning the project work her daughters were involved in using iMovie to present their results in natural science.

> My girls are academically weak because they both have dyslexia and during the years in primary school they have struggled all the time with not being able to prove themselves in any subject-oriented way. I think it was incredibly positive for them to come here . . . to be able to work on computers and film and edit and such things. They have done a bit of that at home before, so they had knowledge that the other students could get from them, and through that they got a higher status in the group. So for them it has been like . . . I don't

know . . . almost like a new life. It is very important that they gain ownership of their work. I think that is one of the keys to create engagement. For adults it is like this, and I do not think this is different for children.

(Mother, 2003)

The teacher of these students added that:

Suddenly these students come into a learning environment where they have experiences related to a new tool that become available for them without only focusing on reading and writing. But also for the students that are clever and learn things fast, this seems to give them more. Also for them it is a growth environment to produce good results.

(Teacher, 2003)

The two important aspects for changing the learning process for these girls were, first, the importance of coming to a school with a much more open and flexible learning environment where they could use their strong competencies (visually) to strengthen their weaker competencies (reading, writing), and, second, the digital resources available at the school that support different learning activities among the students in a more flexible way than before.

All in all these data tell us that there is a strong connection between the schools that are working holistically with school development and their success in developing their educational practices and their use of ICT. The important factors for achieving this were the way actors within these schools managed to see the link between the use of ICT, contextual processes and change. Conceptions of digital literacy are in this way closely linked to the way teachers define their own contextual settings for working with computers as part of their activities.

Changing contextual constraints

The research referred to above indicates that the change processes that teachers, and students, are involved in using ICT as part of their learning activities deal with many more aspects of digital literacy than just using the technology. The teachers report on changes in the contextual situation they are involved in as the technology becomes more present in their practice. In projects like PILOT we see many examples that the teachers are reflecting on different aspects of their educational practices rather than just the technology itself. Their statements relate to institutional processes, about the community and the school culture they are part of and activities they are oriented towards with their students. It is how they experience the contextual changes that are important. And in line with Cole (1996), this is not context-understood as something in the environment outside themselves, but as different 'threads' that are woven together. The use of technology is embedded in their social practices with the institutional routines and regulations, the distributed cognitions and shared spaces, and the situatedness of knowledge practices in the classroom. All this weaves together when studying digital literacy as social practice and the pedagogical use of ICT in schools.

As shown above, the major challenges for the schools in the PILOT project were related to how they dealt with changes in the contextual constraints when ICT was implemented and used in the school practice. This project illustrates the importance of seeing these constraints on different levels within the school community in order to establish new literacy practices by using digital technologies.

In this way we need to abandon the notion of literacy as a set of disembodied skills, and to recognize that literacies are always inevitably situated within specific practices and specific social contexts, what some educationalists term a social theory of media literacy (Street, 1984; Buckingham, 2003).

Literacy and citizenship in the digital age

I have used activity theory and different levels at which activities can be analysed as an approach to studying digital literacy as something more than a specific set of skills. This approach was then related to different aspects of context as important for studying digital literacy in schools. In addition, 'mediated action' and mastery and appropriation were used as a way of stating the connection between technological development and issues of literacies in the way people use the technology.

There is a real danger today that both policy-makers and research initiatives see 'digital literacy' as just being able to use the technology in school-based learning, as shown by different initiatives of developing standards for digital literacy. If using computers in schools is just seen as a skill and cognitive tool, the appropriation of how such tools can enhance learning will not be taken up by the students. I see activity theory as a theoretical framework for expanding our conceptual understanding of such literacies. These theoretical perspectives will allow us to develop a multilevel approach, combining institutional effects and theories of mind (Olson, 2003), to 'digital literacy' as part of school-based learning.

The social and cultural developments we experience today point to the importance of digital literacy as a social practice with huge implications for being considered a citizen in the digital society, with its emphasis on information, knowledge and networks. As Gunter Kress (2003) has pointed out, the development of media technologies affects what new kinds of literacies may be developing, and what types of meanings, cultural effects and transformations they will produce, as well as the question of the likely distribution of access to or exclusion from these literacies. Within educational settings it is print that traditionally has been at the centre of knowledge-production, and literacy has often been conceived as a collection of culturally independent cognitive skills. Learning to read and write was associated with a particular kind of cognitive development, through which people became more logical, analytical, rational and 'civilized'. One unfortunate consequence is drawing a distinction between the literate and the illiterate, and between the media and education as competitors in the reproduction of culture and the formation of social and cultural subjects.

"activity theory as a theoretical framework for expanding conceptual understanding"

What is important is to view both education and the media as interwoven systems in culture, and not as islands outside of it. This raises questions about the cultural resources made available to people in order to cope, and how aspects of those resources are made available through 'education', institutionally conceived. Major implications of these developments will emerge in areas such as; an evaluation system that takes the wide variety of available resources into consideration, new conceptions of relevant contexts for learning, ways of collaborating, what counts as literacy and so forth. And from this perspective it is the culture that provides the tools for organizing and understanding our worlds in communicable ways.

This also points to the broader debate about the 'digital divide', understood as 'social stratification due to unequal ability to access, adapt, and create knowledge via use of information and communication technologies' (Warschauer, 2007), and participation in democratic processes. The important message is to integrate a critical dimension into how we use and are shaped by technological developments, and have the possibility to make such judgments. How our education system relates to 'digital literacy' as a set of competencies in our culture has impact on such cultural processes, and who will be included and excluded as citizens with the ability and empowerment to make decisions and to be able to take part in social development.

References

Ba, H., Tally, W. and Tsikalas, K. (2002). Investigating Children's Emerging Digital Literacies. *The Journal of Technology, Learning, and Assessment*, 1(4).

Barton, D. (1994). *Worlds of Literacy*. Amsterdam: John Benjamins.

Bereiter, C. (2002). *Education and Mind in the Knowledge Age*. Mahwah, NJ: Lawrence Erlbaum.

Bliss, J., Säljö, R. and Light, P. (eds) (1999). *Learning Sites. Social and technological resources for learning*. Amsterdam: Pergamon.

Buckingham, D. (2003). *Media Education. Literacy, learning and contemporary culture*. Cambridge: Polity Press.

Castells, M., Flecha, R., Freire, P., Giroux, H. A., Macedo, D. and Willis, P. (1999). *Critical Education in the New Information Age*. Lanham, MD: Rowan and Littlefield.

Cope, B. and Kalantzis, M. (ed.). (2000). *Multiliteracies: Literacy Learning and the Design of Social Futures*. London: Routledge.

Cole, M. (1996). *Cultural Psychology: A once and future discipline*. Cambridge, MA: Harvard University Press.

Daniels, H. (2005). *Analysing Institutional Effects: First steps in the development of a language of description*. Paper presented at the ISCAR Conference, Seville, Spain, September 20–24.

De Corte, E., Verschaffel, L., Entwistle, N. and van Merriënboer, J. (eds) (2003). *Powerful Learning Environments: Unravelling basic components and dimensions*. Amsterdam: Pergamon.

DiSessa, A. A. (2001). *Changing Minds: Computers, learning, and literacy*. Cambridge: MA, The MIT Press.

Engeström, Y. (1987). *Learning by Expanding: An activity-theoretical approach to developmental research*. Helsinki: Orienta-konsultit.

Erickson, F. and Schultz, J. (1997). When is Context? Some issues and methods in the analysis of social competence. In M. Cole, Y. Engseström and O. Vasquez (eds) *Mind, Culture and Activity*. Cambridge: Cambridge University Press.

Erstad, O. (2004). *PILOTER for Skoleutvikling.* (*PILOTS for School Development.*) ITU publication series no. 28, University of Oslo, UniPub.

Erstad, O. (2005). Expanding Possibilities: Project work using ICT. *Human Technology: An interdisciplinary Journal on Humans in ICT environments.* 1(2): 109–264.

European Charter for Media Literacy (2006). Retrieved from: http://www.euromedialiteracy. eu/ (accessed 19 October 2009). The European Charter for Media Literacy.

Freire, P. and Macedo, D. (1987). *Literacy: Reading the word and the world.* London: Routledge & Kegan Paul.

Gee, J. P. (2003). *What Video Games Have to Teach Us About Learning and Literacy.* New York: Palgrave Macmillan.

Graff, H. J. (1987). *The Labyrinths of Literacy: Reflections on literacy past and present.* London: The Falmer Press.

Heath, S. B. (1983). *Ways with Words.* Cambridge: Cambridge University Press.

Kozma, R. B. (ed.) (2003). *Technology, Innovation and Educational Change. A global perspective.* Eugene, OR: International Society for Technology in Education (ISTE).

Kress, G. (2003). *Literacy in the New Media Age.* London: Routledge.

Land, S. M. and Hannafin, M. J. (2000). Student-centered Learning Environments. In D. H. Jonassen and S. M. Land (eds) *Theoretical Foundations of Learning Environments* (pp. 1–24). Mahwah, NJ: Lawrence Erlbaum.

Lankshear, C. and Knobel, M. (2003). *New Literacies: Changing knowledge and classroom learning.* Berkshire: Open University Press.

Lankshear, C. and Knobel, M. (2006). Digital Literacies: Policy, pedagogy and research considerations for education. *Nordic Journal of Digital Literacy,* 1, 12–24.

Lemke, J. (1998). Metamedia Literacy: Transforming meanings and media. In D. Reinking, M. C. McKenna, L. D. Labbo, and R. D. Kieffer (eds) *Handbook of Literacy and Technology: Transformations in a post-typographic world* (pp. 283–301). Mahwah, NJ: Lawrence Erlbaum.

Mattelart, A. (2003). *The Information Society.* London: Sage.

Minick, N., Stone, C. A. and Forman, E. A. (1993). Introduction: Integration of individual, social, and institutional processes in accounts of children's learning and development. In E. A. Forman, N. Minick, and C. A. Stone, (eds) *Contexts for Learning: Sociocultural dynamics in children's development.* New York: Oxford University Press.

Nardi, B. (1996). Studying Context: A comparison of activity theory, situated action models, and distributed cognition. In B. Nardi (ed.) *Context and Consciousness: Activity theory and human-computer interaction* (pp. 69– 102). Cambridge, MA: The MIT Press.

New Media Consortium (2005). *Global Imperative: The report of the 21st Century Literacy Summit.* Retrieved from: http://www.nmc.org/projects/literacy/index.shtml (accessed 19 October 2009).

Olivier, M. and Pelletier, C. (2006) 'Activity theory and learning from games: implications for game design', in D. Buckingham and R. Willet (eds) *Digital Generations* (pp. 67–92). London: Lawrence Erlbaum.

Olson, D. R. (2003). *Psychological Theory and Educational Reform. How school remakes mind and society.* Cambridge: Cambridge University Press.

Pahl, K. and Rowsell, J. (2005). *Literacy and Education. Understanding the New Literacy Studies in the Classroom.* London: Paul Chapman.

Perkins, D. N., Schwartz, J. L., West, M. M. and Wiske, M. S. (1995). *Software Goes to School. Teaching for understanding with new technologies.* New York: Oxford University Press.

Rassool, N. (1999). *Literacy for Sustainable Development in the Age of Information.* Clevedon: Multilingual Matters.

Scribner, S. and Cole, M. (1981). *The Psychology of Literacy.* Cambridge, MA: Harvard University Press.

Street, B. V. (1984). *Literacy in Theory and Practice.* Cambridge: Cambridge University Press.

Säljö, R. (2005). *Lärande and Kulturella Redskap – Om lärprocesser och det kollektiva minnet* (Learning and Cultural Tools – On learning processes and collective memory). Stockholm: Norstedt Akademiska Förlag.

Warschauer, M. (2007). A Literacy Approach to the Digital Divide. In M. A. Pereyra (ed.) *Las mulialfabetizaciones en el espacio digital.* Malaga, Spain: Ediciones Aljibe. Retrieved from: http://www.gse.uci.edu/faculty/markw/lit-approach.pdf (accessed 19 October 2009).

Wells, G. and Claxton, G. (2002). *Learning for Life in the 21st Century.* Oxford: Blackwell.

Wertsch, J. (1998). *Mind as Action.* New York: Oxford University Press.

White paper (2004). *A Culture for Learning* White paper nr. 30, 2003–04. Oslo: Ministry of Education and Research.

Section 4

Design environments and new tools and representations

Using Bakhtin to re-think the teaching of Higher-order thinking for the network society

Rupert Wegerif and Maarten De Laat

Introduction

We borrow the term 'network society' from Manuel Castells, one of the most widely quoted commentators on the impact of the internet revolution. In his trilogy, *The Information Age: Economy, society and culture*, he analyses data on current trends to argue that there is a convergence towards a new form of social organisation which he calls the 'network society', defining this as: 'a society where the key social structures and activities are organized around electronically processed information networks' (Castells, 2001). Of course there have always been networks but Castells advances the claim that the advent of the internet has transformed the nature of these networks. The difference now is the mediating role played by near-instantaneous electronic communication. In particular Castells claims that a global economy is different from a world economy because: 'it is an economy with the capacity to work as a unit in real time on a planetary scale' (1996, p. 92). We think that this interesting claim suggests a new and more situated way of conceptualising what it might mean to teach 'Higher-order' thinking skills.

In the introduction to this volume the editors emphasise the convergence between new tools and new competencies (Ludvigsen, Lund, Rasmussen & Säljö, this volume). While some of the new competencies implied by new technologies are highly situated in the specific practices associated with the use of new tools, others have been conceptualised in a much more general way. It has long been argued, for example, that the increasing automation of low-skilled and semi-skilled work puts a premium on 'Higher-order' skills, such as making reasoned decisions between alternatives and innovating new approaches (e.g. Ennis, 1996; Wegerif, 2003; Anderson & Krathwohl, 2001). Some argue further that the accelerating rate of technological and social change associated with globalisation also puts a premium on adaptability or 'learning to learn' throughout the lifespan (e.g. Levin & Rumberger, 1995; Quisumbing, 2005). Castells follows this trend in describing education for the network society in terms of flexible and general thinking and learning skills relating these to the skills required to make full use of the internet. Real education, he writes, is

[handwritten margin note: Accelerating rate of change + learning]

to acquire the intellectual capacity of learning to learn throughout one's whole life, retrieving the information that is digitally stored, recombining it, and using it to produce knowledge for whatever purpose we want.

(Castells, 2001, p. 278)

This understanding of education, he continues, 'calls into question the entire education system developed during the industrial era' (p. 278) and demands that we develop a new pedagogy.

But what kind of new pedagogy do we need? Pundits of knowledge age skills tend to combine Higher-order thinking skills such as critical thinking with more situated skills such as media literacy (Trilling & Hood, 2001). The model of mental activity as data-processing favoured by cognitive psychology makes it easy to conceptualise Higher-order skills in general and 'meta-cognition' in particular, as strategies for processing more basic 'lower-order' processes (e.g. Pinker, 1998). Increasingly, however, thinking and learning are also being conceptualised in more socially situated ways, as the properties of communities of practice for example (Lave & Wenger, 1991), or of activity systems (Engestrom, 1987) or as about learning to use tools in contexts (Wertsch, 1998; Hutchins, 1995; Scribner & Cole, 1978).

It is perhaps not surprising that while the literature of sociocultural and situated-learning theory contains many accounts of how specific practices with specific tools leads to specific cognition in specific social contexts, there are fewer studies in this tradition, that focus on how we might learn general 'Higher-order' thinking skills unbounded by a culturally specific tool system. However, while it is not surprising that sociocultural theory has focused on cognition as using tools in specific social contexts, this might raise a problem for education if what is really required by the emerging network society are, as Castell and others appear to suggest, more general 'Higher-order' thinking skills, such as creativity, decision-making and 'learning to learn' (e.g. Trilling & Hood, 2001).

In this chapter we use Bakhtin's account of dialogue and of dialogic to argue that, while accepting the shift away from individualistic cognitive psychology towards understanding cognition as embedded in socially situated practices, it is still possible to preserve the pedagogic aim of teaching for Higher-order thinking and learning skills. First we argue for a reconceptualisation of Higher-order thinking and learning skills as primarily a property of dialogues, elaborating on the importance of 'dialogic reflection' as the primary 'Higher-order thinking skill' upon which all others are derivative. We then support and develop this argument with two case studies that illustrate the value of this theoretical perspective for technology enhanced pedagogy.

A dialogic reconceptualisation of Higher-order thinking

Bakhtin's dialogic perspective is often presented within a sociocultural tradition which emphasises the social situatedness of cognition. Bakhtin is sometimes referred to in support of the claim that cognition occurs within dialogues in which all utterances are spoken by someone and have a specific addressee, an idea which may carry with it the implication that there is no general cognition but only specific cognition. Bakhtin was certainly concerned to bring our understanding of cognition back from the abstract heights of dialectic argument down to the concreteness of dialogues between personalities but it is interesting that for Bakhtin dialogic was also about escaping from what he referred to dismissively as 'the narrow space of small time' (Bakhtin, 1986, p. 167). He writes that:

> In order to understand it is immensely important for the person who understands to be located outside the object of his or her creative understanding – in time, in space, in culture.
>
> (Bakhtin, 1986, p. 7)

Utterances in a dialogue, he pointed out, are never only directed at a specific addressee but also at a superaddressee, the ideal of a third party to the dialogue who has a capacity to understand what is really meant by the utterance even when the specific addressee cannot understand it due perhaps to his or her limitations (Bakhtin, 1986, p. 126). The superaddressee evokes for some the idea of God as someone who understands everything but is also similar to the ideal of an unsituated universal perspective aspired to by science and often referred to as a 'God's eye point of view on the world'. This ideal of an unsituated perspective is understood by Bakhtin as a projection out of situated dialogues since meaning, for Bakhtin, is always a product of an interaction of perspectives.

However, if the ideal of unsituatedness is a product of dialogue, then so is the equal and opposite ideal of situatedness. In fact these two ideals are interdependent. The extent that one thinks that one can accurately specify the key features of a situation is the extent that one thinks that one has a comprehensive overview or map. From a more dialogic perspective one cannot know one's situation except through taking the perspective of another in a dialogue and since that dialogue is open-ended the salient features of one's situation are always open to interpretation.

Bakhtin dismisses the superficial understanding of dialogue as the opposite of monologue (Bakhtin, 1986, p. 117). In doing this he distinguishes the living internal reality of dialogue from any external empirical account of a dialogue. This is important because while viewed from the outside other people's dialogues appear as situated in time and space, our own dialogues on the inside appear unsituated and open to infinite potential. He turned this double nature of dialogue into a joke, writing, 'the ancient Greeks did not know the main thing about themselves, that they were *ancient* Greeks' (1986, p. 6). It can be argued that the essence of Bakhtin's account of dialogic is the holding of two irreducibly different perspectives together at once in creative tension (Wegerif, 2007, p. 28). For Bakhtin meaning is a product of dialogues. Things do not simply mean on their own but only in the context of a dialogue in which they mean something for someone as an answer to a question. Any idea we have of the nature of our 'situation', for example, must be constructed in a dialogue in this way. Meanings, interpretations of our situation for example, can never be fixed because they are always open to re-interpretation in an ongoing dialogue. As Bakhtin puts it clearly:

> There is neither a first nor a last word and there are no limits to the dialogic context (it extends into the boundless past and the boundless future)
> (Bakhtin, 1986, p. 170)

This way of understanding dialogic offers a new way of understanding that which is general to human thought. Thinking always occurs within dialogues (both internal and external to individual minds) and dialogues, however apparently superficial and clear-cut, always have an unbounded potential for meaning (ibid. p. 162). Bakhtin points out in his studies of literature that texts can be more or less dialogic which means more or less multi-voiced, open to the other and open to the possibility of something new emerging (this emerges from Bakhtin's study of poetics in Doestoevsky: Bakhtin, 1973). Developing from Bakhtin we are using dialogic in two ways, first as a kind of noun referring to the essence of dialogue in the apparent state of holding two incommensurate perspectives together in tension and second, as an adjective describing the degree of dialogicality of dialogues, which means the extent to which they are multi-voiced, open to the otherness of the other and open to the possibility of the new. This second definition of dialogic, dialogic as a direction from relatively closed dialogues to relatively open dialogues, is the basis of a new approach to understanding the teaching and learning of 'Higher-order' thinking skills (Wegerif, 2007).

The phrase 'Higher-order thinking' originated in a questionable distinction made between lower-order skills such as remembering and Higher-order skills such as evaluating (Bloom, 1956). The sort of distinction being made by Bloom is suspect but the phrase 'Higher-order' is still useful to distinguish distinctively human creative thinking from the kind of 'cognition' which has been ascribed to animals and to machines. The essential dialogicality of normal human thinking is increasingly pointed to by developmental psychology as a contrast to the more algorithmic cognition found in psychopathologies such as autism and in non-human contexts (e.g. Hobson, 2002; Tomasello, Carpenter, Call, Behme & Moll, 2005).

The potential relevance of engagement in dialogue as shared enquiry to the tradition of teaching Higher-order thinking is evident if we adopt Resnick's definition of Higher-order thinking. Resnick chaired a US government commission into the teaching of thinking skills which took evidence from many practitioners and other experts. Her main conclusion was that:

> Thinking skills resist the precise forms of definition we have come to associate with the setting of specified objectives for schooling. Nevertheless, it is relatively easy to list some key features of higher order thinking. When we

do this, we become aware that, although we cannot define it exactly, we can recognize higher order thinking when it occurs.

(Resnick, 1987)

Although Resnick was conceptualising Higher-order thinking skills as individual skills the skills she refers to are all evidently the kind of skills found in a complex open-ended dialogue (where a dialogue is defined with Bakhtin as a 'shared inquiry' 1986, p. 168). Research findings on the effectiveness of teaching general thinking skills programmes suggest that the depth of dialogic engagement is relevant to evidence of learning that supports problem-solving and general thinking and learning skills and dispositions generally beyond the context in which they are learnt (e.g. Mercer, Daws, Wegerif & Sams, 2004; Wegerif, Mercer & Daws, 1999: Trickey & Topping, 2004).

What is offered by the dialogic paradigm we have briefly outlined is a way to understand how education can promote general thinking and learning beyond the use of specific cultural tools but without returning to the questionable individualistic abstractions of cognitive psychology. The big idea for education that emerges from this particular reading of Bakhtin is that development in the direction of dialogue considered as an end in itself lies behind the teaching and learning of Higher-order thinking. Teaching for Higher-order thinking can thus be translated into opening, expanding and deepening dialogic spaces wherever they occur (Wegerif, 2007).

Where in the neo-Vygotskian sociocultural tradition technology is conceptualised as a mediating means for cognition, from this more dialogic perspective technology is seen as a facilitator opening and shaping dialogic spaces that would not otherwise be there. A dialogic perspective on cognition does not render the networked perspective on learning obsolete because dialogues always occur within networks. The dialogic perspective reveals, however, that the question 'how can networks be made more intelligent?' is misleading and should be replaced with the very different question 'how can networks open up, expand, deepen and generally resource creative dialogic spaces of reflection?'

Designing for networked and dialogic Higher-order thinking and learning

'Networked learning' is used to refer to the kind of learning appropriate to Castells' concept of the network society. Both metaphors take the use of electronic networks as the prime source through which social activities are structured and mediated. Networked learning is defined as the use of information and communication technologies to support collaborative and cooperative connections: between one learner and other learners; between learners and tutors; between a learning community and its learning resources, so that participants can extend and develop their understanding and capabilities in ways that are important to them, and over which they have significant control (Banks, Goodyear, Hodgson & McConnell, 2003).

As we have already noted, Castells draws a contrast between electronic networks and traditional networks based on the way in which electronic networks create a new sense of space and time that contrast to the space and time of places linked together. He refers to this as a 'space of flows'. In the emerging network society, he writes, elites identify themselves more with the space of flows and less with the space of places. This is perhaps apparent in the brief account Castells gives of a reformed education which we quoted earlier as being all about accessing information and working with it to produce knowledge, in other words it is about the skills required for participating more centrally in information and knowledge flows.

While the space and time of networks ('the space of flows': Castells, 2004, p. 147) and the space and time of dialogues ('dialogic space': Wegerif, 2007, p. 4) are both to be distinguished from the space and time of places, they also need to be distinguished from each other. While networks are nodes related externally to each other, dialogic is characterised by internal relationship: the outside addressee is already on the inside of the utterance as it forms which is the concrete meaning of the definition of dialogic as holding two or more perspectives together in tension. Networks do not think; thinking occurs in dialogues. But dialogues occur within networks and are resourced by networks. So our reconceptualisation of Higher-order thinking skills in the context of the idea of the network society must combine the critical and creative thinking skills that are derivative of dialogic reflection with the more embodied skills characteristic of networked learning and participation in flows of knowledge.

The networked and dialogic interpretative framework we propose implies the need for a pedagogy of teaching for dialogic and also for networked learning skills and competencies, aimed at the ability to constructively participate and facilitate networked environments combined with the need to sustain in creative tension more than one perspective simultaneously. This pedagogy can be described in terms of moving learners into the space of flows and also into the space of dialogue. Dialogues occur within networks and networked learning skills augment and realise a capacity for dialogic reflection. Tools, including language and computer environments, can be used for opening up and maintaining dialogic spaces and for deepening and broadening dialogic spaces (Wegerif, 2006; 2007).

Walton points out that there are some general network competencies and skills people must possess in order to learn and participate in a set of relationships (see Walton, 1999, p. 541):

- Spanning structural boundaries – establish broad networks across existing hierarchy and work them directly, making opportunistic use of meetings.
- Making transitions – use transitions as opportunities to learn new skills, look for alternatives/role models, tend to dive in and enter quickly, stay focused on needs being served, facilitate major change through lots of communication, set new expectations, and build trust.

- Communication skills – engage in building shared meaning, focus on the need of others and anticipate questions, the real communication tends to go on outside meetings.
- Problem-solving – look at the whole situation (out of boundary or lateral thinking) or the big picture, and coaching others.
- Power relationships – treat teachers, coaches or mentors, as supporters or as people who could add value to an idea. Play leaderships roles without authority.

Networked learning competencies and social meta-cognitive strategies, for example, can be supported by tools built into online learning environments that enable students to become more aware of, and to take charge of, their own networked learning (De Laat, 2006). To illustrate this framework for creative technology-enhanced pedagogical design, we describe the development and empirical evaluations of two tools to support dialogic networked learning. *Online Tools*

Baker, Quignard, Lund and Séjourné (2003) make a useful distinction between deepening and broadening a space of debate, where deepening can be translated roughly as increasing the degree of reflection on an issue and broadening as increasing the range of relevant perspectives and relevant knowledge brought into the dialogue. In a similar way the two cases we present below illustrate how specifically designed tools can help to both deepen and to broaden dialogic spaces. In the first study learners are encouraged to deepen dialogic reflection through constructing and modifying a shared external representation of a dialogue. The tools provided support reflection through allowing shared access to the 'inner' thoughts of participants in dialogue next to their 'outer' words and allowing the replay of the dialogue with changes to explore the impact of different choices. The second case has this same capacity to deepen reflection but adds tools designed to expand the dialogue first with a range of social roles or 'voices' and then with a breakdown of the dialogue into 'stages' with different functions. The second case raises the need for networked learning competencies to coordinate and regulate dialogues in groups and therefore the need to provides tools to support this. *Deepening + broadening learning Space*

Case I: Designing for deepening dialogue

Talk in face-to-face dialogues exists only momentarily and only for those immediately present. Technologies that support drawing and writing can thus be thought of as a way of deepening dialogues, by turning transitory talk and thoughts into external objects that are available to learners for discussion and shared reflection (Ong, 1982). Computer documents can offer a kind of halfway stage between the evanescence of talk and the permanence of written texts. Harry McMahon and Bill O'Neill, the originators of Bubble Dialogue software, use the term 'slow-throwness' to refer to the way that their tool can externalise the thoughts and feelings of the participants and also support reflection and the possibility of returning and retrospectively changing dialogues (McMahon & O'Neill, 1993). At the heart of Bubble Dialogue is the simple idea of combining pictures with speech and thought bubbles. The pictures are easy to load into the software and can represent dialogues in any situation. In addition to the bubbles there is a facility to review the dialogue created so far and to change it. Bubble Dialogue was originally developed in HyperCard but we have designed a multimedia version (BubbleDialogue II) incorporating more features to support reflection. Bubble Dialogue has now been extensively used to promote social awareness amongst children with social and behavioural difficulties (Jones & Price, 2001; Wegerif, Littleton & Jones, 2003). The findings of this research support the claim that features of Bubble Dialogue allow children to externalise their own image and reflect upon it, to consider the difference between what they say and what they really think in order to explore the consequences of their speech in a context where they can go back and change what they say until they get the outcome that they want. Although McMahon and O'Neill originally articulated this as 'sociocultural' design, their approach to supporting the deepening of dialogue makes more sense within the dialogic paradigm we have outlined since the technology is not a mediating means to the cognition and the construction of knowledge but a resourcing of a dialogic space. Qualitative discourse analysis shows that the capacity of Bubble Dialogue to support social metacognition, with the right pedagogy, is related to features of the interface design.

An example of such dialogue is provided in the Bubble Dialogue reproduced in Figure 19.1 and Extract 1. This was created by Charlene and Rory, both aged 10 years, and both excluded from their previous schools because of behavioural

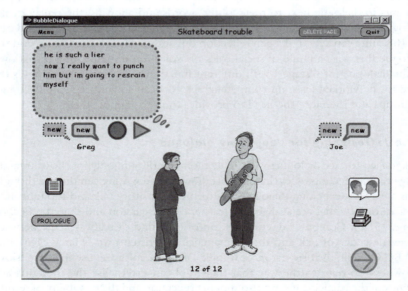

Figure 19.1 Bubble Dialogue

difficulties. They are discussing a Bubble Dialogue scenario about a personal conflict involving characters called Joe and Greg. In the story Greg was using his new skateboard in the playground when Joe, a bigger boy, grabbed it from him.

In the first exchanges both characters 'square up' for a physical fight. However, the next set of think bubbles that Charlene and Rory produced (see Transcript Extract 1) indicate that while both parties are prepared to fight over the skateboard 'asking nicely' or apologising would diffuse the situation.

Transcript extract 1 (Bubble Dialogue): I'm not scared

(*Joe thinks:*	he just have to ask nicely)
Joe says:	I'll kick your head in you fat brat head
Greg says:	yeah come on then, I'm not scared of you if im a big fat brat head what does that make you, you peebrain
(*Greg thinks:*	im not scared of him all hes got to do is give me my skateboard back and apologise to me, if he doesn't im going to break his big fat ugly bogied up nose)

Charlene and Rory's story goes on to have Joe give Greg the skateboard back. When Greg insists on an apology, Joe denies having taken the board and says that Greg should say sorry for threatening to punch his lights out when he was only playing. Eventually they both manage to apologise in a guarded way and agree to be friends.

Transcript Extract 1 shows that, as well as their obvious enjoyment in the use of insulting language, they were also able to explore the distinction between what their proxy characters were saying and what they were thinking. This implies a reflective exploration of their own motives. Although the characters were acting tough, they did not actually want to fight and through using the Bubble Dialogue program, they rehearsed a way to talk themselves out of the fight that had at first seemed to be inevitable. The features of Bubble Dialogue allowed them to xternalize their own image and reflect on it, to consider the difference between what they say and what they really think in order to explore the consequences of their speech in a context where they can go back and change what they say until they get the outcome that they want. All these features deepen the space of reflection involved in a dialogue in a way that increases the degrees of creative freedom because it is only through becoming more aware of who one is through a dialogue that one is able to change.

Case 2: Designing for expanding and resourcing dialogue

Discuss is an online environment with role-play and staging to raise awareness of networked competencies needed to coordinate and regulate dialogues. A criticism often heard by students and teachers is the difficulty of structuring and moderating social learning processes by members of the group (Clouder & Deepwell, 2004;

Ferry, Kiggins, Hoban & Lockyer, 2000; Kear, 2004; Light, Nesbit, Light & Burns, 2000; Strijbos, 2004).

Virtual learning environments (VLEs) and groupware applications may offer the possibility for a shared workspace for networked learning communities, but may not provide enough support or scaffolding, by themselves, for the community to regulate its own learning activities most effectively. It has been argued by various researchers (Duffy & Jonassen, 1992; Hakkarainen, 1998; Koschmann, Kelson, Feltovich & Barrows, 1996; Scardamalia & Bereiter, 1994; Wegerif, 1998) that group members working in a networked learning environment may be able to work and learn more productively if pedagogical guidance and modelling is provided within the shared space to regulate learning activities. In a traditional 'classroom' the teacher is an ever-present regulator of the learning activities of the group. In an online learning environment, however, this function may be less apparent, and the participants may have to be more self- and group-reliant in order to be con-structive learners. We argue therefore for a more group- or community-centred pedagogical model to raise the social metacognitive awareness amongst participants of networked learning environments (De Laat, 2006) and enable them to take ownership of their dialogic space through a process of shared design, coordination and regulation.

Discuss aims to provide pedagogically driven models and methods, by incor-porating them into the design of the tool and as such scaffolding social learning activities from within.

In our view, it is important to support collaborative learning through informa-tion and communication technologies (ICTs) by focusing on the group dynamics that are needed to organise and coordinate learning and to support the clarifica-tion and the aim of the discourse by providing insight into how knowledge is created. Collaborative learning requires that the participants make their learning goals explicit and necessitates particular learning skills to achieve them (De Laat & Simons, 2002). We argue that designing groupware that focuses specifically on facilitating the collaborative learning processes may help participants to regulate their discussion. The hypothesis is that integrating models for collaborative learning in the learning activities will stimulate the students to actively think and discuss the social processes needed to successfully work on their group learning tasks.

In Discuss we introduce two models through which collaborative learning proc-esses might be stimulated. The first model is aimed at raising awareness among the participants of the management roles that might help in the coordination of the online discussion. These roles aim to stimulate interdependence and collaboration (Forsyth, 1999; Johnson & Johnson, 1999). The roles introduced (see Figure 19.2) are: discussion manager, process manager, content manager, knowledge manager and technical manager.

These roles focus on tasks required to support the overall collaborative learning and tutoring process. By giving each member some explicit responsibility for the community's coordination of their collaborative learning, a heterogeneous com-munity is created that may be able to accomplish something that an individual

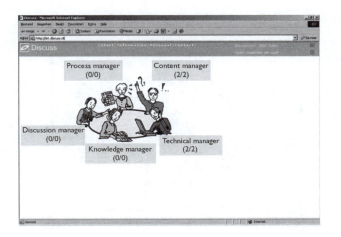

Figure 19.2 The management role model used by Group One in "Discuss"

could not achieve alone (Johnson & Johnson, 1999).

The second model is aimed at raising awareness among participants of a discussion structure that will help to regulate the content of the discussion. This is done by presenting the community with a problem-solving cycle, called progressive enquiry developed by Hakkarainen (1998), which is based upon a pedagogical model of the way knowledge is socially constructed in scientific communities. Progressive enquiry engages members of the community in a step-by-step process of question and explanation-driven enquiry (see Figure 19.2) as a way to develop shared expertise on their collaborative task.

The participants in a PE-structured activity commence by creating a shared context, followed by formulating a question to guide their work. The next four steps are a process of brainstorming, evaluating, deepening and (re)structuring their community knowledge as a way to derive at their final stage, the conclusion, to round up the discussion.

Progressive enquiry

It is important to make clear that the awareness by participants of a certain type of support model can only stimulate the learning process if they actually appropriate the model. Ludvigsen and Mørch (2003) found, for example, that the PE is a useful model because it makes the students aware of the systematic parts of the knowledge-building process. However they warn of the danger of overgeneralising the model to different learning contexts where it may not be appropriate. Software should therefore not impose these models on individuals and user groups, but rather make them available according to the needs and abilities of the group (Spencer, 2000).

This is why in future versions of Discuss we aim to offer groups the possibility to make their own collaborative models to suit each group's unique ways and needs

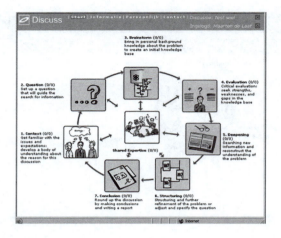

Figure 19.3 The progressive enquiry structure used by Group Two in "Discuss"

of working collaboratively as well as stimulating group discussion and reflection how to design their own dialogical space.

Qualitative discourse analysis between one group using the roles model, another using the progressive enquiry model and a third group using no additional structure showed an increase of learning and tutoring processes amongst the students using Discuss models compared to students using Discuss with no additional structure (see De Laat & Lally, 2005).

Supports for interaction

The analysis of the interaction patterns within each group indicated that more discussion amongst the members is devoted to discussing the regulation, design and coordination of their collaborative task, especially within the group using the management roles indicating that the tools provided did help to widen the dialogic space and, through this, helped to support an increased social metacognitive understanding of the group's needs.

Additional student recall interviews showed that the inbuilt pedagogic models helped stimulate debate about how to work and learn together but the students also mentioned that the tool needs to allow for more flexibility to redesign and tailor the models by the group members to make it fit the task at hand.

Discussion and conclusions

We propose that education is similar to architecture in being a creative design discipline and our discussion of these different technologically enhanced pedagogical designs borrows from architecture, the idea of 'design patterns' which are ways to solve similar recurring design problems (Goodyear, 2005). An illustration of a design pattern is supporting dialogic reflection by replaying the process of the dialogue which is a design feature of Bubble Dialogue and other software designed to support reflection on dialogue such as DIGALO (www.argunaut.net). We focus not only on the design of the tools but also on the design of the way in which the tools are used in educational contexts. For example, the aims of creative, critical and reflective dialogic thinking are made explicit in the teaching and the ground rules of taking risks, listening with respect and accepting challenges are established in the classrooms or groups in which these tools are being used. Implementing collaborative support models as we do in the Discuss system might provide the design patterns to help the students to learn to reflect collectively. Teaching these networked thinking and learning skills requires a delicate balance between teacher responsibility and student's ability to act and take over control of the dialogical space.

Research has indicated that the teacher's presence in networked learning spaces is essential to improve learning and that students are in need of support for preparation and regulation especially at the beginning phase of a collaborative project (De Laat, 2006). On the other hand, we have seen that students are capable of taking over some of the teacher roles, and starting to develop leadership roles themselves within the group as a way to guide and support each other to participate in their activity. Students, in other words, are acting as active learners by assuming some control of teaching and learning dialogues and relationships. Therefore, when employing networked learning it seems important to carefully introduce students into taking over these responsibilities by gradually handing over control from the teacher to the students. In this process-oriented teaching there is a need to manage the interplay between self-regulation and external regulation (Vermunt & Verschaffel, 2000).

The teaching and learning of general thinking skills, especially creativity and learning to learn, is hard to understand through that neo-Vygotskian perspective which focuses on the use of tools for the social construction of knowledge. Understanding is an event within a dialogue between perspectives and is not reducible to a constructed representation. A narrow focus on tools as mediators of cognition cannot explain creative insights and is hard to convert into a pedagogy for teaching general thinking skills since tools are always specific to tasks. Teaching Higher-order thinking, adopting Resnick's definition, is much easier to understand through a dialogic perspective which focuses on the opening, deepening and broadening of reflective spaces. It is the implicit space of possibilities opened up by dialogue which allows for creative emergence and which is the irreducible context for all interpretations of signs and representations (Wegerif, 2006; 2007). This dialogic interpretative framework implies the need for a pedagogy of teaching dialogic, that is, the ability to sustain more than one perspective simultaneously, as an end in itself and as the primary thinking skill upon which all other thinking skills are derivative. This pedagogy can be described in terms of moving learners into the space of dialogue. In addition, since dialogues occur within networks, it is important to encourage the networked learning skills and competencies that enable students to actively participate in networked learning. De Laat (2006, p. 185) proposes a community-centred framework to networked learning where both the individual and collective learning processes and outcomes are accounted for and (re)negotiated by the group during various stages of their collaboration. Tools, including language and computer environments, can be used for opening up and maintaining dialogic spaces and for deepening and broadening dialogic spaces. In many cases the pedagogic practices that follow from this dialogic interpretative framework are already happening, this includes the promotion of communities of enquiry and dialogue skills, the use of forums of alternative voices to induct students into debate, engagement in real dialogues across cultural and geographic differences using the internet, scaffolding induction into such dialogues using synchronous and asynchronous environments, amongst others. The purpose of the dialogic and networked learning framework proposed is therefore not only in suggesting new pedagogical designs but also in providing an interpretative framework that can be applied retrospectively to pedagogical designs that have emerged through the intuition of practitioners but that need theorising in a way that can show which features work and why and which features are not necessary.

The dialogic and networked framework proposed in this chapter responds to the educational needs of our cultural and historical situation articulated by Ludvigson, Lund and Saljo in the introduction to this volume and also by Castells (2001). The advent of the internet, which has transformed our world, is not best understood as a tool system but rather as an expanding cacophony of competing voices. Teaching general thinking and learning skills, in the context of the shift to a global network society, is at least partly about teaching students how to use the internet for thinking and learning. Whilst being able to participate in the construction of shared knowledge is clearly an important aim of education, the networked dialogic perspective argued for in this chapter claims that it is even more important, as both a preliminary requirement for construction and as the context of construction, that students in the networked society learn how to listen and respond to other voices.

References

Anderson, L. W. and Krathwohl, D. R. (2001). *A Taxonomy for Learning, Teaching, and Assessing*. New York, NY: Longman.

Bakhtin, M. (1973). *Problems of Dostoevsky's Poetics* [B. Rotsel, trans.]. New York: Ardis.

Bakhtin, M. (1986). *Speech Genres and Other Late Essays*. Austin, TX: University of Texas Press.

Baker, M. J., Quignard, M., Lund, K. and Séjourné, A. (2003). Computer-supported Collaborative Learning in the Space of Debate. In B. Wasson, S. Ludvigsen and U. Hoppe, (eds). *Designing for Change in Networked Learning Environments: Proceedings of the International Conference on Computer Support for Collaborative Learning 2003*, (pp. 11–20). Dordrecht: Kluwer Academic Publishers.

Banks, S., Goodyear, P., Hodgson, V. and McConnell, D. (2003). Introduction to the Special Issue on Advances in Research on Networked Learning. *Instructional Science, 31*, 1–6.

Bloom, B. S. (ed.) (1956). *Taxonomy of Educational Objectives: The classification of educational goals: Handbook I, cognitive domain*. New York, NY: Longmans Green.

Castells, M. (1999). *The Information Age: Economy, Society and Culture*, 3 Vols. Oxford: Wiley-Blackwell.

Castells, M. (2004). An Introduction to the Information Age. In Webster *et al.* (eds) *The Information Society Reader* (pp. 138–49). London and New York: Routledge.

Castells, M. (2001). *The Internet Galaxy: Reflections on the Internet, business, and society.* Oxford: Oxford University Press.

Castells, M. (1996). *The Rise of the Network Society.* Oxford: Blackwell.

Clouder, L. and Deepwell, F. (2004). Reflections on Unexpected Outcomes: Learning from student collaboration in an online discussion forum. In S. Banks, P. Goodyear, C. Jones, V. Lally, D. McConnel and C. Steeples (eds) *Proceedings of the Fourth International Conference on Networked Learning 2004* (pp. 429–435). Lancaster: Lancaster University.

De Laat, M. (2006). *Networked Learning.* Apeldoorn, the Netherlands: Politie Academy.

De Laat, M. and Simons, P. R. J. (2002). Collective Learning: Theoretical perspectives and ways to support networked learning. *Vocational Training: European Journal, 27*, 13–24.

De Laat, M. and Lally, V. (2005). Investigating Group Structure in CSCL: Some new approaches. *Information Systems Frontiers, 7*, 13–25.

Duffy, T. M. and Jonassen, D. H. (1992). Constructivism: New implications for instructional technology. In T. M. Duffy and D. H. Jonassen (eds). *Constructivism and the Technology of Instruction: A conversation* (pp. 1–16). Mahwah, NJ: Lawrence Erlbaum.

Engestrom, Y. E., (1987). *Learning by Expanding: An activity-theoretical approach to developmental research.* Helsinki: Orienta-Konsultit. Retrieved from http://lchc.ucsd.edu/MCA/Paper/Engestrom/expanding/intro.htm (accessed April 2005).

Ennis, R. H. (1996). *Critical Thinking.* Englewood Cliffs, NJ: Prentice-Hall.

Ferry, B., Kiggins, J., Hoban, G. and Lockyer, L. (2000). Use of Computer-mediated Communication to Form a Knowledge-building Community in Initial Teacher Education. *Educational Technology and Society, 3*, [online journal].

Forsyth, D. R. (1999). *Group Dynamics.* Belmont: Brooks/Cole-Wadsworth.

Goodyear, P. (2005). Educational Design and Networked Learning: Patterns, pattern languages and design practice, *Australian Journal of Educational Technology, 21*(1), 82–101.

Hakkarainen, K. (1998). *Epistemology of Scientific Inquiry in Computer-supported Collaborative Learning.* Toronto: University of Toronto.

Hobson, P. (2002). *The Cradle of Thought: Exploring the origins of thinking.* London: Macmillan.

Hutchins, E. (1995). *Cognition in the Wild.* Cambridge, MA: The MIT Press.

Johnson, D. W. and Johnson, R. T. (1999). *Learning Together and Alone: Cooperative, competetive and individualistic learning.* Boston, MA: Allyon and Bacon.

Jones. A. and Price E. (2001). Using a Computer Application to Investigate Social Information Processing in Children with Emotional and Behavioural Difficulties. In I. Hutchby, and J. Moran-Ellis (eds) *Children, Culture and Technology* (pp. 133–150). London: Falmer Press.

Kear, K. (2004). Peer Learning Using Asynchronous Discussion Systems in Distance Education. *Open learning, 19*, 151–164.

Koschmann, T., Kelson, A. N., Feltovich, P. J. and Barrows, H. S. (1996). Computer-supported problem-based learning: A principled approach to the use of computers in collaborative learning. In T. Koschmann (ed.) *CSCL: Theory and Practice of an Emerging Paradigm* (pp. 83–123). Mahwah, NJ: Lawrence Erlbaum.

Lave, J. and Wenger, E. (1991). *Situated Learning: Legitimate periperal participation.* Cambridge: Cambridge University Press.

Levin, H. and Rumberger, R. (1995) Education, Work and Employment in Developed Countries: Situation and future challenges. In J. Hallak and F. Caillods (eds) *Educational Planning: The international dimension* (pp. 69–88). UNESCO Bureau of Education, International Institute for Educational Planning. London: Garland.

Light, V., Nesbitt, E., Light, P. and Burns, J. R. (2000). Let's You and Me Have a Little Discussion: Computer-mediated communication in support of campus-based university courses. *Studies in Higher Education, 25,* 85–96.

Ludvigsen, S. and Mørch, A. (2003). Categorisation in Knowledge Building. In B. Wasson, S. Ludvigsen and U. Hoppe (eds) *Designing for Change in Networked Learning Environments. Proceedings of the 6th International Conference on Computer Support for Collaborative Learning* (CSCL 2003) (pp. 67–76). Dordrecht: Kluwer.

McMahon, H. and O'Neill, W. (1993). Computer-mediated Zones of Engagement in Learning. In T. Duffy, J. Lowyck and D. Jonassen (eds) *Designing Environments for Constructive Learning* (pp. 37–57). Berlin: Springer.

Mercer, N., Dawes, R., Wegerif, R. and Sams, C. (2004). Reasoning as a Scientist: Ways of helping children to use language to learn science. *British Educational Research Journal, 30,* 367–385.

Ong, W. J. (1982) *Orality and Literacy: The technologizing of the word.* London: Methuen.

Pinker, S. (1998). *How the Mind Works.* London: Allan Lane.

Quisumbing, L. R. (2005). Education for the World of Work and Citizenship: Towards sustainable future societies. *Prospects: Quarterly review of comparative education, 35,* 289–301.

Resnick, L. (1987). *Education and Learning to Think.* Washington, DC: National Academy Press.

Scardamalia, M. and Bereiter, C. (1994). Computer Support for Knowledge-building Communities. *The Journal of the Learning Sciences, 3,* 265–283.

Scribner, S. and Cole, M. (1978). Literacy Without Schooling: Testing for intellectual effects. *Harvard Educational Review, 48,* 448–466.

Spencer, D. (2000). *Computer-mediated Communications: State of the art group facilitation, collaboration and asynchronous learning networks. 2003.* Retrieved 25 July, 2003, from http://web.njit.edu/~hiltz/CMC_SOTA_David.doc

Strijbos, J. (2004). *The Effect of Roles on Compter-supported Collaborative Learning.* PhD dissertation, Open Universiteit Nederland, Heerlen.

Tomasello, M., Carpenter, M., Call, J., Behne, T. and Moll, H. (2005). Understanding and Sharing Intentions: The origins of cultural cognition. *Behavioral Brain Sciences, 28*(5), 675–91, and discussion, 691–735.

Trickey, S. and Topping, K. J. (2004). *Philosophy for Children: A systematic review.* Research Papers in Education, *19*(3), 365–380.

Trilling, B. and Hood, P. (2001). Learning, Technology and Education Reform in the Knowledge Age, or 'We're Wired, Webbed and Windowed, Now What?' In C. Paechter, R. Edwards, R. Harrison and P. Twining (eds) *Learning, Space and Identity.* London: Paul Chapman Publishing and The Open University. Also at: http://www.wested.org/cs/we/view/rs/654

Vermunt, J. and Verschaffel, L. (2000). Process-oriented Teaching. In P. R. J. Simons, J. Van der Linden and T. Duffy (eds) *New Learning* (pp. 209–225). Dordrecht: Kluwer Academic Publishers.

Walton, J. (1999). *Strategic Human Resource Development*. London: Prentice Hall.

Wegerif, R. (1998). The Social Dimension of Asynchronous Learning Networks. *Journal of Asynchronous Learning Networks, 2,* 34–49.

Wegerif, R. (2003). *Thinking Skills, Technology and Learning: A review of the literature.* Bristol: NESTA FutureLab (http://www.nestafuturelab.org/).

Wegerif, R., Littleton, K. and Jones, A. (2003). Stand Alone Computers Supporting Learning Dialogues in Primary Classrooms. *International Journal of Education Research, 39,* 851–860.

Wegerif, R. (2005). Reason and Creativity in Classroom Dialogues. *Language and Education, 19,* 223–238.

Wegerif, R. (2006). Towards a Dialogic Understanding of the Relationship Between Teaching Thinking and CSCL. *International Journal of Computer Supported Collaborative Learning, 1,* 143–157.

Wegerif, R. (2007). *Dialogic, Education and Technology: Expanding the space of learning.* New York, NY: Springer.

Wegerif, R., Mercer, N. and Dawes, L. (1999). From Social Interaction to Individual Reasoning: An empirical investigation of a possible socio-cultural model of cognitive development. *Learning and Instruction, 9*(5), 493–516.

Wertsch, J. V. (1998). *Mind as Action.* New York, NY: Oxford University Press.

Chapter 20

Self-regulation and motivation in computer-supported collaborative learning environments

Sanna Järvelä, Tarja-Riitta Hurme and Hanna Järvenoja

Introduction

Postindustrial society is changing, both quantitatively and qualitatively. Population is not only increasing in number, but also growing older and more diverse. Life expectancy has almost doubled in the past century and the exponential growth of the world's population, along with its increased longevity, diversity and mobility, has significant implications for teaching and learning (Murphy & Alexander, 2000). The changing character of the population also demands a re-examination of what being a lifelong learner means. The learner is required to study effectively by self-regulated learning and use many learning tools and work collaboratively with other learners at the same time. Theory of learning, empirical experiments and learning tools are developed to guide the learners to improve how they learn, as they learn (Alexander, 2004). Self-regulated learning theory concerns how learners develop learning skills and use learning skills effectively (Boekaerts, Pintrich & Zeidner, 2000). In this chapter, arguments are given regarding why self-regulated learning is an important issue in future learning in social practices. During the past few years we have been studying self-regulated learning in computer-supported collaborative learning environments. In this chapter, we review findings from our studies and other studies to demonstrate a need to focus on students' engagement and cognitive and motivational coping while working in modern collaborative and computer-supported learning environments. The basic idea of self-regulated learning will be introduced and metacognition as a form of cognitive regulation, as well emotion and motivation regulation models, will be introduced. Finally, we will discuss how self-regulated learning skills can be supported with various new computer-supported regulation tools.

Why self-regulation is topical in social learning situations practices

Multiple new forms of social and collaborative learning practices (Barab, Kling & Grey, 2004; Strijbos, Kirschner & Martens, 2004) have been developed from the recent ideas of social cognition (Higgins, 2000; Thompson & Fine, 1999) and more cognitive-oriented approaches (Dillenbourg, 1999). From a motivation point of view, the implication is that learners' adaptation to complex social-learning practices, such as sharing knowledge and maintaining coordinated activities, requires cognitive, motivational and socio-emotional skills that are different to, and often more challenging than, more conventional and well-structured learning situations. Recent student-centered learning methods (Singer, Marx, Krajcik & Chambers, 2000; Randi & Corno, 2000; Hakkarainen, Lipponen & Järvelä, 2002) afford student opportunities to engage in self-regulated learning including encouraging students to set their own goals, emphasizing collaboration and negotiation and proving scaffolding during learning. The results of these studies have provided evidence that by using computer-supported pedagogical models it is possible to create more challenging learning situations for students. Challenging conceptual work can be more intrinsically interesting than more traditional learning tasks (Stipek, 2002) because pushing students to explain and analyze their answers and problem-solving strategies has resulted in high levels of engagement among the students (Turner, Meyer, Cox, Logan & DiCintio, 1998).

Recent research, however, reveals that students face difficulties engaging in learning and achieving their goals in a variety of learning contexts (Volet & Järvelä, 2001). The results of these studies consider what kind of emotional and motivational experiences the students have during the computer-supported learning projects and indicate that students with different socioemotional orientation tendencies will interpret the novel instructional designs in ways which subsequently will lead to different actual behaviours among them. Our own studies have shown (Järvelä, Veermans & Leinonen, 2008; Järvenoja & Järvelä, 2005; Salovaara & Järvelä, 2003) that students may adopt context specific interpretations of motivational goals and self-regulation when confronted with atypical learning demands. By these demands it is meant pedagogical practices with increased orientations toward social learning and collaboration in the service of solving problems. For example, social processes are highlighted in students' contextual interpretations of their self-regulation (Järvelä & Salovaara, 2004).

Wosnitza and Volet's (2005) study examined the origin, direction and impact of emotions in social online learning. Their analysis of social online-learning situations revealed a range of other-directed emotions, in addition to self-, task- and technology-directed emotions. Emotions generated in social online environments are not different in nature from those generated in face-to-face learning situations. What is different in social online learning is the fact that emotions are expressed via technology, and that the disclosure of emotions is necessarily voluntary. The results highlight the multiple directions emotions can take and the significance of students' interpretations of their emotions on the learning process.

In general, academic emotions are significantly related to student motivation, learning strategies, cognitive resources, self-regulation and academic achievement (Pekrun, Goetz, Titz & Perry, 2002). Anyhow, not only the emotions themselves vary but also the sources that cause emotions. Learning situations are important sources of emotions that instigate a variety of self-referenced, task-related and social emotions. Some of the recent studies show that when more contextual attempts at investigating classroom motivation have been made, the need to examine emotions tends to emerge (Meyer & Turner, 2002; Volet & Järvelä, 2001). Järvenoja and Järvelä's (2005) study investigated what kind of explanations students gave to their emotional experiences related to computer-supported collaborative learning. The process-oriented interviews were conducted during and after the lessons and questions were asked about students' self-related beliefs and feelings. By looking at the ways the students explain the different emotions in new pedagogical contexts it was possible to find out their subjective and contextual specific explanations. Four categories were composed to describe the differences in reasons for emotional experiences. One of the critical features was that, especially in the beginning of the learning project, the self-driven emotions played an important role in inhibiting or facilitating task-involvement.

Self-regulated learning

After three decades of research, self-regulation is a well-established concept with empirical support from developmental and intervention research. The nature and assumptions underlying self-regulation in learning have been widely discussed (e.g. Winne, 1995; Zimmerman, 1989). Self-regulated learning has been defined as an active, constructive process whereby learners set goals for their learning and then attempt to plan, monitor, regulate and control their cognition, motivation, behaviour and context (Boekaerts, Pintrich & Zeidner, 2000; Pintrich, 2000). Self-regulated learners take charge of their own learning by choosing and setting goals, using individual strategies in order to monitor, regulate and control different aspects which influence the learning process and evaluating his or her actions. Eventually, they become less dependent on others and the contextual features in a learning situation (Boekaerts, Pintrich & Zeidner, 2000; Schunk & Zimmermann, 1994; Winne & Hadwin, 1998). Studying effectively by self-regulated learning itself can be seen as a skill powered by will.

Self-regulated learning includes several sub-processes. Accordingly, different studies on self-regulated learning have stressed different aspects; for example, metacognitive processes (Winne, 1995), learning strategies (Zimmerman & Martinez-Pons, 1989), self-efficacy (Schunk & Zimmerman, 1997), motivational regulation (Wolters, 2003), emotional self-regulation (Pekrun Goetz, Titz & Perry, 2002) and volition (Corno, 2001). Depending on the studies, there are differences in how self-regulatory processes are portrayed. Based on these studies there is strong evidence of how cognitive strategies contribute to students' learning and how different motivational perceptions (e.g. achievement goals, the beliefs of self-efficacy) reciprocally affect the use of strategies.

Although self-regulation research has traditionally focused on an individual perspective, there is an increasing interest in considering these processes at the social level with reference to concepts such as social regulation, shared regulation or co-regulation (Jackson, McKenzie & Hobfoll, 2000). All these regulation types contribute to how students reach their goals, even though they are directed differently. These processes are self-regulation, where the individual aims to regulate her-/himself; other-regulation, where an individual aims to affect others; and finally shared regulation where some or all of the group members simply cooperate to regulate others or in the best cases, regulate themselves consensually in shared regulation (Järvelä, Volet & Järvenoja, 2010; Vauras, Iiskala, Kajamies, Kinnunen, & Lehtinen, 2003).

self other + shared regulation

Metacognition as a form of cognitive regulation

One important aspect of the self-regulated learning models is that students can monitor, control and regulate their own cognitive actions (Pintrich, 2000; Zimmerman, 2001) which could also be referred to as metacognition (Flavell, 1979; Brown, 1987). In general, metacognition refers to the awareness that learners have of their general cognitive strengths and weaknesses, and of the cognitive resources they can apply to meet the demands of particular tasks (*knowledge of cognition*). It also concerns learners' knowledge and skill about how to regulate learning processes and engagement in tasks (the *regulation of cognition*) to optimize learning outcomes (Winne & Perry, 2000; Pintrich, Wolters & Baxter, 2000).

In order to engage the learners into joint problem-solving and the use of metacognitive skills, computer-based learning environments, like asynchronous discussion forums, have been utilized to support students' metacognitive activity – for example, in mathematical problem-solving (Hurme & Järvelä, 2005). The main idea is that in networked discussion the students make their thinking visible (Lehtinen, 2003) and externalize their thinking by writing computer notes to the discussion forum (Scardamalia & Bereiter, 1996). The students are encouraged to construct explanations, pose questions and provide further information to each other (Cohen & Scardamalia, 1998). The processes of explanation construction (Ploetzer, Dillenbourg, Preier & Traum, 1999), help providing, and help seeking (Newman, 1994) are essential for students' metacognitive activity. While constructing explanations, the students become aware of their thinking, of the missing knowledge and lack of understanding (Webb, 1989). While contributing their ideas and making their thinking visible the students are able to reflect their cognitive processes and discuss what they do or do not know and understand with others. In addition, the messages saved to the database are continuously available to the students for further review afterwards.

In networked mathematical problem-solving, the learners can explain how they have solved the problem, how the given task influences the problem-solving or they can ask for support and advice on their own problem-solving and regulate the group's working. For example, in one of our studies, Hurme and Järvelä (2005) analyzed the metacognitive content of the discussion forum data of 13-year-old secondary school students' mathematical problem-solving in geometry and probability courses. The main finding was that even though there were a quite lot of messages in the database, only a few of them were characterized as metacognitive.

In their study, Hurme and Järvelä provide an example of a joint problem-solving session where the three student pairs were working with a probability problem given by the mathematics teacher. The problem was the following: "Rolling one dice twice makes a two-digit number. What is the probability that the number you get is bigger than 46?" The purpose of this task was not just to solve the problem but also to make an inquiry with three phases: *planning the inquiry, implementing an experiment with dice* and *making a report of the inquiry*. In the beginning of the task the students must first understand what the concept of probability means and how to apply it in this problem. One pair of girls had published their inquiry plan in the knowledge forum learning environment and the three groups had the following discussion, presented in Example 1.

Example 1. "Rolling dice" – discussion in knowledge forum learning environment (Hurme & Järvelä, 2005)

Bob and Michael: The number of rolling dice . . . Aren't there actually 72 possibilities because the dice can be tossed vice versa . . .

Tina and Helen: It could be . . . but we don't think that it is calculated that way because in the formulation of the problem there is not mentioned the dice as separate (e.g. dice 1 and dice 2)

Bob and Michael: A little bit more about the total number of tossing dice . . . But in the problem the same dice is tossed twice and it doesn't matter if you toss one dice or use two different dice.

Jack and Sam: We agree. We think so too but there are still altogether 36 possibilities. At every number [1, 2, 3, 4, 5, 6] in first dice there is 6 possibilities, in other words 6 × 6 =36. This is a quite complicate[d] explanation but think about it.

Jack and Sam: No it is not. It is not possible because the dice are tossed TWICE and not FOUR times.

Tina and Helen: Tell us about it . . . let's start all over again . . . there are 6 numbers in the number cube, and if we toss it twice we have to MULTIPLY 6 by itself, so 6 × 6 =36? So how to get 72 [possibilities]? There is no reason to multiply 36 with 2 . . .

In this discussion, the students made their thinking visible by asking questions and providing explanations. Bob and Michael have not completely understood the problem and the question they posed to the girls requires an analysis of the premises of the given task. Tina and Helen reply to them in order to make their understanding visible. Bob and Michael continue their analysis of the problem by suggesting that it is the same thing to use one dice twice or have two different dice. This can be seen as a *regulation of cognition* because they are providing an explanation in order to facilitate others' problem-solving. Jack and Sam's first discussion comment can also be interpreted as *a regulation of cognition*: they have an attempt to make the others think about the problem and its prerequisites by providing a detailed explanation. Jack and Sam's second comment is a reply to Bob and Michael's first suggestion of having a total of 72 possibilities for rolling a dice and it continues their previous explanation how to count the probability. In the last message Tina and Helen are monitoring and evaluating their own understanding (*the regulation of cognition*) rather than asking for a further explanation.

Example 1 shows that metacognitive activity is an essential part of joint problem-solving where the students are working with an inquiry task. The students are not only metacognitively monitoring and controlling their own, but also the others' cognitive activity, requiring reciprocal interaction (Hurme, Palonen & Järvelä, 2006). In a similar way, previous research has seen metacognition as socially mediated (Goos, Gailbraith & Renshaw, 2002) or as socially shared metacognition, in terms of inter-individual awareness of joint problem-solving (Iiskala, Vauras & Lehtinen, 2004). Thus, metacognition is an essential part of collaboration where the group's cognitive activity is regulated by planning, monitoring and evaluating in order to achieve meaningful thinking and new approaches to solve the problem. This kind of shared metacognitive activity is presented in Example 2 where the first year pre-service teachers are jointly trying to solve the given mathematical problem called "Dark Stairs" in Workmates asynchronous learning environment (see Hurme, Merenluoto, & Järvelä, 2009):

> Matt, Grandmother, little sister and Dad are standing upstairs in the dark and they need to go downstairs. The stairs are really narrow and are in bad shape and about to crash, so they can take only two people's weight at a time. The stairs will collapse in 18 minutes. The family has only one flashlight and it is impossible to use the stairs without the light being on. The sinuous stairs are also so long that it is impossible to throw the flashlight upstairs from the downstairs. The members of the family are aware of how much time it requires for them to get down the stairs. Because Grandmother is in poor health it takes seven minutes for her to go down the stairs. The little sister walks down the stairs in five minutes and Dad in three minutes. Matt runs the stairs in two minutes. Is there enough time for them to get everybody downstairs in 18 minutes?
> (Modified, Björklund, Lehto, Pasanen & Viljanen, 2002)

The Dark Stairs was a brain-teaser problem, where the solver needs to build an efficient situation model and be ready to test different kinds of solutions. The most obvious but incorrect strategy would be to choose the fastest one to run up and down the stairs. The crucial elements for solution are that the two slowest people go downstairs together and the two fastest people change which one of them runs up or down the stairs.

Example 2. Socially shared metacognition in joint problem-solving in triad A (Hurme, Merenluoto, & Järvelä, 2009)

Alina: Matt is the fastest one to dribble the flashlight up and down, but should it be someone slower to go together with Grandmother . . .? I've tried several ways to solve this but I always get 19 minutes.

Tapio: I've also the same 19, that's why someone slower should take Grandmother down but I don't get it.

Anna: I noticed that there is an error in my thinking . . . So if for Grandmother it takes 7 minutes anyway, it would be reasonable for example to put little sister to go with her because for little sister it takes for 5 minutes. But now the Grandmother and little sister are going together and it takes altogether 7 minutes. The little sister goes up – 5 minutes. Sister goes down with dad and it takes 5 minutes . . . Does this sound reasonable . . .?

In Example 2, Alina's message illustrates the *regulation of cognition* because she is channeling the group's thinking into a new approach: having two slowest persons going down at the same is an essential part of successful problem-solving. Tapio agrees with her and he appropriates Alina's idea but he still does not quite understand how the prerequisites of the task are fitting together. Anna participates in the discussion first by monitoring her own thinking (the *regulation of cognition*) and then she adopts Alina's idea and develops it further. This kind of regulation of the group's cognitive activity could be considered as a sign of socially shared metacognition.

The group continues to work collaboratively for an hour by supporting each other and constructing new ideas to solve the problem. On the basis of their several joint attempts, Anna presents the effort which leads them to the solution: Dad and Matt go down (three minutes), Matt runs up (two minutes), Grandmother and little sister go down (seven minutes) and Matt goes down with Dad (three minutes).

To sum, in this section, we have presented metacognition in joint technology-based problem solving in mathematics at secondary school level and among pre-service teachers. In the first two examples, the groups were working together collaboratively which allowed the members not only to regulate their own cognitive processes but also to affect how others thought and proceeded in problem-solving. Particularly in the first pre-service teacher's group they took each other's ideas into account and jointly developed them further.

Motivation regulation in self-regulated learning

In every learning situation a student has to cope with his or her own emotional and cognitive demands and conflicts as well as social settings and environmental cues (Volet & Järvelä, 2001). This is to say, that students have to regulate their cognitive, motivational and emotional learning processes (Boekaerts, Pintrich & Zeidner, 2000). Learners' capabilities for exerting motivational and emotional control have been shown to be useful in describing these individual differences of learning processes.

Regulation of motivation refers to "the activities through which individuals purposefully act to initiate, maintain, or supplement their willingness to start, to provide work toward, or to complete a particular activity or goal" (Wolters, 2003, p. 190). *Motivation regulation* is a key to successful self-regulated learning (Järvelä & Niemivirta, 2001). It consists of means by which students' select and manage goals, and how they follow through when challenges arise as learning unfolds. While goals set standards for students' achievement (Pintrich, 2000), *motivation control* strategies operationalize how self-regulated learning is applied. Regulation of motivation is conceptually distinct from motivation even though it may be difficult to differentiate empirically between these two phenomena, and the relation between students' motivation and motivation regulation is reciprocal (Järvenoja & Järvelä, 2005; Wolters & Rosenthal, 2000). Theories of motivation emphasize the subjective control that various beliefs and attitudes have on student choice, effort, and persistence, whereas the regulation of motivation concerns students' active control of the processes that influence these outcomes (Kuhl, 1985).

A concept of volition can be seen as a part of the regulation of motivation. Kuhl (1984) as well as Corno (1993) discussed under the label of volitional control various strategies that individuals might use to control their motivation. Corno has defined volition as a tendency to maintain focus and effort toward goals despite distractions. Volition is needed particularly in the executive phase of a learning process, when motivation and goal commitment is established, but a student still needs to sustain and support the decisions made. Volitional processes strengthen the motivational aspects that back up the goal-oriented actions and also the control of emotional reactions. Traditional research on volition divides into specific volitional control strategies for covert and overt processes. Covert processes involve the control of cognition, emotional control and motivation control. Overt processes deal with environmental control, such as task control or control of others.

What is the role of motivation and emotion control in collaborative learning situations?

Motivation and emotion control is an emerging area of study that is gaining interest in the field of collaborative learning research. Collaborative learning includes a variety of shared processes where individuals aim to regulate the prerequisites for learning together, and an increasing amount of studies emphasise the meaning of motivation and emotions for successful collaboration (Crook, 2000). Social learning situations, where individuals' characteristics, goals and demands meet, can evoke emotions and create novel motivational challenges for individuals (Järvelä, Lehtinen & Salonen, 2000; Järvenoja & Järvelä, 2005). In collaborative learning processes these socio-emotional conflicts can emerge due to a variety of reasons originating from, for example, individual differences, cognitive conflicts or modes of interaction. For instance, collaborative learning models presume that group members create a shared conception of a task and then try to reach this goal by equally sharing the responsibility of the learning process respectively (Roschelle & Teasley, 1995). Collaborative learning creates new challenges for motivation maintenance. This requires constant negotiation and argumentation between the students, as well as adjustment of individual conceptions and goals, and also control of emotional reactions to these conflicts.

Several studies have shown how different elements, such as lack of common ground in shared problem-solving (Mäkitalo, Häkkinen, Järvelä & Leinonen, 2002) or multiple cognitive perspectives and complex concepts (Feltovich, Spiro, Coulson & Feltovich, 1996), can inhibit collaborative knowledge construction. Often these same situations are also socio-emotionally challenging and they can act as competitive motives or interruptions or obstacles to motivated action in different phases of the learning process. Therefore, these situations invite the need to control motivation and emotions of individuals and their group members. In other words, it can be argued that the regulation of emotion, at both the individual and group level, is critical for successful collaboration.

When considering self-regulation in collaboration, regulation processes can be seen as a form of individual participation in the collaborative activity (Hurme *et al.*, 2006). In other words, with regulation actions, individual group members take part in the formation of a group's common ground and emotional stability. For example, in order to reach personal goals, individual group members have to try to reciprocally regulate each other (Vauras, Iiskala, Kajamies, Kinnunen, & Lehtinen, 2003). Also, in order to reach the shared goal, the group members may need to regulate their motivation or emotional conflicts together through equally sharing the responsibility of the learning task requirements. For example, individual students who are required to form a group and work toward a common objective must define their aims and standards to create a shared goal. They need to be able to negotiate compromise, change their opinions, explain and listen. These actions expect an ability to control personal emotions and support others in this process.

In the Hurme *et al.* (2006) study, 99 first-year educational psychology students participated in an educational psychology course, which was part of their teacher-education studies. Forty-one of the students worked in a virtual setting and studied in groups of 3–5 members in three different collaborative learning tasks. Example 4 illustrates the students' motivation regulation in collaborative online learning tasks. It is a brief review of a virtual discussion from a group of three students illustrating how students use social comments in order to maintain motivation and a socio-emotionally secure atmosphere in the group (A review includes examples in a discussion from a one-week virtual course discussion).

Example 4

DAY 1
I think *Maria had found a good point* . . .
What do you think about . . .*?*
What else comes to your mind about . . .*?*
OK, what have *we* got from here?
Laura had found a good thing . . .
What do you think if I say . . .*?*

DAY 3
It seems that *as shared things* we have . . .
In Laura's text it was emphasized well that . . .
This time *we* found pretty much the same things. We also found different things
and same things but in different names.
What do you think about . . .*?*
I agree with you Anna . . .
What do you think?
Sure, those things that Anna suggested are important . . .
What else would come to your minds about this?

DAY 6
In the future *we* could develop . . . *I want to thank my group for success in
teamwork.*

In Example 4 it is seen that even when the focus of three students is on the topic
and they all agree that they are willing to find solutions, the students also aim to
regulate their shared efforts to complete the task. Example 4 demonstrates what
kind of non-cognitive, socially constructive comments the students used in order
to motivate each other. With these comments, the students aimed at explicitly
acknowledging and giving support to others' ideas, and at building and maintaining
the motivation and socio-emotional ground by, for example, asking each others'
opinions, referring to their shared goals, using other group members' first names
and talking about "us" or "we."

Conclusions

In this chapter we have discussed how effective learning in social practices, with
and without computers, necessitates that students self-regulate their learning. A
long research tradition in self-regulated research has identified the core regulatory
processes of cognition, motivation and emotion. As Winne (2006) puts it, studying
effectively by self-regulated learning is a skill powered by will. Learners apply this
with varying expertise. Is there anything we can do to support effective learning
skills and active self-regulation?

Among educational psychologists and instructional designers it has been popular to create "powerful" often technology supported learning environments. The adaptation of constructivist epistemological principles has particularly encouraged researchers to analyze how technology-based environments would provide learners with new opportunities for activities which are beneficial for knowledge construction (Roschelle, Pea, Hoadley, Gordin & Means, 2000). Technology has contributed to many attempts for supporting Higher-order learning and the development of metacognition and self-regulation (De Corte, Verschaffel, Entwistle & Van Merriëboer, 2003). Recently, there have particularly been efforts by people working on self-regulated learning theory to find ways to design technology to assist in helping students' to develop better learning strategies and regulate their learning process (e.g. Hadwin, Winne & Nesbit, 2005).

In this chapter we have also discussed the competencies needed to participate in future social learning practices, with an emphasis put on motivated and self-regulated learning and how these processes emerge in various computer-supported learning environments. New opportunities for scaffolding self-regulated learning have been searched from computer-based regulation tools, which aim to promote cognitive regulation processes (Hennessy & Murphy, 1999). Learning tools are to promote motivated learning from the individual learning point of view, as well as in opening new learning opportunities for social and interactive learning (Azevedo, 2005). Another promising line of research comes from Winne and his colleagues (2006) who have developed the gStudy computer environment that provides environment for learning kits. Tools in gStudy are being researched to investigate their capacity to help learners learn more effectively by enhancing self-regulated learning. The environment gathers the detailed process data of students' actions that can be provided for students to enhance their awareness of their learning process.

Emerging learning practices (Ludvigsen, Lund, Rasmussen & Säljö, this volume) in a variety of contexts are so complex and multidimensional that a strong theoretical and conceptual understanding is needed to elaborate learning processes in research and practice. In addition to motivation, emotion and cognition the self-regulated learning theory takes into account the behavioral and environmental features when analyzing the effectiveness of learning in computer-supported learning environments. The future progress in research presumes theoretical and empirical analysis made in real contexts, embedded into authentic learning. Salomon (1992) has claimed that the traditional focus of researchers' attention has been on how the individuals and their cognitions and motivations change when studying in new learning environments. According to him, however, it is the whole system that changes in interaction with the individuals in it, not just the single and isolated individuals' perceptions and motivations. Thus, the focus should also be on analyzing how individual characteristics interact with situational features and social factors, and furthermore, how technology forges learning processes.

In the contemporary computer-supported collaborative learning environments social interaction is often taken for granted because the tools are made available

(Kreijns, Kirschner & Jochems, 2003). Beyond tools for collaboration, learners need structured and scaffolded support for enacting the collaboration process. Recently, there have been efforts to combine ideas from instructional design and collaborative learning, to structure the collaboration process in order to promote specific types of interactions (Weinberger, Ertl, Fischer & Mandl, 2005). However, the focus has been on orchestrating and emphasizing collaborative interactions on the task, but not on the development of the collaborative community, and individuals' engagement in the community. Successful engagement in collaborative learning presumes norms that allow members to feel safe, take risks and share ideas. This actually involves core processes of self-regulated learning; effective use of learning strategies to participate in collaborative interactions; metacognitive control and regulation of motivation and emotions. There is not yet much research on these aspects, but our own findings already show that in a collaborative learning situation an individual group member can play a leading role in activating motivation regulation (Järvenoja & Järvelä, 2009). Socially shared learning tasks may also stimulate new strategies for motivation regulation (Järvelä, Järvenoja & Veermans, 2008), as well as collaborative knowledge construction and joint metacognitive regulation (Hurme *et al.*, 2006).

To conclude, broadening research perspectives on computer-supported collaborative learning to self-regulated learning can increase understanding about how students are able to engage in studying more deeply and continuously improve skills in socially learning practices. From teachers' as well as instructional designers' points of view, this type of research can offer information and methods concerning how to support motivation regulation in practice, which will open new opportunities for fostering students' motivation to learn.

References

Alexander, P. A. (2004). Envisioning the Possibilities for Educational Psychology. *Educational Psychologist*, *39*, 149–156.

Azevedo, R. (2005). Computer Environments as Metacognitive Tools for Enhancing Learning. *Educational Psychologist, 40*, 193–197.

Barab, S. A., Kling, R. and Gray, J. (eds). (2004). *Designing for Virtual Communities in the Service of Learning*. Cambridge: Cambridge University Press.

Björklund, J., Lehto, S., Pasanen, S. and Viljanen, M. (2002). *Teacher's Guide to Fun Math*. Helsinki: MFKA-Kustannus OY.

Boekarts, M., Pintrich, P. R. and Zeidner, M. (eds). (2000). *Handbook of Self-regulation*. San Diego, CA: Academic Press.

Brown, A. L. (1987). Metacognition, Executive Control, Self-regulation and Other Mysterious Mechanisms. In F. Weinert and R. Kluwe (eds). *Metacognition, Motivation and Understanding* (pp. 65–115). Hillsdale, NJ: Lawrence Erlbaum.

Cohen, A. and Scardamalia, M. (1998). Discourse about Ideas: Monitoring and regulation in face-to-face and computer-mediated environments. *Interactive Learning Environments*, *6*, 93–113.

Corno, L. (2001). Volitional Aspects of Self-regulated Learning. In B. J. Zimmerman and

D. H. Schunk (eds). *Self-regulated Learning and Academic Achievement: Theoretical perspectives* (pp. 191–225). Mahwah, NJ: Lawrence Erlbaum.

Corno, L. (1993). The Best-laid plans: Modern conceptions of volition and educational research. *Educational Researcher, 22,* 14–22.

Crook, C. (2000). Motivation and the Ecology of Collaborative Learning. In R. Joiner, K. Littleton, D. Faulkner and D. Miell (eds). *Rethinking Collaborative Learning* (pp. 161–178). London: Free Association Books.

De Corte, E., Verschaffel, L., Entwistle, N. and Van Merriëboer, J. (eds). (2003). *Powerful Learning Environments: Unravelling basic components and dimensions* (pp. 35–54). Amsterdam: Pergamon.

Dillenbourg, P. (1999). Introduction: What do you mean by "collaborative learning"? In P. Dillenbourg (ed.). *Collaborative Learning: Cognitive and computational approaches* (p. 119). Amsterdam: Pergamon.

Feltovich, P. J., Spiro, R. J., Coulson, R. L. and Feltovich, J. (1996). Collaboration Within and Among Minds: Mastering complexity, individually and in groups. In T. Koschmann (ed.) *CSCL: Theory and practice of an emerging paradigm,* (pp. 25–44). Mahwah, NJ: Erlbaum.

Flavell, J. (1979). Metacognition and Cognitive Monitoring: A new area of cognitive-developmental inquiry. *American Psychologist, 34,* 906–911.

Goos, M., Galbraith, P. and Renshaw, P. (2002). Socially Mediated Metacognition: Creating collaborative zones of proximal development in small group problem solving. *Educational Studies in Mathematics, 49,* 193–223.

Hadwin, A. F., Winne, P. H. and Nesbit, J. C. (2005). Roles for Software Technologies in Advancing Research and Theory in Educational Psychology. *British Journal of Educational Psychology, 75,* 1–24.

Hakkarainen, K., Lipponen, L. and Järvelä, S. (2002). Epistemology of Inquiry and Computer-supported Collaborative Learning. In T. Koschmann, N. Miyake and R. Hall (eds). *CSCL2: Carrying forward the conversation* (pp. 129–156). Mahwah, NJ: Erlbaum.

Hennessy, S. and Murphy, P. (1999). The Potential for Collaborative Problem Solving in Design and Technology. *International Journal of Technology and Design Education, 9,* 1–36.

Higgins, E. T. (2000). Social Cognition: Learning about what matters in the social world. *European Journal of Social Psychology, 30,* 3–39.

Hurme, T.-R. and Järvelä, S. (2005). Students' Activity in Computer Supported Collaborative Problem Solving in Mathematics. *International Journal of Computers for Mathematical Learning, 10,* 49–73.

Hurme, T.-R., Merenluoto, K. and Järvelä, S. (2009). Socially Shared Metacognition of Pre-service Primary Teachers in a Computer Supported Mathematics Course and Their Feelings of Task Difficulty: A case study. *Educational Research and Evaluation, 15*(5), 503–524.

Hurme, T.-R., Palonen, T. and Järvelä, S. (2006). Metacognition in Joint Discussions: An analysis of the patterns of interaction and the metacognitive content of the networked discussions. *Metacognition and Learning, 1,* 181–200.

Iiskala, T., Vauras, M. and Lehtinen, E. (2004). Socially-shared Metacognition? *Hellenic Journal of Psychology, 1,* 147–178.

Jackson, T., McKenzie J. and Hobfoll, S. E. (2000). Communal Aspects of Self-regulation. In M. Boekaerts, P. R., Pintrich and M. Zeidner (eds). *Handbook of Self-regulation* (pp. 275–300), San Diego: Academic Press.

Järvelä, S., Järvenoja, H., Veermans, M. (2008). Understanding Dynamics of Motivation in Socially Shared Learning. *International Journal of Educational Research, 47*(1), 122–135.

Järvelä, S., Lehtinen, E. and Salonen, P. (2000). Socio-emotional Orientation as a Mediating Variable in the Teaching-learning Interaction: Implications for instructional design. *Scandinavian Journal of Educational Research, 44,* 293–306.

Järvelä, S. and Niemivirta, M. (2001). Motivation in Context: Challenges and possibilities in studying the role of motivation in new pedagogical cultures. In S. Volet and S. Järvelä (eds). *Motivation in Learning Contexts* (pp. 105–127). Amsterdam: Elsevier.

Järvelä, S. and Salovaara, H. (2004). The Interplay of Motivational Goals and Cognitive Strategies in New Pedagogical Culture: A context oriented and qualitative approach. *European Psychologist, 9,* 232–244.

Järvelä, S., Veermans, M. and Leinonen, P. (2008). Investigating Students' Engagement in a Computer-supported inquiry: A process-oriented analysis. *Social Psychology in Education, 11,* 299–322.

Järvelä, S., Volet, S. and Järvenoja, H. (2010). Research on Motivation in Collaborative Learning: Moving beyond the cognitive-situative divide and combining individual and social processes. *Educational Psychologist, 45*(1), 15–27.

Järvenoja, H. and Järvelä, S. (2009). Emotion Control in Collaborative Learning situations: Do students regulate emotions evoked from social challenges? *British Journal of Educational Psychology, 79*(3), 463–481.

Järvenoja, H. and Järvelä, S. (2005). How Students Describe the Sources of Their Emotional and Motivational Experiences During the Learning Process: A qualitative approach. *Learning and Instruction, 15,* 465–480.

Kreijns, K., Kirschner, P. A. and Jochems, W. (2003). Identifying the Pitfalls for Social Interaction in Computer-supported Collaborative Learning Environments: A review of the research. *Computers in Human Behaviour, 19,* 335–353.

Kuhl, J. (1985). Volitional Mediators of Cognition-behaviour Consistency: Self-regulatory processes and action versus state orientation. In J. Kuhl and J. Beckmann (eds). *Action Control: From cognition to behaviour* (pp. 101–128). New York: Springer-Verlag.

Kuhl, J. (1984). Volitional Aspects of Achievement Motivation and Learned Helplessness: Toward a comprehensive theory of action control. *Progress in experimental personality research, 13,* 99–171.

Lehtinen, E. (2003). Computer-supported Collaborative Learning: An approach to powerful learning environments. In E. De Corte, L. Verschaffel, N. Entwistle and J. Van Merriëboer (eds). *Powerful Learning Environments: Unravelling basic components and dimensions* (pp. 35–54). Amsterdam: Pergamon.

Meyer, D. K. and Turner, J. C. (2002). Discovering Emotion in Classroom Motivation Research. *Educational Psychologist, 37,* 107–114.

Murphy P. K. and Alexander P. A. (2000). A Motivated Exploration of Motivation Terminology. *Contemporary Educational Psychology, 25,* 3–53.

Mäkitalo, K., Häkkinen, P., Järvelä, S. and Leinonen, P. (2002). Mechanisms of Common Ground in Case-based Web Discussions in Teacher Education. *The Internet and Higher Education, 5,* 247–265.

Newman, R. S. (1994). Adaptive Help Seeking: A strategy of self-regulated learning. In D. H. Schunk and B. J. Zimmerman (eds). *Self-regulation of Learning and Performance: Issues and educational applications* (pp. 283–301). Hillsdale, NJ: Lawrence Erlbaum.

Pekrun, R., Goetz, T., Titz, W. and Perry, R. P. (2002). Academic Emotions in Students' Self-regulated Learning and Achievement: A program of qualitative and quantitative research. *Educational Psychologist*, *37*, 91–105.

Pintrich, P. R. (2000). The Role of Goal Orientation in Self-regulated Learning. In M. Boekaerts, P. R. Pintrich and M. Zeidner (eds). *Handbook of Self-regulation* (pp. 451–502). San Diego, CA: Academic Press.

Pintrich, P. R., Wolters, C. and Baxter, G. (2000). Assessing Metacognition and Self-regulated Learning. In G. Schraw and J. Impara (eds). *Issues in the Measurements of Metacognition* (pp. 43–98). Lincoln, NB: Buros Institute of Mental Measurements, University of Nebraska.

Ploetzner, R., Dillenbourg, P., Preier, M. and Traum, D. (1999). Learning by Explaining to Oneself and to Others. In P. Dillenbourgh (ed.). *Collaborative Learning: Cognitive and computational approaches* (pp. 103–121). Amsterdam: Pergamon.

Randi, J. and Corno, L. (2000). Teacher Innovations in Self-regulated learning. In M. Boekarts, P. R. Pintrich and M. Zeidner (eds). *Handbook of Self-regulation* (pp. 651–685). San Diego, CA: Academic Press.

Roschelle, J., Pea, P., Hoadley, C., Gordin, D. and Means, B. (2000). Changing How and What Children Learn in School with Computer-Based Technologies. *The Future of Children and Computer Technology*, *10*, 76–101.

Roschelle, J. and Teasley, S. (1995). The Construction of Shared Knowledge in Collaborative Problem Solving. In C. E. O'Malley (ed.). *Computer Supported Collaborative Learning* (pp. 69–97). Heidelberg: Springer-Verlag.

Salomon, G. (1992). New Challenges for Educational Research: Studying the individual within learning environments. *Scandinavian Journal of Educational Research*, *35*, 167–182.

Salovaara, H. and Järvelä, S. (2003). Students Strategic Actions in Computer Supported Collaborative Inquiry. *Learning Environments Research*, *6*, 267–284.

Scardamalia, M. and Bereiter, C. (1996). Computer Support for Knowledge-building Communities. In T. Koschmann (ed.). *CSCL: Theory and Practice of an Emerging Paradigm* (pp. 249–268). Mahwah, NJ: Lawrence Erlbaum.

Schunk, D. H. and Zimmerman, B. J. (eds). (1994). *Self-regulation of Learning and Performance. Issues and Educational Applications.* Hillsdale, NJ: Erlbaum.

Schunk, D. H. and Zimmerman, B. J. (1997). Social Origins of Self-regulatory Competence. *Educational Psychologist*, *32*, 195–208.

Singer, J., Marx, R. W., Krajcik, J. and Chambers, J. C. (2000). Constructing Extended Inquiry Projects: Curriculum materials for science education reform. *Educational Psychologist*, *35*, 165–178.

Stipek, D. J. (2002). *Motivation to Learn: From theory to practice* (4th edn). Boston: Allyn and Bacon.

Strijbos, J. W., Kirschner, P. and Martens, R. (2004). What We Know about CSCL and Implementing it in Higher Education, In P. Dillenbourg (Series ed.). *Computer-supported Collaborative Learning* (Vol 3). Boston: Kluwer Academic Publishers.

Thompson, L. and Fine, G. (1999). Socially Shared Cognition, Affect, and Behavior: A review and integration. *Personality and Social Psychology Review*, *3*, 278–302.

Turner, J. C., Meyer, D. K., Cox, K. E., Logan, C. and DiCintio, M. (1998). Creating Contexts for Involvement in Mathematics. *Journal of Educational Psychology*, *90*, 730–745.

Vauras, M., Iiskala, T., Kajamies, A., Kinnunen, R. and Lehtinen, E. (2003). Shared

Regulation and Motivation of Collaborating Peers: A case analysis. *Psychologia, 46,* 19–37.

Volet, S. E. and Järvelä, S. (eds). (2001). *Motivation in Learning Contexts: Theoretical advances and methodological implications.* Amsterdam: Elsevier Science.

Webb, N. (1989). Peer Interaction and Learning in Small Groups. *International Journal of Educational Research, 13,* 21–40.

Weinberger, A., Ertl, B., Fischer, F. and Mandl, H. (2005). Epistemic and Social Scripts in Computer-supported Collaborative Learning. *Instructional Science, 33,* 1–30.

Winne, P. H. (2006). How Software Technologies Can Improve Research on Learning and Bolster School Reform. *Educational Psychologist, 41,* 5–17.

Winne, P. H. (1995). Inherent Details in Self-regulated Learning. *Educational Psychologist, 30,* 173–187.

Winne, P. H. and Hadwin, A. F. (1998). Studying as Self-regulated Learning. In D. J. Hacker, J. Dunlosky, and A. C. Graesser (eds). *Metacognition in Educational Theory and Practice* (pp. 277–304). Mahwah, NJ: Lawrence Erlbaum Associates.

Winne, P. H., Nesbit, J. C., Kumar, V., Hadwin, A. F., Lajoie, S. P., Azevedo, R. A. and Perry, N. E. (2006). Supporting Self-regulated Learning with gStudy Software: The Learning Kit Project. *Technology, Instruction, Cognition and Learning, 3,* 105–113.

Winne, P. H. and Perry, N. E. (2000). Measuring Self-regulated Learning. In M. Boekaerts, P. R. Pintrich and M. Zeidner (eds). *Handbook of Self-regulation* (pp. 531–566). San Diego, CA: Academic Press.

Wolters, C. A. (2003). Regulation of Motivation: Evaluating an underemphasized aspect of self-regulated learning. *Educational Psychologist, 38,* 189–205.

Wolters, C. A. and Rosenthal, H. (2000). The Relation Between Students' Motivational Beliefs and Their Use of Motivational Regulation Strategies. *International Journal of Educational Research, 33,* 801–820.

Wosnitza, M. and Volet, S. E. (2005). Significance of Social and Emotional Dimensions in Online Learning. *Learning and Instruction, 15,* 446–463.

Zimmerman, B. J. (1989). A Social Cognitive View of Self-regulated Learning. *Educational Psychologist, 81,* 329–339.

Zimmerman, B. J. (2001). Theories of Self-regulated Learning and Academic Achievement: An overview and analysis. In B. J. Zimmerman and D. H. Schunk (eds). *Self-regulated Learning and Academic Achievement. Theoretical perspectives.* (pp. 1–37). Hillsdale, NJ: Lawrence Erlbaum Associates.

Zimmerman, B. J. and Martinez-Pons, M. (1989). Student Differences in Self-regulated Learning: Relating grade, sex, and giftedness to self-efficacy and strategy use. *Journal of Educational Psychology, 82,* 51–59.

Chapter 21

Interactive whiteboards

Does new technology transform teaching?

Neil Mercer, * *Julia Gillen,*[†] *Judith Kleine Staarman,*[‡] *Karen Littleton*[§] *and Alison Twiner*[§]

Introduction

In this chapter we will discuss the pedagogical use of computer-based technology in schools through considering the emergent use of a new form of that technology, the interactive whiteboard (IWB). We examine it from a sociocultural perspective, taking Wertsch's notion (1991) of the 'heterogeneous mediational tool kit' as a frame for this study. This particular perspective emphasises the study of tools as they are used in specific sites of activities of learning and teaching, rather than just the designed properties of these tools. It captures the broad multifunctionality of a tool such as the PC or the IWB, as it can be drawn upon in the course of classroom activities. As Wertsch comments, 'only by being part of action do mediational means come into being and play their role. They have no magical power in and of themselves.' (Wertsch, 1991, p. 119). Actions take place in specific settings and circumstances, and our research has attempted to take this into account. This sociocultural perspective has led us to examine critically some ways in which technological innovations have been represented and researched, and how their use is promoted in educational settings. Our discussion is informed by our past involvement in a range of research projects on the use of computer-based technology in education, but we will here draw our illustrative examples from one recent, classroom-based study in British primary schools.

We begin with a brief review of the introduction of computer technology into schools, taking the UK as an example, and set out our own critical perspective on this process. We then describe the multiple capacities of the IWB in order to show that the potential of this tool as a mediational means is not constrained in a narrow, or heavily pre-determined way. Through the analysis of observational data, we show how its affordances relate to teachers' established practices, and discuss the extent to which its introduction has been supportive, transformative or disruptive of those practices. We end with some comments about the potential

* University of Cambridge
† Lancaster University
‡ University of Exeter
§ The Open University

educational significance of this tool and draw more general conclusions about the introduction, use and evaluation of new forms of ICT in schools.

Background

The introduction of interactive whiteboards in the UK

In the UK, the IWB has been commandeered to support broad claims about the value of information and communications technology (ICT) for the improvement of teaching and learning in schools. The recent widespread and rapid introduction of the IWB into British schools occurred at the direct instigation of the government. This might be characterised as the third major wave of UK government-led initiatives introducing computer-based technology into schools in the last 30 years. The first of these was around the end of the 1980s, when the first PCs were placed in schools. At that stage, the number of machines per school was very small, perhaps no more than one or two. The second was in the late 1990s, when the number of PCs was massively increased, and a national professional development programme for teachers on the use of computers was also launched. With this third wave, government funding has provided IWBs for all schools in England and Wales. By the end of 2005, 94 per cent of primary schools were estimated to have at least one IWB – increased from 63 per cent in 2004 (Becta, 2006a; Becta, 2005). The mean number of IWBs per primary school was reported to be five in 2005, compared to just two in the previous year (Becta, 2006b).

ICT innovations in education are often surrounded by optimistic rhetoric, dating back to Papert's (1980) claims for the 'powerful machine'. The same rhetoric can be found in the discussion of the introduction of IWBs. For instance, during the time that IWBs were being introduced into English schools, MirandaNet (an association of educational researchers and developers of ICT) had on its website: 'the technology can effect a profound change in the ways in which our students learn, the ways in which we teach and, more fundamentally, the ways in which we organize the curriculum and our schools.' (MirandaNet, 2005). The Secretary of State for Education who promoted the UK whiteboards initiative, Charles Clarke, was quoted as saying, 'ICT transforms education and the way that children learn.' (Public Technology, 2004), and 'I have been hugely impressed myself by the use of electronic whiteboard technology. I have seen really exhilarating lessons taking place, engaging children in an entirely different way.' (Hitachi, 2004). Evaluations of a more careful kind are well summarised by Weller (2002, p. 7): 'It is the impact upon teaching practice where educational technology seems to have been much less significant than the investment, discussion and optimism surrounding it would warrant.'

Teachers' apparent reluctance to wholeheartedly embrace technology as a transformational force is often seen by ICT advocates as simply reflecting their professional conservatism or lack of vision. As Secretary of State Clarke again said: 'The first problem is that the culture of using ICT is not deeply founded in the teaching of education – it is a long mountain we have to climb . . . Teachers have to be convinced to use ICT for the betterment of students' education.' (Clarke, 1999, p. 2). Many of these advocates of ICT simply trust the technology to somehow deliver in and of itself the 'transformation' and 'revolution' of educational practice. In all these initiatives, there has been little recognition of the potentially disruptive effect of introducing new technology into an established domain of work, especially given the inevitable unreliability of that technology in its early stages. Only rarely, and relatively recently, has it been suggested that computers might help teachers do the job they already do more effectively, rather than be a force for changing it. (Compare the way that computers are provided for secretaries, accountants, research scientists and graphic designers.) But of course the computers offered to schools, in the first waves of initiatives, were not expressly designed for use in the kinds of collective endeavours which take place in classrooms. In the form of 'personal computers' (PCs), they were essentially hand-me-downs from the office, well-designed only for individual activity. The tools being provided were not really fit for purpose. Moreover, educational software has often been designed without the close involvement of teachers (or even educational researchers), and so often has had little direct relationship with the aims and constraints of the curriculum. It has therefore been difficult for teachers to properly integrate the use of ICT into their normal practice (Hennessy, 2006).

New technology is brought into schools for the use of teachers with generally well-established practices, often grounded in many years of experience, and often generating appropriate and successful educational outcomes. A technology-led mode of introduction which ignores this is very likely to create problems, especially regarding teachers' take-up of the technology as a pedagogic tool (Dawes & Selwyn, 1999; Dawes, 2000). The material situation facing teachers in the face of innovations is that the new tools, whatever they are, must be integrated into pedagogical practices of teachers (Hennessy, 2006). As the classroom researchers Burnett, Dickinson, Myers, and Merchant (2006, p. 12) explain: 'The problem with transformation is that it always seems out of reach . . . Whilst waiting for the bright new future, teachers have to get on with coping with the present.'

We suggest that a different perspective should be taken in introducing and evaluating new technology. The important issue is not whether or not technology transforms teaching, but how effectively it contributes to teaching and learning, in the context of normal pedagogic practice.

Researching the interactive whiteboard

The IWB, with its large, touch-sensitive display, is perhaps the only type of educational technology well-suited for whole-class interaction. Typical functionalities of IWBs include:

- Large, touch sensitive, full colour displays on which teacher and pupils can write their own text, call up images from a hard disk, internet or intranet and run a range of software, including simulation software;

- The option to select, display, move and manipulate images (including video) and texts;
- The possibility to save and recall current and previous lesson activities, which may be revisited, reviewed and amended as and when required;
- The option of connecting the IWB to a range of other ICT equipment, including laptops operated by children in the class, digital cameras, video-players and microscopes.

By conceptualising the IWB as a tool or mediating artifact (Wertsch *et al.*, 1993), we aim to take into account the relationships between the affordances of IWBs, the pedagogical practices of teachers and the communicative repertoires of teachers and pupils within the particular context of whole-class teaching. In our recent research, we have observed sequences of lessons in the primary classrooms of teachers who have taken up the IWB with at least some measure of enthusiasm and declare themselves to be relatively keen users of this technology. Our investigation is not therefore an objective evaluation of this technological innovation per se. It is rather an exploration of some of the ways in which keen, relatively competent early adopters of the new technology are making use of the IWB within their whole-class teaching. We focus upon the activities of the teacher as she or he utilises the IWB in pursuit of pedagogic goals, typically – but not always – in the context of whole class interaction. This allows us to examine not only the ways the IWB is integrated into practice, but also its 'transformational' potential. For example, research has shown that teachers typically use interactions with students to build a contextual foundation of 'common knowledge', based on past experience shared with students, to underpin classroom activity (Edwards & Mercer, 1987). Is the IWB employed for this very legitimate purpose – and does its use help the building of such a useful foundation? Research internationally has also shown that classroom dialogue normally has a regular pattern of Initiation–Response–Follow-up (IRF) (Sinclair & Coulthard, 1975) in which teacher's talk and teacher's questions predominate and students only make short responses (see, for example, Edwards & Westgate, 1994; Mercer, 1995; Burns & Myhill, 2004). Although in some other countries extended contributions from pupils have been observed as more common (Alexander, 2000), this seems to typify life in most British classrooms. There have been recent attempts by both researchers and government agencies in the UK to create a more 'dialogic' climate in schools (Mortimer & Scott, 2003; Alexander, 2004; QCA, 2003; DfES, 2002), and our own research has shown that more active discursive involvement of pupils is associated with better learning outcomes (Rojas-Drummond & Mercer, 2004). We were therefore interested to know if the use of the IWB was associated with changes in the normative patterns of whole-class interaction, or if it was employed to sustain the discursive status quo which has been so persistently documented by classroom researchers. More generally, we have sought evidence of how teachers use the IWB as part of their communicative toolkit and considered which of its functionalities are actually used. Elsewhere, for example, we have examined how its multifunctionality can be applied to the teaching of primary science (Gillen, Littleton, Twiner, Staarman & Mercer, 2008).

Methods

Our research project focused on four teachers and four classes of children aged 7–11 years, in primary schools in the south of England. Each teacher was video-recorded during two sequences of two lessons, providing 16 lessons overall. Recordings were transcribed, with context notes added from the team's viewing of the videos. Teachers were also interviewed to discover how they account for their use of IWBs. The interviews addressed their individual perceptions of the advantages and disadvantages of the equipment, as well as any ways in which they saw its use enabling or inhibiting their effective pedagogical practice.

The analysis consisted of two main stages. The first involved a preliminary consideration of all recorded data and associated transcriptions. The second consisted of a more detailed examination of video and transcript data to create notes on topic themes, lesson content and non-verbal aspects of interpersonal interaction (including the use of technical equipment and other artifacts). Guided by the research questions, particular sequences were then selected for closer examination. The process then became one of: (a) tracing ways in which the IWB functioned as a communicative and pedagogic tool in the teacher-pupil interactions of the classroom and (b) describing and distinguishing specific features of the interaction around the use of IWBs. This was not a coding procedure, because any emergent descriptors were not used to replace the original data. Instead, we generated descriptions of interactions between teachers and pupils in particular data examples and then attempted to generalise across examples. Descriptors of types of teacher-pupil interaction generated in earlier research provided an initial resource, but new descriptors were created as necessary.

In our analysis, we have drawn on the work of Mortimer and Scott (2003) who have devised a matrix for distinguishing different types of 'communicative approach' in teacher-led talk, as shown in Figure 21.1.

The *interactive-non-interactive* dimension represents the extent to which the students, as well as the teacher, are actively involved in the dialogue. The *dialogic-authoritative* dimension represents the relative extent to which the students' or teachers' ideas influence the content and direction of the classroom talk. These two dimensions allow any episode of classroom dialogue to be defined as being interactive or non-interactive on the one hand, and dialogic or authoritative on the other. Four classes of 'communicative approach' can thus be identified: interactive/dialogic, interactive/authoritative, non-interactive/dialogic and non-interactive/authoritative. In a dialogic/interactive episode, a teacher might ask students for their ideas on a topic. The teacher might record those ideas on the IWB for future reference, or ask other pupils whether or not they agree with what has been said. The teacher might ask students to elaborate their ideas ('Oh, that's interesting,

	INTERACTIVE	NON-INTERACTIVE
DIALOGIC	A. Interactive/ Dialogic	B. Non-interactive/ Dialogic
AUTHORITATIVE	C. Interactive/ Authoritative	D. Non-interactive/ Authoritative

Figure 21.1 Four classes of communicative approach (Mortimer & Scott, 2003, p. 35)

what do you mean by that?'). But the teacher would not evaluate these ideas in terms of their correctness, or lead the discussion along a narrow, pre-defined track. Classroom talk becomes more 'authoritative' when the teacher acts more explicitly as an expert, keeps to a given agenda and directs the topic of the discussion clearly along certain routes (which may reflect the structure and content of the curriculum topic being dealt with). In a non-interactive/authoritative episode the teacher would typically be presenting ideas in a 'lecturing' style. These different types of talk do not represent better or worse teaching strategies in any absolute sense: the quality of teaching depends on making the right strategic choices about which to use, and the different types of talk can function in complement. But they do suggest that there is typically too little interactive/dialogic talk in classrooms, thus limiting opportunities for students' active involvement in the construction of knowledge.

Results

We will present two case studies based on data from lessons observed in the classes of two teachers in one of our project schools.

Case Study 1: Mr Henderson, Year 3 (ages 7–8) English (literacy) lesson

Extracts 1, 2 and 3 are from a literacy lesson, on writing instruction texts. This teacher had just three years' professional experience, but had had access to an IWB for most of this time.

Extract 1: Using pictures of previous lesson as resource

In a cookery lesson the previous day, the children had made pancake batter, and after this literacy lesson they went on to make pancakes (as it was Pancake Day/ Shrove Tuesday). The literacy lesson is linked to this activity, as the students are learning how to structure and write a recipe for making pancakes. The teacher had taken photographs of the cooking lesson the day earlier, and put four of these photographs, showing sequential stages of making the batter, on the IWB. Also on the board, as Extract 1 begins, is a set of labels for each of the activities shown (e.g. 'mixing the batter'), but not yet attached to the pictures. The first extract is at the beginning of the lesson (after four minutes) when the teacher asks one of the pupils to label the pictures. The pupils are all seated on the floor in front of the IWB (a common seating arrangement in the UK). Our transcription conventions are described in a note at the end of the chapter.

Teacher:	OK, here we go. Here are some pictures of you doing it yesterday (*making pancake batter*). Let's see, first of all, let's see if we can get somebody to come and label, what, some of these up correctly. Who would like to come and label the instructions to the pictures? Eh, Ruben, you come and do the first one? (And let you think) just move the, move the label onto the picture you think it goes with.	*Teacher gives IWB pen to pupil, who walked up to the IWB. Pupil puts pen to label in order to move it on the IWB*
Teacher:	Mmm, yeah: Is that right? (*to other pupils*). That's, why don't you do the one, that's got you on there?	*Pupil moves a label to the top right picture*
Ruben:	OK.	
Teacher:	What are you doing there? Right, OK, so move that onto, right, that's it, onto that picture. Very good, right.	*Pupil moves label to picture of himself*

Extract 1 shows an imaginative use of digital photographs which, by engaging the children in an engaging way, cued common knowledge of past shared experience and thus linked yesterday's activity to today's lesson. This could provide some coherence for pupils' experience of classroom education which, as Alexander (2000), Crook (1999) and other researchers have argued, may not naturally emerge for pupils through participation in classroom activities. The use of the actual photographs of the pupils also made the literacy activity (writing a recipe for pancakes) personal and more authentic. The IWB allows elements of instructional texts to be moved and ordered, and in a way that encourages children to think about the practical implications of the order. While this can of course be achieved in other ways, it is hard to imagine how this could be done so well, or so relatively easily, without this digital technology (i.e. camera + IWB). However, as a piece of classroom interaction, this extract has all the usual structural features: the teacher asks the questions, does most of the talking and follows up children's responses with an evaluative comment. In Mortimer & Scott's terms, this is interactive/authoritative discourse.

Extract 2: Block-reveal: structure and pace

This extract comes from somewhat further in the lesson, when the children are required to think about what they will have to put in the recipe text, after the instructions of making the batter.

Teacher:	Right, OK. This is what we're going to be doing the next part of the recipe, so this is now the part that we haven't done yet. Can anybody think what we might be doing next? What would be the next stage in the, to make the pancake? James?	
James:	Put in the pan and let it cook.	
Teacher:	Putting the?	
James:	Put it inside and let it cook	
Teacher:	Alright, putting it in the pan and letting it cook, let's see if you're right with that one. Right, very good, yes. Heat frying pan and pour in the batter. What was the verb there? Which verb did we, what did we use there, which is the, what's the doing word in that case? (Liam)	*Moves block that was covering text on IWB slightly down to reveal text: "heat frying pan and pour in batter"*
Liam:	Heat?	
Teacher:	Heat, yes, and again it's coming [up at the front isn't it, it's an instruction	
Pupil:	[(. . .) instruction	*Some children are talking*
Teacher:	There's two actions, two verbs in that sentence, the other one . . .	*Looks to pupils, some of whom are still talking*
Pupil:	You also have to put oil in the pan because it's hard to get it out.	
Teacher:	That's quite right, you do normally put a little bit of oil or butter, haven't put that down on there. Right.	

In Extract 2 we see the teacher using the 'block-reveal' facility to give structure and pace to whole-class discussion. We see the IWB being used as part of a teacher's communicative tool kit. The teacher uses different language genres, of which one (instructional texts) is bound up with his teaching objectives. In his third turn he accepts, and slightly reformulates, a pupil's contribution towards what is the next action in the sequence of cooking a pancake. He then reformulates it more specifically into the target genre, drawing attention to its grammatical structure and giving it a label (an 'instruction'). However, when a pupil makes a relevant suggestion, but which does not fit the more formal instructional style – 'You have to put oil in the pan . . .' – the teacher accepts this contribution but does not act on it. The exchange is interactive/dialogic with respect to the students' and the teacher's talk, but not with respect to the teacher's actions. He chooses not to take advantage of the IWB presentation's provisionality and mutability to revise his original formulation. The written presentation of the recipe can perhaps be considered a powerful form of 'authoritative' discourse, which cannot be easily dislodged by the oral discourse. In this way we see how the IWB is used as a tool for maintaining the discursive *status quo* of the classroom, rather than disrupting or transforming it. However, a key potentiality of the IWB is the ease of making such shifts, of drawing flexibly on the mediational toolkit in a way that Wertsch (1991) captures with the notion of *heterogeneity*, and it is to such an example that we turn now.

Extract 3: Provisionality – adding quantities

The last extract for this teacher is from later in the lesson, after the children have been working in groups on their recipes. The teacher has put a template on the IWB which shows the heading 'Ingredients', a bullet list to be filled in by the pupils, and some pictures of various ingredients. The pupils have to fill in the same template on paper, working together in groups. The teacher walks around the classroom and talks to pupils.

Pupil:	(Do you have to put like) how much to put in?	*Pupil walks over to teacher*
Teacher:	Yes, (*directs attention to rest of the class*) if you can remember how much, remember it is important. Who can remember how much we used of the different ingredients? Katie?	*Pupils raise hands, teacher walks to IWB, where the template of the recipe is still shown*
Katie:	Erm, one hundred grams of flour	
Teacher:	Flour, yes, that was one hundred grams, good. I'll write that one here. One hundred grams, good. Can anyone remember how much milk we used?	*Writes '100g' in the picture of the flour on the IWB*

In Extract 3, we see that the teacher uses the provisionality afforded by the IWB.

During the group work, one of the children notices that the amounts of ingredients are not listed. The teacher acknowledges the importance of this and subsequently adds the quantities to the recipe items on the IWB, while also taking the opportunity to move into the language of weights and measures.

While we cannot explain why the teacher took up this opportunity and not the earlier one, we can say that the affordances of the IWB were used by this teacher to:

1   support both authoritative/interactive dialogue and non-authoritative/interactive dialogue (using children's contributions to modify his formal presentation and hence the task-related information);
2   relate past shared experience and so build a contextual foundation of common knowledge for current tasks;
3   give children opportunities to move from everyday language into the more specialized forms of a target genre;
4   make a lively and engaging presentation;
5   maintain a balance between planned lesson structure and spontaneous reactions to contributions and events as they unfolded.

It is evident from our observations and interview data that this teacher had integrated the IWB fully into his lesson planning and teaching strategies. The technology seems to serve effectively as a tool for pursuing his normal, and legitimate, teaching goals. Its use is not in any sense disruptive of his practices. It seems to make a very useful enhancement to his teaching tool kit, but it is not in any pedagogical sense 'transformational'.

Case Study 2: Mrs Patel, Year 5 (age 9–10 years) science lesson

Extracts 4, 5 and 6 were taken from a science lesson on evaporation. This second teacher had the role of providing ICT-related support for other teachers within her education authority, and so was very familiar with the technology. She was not the regular teacher for this class, and while she was often based at this school she was not very familiar with the pupils involved. Nevertheless, her confidence with the IWB was apparent in seamless movement through screens, and incorporation of a variety of the IWB's functionalities.

Extract 4: Video – engagement at lesson start

Extract 4 is from the start of the lesson. After overcoming a few problems in accessing the file, the teacher opens a video file of herself in her kitchen at home. The extract shows her putting water into a hot frying pan, to demonstrate how the water evaporates. This is presented in the form of a 'magic trick'.

Teacher (on video):	Hey, this is Mrs Patel. I'm standing in my kitchen and I'm going to do a magic trick. Are you ready? (*pause*)	*Teacher in classroom moves to side of IWB out of the way*
Pupils:	Yes	
Teacher (on video):	I said are you ready?	*Holds hand to ear in listening gesture*
Pupils:	Yes! (*louder*)	
Teacher (on video):	You see I've got an ordinary frying pan here	*Holds up pan in left hand and runs right hand round*
	and an ordinary glass of water.	*it, lowers pan but keeps left hand on it*
	I'm going to take a bit of the water, and I'm going to put	*Holds up glass in right hand and puts back on side*
	it in the frying pan.	*Takes spoonful of water, and*
	Watch carefully	*moves above pan*
	Now you see it . . .	*Drops water into pan, which*
	(*pause*)	*sizzles*
	Now you don't	*Holds up pan on its side, and no water runs out*
Pupil:	Whoa!	
Teacher (on video):	Tada!	*Looks back at camera keeps holding pan in left hand, and raises right hand to 'show off' her display*
Pupil:	That is a magic trick!	*Pupils clap*

This extract shows the teacher making imaginative and effective use of technology (digital video camera + IWB) to demonstrate to the children how water is evaporated by heat, in a way that clearly engaged the children and avoided the need for staging an event which might create 'health and safety' problems. The children saw something relevant that they would possibly not have been able to see otherwise in a classroom. Also, by presenting the video file as a 'magic trick', the teacher provided the pupils with an 'anchor', which grasped their attention and enabled the building of further understanding (Schwartz, Lin, Brophy, & Bransford, 1999). This was a non-interactive/authoritative piece of discourse which seemed to function well in context.

Extract 5: Pupil involvement – hands up and IRF sequence (Initiation–Response–Follow-up)

This extract is taken from part-way through the science lesson, during a task to categorise various objects on the IWB as solid, liquid or gas. Some class members disagree as to whether ice (the particular object they are categorising at that time) can be considered a solid or liquid. The teacher tries to draw the 'correct' answer from the pupils, to establish the difference between ice as a solid and water as a liquid.

Teacher:	OK, it *could* be liquid. When is that a liquid?	
Pupils:	(*intake of breath*)	*Raise hands energetically*
Teacher:	When is that a liquid? (*pause*) Er, Josh.	
Josh:	(*quietly*) When the temperature is very hot	*Lowers hand before speaking, and other students then lower their hands*
Teacher:	When is, sorry, [when	*Said in a questioning tone*
Josh:	[When the temperature is hot	
Teacher:	When the temperature is hot, it's a liquid?	
Another pupil:	When it melts	
Josh:	(*laughs*)	*He laughs as if he suspects his answer isn't quite right*
Teacher:	Does that make sense? Can somebody try to re-word that for me?	*Pupils begin to raise hands again (including Josh)*
Pupil:	When it's been melted	
Teacher:	When it's been melted and it's (*pause*) what?	
Pupil:	Er, er water	
Teacher:	Water, well done.	

Extract 5 illustrates that the dialogue throughout this lesson was very much of the normal IRF kind, with closed questions from the teacher and short responses from students, and with the teacher relying on the usual 'hands up' system for selecting respondents. The same kind of conventional dialogue structure can be found in Extract 6.

Extract 6: Risk taking and error – exposure or opportunity

This extract is also from the task to categorise various objects as solid, liquid or gas. A girl has been called to the IWB, and selects a picture to categorise (the bottom half of the picture shows a desert, and the top half a blue sky). The girl (Aimee) appears confused about which category it should belong to (solid, liquid or gas), and the teacher poses questions to her and the class to work through the confusion.

		Aimee comes up to the IWB. Teacher gives her the IWB pen, and she hovers the pen over a picture
Teacher:	What is that a picture of, Aimee?	
Aimee:	A desert?	
Teacher:	Yep	*Aimee starts to drag the picture over to the 'gases' column, but then hovers between the 'gases' and 'liquids' columns*
Aimee:	(. . .)	*Aimee looks to teacher, but doesn't let go of the picture*
Teacher:	You think it's a gas?	*Other pupils mutter*
Teacher:	(*to Aimee*) What are we looking at? Which part of the picture are you looking at? (*to rest of class*) No, she [could	*Teacher moves finger to point repeatedly between top and bottom sections of the picture*
Aimee:	[Oh, oh	*Aimee starts to move picture over to 'solids' column*
Teacher:	She could be right. She could put it there, and we'll talk about why (*to Aimee*) What part are we looking at? What do you think that picture is talking about?	*Aimee moves picture slowly to more central position between the three categories*
Aimee:	I don't understand	*Releases the IWB pen's hold of the picture*
Teacher:	Which material are we looking at?	*Teacher points between the top and bottom sections of the picture. Aimee then points to the top section.*
Teacher:	(*to rest of class*) The sky! OK. She's looking at the sky and she wants to put it in the 'gases'. Is that correct?	*Teacher points from picture to the 'gases' column*
Pupils:	[No [Yes	
Teacher:	Oh, put your hands up please, hands up. Do you think she's right Allan?	*Pupils start to put their hands up*
Allan:	Yes	
Teacher:	Yeah. If she's looking at the sky, and she wants to put it in the 'gases' she's correct. Why?	

Allan: Because erm, well gases like,
                erm air, you know, and, and,
                erm, air's gas.
Teacher: Good. Well done.

In Extract 6 there is an interesting use of the IWB for actively involving children in the construction of knowledge. They are asked to come up to the IWB to put images of substances in appropriate frames (i.e. solids, liquids or gases). This activity provides the teacher with an opportunity to establish the children's level of understanding about the topic, as well as interactivity on the part of the pupils. The extract illustrates the power of the IWB to engage pupils, as from the raised hands it seems that they are very eager to be chosen to come up to the IWB for the activity. However, this affordance of the IWB also carries with it risks for pupils of public exposure and ridicule for error, as in the case of the girl who put the 'desert' picture in the 'gases' box. We would argue that since in most research the IWB is reported to be highly motivating for pupils, the issue of managing classroom behaviour when mistakes are exposed is important for teachers. We might note that this teacher paid considerable attention to recasting the perceived error as a legitimate possibility.

Smith (2001) in her evaluation of IWBs in one region of the UK emphasised the importance of pupils as well as teachers using the IWB, but also commented on the difficulties of individual pupil use, where the one-at-a-time nature of this activity means other pupils have to sit and wait their turn (as seen in Extract 5 above). Smith also noted that in such activities where pupils are called up to interact with the board, teachers noted a loss of pace, and boredom of more able pupils. Thus the introduction and utilisation of new interaction opportunities, which pupils tend to find motivating and enjoyable when it is their turn (Smith *et al.*, 2005), raises new issues for classroom management. In this lesson such potential challenges were managed through changes of pace and variation of activities.

Conclusions

As discussed earlier, one common claim made by proponents of ICT in education is that new technology is 'transformational'. This could be taken to mean that simply using the technology will have profound effects on classroom practice, and indeed on pedagogy. The implication then is that if no transformation occurs, the technology is not being used properly. We have questioned this position and argued that a successful introduction of ICT could instead mean that some procedures or strategies within established teaching practices become easier to enact, or quicker to accomplish. In other words, we have argued that new ICT should be conceptualised as an addition to a teacher's toolkit, rather than as a coercive means for changing educational practice. We have illustrated our argument with case studies of teachers' use of the IWB, showing how this specific mediating artifact is used within established procedures, strategies and patterns of interaction.

We have shown that the IWB can be a very effective tool, enabling teachers to:

- consolidate shared experience, and so enhance continuity and coherence across lessons;
- provide a more authentic and engaging whole-class learning experience for children;
- integrate diverse, multimodal learning resources.

In the interpretation of our findings, we draw on a distinction made by Smith *et al.* (2005) between _technical interactivity_ and _pedagogical interactivity_. In terms of technical interactivity, the IWB seems to facilitate a speedy, smooth presentation compared with earlier technology (for instance when a teacher would use a video player, then write on a blackboard, then allow children to manipulate pictures on a magnetic screen and then use the video again). As a mediating artifact, it can justifiably be claimed to transform teaching to the extent that it clearly enables teachers to combine innovative styles of presentation with different kinds of multimodal information.

In terms of pedagogical effects, the picture is more complex. In English schools, the IWB is always located at the front of the classroom, and so the teacher inevitably teaches from there. This can mean that the teacher is well placed to observe and respond to pupils' comments (as Smith, 2001, suggested); but there is evidence also to support the claim by Hall and Higgins (2005) that this may reinforce a traditional style of teaching. There is the danger of a teacher feeling tied to the structure and pace of a previously prepared IWB presentation, thus reducing the opportunity for spontaneous pupil-contributions and extended classroom dialogue. On the other hand, the shared representation of content on the IWB potentially may encourage more interactive/dialogic interaction, in Mortimer and Scott's (2003) terms, if children use the representation on the IWB to challenge the teacher's (or other authority's) claims (as we saw in Extract 2). This illustrates the potential of IWBs for contributing to changes in the quality of pedagogic dialogue.

Overall, we have observed that IWBs enable teachers to produce lively, engaging, well-structured and interactive lessons quite easily, which is likely to have an effect on what teachers realistically *can* do in the time available. The most effective use of IWBs seems likely to involve striking a balance between providing a clear structure for a well-resourced lesson, and retaining the capacity for more spontaneous or provisional adaptation of the lesson as it proceeds. Otherwise there remains a danger of over-reliance on the conventional IRF structure for dialogue, with its associated closed questioning, 'cued elicitations' (Mercer, 1995) and one word answers from pupils. Teachers may use the whiteboard's technical affordances effectively, yet maintain their established, conventional style of teaching. In this sense the use of this new technology cannot be claimed to 'transform teaching', in which interactive/authoritative talk prevails. Indeed, since it is possible to use the IWB to increase the pace of the lesson, for instance, through the quick manipulation of images, opportunities for extended teacher–pupil dialogue may even become more limited.

In summary, we have observed interactive whiteboards being used effectively by teachers in English primary schools to facilitate what they want to do: but we have not seen this technology cause a radical reformulation of how teaching and learning is carried out. Our research therefore reinforces our belief that expectations of ICT in education as a 'transformational' force are often misconceived, and probably counter-productive to the effective use of the technology in schools. If new technology was reconceptualised as a potential means for helping teachers do their job more effectively, rather than as a means for making them change their established practices, it would almost certainly receive a warmer welcome from the professional workforce. It would probably also be more likely then to contribute to better learning outcomes for students. It may well be that some established pedagogic practices need to be criticised, re-evaluated and changed: indeed, there is much evidence that this is the case. But this cannot be achieved simply by introducing new technology. To paraphrase Wertsch's (1991) comments, as quoted at the beginning of this article: the tools of educational technology have no magical power in themselves; only by being embedded in the practices of teachers and learners do their mediational means come into play. It is only when this is properly appreciated that we will be able to make best use of governmental boldness in technological investment, welcome as that may be. In future research on technological innovation in education, we suggest that there is a need to reassess the appropriateness of the 'transformational' image of ICT in education; plan and assess the use of computer technology from an educational, rather than a technological, perspective; and develop a more sophisticated conceptual model of how ICT can facilitate teaching and learning in the classroom.

Note

Transcription conventions

could	indicates emphasis
(making)	indicates partly unintelligible speech, with most likely speech
noted	
(. . .)	indicates unintelligible speech
[	indicates overlapping speech
(*intake of breath*)	indicates contextual note

References

Alexander, R. (2004). *Towards Dialogic Teaching: Rethinking classroom talk*. Cambridge: Dialogos.

Alexander, R. (2000). *Culture and Pedagogy: International comparisons in primary education*. Malden, MA: Blackwell.

Becta (2006a). *Survey of LAN Infrastructure and ICT Equipment in Schools 2005.* Main report. A report by Atkins Management Consultants for Becta (Coventry, Becta). http://partners.becta.org.uk/page_documents/survey_of_lan_infrastructure0306.pdf (accessed 11th May 2006).

Becta (2006b). *The Becta Review 2006: Evidence on the progress of ICT in education* (Coventry, Becta). http://becta.org.uk/corporate/publications/documents/The_Becta_Review_2006.pdf (accessed 11 May 2006).

Becta (2005). *Becta Review 2005: Evidence on the progress of ICT in education.* British Educational Communications and Technology Agency. http://www.becta.org.uk/corporate/publications/documents/Review_2005.pdf (accessed 8 March 2006).

Burnett, C., Dickinson, P. Myers, J. and Merchant, G. (2006). Digital Connections: Transforming literacy in the primary school. *Cambridge Journal of Education,* 36(1), 11–29.

Burns, C. and Myhill, D. (2004). Interactive or Inactive? A consideration of the nature of interaction in whole class teaching. *Cambridge Journal of Education,* 34(1), 35–49.

Clarke, C. (1999). Quoted in 'Charles Clarke Reveals ICT Targets'. *Educational Computing and Technology,* March.

Crook, C. (1999). Computers in the Community of Classrooms. In K. Littleton and P. Light (eds). *Learning with Computers: Analysing productive interaction.* London: Routledge.

DfES (2002). *Key Stage 3 National Strategy: Training materials for the foundation subjects.* London: Department for Education and Skills. http://www.standards.dfes.gov.uk/keystage3/respub/fs_trmat (accessed 8 March 2006).

Dawes, L. (2000). First Connections: Teachers and the national grid for learning. *Computers and Education,* 33(4), 235–252.

Dawes, L. and Selwyn, N. (1999). Teaching With the Dream Machines: The representation of teachers and computers in information technology advertising. *Journal of Information Technology for Teacher Education,* 8(3), 289–304.

Edwards, A. and Westgate, D. (1994). *Investigating Classroom Talk* (2nd edn). Basingstoke: Falmer Press.

Edwards, D. and Mercer, N. (1987). *Common Knowledge: The development of understanding in the classroom.* London: Methuen/Routledge.

Gillen, J., Littleton, K., Twiner, A., Staarman, J. K. and Mercer, N. (2008). Using the Interactive Whiteboard to Resource Continuity and Support Multimodal Teaching in a Primary Science Classroom. *Journal of Computer Assisted Learning,* 24, 348–358.

Hall, I. and Higgins, S. (2005). Primary School Students' Perceptions of Interactive Whiteboards. *Journal of Computer Assisted Learning,* 21, 102–117.

Hennessy, S. (2006). Integrating Technology into Teaching and Learning of School Science: A situated perspective on pedagogical issues in research. *Studies in Science Education,* 42, 1–50.

Hitachi (2004) Hitachi's interactive whiteboards now available through government's new £25 million 'School Whiteboard Expansion' initiative. Press release. http://uk.hitachisoft-interactive.com/uploads/BECTA.pdf (accessed 6 December, 2006).

Mercer, N. (1995). *The Guided Construction of Knowledge: Talk amongst teachers and learners.* Clevedon: Multilingual Matters.

MirandaNet (2005). MirandaNet Fellowship. http://www.mirandanet.ac.uk (accessed 25 April 2005).

Mortimer, E. F. and Scott, P. H. (2003). *Meaning Making in Secondary Science Classrooms.* Maidenhead: Open University Press.

Papert, S. (1980). *Mindstorms: Children, computers and powerful ideas*. New York: Basic Books.

Public Technology (2004). More cash for school IT, to personalise learning, says DfES' Charles Clarke http://www.publictechnology.net/content/423 (accessed 1 December 2006).

QCA (2003). *New Perspectives on Spoken English in the Classroom: Discussion papers*. London: Qualifications and Curriculum Authority.

Rojas-Drummond, S. and Mercer, N. (2004). Scaffolding the Development of Effective Collaboration and Learning. *International Journal of Educational Research*, 39(1–2), 99–111.

Schwartz, D. L., Lin, X., Brophy, S. and Bransford, J. D. (1999). Toward the Development of Flexibly Adaptive Instructional Designs. In C. M. Reigeluth (ed.). *Instructional Design Theories and Models: A new paradigm of instructional theory, Vol. 2* (pp. 183–213). Mahwah, NJ: Lawrence Erlbaum Associates.

Sinclair, J. and Coulthard, M. (1975). *Towards an Analysis of Discourse: The English used by Teachers and Pupils*. London: Oxford University Press.

Smith, H. (2001). Smartboard Evaluation: Final Report. http://www.kented.org.uk/ngfl/ict/IWB/whiteboards/report.html#6 (accessed 10 January 2006).

Smith, H. J., Higgins, S., Wall, K. and Miller, J. (2005). Interactive whiteboards: boon or bandwagon? A critical review of the literature. *Journal of Computer Assisted Learning*, 21, 91–101.

Weller, M. (2002). *Delivering Learning on the Net: The why what and how of online education*. London: Kogan Page.

Wertsch, J. V. (1991). Voices of the Mind: A sociocultural approach to mediated action. Hemel Hempstead: Harvester Wheatsheaf.

Wertsch, J. V., Tulviste, P. and Hagstrom, F. (1993). A sociocultural approach to agency. In E. A. Forman, N. Minick and C. A. Stone (eds), *Contexts for Learning: Sociocultural Dynamics in Children's Development* (pp. 336–356). New York: Oxford University Press.

Chapter 22

Differences that make a difference

Contrasting the local enactment of two technologies in a kinematics lab

Oskar Lindwall and Jonas Ivarsson

This chapter reports a study that is part of a larger project in which we investigate the use of computer-supported learning environments in science education. In the project, teachers and researchers jointly document the workings of educational practices and use this documentation in order to improve the design and enactment of the practices. These revised practices are then investigated to see how they could be further improved, and so on. With such an organization and focus, and by applying a currently popular term, the project can be characterized as *design-based research* (e.g. Brown, 1992; Stahl, this volume). Although there is a great variety among design-based research projects, a common aim is to provide analyses and theories that have the potential of doing "real work in practical educational contexts" (Cobb, Confrey, diSessa, Lehrer, & Schauble, 2003, p. 13). In addition, a frequent and distinguishing feature is that the projects include separable phases – they are usually conducted "through continuous cycles of design, enactment, analysis, and redesign" (Design-based Research Collective, 2003, p. 5). Thus, by repeatedly comparing interventions that emerge through successive iterations, design-based research projects, including ours, aim to be relevant to practical educational contexts as well as contributing to the scientific community.

Since design-based research is conducted in and through continuous cycles, an important part of the research practice is to compare or contrast various learning environments in order to explicate the differences between them. In striving for results with the potential of changing educational practices, however, not all differences are equally interesting. To paraphrase Bateson (1972), the aim is to discover and describe *differences that make a difference* with regard to the design for and enactment of educational activities. Of course, the search for differences that make a difference is not unique to designed-based research. Nevertheless, in the search for differences with practical consequences for educational contexts, how to uncover, describe and analyze these differences are central and far from trivial questions.

In a previous analysis (Lindwall & Ivarsson, 2004), these questions surfaced when contrasting activities afforded by two technologies, known as *probeware* and *Graphs & Tracks*. Since the literature describes the strengths and characteristics of probeware and Graphs & Tracks in similar ways, and since the two technologies are both designed to develop students' understanding of kinematics and graphs, one could expect the activities supported by the two technologies to be somewhat similar. This, however, was not the case. By carrying out detailed investigations of students' interaction, it became evident that the students did strikingly different things in activities afforded by the two technologies.

In this chapter, we provide a re-examination of our previous analyses. Our aim is to show that some important differences that make a difference are to be found in the practical work of the students; more specifically, in the ways that students orient to the subject matter content. We will also argue that it is easy to lose sight of these differences when trying to generalize and abstract from the lab work of the students – for instance by explaining the success of probeware with reference to characteristics of the technology, such as the real-time graphing and the multiple modalities, or by describing the students' interaction as explorative or actively engaged. In order to keep sight of certain differences that make a difference, that is, one has to stay close to the particular and concrete. This does not mean that such findings only have to be locally relevant. Rather, and in line with Erickson, we make the seemingly paradoxical claim "that to achieve valid discoveries of universals one must stay very close to concrete cases" (1986, p. 130). Before we continue with this argumentation and the empirical illustrations, we will provide a short recapitulation of what sparked our interest in the activities afforded by the two technologies.

Probeware and Graphs & Tracks: Two technologies with similar characteristics

Probeware, also referred to as *computerized data-logging* or *microcomputer-based labs*, consists of a computer connected to probes via an interface, which measures and visualizes scientific phenomena, such as velocity or temperature. For over two decades, probeware has attracted the attention of science educators and researchers, as it is suggested that the technology can offer a remedy for the students' conceptual difficulties in domains such as mechanics (e.g. Tinker, 1996). In relation to other educational technologies, the claims concerning the strengths of the technology have been particularly strong. Euler and Müller (1999), for instance, argue that probeware is the only computer-based learning environment in physics education that has a proven positive learning effect.

As a result of the learning outcomes, there have been several efforts to find the "mechanisms governing success" (Linn, Layman, & Nachamias, 1987, p. 252). In an early and influential study, Mokros and Tinker (1987) suggested four possible explanations of the effectiveness of probeware: the use of multiple modalities, the real-time pairing of events and their representations, the genuine scientific experiences made available and the elimination of the drudgery of graph production. These suggestions have been supported and expanded in an ongoing dialogue about probeware. In addition to the characteristics mentioned, it has been argued that probeware supports collaboration, active student engagement and an interactive learning experience (Beichner, 1990; Bernhard, 2003; Thornton & Sokoloff, 1990).

In our investigations of computer-supported learning environments for the learning of kinematics, attention was also drawn to a technology called Graphs & Tracks. In contrast to probeware, Graphs & Tracks is a purely virtual environment that does not involve "physical reality." Nevertheless, this technology shares the educational goals as well as many of the characteristics of probeware: the simulation makes use of multiple modalities, has a real-time pairing of events and representations and eliminates the drudgery of graph production. In addition, the literature suggests that this technology and associated assignments support collaboration, interaction and active student engagement (e.g. McDermott, 1990). Consequently, most of the "mechanisms governing success," which have been used to explain the positive results of probeware, are also used to characterize Graphs & Tracks.

Even though the use of Graphs & Tracks cannot end up in the same activities and learning outcomes as the use of probeware, we hypothesized that activities based on the two technologies would resemble each other and that the students would approach kinematics in similar ways. By observing what the students actually did in activities afforded by the two technologies, however, it became obvious that they were not equivalent: activities based on probeware functioned as anticipated while activities that included Graphs & Tracks did not (Lindwall & Ivarsson, 2004). This observation brings to the fore some important issues in relation to common explanatory constructs found in the research literature. Given that the proposed "mechanisms governing success" do not differentiate the two learning environments, the constructs are not particularly suited to pinpoint differences that make a difference. This is not to say that the characterizations of the technologies and activities are wrong or irrelevant. Real-time graphing and multiple modalities are defining qualities of the technologies, and students using Graphs & Tracks can be seen as being as active as those who use probeware. Still, in observing what the students do in the two learning environments, one can note several potentially significant differences that cannot be captured with such characterizations.

Design-based research and studies of interaction

In the educational research community, several authors have provided arguments for the need for detailed investigations of educational interventions based on first-hand observations. Erickson and Gutierrez, for instance, point out that observational studies are necessary in most educational research projects since "a logically and empirically prior question to 'Did it work?' is 'What was the "it"?' – 'What was the treatment as actually delivered?'" (2002, p. 8) Similarly, Winn, although clearly not rejecting experimental research, states that he prefers detailed information "about how an intervention works, and the opportunity to fix it if it does not work, than a statistically derived estimate of the probability that what I was observing was due to chance and not to the intervention" (2003, p. 371). That is, even though pre- and post-tests and experimental procedures might say a lot concerning the effectiveness of an intervention, the intervention itself has to be investigated in order to gain certain insights that are useful to its design.

Among science and mathematics educators, these and similar arguments have resulted in a number of projects that address the relation between detailed investigations of interaction and educational design. In a series of early studies, relevant to our study, Roschelle investigates a Newtonian microworld simulating velocity and acceleration. Roschelle (1990) presents and discusses a number of principles that have guided the design of the technology, including an overall metaphor of scientific visualization, a specific emphasis on epistemic fidelity, extending engagement with the problematic situation, supporting focus and context, enabling communicative action and learning by doing. Despite these careful considerations, he later notes that, "only 6 of 14 students converged on explanations that were like scientists explanations" (Roschelle, 1992, p. 241). Focusing on a single case where two of these six "successful" students were working with the microworld, Roschelle asks, "How can two (or more) people construct shared meanings for conversations, concepts, and experiences?" (ibid., p. 236). By analyzing the interaction, he shows how the students' achieve what he calls a *convergent conceptual change* even though they did not present articulations in the form of scientific definitions such as "acceleration is the derivative of velocity with respect to time." Instead of talking in versions of textbook science, the students' interaction was filled with utterances such as the following, "Ooh, you know what I think it is? It's like the line. Fat arrow is the line of where it pulls that down. Like see how that makes this dotted line. That was the black arrow. It pulls it." (ibid., p. 244). Without access to what the students are doing or the graphical symbols referred to, these utterances lose their meaning. It is hard to see that they are talking about physics at all. Despite this, Roschelle argues that this kind of discussion is important for the students' convergent conceptual change. In fact, he notes that this particular utterance contains a key phrase "it pulls it," which is present in the interaction of successful groups and absent in the unsuccessful groups. Thus, utterances like the one above are used as examples of productive ways of reasoning in the lab.

Analytical approach and research methods

While Roschelle investigated several students working with one particular technology, and to some extent divided the students into successful and unsuccessful ones, we are interested in contrasting the local enactments of two technologies. In contrasting activities afforded by probeware and Graphs & Tracks, we do not claim that the technologies force the students work in certain ways: we do not argue for any version of technological determinism. Nevertheless, the local organization of the students' practical actions and practical reasoning – when using probeware and Graphs & Tracks respectively – were relatively uniform, which makes it possible to uncover, describe and analyze some of the differences between the investigated settings. In the analysis, we draw on a corpus of studies that are conducted under the auspices of *ethnomethodology* (Garfinkel, 1967, 2002; Livingston, 1987) and *conversation analysis* (Sacks, 1992; Schegloff, 2007). What these studies have in common is that social actions are examined as practical accomplishments and that "the logic and organization of such actions is a practical logic, an achieved organization, locally produced, *in situ*, in the 'there and then' and the 'here and now'" (Psathas, 1995, p. 3). As argued for elsewhere, a consequence of this approach, when applied to educational situations is that we have "to bracket our preconceived notions about good teaching, learning, scientific reasoning, and the subject matter content in order to focus on what the students are actually doing and how they understand the task and each other's actions" (Lindwall & Lymer, 2008, p. 190).

By sharing these presumptions, the approach taken in this study is similar to the study by Roschelle (1992). The question posed in that study, "how can two (or more) people construct shared meanings for conversations, concepts, and experiences?" (ibid., p. 236) indicates an interest in how the students actually are working together, what they do, what they make relevant, and how they orient towards a subject matter content in certain ways. This interest is addressed throughout the analyses of Roschelle and is partially addressed by showing, for instance, how the students talk in ways that differ from textbook science. In leaving the specifics of the interaction in order to characterize "the nature of the process through which convergent conceptual change occurred" (ibid., p. 246), Roschelle highlights: (i) the production of a deep-featured situation, in relation to (ii) the interplay of physical metaphors, through the constructive use of (iii) interactive cycles of conversational turn-taking, constrained by (iv) the application of progressively higher standards of evidence for convergence (ibid., p. 237). In the end of our study, we provide a similar list of characteristics. By taking an interest in the differences that make a difference between activities afforded by Graphs & Tracks and probeware, however, the list will be more specific as to what differentiate the two activities. We would also urge the reader to understand the list of characterizations in relation to the analyses rather than in the abstract. In fact, since none of the identifying details of the students' work is preserved in the transformation, the reasons for doing detailed analyses of students' interaction are lost if it is read by itself.

The analysis reported in Lindwall and Ivarsson (2004), where we initially contrasted the activities afforded by probeware and Graphs & Tracks, was performed in several steps. First, approximately 60 hours of recorded interaction were reviewed in search for some recurrent differences in the ways the students approached the tasks in the two learning environments. Later, it was decided to pick out one task from each lab and to analyze how all (eight) groups solved the tasks on the two occasions. After the iterative procedure of viewing and analyzing the videotapes and transcripts, some ways of acting in the environments – arguably relevant for their developing understanding of kinematics – were identified. In an attempt to depict the students' conduct, so as to maintain the identifying details of the activities analyzed, we have used some conventions taken from comics. Sometimes, comics are referred to as sequential art (Eisner, 1985) and it is this sequentiality, together with the possibility of visually presenting what the students do and say, that makes this mode of representation suitable for our aim of contrasting the local enactment of the two technologies.

Illustrations of students' work

Below, we illustrate two episodes taken from an introductory course in physics. The course was part of a thematic teacher-education program where most of the students had a background in social science and in the humanities. This meant, among other things, that they had little previous experience of natural science. Even though a central idea in the thematic teacher education program was to integrate different aspects of science, the course in mechanics was a delimited and well-defined segment with a teacher especially assigned to the lab work. According to this teacher, the activities could be described as *interactive-engagement labs*, where written instructions guide students through an inquiry focusing on conceptual issues, rather than as *cookbook labs*, where students are instructed to verify some textbook equation by following a step-by-step recipe. More specifically, most of the assignments consisted of a so-called *predict-observe-explain procedure* (White & Gunstone, 1992), where students should state a hypothesis, then observe the results and afterwards discuss discrepancies between the hypothesis and the outcome. The examples were based on analyses of the first two labs, in which the students worked with kinematics. During the first lab, the students were instructed to use probeware to construct graphs of position, velocity and acceleration versus time with the help of probes. One week later, in the second lab, they were asked to investigate the relationship between graphs by using Graphs & Tracks. According to the instructions, the goal of the labs – and the purpose of the use of both probeware and Graphs & Tracks – was "to give a basic understanding of the representation of motion in the form of a position vs. time, velocity vs. time, and acceleration vs. time graph and give an understanding of the relationship between position, velocity, acceleration and time."

The first lab: Probeware

In the assignment illustrated here, the students were provided with a position vs. time or a velocity vs. time graph and they were instructed to walk in front of the motion sensor in such a way that a graph similar to a graph specified by the tutor was produced (see Figure 22.1). Most of the times, the activity involved in performing this assignment could be divided into three separate phases. First, the students interpreted the graph presented on the computer screen in terms of how they were going to move in front of the detector in order to replicate it. These interpretations were usually filled with hesitations, omissions and reformulations. After having made an initial interpretation, the students turned the measurement on and walked towards and away from the detector while trying to match the predefined graph.

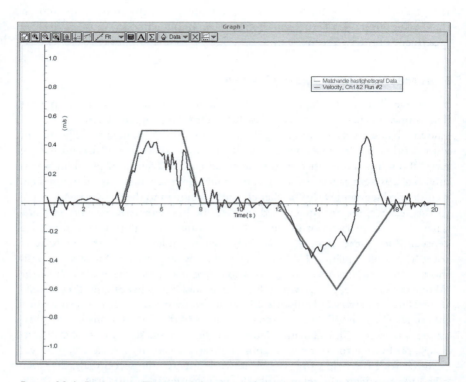

Figure 22.1 Probeware. The pre-defined graph used in the task and a graph produced
by a student. When constructing the graph, the student changed the
direction instead of decreasing the velocity, which resulted in the anomaly
represented in the right part of the graph

In their attempts to replicate the graph, the students received direct feedback
from the screen in the form of a new graph corresponding to the students' movements plotted on top of the existing graph. Sometimes, the students stuck to their
initial interpretation despite discrepancies between the predefined graph and the
produced graph. Most of the time, however, students reacted to discrepancies
between the two graphs, either by changing the direction and speed or by aborting
the attempt to replicate the graph altogether. Once the students had constructed
a graph, they discussed similarities and dissimilarities between the two graphs and
decided whether to make a new attempt or to print out the current graph and
hand it in to the instructor.

Figure 22.2 illustrates the students' fourth attempt to construct this particular
graph, which was the first velocity vs. time graph they had confronted. The episode
starts with Emily taking a step backwards while watching the graph being plotted on
the computer screen. She then stops and the graph drops to the x-axis, producing
an observable discrepancy between the pre-defined graph and the produced graph.

In the sequence, the discrepancy is not only represented by the computer but also responded to by the students. While Felicia's "oops" indicates that something went wrong, Emily, with laughter in her voice, exclaims, "what's it doing." Their previous encounters with probeware were limited to the production and interpretation of position vs. time graphs, and with this lack of familiarity with the technology, they were still not sure what they had to do in order to produce velocity vs. time graphs. By using a concept from Nemirovsky *et al.* (1998), the students gradually *adopt a tool perspective* by investigating what kind of actions make a difference in

Figure 22.2 Two students interacting with the motion sensor and the interface

relation to the task of making a graph similar to the predefined one. Thus, the students' inquiries are oriented towards the tool's responses – to what it is doing in relation to what they are doing.

In contrast to other situations, where the students' concerns with the technology became the topic of the activity for quite some time, the students in this episode soon resolve this issue. While Emily's initial reaction to the graph expressed surprise or frustration, her subsequent utterance – with a clearly marked change in her voice – relates the graph to her actions "it is 'cause you stand still here." This utterance is interesting not only because it identifies the dilemma they had confronted, and implicitly resolves it, but also because Emily refers to the action of "standing still" while simultaneously indexing a place in the graph, "here." Nemirovsky *et al.* use the notion of *fusion* to characterize episodes where students are "talking, gesturing, and envisioning in ways that do not distinguish between symbols and referents" (1998, p. 141). As they point out, fusion is both "ordinary and pervasive" (ibid., p. 144). It is not relevant *that* fusion takes place. What matters is *how* fusion takes place. In this episode, the students do not relate to the graph by referring to visual or mathematical characteristics, but in terms of what they did when producing the graph. A particular place in the graph is linked to a certain movement and, consequently, the graph very concretely indexes places and movements in the room. After noting that they "stand still" at a certain point, Emily clarifies her observation by saying the graph "goes down" because of that. Excitedly, Felicia responds to Emily's utterances by proposing that they should not stand still, and that "it is the *velocity* that should be constant." Thus, by referring to the movements and to how these movements result in certain visual properties of the graphical representation, the two students establish a distinction between position vs. time and velocity vs. time graphs.

In the words of Marton, learning to perceive something in disciplinary relevant ways "amounts to learning to find the differences that are most critical in relation to our goal" (2006, p. 521). In the episode illustrated here, the difference between velocity vs. time graphs and position vs. time graphs is made salient through the practical task of reproducing graphs by moving back and forth. The critical part of the task, then, is to understand to what movements the graph corresponds. Since the students initially make interpretations of the velocity vs. time graph in a way that correspond to a position vs. time graph, arriving at an understanding of the differences between the two types of graphs becomes critical. The students' prior understanding of the graph – as a position vs. time graph – becomes a background for subsequent utterances such as "it is the *velocity* that should be constant."

By looking at what the students have said and done prior to this episode, one can note that this is the first time they talk about *constant* velocity. When using undifferentiated concepts of *speed* and *motion* – which do not handle change in speed or change in direction – the students initially had problems in interpreting the increasingly complex graphs: central differences that made a difference were not brought up in the students' interaction. Gradually, however, the concepts were replaced with ones that were more distinctive, and distinctions between *constant velocity* and *acceleration* and between *positive* and *negative velocity* evolved as helpful resources. The graph matching assignments made some distinctions more useful than others and eventually, the interpretations of the graphs became very similar, with the students focusing on approximately the same things, dividing the graph into the same sections and using the same concepts.

To sum up, we have illustrated: (i) how the students tried to discern what the sensor was measuring in relation to their own movement; (ii) how places in the graph indexed concrete places and movement in the room; and (iii) how the concepts the students used gradually developed over time as they became relevant for the completion of the assignments. Next, we turn to the students' work with Graph & Tracks with the aim of showing an example of how a learning environment, which has the same goal, concerns the same content as the previous lab and includes a tool that – at least on a superficial level – has many structural similarities with probeware, could lead to very different courses of action.

The second lab: Graphs & Tracks

The second lab on kinematics took place about one week later. This time, the same eight groups of students were working with Graphs & Tracks, a program that was new to them. Although the purpose of this lab was the same as the previous one, there were some differences between the tasks that included probeware and the tasks afforded by the simulation. Since Graphs & Tracks is a purely virtual environment, nothing "real" outside the computer was measured. Instead, the students, in eight tasks of increasing difficulty, were supposed to arrange a symbolized track and some initial conditions in such a way that the motion of a ball corresponded to a predefined graph.

For each problem, the computer presented a position-versus-time graph, a diagram of a ball on a set of tracks and a number of initial conditions (see Figure 22.3). The students could also choose to observe the corresponding velocity vs. time and acceleration vs. time graphs. In the simulation, six posts support the five segments of the track and the user can alter the height of these posts. The simulation started when "roll" was pressed at which time the ball rolled down the track and the resulting graph was generated. The general task was to arrange the track and the initial conditions in a way that made the motion of the ball correspond to the predefined graph. The evaluation was automated, and the computer displayed the message "congratulations" when the students reached the correct solution. A central idea in the design of Graphs & Tracks is the intertwinement of different representations (McDermott, 1990) since the students were supposed move between the three different graphs and, in this way, compile information about the motion of the ball. One of the easiest ways of solving the tasks is to use the position vs. time graph for the initial position, the velocity vs. time graph for the initial velocity and the acceleration vs. time graph for the slope of the track. This, however, was not a strategy used by many students. Instead, a trial-and-error approach was fostered in most groups.

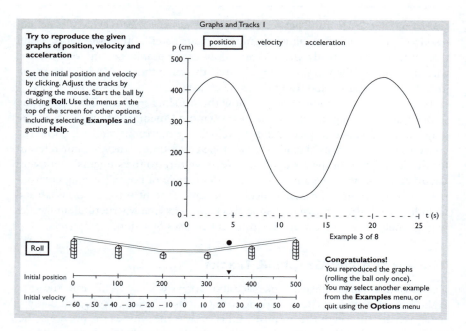

Figure 22.3 Graphs & Tracks. The position vs. time graph and the track match each other

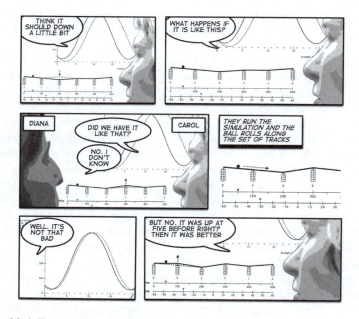

Figure 22.4 Two students interacting with Graphs & Tracks

Prior to the episode illustrated in Figure 22.4, Diana and Carol had made many small adjustments to the track. In the episode, they return to an earlier configuration, but they do not remember whether it is similar to an earlier trial. They confer with each other on how to proceed with the assignment and reason about various outcomes. Carol, "think it should down a little bit," then moves one of the posts and asks, "what happens if it is like that." Looking at the episode, one might reasonably characterize the students' conduct as both collaborative and exploratory; they ask each other questions and make conjectures about the setup of the track. Nevertheless, the rationale for changing the height of the posts, as expressed in and through the students' actions, is considerably different from that exhibited in the previous episode where the students were working with probeware. Rather than introducing conceptual distinctions or discussing the relation between graphs and motions, the students make small adjustments based on how much the two graphs visually resemble each other in relation to earlier setups. With this approach, it became important to remember earlier arrangements of the track. When Carol addresses Diana, asking, "did we have it like that," she is referring to the track's current configuration in relation to earlier attempts. As the different configurations are similar in appearance, and since they had made a number of attempts, it is understandable that Diana responds by saying "don't know."

When evaluating the result of the trial, Diana comments that the newly produced graph is "not that bad." Carol does not fully agree with this and states that "it was better" before when one of the posts was elevated. The lack of progression here is assessed with reference to visual similarities between the predefined graph and the produced graph. In order to complete the assignment, the two graphs had to overlap entirely. Less discrepancy in appearance between the two graphs, however, does not automatically mean that one is closer to a solution. Especially not when just one of the three graphs are considered. What looks "better" in the position vs. time graph might be seen as a clear deviation from the required configuration if the acceleration vs. time graph was consulted.

After the episode shown in Figure 22.4, the same procedure is done all over again: some adjustment is made, the simulation is run, and this is repeated until the two graphs are calibrated. Throughout the assignment, this group as well as most of others repeatedly forgot what setups they had already tried out. It turns out that Carol and Diana needed to make forty attempts before the two graphs matched. In contrast, another group, using a different strategy that involved all three graphs, solved the same task in five attempts. While Graphs & Tracks is intended to provide a tool for the pooling of multiple representations of the same phenomena, this feature of the software is not mandatory. Most students in this study managed to solve the tasks by approaching it in a similar way to the group presented here. Although the tasks could be solved by picking out the most critical information from each graph, it was more common that trial-and-error strategies were used. Some groups managed to solve the tasks using only the position vs. time graph while other groups only used the velocity vs. time graph, a fact that indicates that a distinction between these two graphs was not a prerequisite for solving the tasks. One can further note that when working together on these tasks, the students often talked about adjustments of the track, but they hardly ever used any concepts concerning motion. The verbal communication was directed at specific details, like the height of individual posts or the inclination of a certain section, and it never concerned the overall character of the represented motion.

In comparison with the students' use of probeware, the differences are striking. These differences can be found in: (i) how graphical representations and references to concrete movements were made; (ii) the use of conceptual distinctions; (iii) and the progression of the students' interpretations of the graphs. It is at this point, we argue, that one can begin to understand the success of probeware. Although both probeware and Graphs & Tracks have been described as having almost the same set of characteristics, the analysis shows that there are huge differences in how the students approach and enact kinematics in the two environments investigated.

Differences that make a difference

Originally, the oft-cited quote of Bateson states that "information is a difference that makes a difference" (1972, p. 99). When employed by others, the quote commonly acquires meanings not originally emphasized, or even intended, by Bateson. According to Lehmann, for instance, several pragmatist philosophers hold that"a difference is only interesting if it actually has practical consequences [and, consequently, that] many differences that would count as information in the sense of Bateson do not qualify as differences that make a difference" (2004, p. 77). This comment echoes much of the rhetoric in design-based research. At the beginning of this chapter, we introduced the notion of differences that make a difference to highlight the fact that design-based research, including the project reported here, strives to uncover, describe and analyze differences with practical consequences for educational contexts. Of course, finding such differences is not only, or even primarily, a concern for educational researchers. Mainly, it is something that occupies teachers and educational designers in their everyday work (cf. Marton & Pang, 2006). Although this work is not directly observable in our examples, the tools that the students use and the tasks they are occupied with have a history and an aim that is consequential to the students' conduct. For instance, the tasks afforded by both probeware and Graphs & Tracks have been designed in ways that enable the students to make connections between phenomenon and representations.

Since students are not "passive recipients of instructional treatment" (Doyle, 1979, p. 203), however, the intentions of teachers and designers do not always result in the desired activity. It is not enough that the technology itself embodies the possibility of approaching kinematics in certain ways. As the literature on educational assignments repeatedly shows, it is common that students exclusively focus on the operational aspects of the task without actually approaching the subject matter content and, consequently, the examples provided by the teacher fail to exemplify anything (e.g. Edwards & Mercer, 1987; Säljö & Bergqvist, 1997).

When working with Graphs & Tracks, changing the height of one of the posts from four to five might well distinguish between the correct and the incorrect solution; in the unfolding chain of events, this action becomes temporarily significant and meaningful to the student. Still, this move would hardly be deemed a central part of mechanics; neither will it suffice as an account of what they know after completing the course in question. In contrast, what the students oriented towards when working with probeware could be considered central to an understanding of kinematics and graphs. The developing coherence of the students' work had structural similarities with what students are traditionally held accountable for in having an understanding of mechanics. Because of this, their work could function as a resource in relation to teachers' questions or subsequent tests. As the metaphor of *pulling* used by the successful groups in Roschelle's study became useful in later discussions about force, so might the distinctions, interpretations and concepts that emerged in and through the students interaction with probeware become useful in later conversations about mechanics and interpretations of graphs.

Mechanisms, design principles and explications

When describing and analyzing the two episodes, we stayed close to the local rationality of the students as it was achieved and maintained there and then, *in situ*. In the previous section, we discussed what the students oriented to in relation to what they were supposed to learn. In a strict sense, we thus departed from what is observable for us as analysts – the students' sayings and doings – and began to make normative judgments based on criterial relationships (cf. Heyman, 1984). Instead of analyzing the differences that make a difference for the students in their effort to complete certain tasks, we discussed the differences that make a difference for us as researchers by relating what the students actually oriented to in relation to what was intended on *local pragmatic grounds* (Lindwall & Lymer, 2005, p. 392). A next step, with a starting point in what the students were doing and on how their doings relate to the intended object of learning, might be to compare and contrast the enactment of the two technologies. What are the differences that make a difference between the two activities? On the one hand, the ways students approach the tasks in the two episodes can be seen as relatively alike: they are equally involved, explorative and collaborative. Moreover, the technologies they use have similar characteristics. On the other hand, and as we have shown, there are striking differences in how kinematics was approached in the two episodes, how graphs were interpreted and how concepts were used.

In an effort to provide highly generalizable and consequential results, one may feel the need to formulate these differences in terms of mechanisms or design principles. The problems of explanatory constructs such as "mechanisms governing success" were highlighted at the beginning of the chapter. Expanding the list of mechanisms with some characteristics based on our observations would not help overcome these problems. In abstracting from the students' conduct, the descriptions would always risk losing the particular features that differentiate what the students actually were doing and how they approached the subject matter content. The striving for generalization comes at a price, as such constructs "could be taken as pointing out the series of objects between which one couldn't choose (hence the appearance of generalisation)" (Sacks, 1963, p. 12). Moreover, as students certainly could learn kinematics even if they did not work collaboratively or use real-time graphing, the list of mechanisms would specify neither the sufficient nor the necessary conditions for learning.

Taking another route and summarizing the exhibits of the students' work in terms of design guidelines would be similarly problematic. Even though design principles – such a specific emphasis on extending engagement with the problematic situation, supporting focus and context, enabling communicative action and learning by doing (Roschelle, 1990) – can be important in the design process, transforming detailed studies of students' work into such "highly generalizable and semi-intuitive recommendations" (Plowman, Rogers, & Ramage, 1995) is not the best way of presenting the insights from studies such as the one reported here. In fact, since none of the identifying details of the students' work is preserved through such transformation, one loses the reasons for carrying out detailed studies in the first place.

Previously, we highlighted the fact that one could find differences between the two settings in: (i) how graphical representations and references to concrete movements were made; (ii) the use of conceptual distinctions; and (iii) the progression of the students' interpretations of the graphs. Even though these formulations summarize the observations in a way that might resemble the mechanisms or the design principles, they should be read as pointing towards the illustrations presented in this chapter. In order to understand what these formulations are talking about, one must therefore return to the illustrated episodes. That is, in order to in order to keep these formulations from becoming empty, one must understand them in relation to concrete displays of students conduct.

Acknowledgements

This work has been carried out within the Linnaeus Centre for Research on Learning, Interaction and Mediated Communication in Contemporary Society (LinCS) and has been funded by The Swedish Science Council and the Knowledge Foundation, through its research program LearnIT. We are grateful to a number of colleagues, particularly Jonte Bernhard and Gerry Stahl, for comments on earlier manuscripts.

References

Bateson, G. (1972). *Steps to an ecology of mind.* New York: Ballantine Books.
Beichner, R. J. (1990). The effect of simultaneous motion presentation and graph generation in a kinematics lab. *Journal of Research in Science Teaching, 27*(8), 803–815.
Bernhard, J. (2003). Physics learning and microcomputer based laboratory (MBL):

Learning effects of using MBL as a technological and as a cognitive tool. In Psillos, D., Kariotoglou, P., Tselfes, V., Fassoulopoulos, G., Hatzikraniotis, E. and Kallery, M. (eds), *Science education research in the knowledge based society* (pp. 313–321). Dordrecht: Kluwer Academic Press.

Brown, A. L. (1992). Design experiments: Theoretical and Methodological challenges in creating complex interventions in classroom settings. *The Journal of the Learning Sciences*, 2(2), 141–178.

Cobb, P., Confrey, J., diSessa, A. A., Lehrer, R. and Schauble, L. (2003). Design experiments in educational research. *Educational Researcher*, 32(1), 9–13.

Design-based Research Collective. (2003). Design-based research: An emerging paradigm for educational inquiry. *Educational Researcher*, 32(1), 5–8.

Doyle, W. (1979). Classroom tasks and student abilities. In Peterson, P. L. and Walberg, H. J. (eds), *Research on teaching: Concepts, findings, and implications*. Berkeley, CA: McCutchan.

Edwards, D. and Mercer, N. (1987). *Common knowledge: The development of understanding in the classroom*. London: Routledge.

Eisner, W. (1985). *Comics and sequential art*. Tamarac, FL: Poorhouse Press.

Erickson, F. (1986). Qualitative methods in research on teaching. In Wittrock, M. (ed.), *Handbook of research on teaching* (3rd edn). New York: Macmillan.

Erickson, F. and Gutierrez, K. (2002). Culture, rigor, and science in educational research. *Educational Researcher*, 31(8), 21–24.

Euler, M. and Müller, A. (1999). *Physics learning and the computer: A review, with a taste of meta-analysis*. Paper presented at the Second International Conference of the European Science Education Research Association.

Garfinkel, H. (1967). *Studies in ethnomethodology*. Englewood Cliffs, NJ: Prentice Hall.

Garfinkel, H. (2002). *Ethnomethodology's program: Working out Durkheim's aphorism*. Lanham, MD: Rowman & Littlefield.

Heyman, R. D. (1984). Language use and school performance in a native classroom. *The Canadian Journal of Native Studies*, 4(1), 11–28.

Lehmann, N. (2004). On different uses of difference: Post-ontological thought in Derrida, Deleuze, Luhmann, and Rorty. *Cybernetics and Human Knowing*, 11(3), 56–80.

Lindwall, O. and Ivarsson, J. (2004). What makes the subject matter matter? Contrasting probeware with Graphs and Tracks. In Ivarsson, J. (ed.), *Renderings and reasoning: Studying artifacts in human knowing* (pp. 115–143). Göteborg: Acta Universitatis Gothoburgensis.

Lindwall, O. and Lymer, G. (2005). Vulgar competence, ethnomethodological indifference and curricular design. In Koschmann, T., Suthers, D. D. and Chan, T.-W. (eds), *Computer support for collaborative learning: The next 10 years* (pp. 388–397). Mahwah, NJ: Lawrence Erlbaum Associates.

Lindwall, O. and Lymer, G. (2008). The dark matter of lab work: Illuminating the negotiation of disciplined perception in mechanics. *Journal of the Learning Sciences*, 17(2), 180–224.

Linn, M. C., Layman, J. W. and Nachamias, R. (1987). Cognitive consequences of microcomputer-based laboratories: graphing skills development. *Contemporary Educational Psychology*, 12(3), 244–253.

Livingston, E. (1987). *Making sense of ethnomethodology*. London: Routledge & Kegan Paul.

Marton, F. (2006). Sameness and difference in transfer. *The Journal of the Learning Sciences*, 15(4), 501–537.

✦ Marton, F. and Pang, M. F. (2006). On some necessary conditions of learning. *The Journal of the Learning Sciences*, 15(2), 193–220.

McDermott, L. C. (1990). Research and computer-based instruction: opportunity for interaction. *American Journal of Physics*, 58(5), 452–462.

Mokros, J. R. and Tinker, R. F. (1987). The impact of microcomputer-based labs on children's ability to interpret graphs. *Journal of Research in Science Teaching*, 24(4), 369–383.

Nemirovsky, R., Tierney, C. and Wright, T. (1998). Body motion and graphing. *Cognition and Instruction*, 16(2), 119–172.

Plowman, L., Rogers, Y. and Ramage, M. (1995). *What are workplace studies for* (Technical Report No. CSEG/12/1995). Lancaster: Computing Department.

Psathas, G. (1995). *Conversation analysis: The study of talk-in-interaction*. Thousand Oaks, CA: Sage.

Roschelle, J. (1990). *Designing for conversations*. Paper presented at the AAAI Symposium on Computer Based Environments for Learning and Teaching, Stanford, CA.

✦ Roschelle, J. (1992). Learning by collaborating: Convergent conceptual change. *The Journal of the Learning Sciences*, 2(3), 235–276.

Sacks, H. (1963). Sociological description. *Berkeley Journal of Sociology*, 8(1), 1–17.

Sacks, H. (1992). *Lectures on conversation* (Vol. 1 and 2). Oxford: Blackwell.

Schegloff, E. A. (2007). *Sequence organization in interaction*. Cambridge: Cambridge University Press.

Säljö, R. and Bergqvist, K. (1997). Seeing the light: Discourse and practice in the optics lab. In Resnick, L. B., Säljö, R., Pontecorvo, C. and Burge, B. (eds), *Discourse, tools, and reasoning: Essays on situated cognition* (pp. 385–405). Berlin: Springer-Verlag.

Thornton, R. K. and Sokoloff, D. R. (1990). Learning motion concepts using real time microcomputer-based laboratory tools. *American Journal of Physics*, 58(9), 858–867.

Tinker, R. F. (ed.). (1996). *Microcomputer-based labs: Educational research and standards*. Berlin: Springer-Verlag.

White, R. T. and Gunstone, R. (1992). *Probing understanding*. London: The Falmer Press.

Winn, W. (2003). Research methods and types of evidence for research in educational technology. *Educational Psychology Review*, 15(3), 367–373.

Index

Note: page numbers in **bold** refer to figures and tables.